FROM HERE TO THERE

A father and son
roadtrip adventure from
Melbourne to London

JON FAINE & JACK FAINE

ABC
Books

0039332

London
Paris
Geneva
Milan
Thessaloniki
Antalya

Ulaanbaatar

Urumqi

Bishkek

Tashkent

Ashgabat

Kashgar

Tehran

Xi'an

Lijiang

Vientiane

Bangkok

Phnom Penh

Singapore

Jakarta

Timor-Leste

Darwin

Melbourne

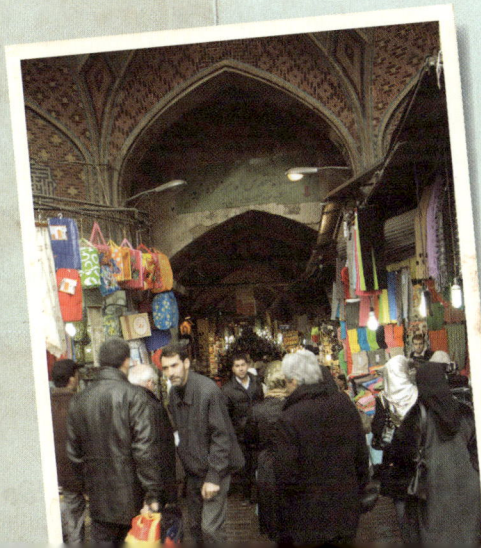

08697 0 1 AUG 2008
araan Air

modo

CONTENTS

	CHRONOLOGY	11
1	INDULGENT CONCEIT	13
2	ANYTHING EXCITING THESE HOLIDAYS?	16
3	MAN OF LISTS	18
4	FIRST YOU HAVE TO LEAVE AUSTRALIA	26
5	MV *KATHRYN BAY*	30
6	THE WORLD'S NEWEST NATION	37
7	SCARY FERRY	54
8	KELIMUTU SUNRISE	61
9	DRAGONS – FLORES, INDONESIA	63
10	THE MISSING LINK	71
11	PLASTIC CHAIRS	85
12	BBQ DOG	98
13	CHINESE CHECKERS	114
14	CHINA FOR BEGINNERS	118
15	LIJIANG HOTPOT	129
16	TIGER LEAPING GORGE	131
17	CHINESE MEDICINE MAKES US SICK	145
18	MONGOLIA RAMBLINGS	158
19	WELCOME TO MONGOLIA	162
20	DIARRHOEA AND NEAR DISASTER IN THE DESERT	172

21	YURTS, YAKS, YOGHURT AND YUCKY FOOD	189
22	THE BROTHEL	199
23	THE SILK ROAD AT LAST	206
24	THE TORUGART PASS	222
25	WHY THE SOVIETS RAN AWAY	231
26	LOVE THY NEIGHBOUR, NOT	235
27	TASHKENT RAMBLINGS	239
28	VISALOTTO	245
29	TASHKENT	250
30	SAMARKAND AND BUKHARA	254
31	WHO CAN YOU TRUST?	262
32	THE PLAY	270
33	TURK-MAD-MENISTAN	277
34	SAM	280
35	HOW TO BRIBE A POLICEMAN	294
36	DOES THE AYATOLLAH APPROVE?	297
37	TEHRAN	304
38	THE GREATEST DISAPPOINTMENT AND A MARVELLOUS REBOUND	306
39	THE GOLDEN ARCHES REAPPEAR	315
40	TURKEY BY A TWENTY-YEAR-OLD	321
41	TO GALLIPOLI BY A FIFTY-TWO-YEAR-OLD	326
42	THE EASY WAY OUT	330
43	PARIS FOR CHRISTMAS	333
44	EMOTION	338
45	MISTAKES WE MADE, THINGS TO AVOID	342
46	TOP TEN	348
47	THANK YOU	350

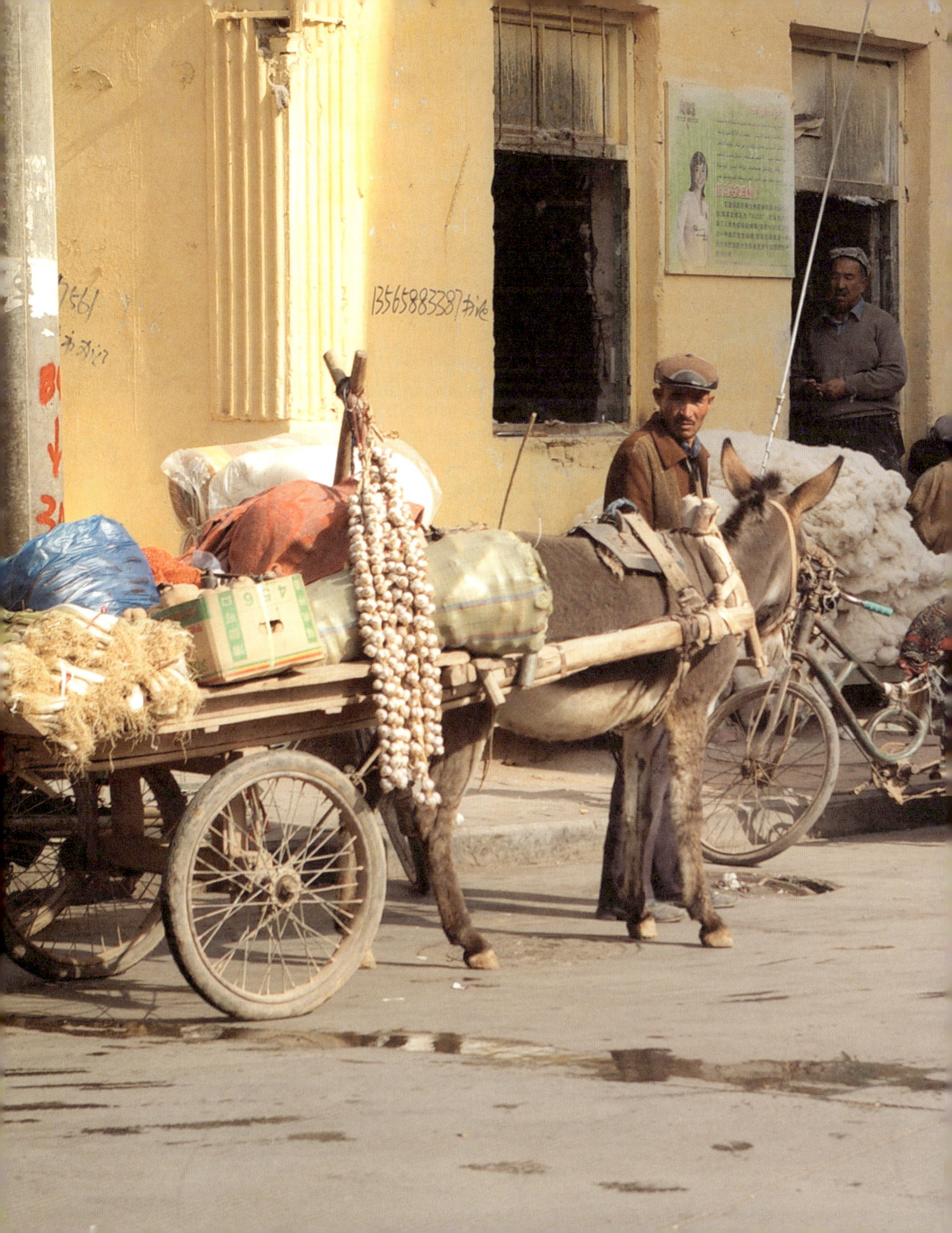
13565883387
456

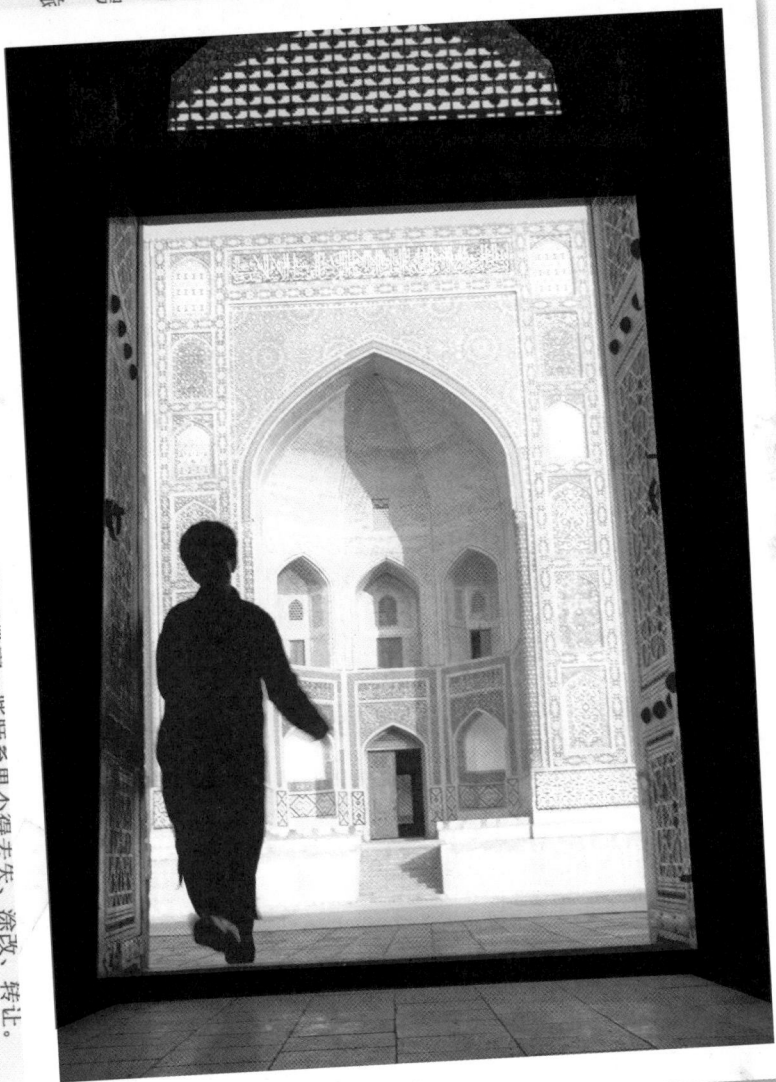

车辆联系单编

联系单编

存

车号：WIM

入境日期

经营单位

申报名称

货场：02库

捏/远单号

接车人：旅

值班关员：

……此联系单不得丢失、涂改、转让。

9084373

02库

CHRONOLOGY

WHERE WE WERE EACH SUNDAY : JUNE 2008 – JANUARY 2009

JUNE 29 2008	Melbourne, Victoria ⟶ Port Augusta, South Australia
JULY 6	Darwin, Northern Territory
JULY 13	Darwin, Northern Territory
JULY 20	Dili, Timor-Leste
JULY 27	Kupang, Timor ⟶ Larantuka, Flores, Indonesia
AUGUST 3	Bima ⟶ Sumbawa Besar, Sumbawa, Indonesia
AUGUST 10	Bali ⟶ Surabaya, Indonesia
AUGUST 17	Bandar Lampung, Sumatra, Indonesia
AUGUST 24	Singapore
AUGUST 31	Bangkok, Thailand
SEPTEMBER 7	Phnom Penh ⟶ Stung Treng, Cambodia
SEPTEMBER 14	Luang Prabang, Laos
SEPTEMBER 21	Luang Namtha, Laos
SEPTEMBER 28	Lijiang ⟶ Yunnan, China
OCTOBER 5	Xiangfan ⟶ Xian, China
OCTOBER 12	Jining ⟶ Erinhot, China/Mongolia border
OCTOBER 19	Tsetserleg, Mongolia
OCTOBER 26	Takeshiken, China/Mongolia border ⟶ Urumqui, China
NOVEMBER 2	Kashgar, China
NOVEMBER 9	Tashkent, Uzbekistan
NOVEMBER 16	Samarkand ⟶ Bukhara, Uzbekistan
NOVEMBER 23	Tehran, Iran
NOVEMBER 30	Pamukkale, Turkey
DECEMBER 7	Kavala ⟶ Igoumenitsas, Greece – ferry to Italy
DECEMBER 14	Geneva, Switzerland ⟶ Bourges, France
DECEMBER 21	Paris, France
DECEMBER 28	Paris, France
JANUARY 4 2009	Lisieux ⟶ Bayeux, France
JANUARY 11	London, England

MelbourneToLondon.com
CONSULAR
V<TAS<JONATHAN ERIC<<FAINE<<<<<<<<<
8005696<<8UZB2109561M1312089<S301113
NO OF ENTRIES ONCE
DURATION OF STAY 20
VALIDITY FROM 13/11/2008
UNTIL 13/12/2008
ACC. NONE
eccetto

1 | Indulgent Conceit

An indulgent conceit. Does travel broaden the mind? Or does travel broaden your ego? Convincing yourself that you are an intrepid adventurer is only a small part of the delusion involved in outlandish overland adventures. Charging through impoverished Third World landscapes in an air-conditioned, turbo-charged, self-contained mechanical bubble, barrelling into miscellaneous villages, and barely glimpsing vistas and landscapes worthy of meditation – this was the inevitable collateral damage in the rampage that our road trip became.

Don't get me wrong, we had a fabulous time, but rather than romanticise our expedition I prefer to accentuate its shortcomings and let the reader judge, on balance, where the truth lies.

Somehow, I convinced myself that it was a good idea. Somehow, I convinced myself that it was doable. Now I shake my head when I realise we drove 39,231 kilometres in six months and play a slide show of highlights in my head. We crossed twenty countries and went from our front gate in Melbourne to Trafalgar Square in London without using an airplane. We drove through a snowstorm in the Gobi Desert in Mongolia, and across the Torugart Pass at Kashgar in western China into Kyrgyzstan in winter, all without snow chains. We diverted around horrific car crashes on mountain roads in teeming rain at Tongren in central China and avoided an Iranian Paykal sedan doing cartwheels on the freeway near Tehran. We wove around the shores of the Caspian Sea, navigated the desert in Turkmenistan and island-hopped by ferry from Timor to Flores to Sumbawa to Lombok and Bali in Indonesia, then on to Java and Sumatra.

We learned to say 'hello' and 'thank you' and 'please' in nearly thirty languages and dispensed fluffy toy koalas that traumatised small children in obscure mountain pockets from Laos to Kurdistan. We threw a frisbee across borders and taught customs officers from Timor-Leste to Uzbekistan how to drop-punt an Aussie Rules football. We gave a hitchhiking soldier a lift on the Armenia–Azerbaijan border, earning smooth passage through roadblocks for our charity.

We ate bark and ox blood and dog and worms and pigs' ears and eel and blood sausage and curries so hot we nearly fell off our chairs. We bribed police across Indonesia, Cambodia, China and Turkmenistan. We ignored parking tickets in Jakarta, Ulaan Baatar, Milan, London and nearly got towed away in Paris. We still have credit on our freeway passes in Singapore and Switzerland. We flouted London's congestion charge and Ashgabat's curfew. We went down one-way streets and were threatened with traffic fines in Tehran and Samarkand. We had one puncture in -13 degrees in snow in No Man's Land between China and Kyrgyzstan and a buckled wheel and ruined tyre from a massive rock in the Altai Mountains in Kazakh Mongolia.

We dented someone's bumper bar in Cambodia (US$5 compensation) and left black rubber tyre marks on the side of a marauding swerving taxi in Turpan in Muslim Uyghur China. We got lost everywhere. We did not take a GPS but used maps and a compass. We asked for directions in mime. We never ran out of fuel. We paid a whopping A$2.66 a litre for diesel in Hovd in western Mongolia, and filled up for the total of an astonishing A$2 for 144 litres in Jolfa in western Iran. (That is not a typing error – 144 litres for less than A$2 or A$0.0125 a litre.) Nothing on the car broke except the CD player jammed. We had nothing stolen from our luggage or car anywhere. Jack was pick-pocketed in Jatujak flea market in Bangkok and that was the only time we were preyed upon. People refused payment for food and fruit in Indonesia, Laos, all over China and in Uzbekistan.

We visited Catholic cathedrals in Timor-Leste and Italy and France, Buddhist temples in Indonesia, Cambodia, Laos and China, Hindu shrines in Bali, shamans' tents in Mongolia, mosques in Indonesia, Malaysia, Central Asia and Turkey and an ancient synagogue in Uzbekistan. We went weeks without seeing tourists. When we did see them they reminded us of ourselves and the sad reality of our own journey. We were not intrepid adventurers after all – just tourists with a car and a different journey. We met people who did not know what or where Australia was, and we met people who had never seen Europeans before.

We squabbled over food and farting, snoring and sneezing. We cried about missing home and Jan and Nigel. We laughed about everything. We spent a fortune on phone calls. We met travellers from Slovenia, Holland, Belgium, France, England, Japan, Australia, New Zealand, Canada, Israel, Turkey, the USA, Greece, Spain, Germany, Hong Kong and all across Asia.

We haggled in dollars Australian, American and Singaporean, and in rupiah, ringgit, baht, kip, yuan, tugreg, som, manat, rial, lira, euro and pounds.

We passed armoured cars and tanks in Iran, sandbagged soldiers in Turkey and fighter jets in China. We watched land-mine clearance crews in Laos and got caught in an anti-government protest in Bangkok. We were frisked by soldiers in Uzbekistan and questioned by police in Turkmenistan. We got past internet censorship in Tehran and China and survived with no communications at all in Mongolia.

We were never in fear for our safety nor in danger – except from bad drivers.

We did what so many people say they want to do, but so few actually get to do. We took time out from work and study, and the earth did not swallow us. We spent six months, twenty-four hours a day, in a car or a small hotel room and can still talk to each other. We both missed home far more than expected.

It was a total folly – and it was the best thing you can do. I wouldn't do it again, but I would recommend it to anyone.

2 | Anything Exciting These Holidays?

Our trip now seems like a dream. It was my whole world. It was my existence and everything that I did was part of it; from sleeping to eating to talking in other tongues to venturing outside of normality. Or my normality.

Then, when it finished, when I woke, it no longer had any bearing on my life other than memories tingling my subconscious and an ability to provide anecdotal jokes about Turkmenistan and the like. Bits of it are hazy and come back to me in waves, provoked by news reports of impossibly faraway events and by photos that assure me that these absurdities really happened, and that I was witness to them. Every now and then I begin to recite parts of our trip but I feel as I do when I annoyingly explain dreams. And, like dreams, these memories are only kept alive in my mind and words fail to re-create the past.

The days before we left just ... happened. They were always going to disappear in a flurry of goodbyes and last minutes. I have no clear recollection of them. All I remember is after my last exam, on the Friday before we left, a gorgeous girl from one of my university tutorials asked me, 'So, you up to anything exciting over the holidays?' I wanted to jump up and down and scream that I was about to go on a romp through almost two dozen countries. I wanted to tell her excitedly about the snow-bound borders where the ice disappears into the mountains and the mountains disappear into the clouds, and about the deserts where you go to see nothing but your own footprints sunk in the sand and the occasional Coke can; to tell her that that changing a tyre in no-man's-land between China and Kyrgyzstan in a minus-8-degree snowstorm would leave me with frozen snot on my upper lip, and that I would be threatened by burly Timorese cockfight trainers; that there is still a KGB in Central Asia and that they would grab me and attempt to arrest me; that I would look up and down and across volcanic vistas that would decrease the value of all other views in life; that a blind, four-year old Chinese girl would break my heart and that that same heart would almost be brought to a stop several times by motorists of various nationalities ... and that I'd do all that and more ... With. My. Dad. But I didn't say it because it would have sounded, well, a bit far-fetched.

She would have told me I was dreaming.

3 | Man of Lists

I am a man who makes lists. Once something is on the list, it must get done. Somehow, sometime.

From Jan on www.MelbourneToLondon.com
Sunday evening, June 30, 2008

I feel like my husband has been having an affair for the last six months.

He has been conducting secret telephone calls in a way that women always know is leading to something. He has been constantly emailing elusive and mysterious people to set up endless rendezvous in exotic locations throughout the world. Do not underestimate the amount of time, energy and effort my husband has spent in nurturing this affair. He has investigated, researched and collected every conceivable gadget the twenty-first century can offer him to ensure that the whole world knows about his new fancy.

What makes it even worse is he has seduced my young and impressionable nineteen-year-old son to accompany him on this wild affair.

This obsession my husband has been having has left me with a concoction of emotions. I have felt alienated and anxious because I am no longer the bastion of his life ... the brick, the grounding force that has always brought him back to earth. I have felt insanely jealous because he is going to conduct this deliberate and premeditated affair in such glamorous and bizarre locations throughout the world.

And now I just feel plain abandoned, dumped and jilted. This Sunday morning at 6.20 he decided he was going to consummate the affair he has lusted after for many years. He packed his bags and left ... Well, he did have to wait around for a few extra minutes while Jack downloaded the last CD onto his iPod.

To look on the brighter side he has left me with the house and its contents, chequebook, his dog . . . And has been so distracted he has even left me to determine the future of the contents of his shed . . . his cars and his crap!!!

And just maybe my nineteen-year-old son is not so gullible. Perhaps he can ultimately persuade his father to see this phase as a temporary midlife-crisis thing and in six months' time he will convince him to return home to dodder into old age with me.

Jon and Jack, I miss you already and you have only been gone for ten hours. While there have been, and still are, multiple negative thoughts rushing through my poor befuddled brain I mostly feel ecstatically happy for you both. I know that you keep each other alert mentally and spiritually. Jack, you will probably even be able to persuade Jon to keep fit and healthy. I know the remarkable bond you have both developed will only strengthen.

Aaagh, and when I start sounding a bit pathetic it is obviously time to say . . . Goodnight.

Jon, on www.MelbourneToLondon.com

June 28, 2008 Sniffles and tears

Halfway through the party, no idea why, it suddenly dawned on me. We were not going to see any of these people, all so dear to us, for half a year. We were going to just be gone. No puff of smoke, no 'shazzam' – just an absence.

I cried. Saying goodbye, to Jan, my parents, family, good friends, the dog . . . once I started, I couldn't hold back.

And today, we packed the car with plastic tubs full of . . . well, I am not even sure what anymore. But I am certain it was all terribly important when it went in there.

And now the reality bites. I confess to feeling profound guilt that we are heading off on this incredible indulgence – and Jan will wave us goodbye. I feel selfish beyond words.

Is it in the DNA of the control freak to make a list and then obediently follow it? I always have one underway. It is a constant thread in my life. From the unmanageable (finish tax return) to the mundane (buy dog food). Once a job is on the list, there is no escaping it.

I started the list for our trip nine months before we left. But the yearning really began when I was a twenty-one-year-old backpacker in London, in 1977. I can clearly recall walking one of those identikit London streets, all two-storey homes, no front yard, bay windows and tiny front porches, stairs up from windows buried below the street, cars jammed tight against each other. As I wove through the Austins and the Vauxhalls, a camel-coloured Land Rover demanded closer inspection. What most caught my eye was the numberplate. White letters on a black background, 'VIC' centred above it. On the tailgate, the inevitable Aussie flag and the oval sticker: 'AUS'.

I stopped and stared. I could not move for a long time – someone had driven this car across the world. Then and there I made myself a promise that I would one day do the same.

So thirty and more years later – June 2008 – as Jack and I heroically conquer the first set of traffic lights just after six on a Sunday morning, I visualise arriving in London, hopefully by New Year's Eve, 2009. Six months driving and, by my reckoning, about 25,000 kilometres lying ahead. Huge gaps in our itinerary, chaotic incomplete arrangements for visas and permits, barriers and hurdles to clear all along the way. Six months away from work, six months of adventure – or six months of slog?

I cannot stop thinking of Jan, sobbing at the front gate as we deserted her moments before. Seared into my eyes is the image of Jan jollied along by the ten or twelve hardy family and friends who came in the cold and the dark to wave us off. I feel indescribable guilt and foolishness and seriously consider then and there taking the next turn, admitting defeat and going home. I can cope with the humiliation of retreat. That is a mere trifle against the heartache and pain of separation. Why am I driving away from what I love and care about most, to who knows what?

And now I will admit to a gnawing worry that we might never make it home. Have I hugged Jan for the last time? Am I condemning her to years of cursing me for my recklessness and stubborn selfishness? Will someone have to sort through my junk, the knick-knacks and mementoes in the drawers in my desk, the crammed shelves of hidden treasures in my shed, sort out the clothes for the op-shop and lament at the folly of it all? Will the dog ever rush to the door to jump onto my thigh again? Am I leading our younger son to danger, or worse? Was my mother right when she asked me not to go? My father cautioned against our chosen route, but my mother just bluntly said, 'Please do something else.'

At work, jokes had been made about us disappearing, never to be seen again. 'Just the number plate, drifting down the Mekong River … will we ever find out what happened to Jon?' was one variation on the theme. Colleagues had asked if we were taking a gun, bulletproof vests or bodyguards for the scary bits. Was I naive and foolhardy in my confident assurances that the world was not a scary place, that we must not just overcome but actively dispel fear, that people are people and that we were just going for a drive? My theory is that if you live in Flores it is not a big deal to take the ferry to Sumbawa or Lombok. If you live in Singapore you can drive into Malaysia anytime, if you are in Thailand it is not that special to drive to Cambodia or Laos. The people in Kyrgyzstan drive to Uzbekistan, Turks drive into Greece – we were just stringing a lot of those local trips together, and adding some rarely crossed land borders to spice it up a bit.

Another complication is whether or not I can disguise my profession from the tinpot despots in some of the less hospitable countries we're going to. Journalists are arrested for working without permits in half a dozen of the countries we are to go through. Turkmenistan bans all foreign journalists, no media is allowed into the Ferghana Valley in Uzbekistan, Iran deports undeclared foreign media, China detains them, especially in Xinjiang, the Muslim west, and Indonesia is fussy about who goes to its remote territories. Eastern Turkey is off limits because of the Kurdish rebellion … the list goes on. Can I conceal my identity and profession for six months and get away with it?

And I'm embarking on a career risk as well. It is unheard of for anyone who does what I do to take a long break. A radio host has only one thing to offer – their presence. If you are not there, you do not exist. Media is fickle at the best of times, and the golden rule is 'never take a holiday'. And if you do, make sure that the person who fills in for you is not very good, so that the audience feel relieved when you return. I have no such luxury. My morning show, a voracious monster that I've ridden for twelve years, every morning from half past eight to noon, interviewing around forty or fifty people a week, about anything and everything, is in my absence being looked after by someone far more able than me. Who will I be without my programme and what will my programme be without me? How will I cope without the ego patting and forelock tugging that absurdly seems to be the undeserving lot of my profession? Can I still relate to the real world outside the cocoon of my own comfortable patch? Big fish in small pond …

And then there is the possible cultural clash, the tension of ethnic identity. Will a Jewish adventurer such as I am be less welcome in so many militant Islamic countries, especially Iran? What about a Jewish journalist 'spying' on the Islamic revolution?

Our intentions could so easily be misunderstood. All these and more churn away in the back of my mind while I research how to get a permit to drive a foreign car through Uzbekistan.

Jack wipes his eyes in the passenger seat. He turns up the music on the iPod and plays the same song three times. I do not know Whitley then, but his song with the wonderful refrain 'I want this more than life itself' will become our unofficial anthem. Then he cues The Waifs singing in harmony, 'I'm in London still . . .' as we turn onto the tollway and lock in the cruise control for the first time, tears blurring the view through the windscreen.

Eventually I manage to smile as I look through the windows of other cars on the freeway. Where are they going? Why are they on the road at 6 am on a Sunday? Is anyone going on an exotic journey like ours? The people inside that Ford ahead, are they going to Africa? And the van behind, maybe en route to Russia? Or just to visit their mum in Sunbury?

There is only so much planning you can do for an adventure like this. We have tried to be ruthless in deciding what to take and what to leave. Clothes for hot and cold weather, medicines and first aid, three days of sardines and crackers, a spirit stove, two large water containers, car spares and tools, and an entire tub of electrical chargers, plugs, cables and electronic gadgetry have finished off the load. Two laptops, cameras, a satellite phone and EPIRB rescue beacon have filled the gear bags on the back seat. We have no tent, no GPS, no car fridge, no winch nor weapons. I have been inspired by and absorbed ideas, experiences and regrets from locals who have recently gone down the road less travelled and tried to learn from them all. Shirley Hardy-Rix and Brian Rix rode their BMW motorbike to Australia overland from Britain, before the terrific epics of Ewan McGregor and Charlie Boorman. Heather Burge, a grandmother from Ferntree Gully, cycled from Beijing to Istanbul, intrepid beyond anything I could imagine. Adrian Scott learned to ride his motorbike by falling off along the Road of Bones across Siberia and Russia. A friend from years back, Phil McMillan, together with two mates, rode his motorbike from London across Russia to Vladivostok a few years ago during long-service leave from teaching. We have the cushy seats and huge carrying capacity of a four-wheel drive turbo diesel to get us where we are going.

From each and every traveller's tale, I gleaned knowledge and guidance. Things to take, things to leave behind, skills to acquire, people to talk to, stuff to buy … on and on it went. I became the dinner party bore, rattling off information about visas for Tajikistan, the difference between Thuraya and Iridium satellite phones and animated analysis of the fuel capacity and range of a Prado versus a Pajero. No one else cared, but my mind was firmly locked on to a path with only one end.

Jan and I had always planned on doing 'the drive' when I retired. A few years back, Jan decided not to go, and so I abandoned my fantasy, resigned to lesser adventures. But when we were en route between Amman in Jordan and Damascus in Syria on a Middle East family holiday in 2006, we crossed the land border between the two in a hire car. As we queued at the frontier to have our papers checked and the vehicle searched, Jan turned from the front seat and said: 'This is what the drive would be like. Jack, you should go with your dad in your gap year …' I had just been offered long-service leave and was looking at options on how to use that time. Jan's suggestion was totally out of the blue, but I knew she was serious when soon after we got home from Syria she announced one evening that her good friend Marcia had offered to come and stay for a six-month-long pyjama party while we were away, if we were serious about driving to London.

Jack deliberated for a week and returned with one precondition. 'I have to be in charge of music,' he stipulated and, after I stopped giggling, I agreed before he could change his mind. The opportunity to spend so long together, to share a unique adventure, to get to know your own offspring beyond the daily grind of 'Clean up your room' and 'Have you done your homework?' seemed too good to believe. I knew it would not be a cakewalk, that there could be hiccups, but none that seemed worthy of serious hesitation or negotiation. How many fathers yearn for more time with their kids? Who doesn't?

Some practical things had to happen. We both attended a first-aid course, and Jack was despatched for an advanced driver course as he would have held a driver's licence for less than a year by the time we were to leave. He hated the tag of 'official photographer' but took to it with vigour, learned what all the buttons on the complex camera could do and spent time with brilliant mentors, thus unearthing a capacity to see things through a viewfinder that his father was not even aware were there. A visit to the bank manager secured an overdraft, and multiple visits to specialist off-road garages helped me work out what was sensible and what would be wasted in fitting out a car.

For a few months I flirted with the idea of seeking sponsorship for our trip. Car industry contacts flushed out an offer of a free off-road luxury wagon, but as we discussed what they expected in return it became clear that it would compromise my work on ABC Radio. How could I return to my job and be seen to be independent in asking questions about, for example, the future of the car industry, if I had accepted a free car from one of those very companies? How could I hold a business to account for a consumer complaint if I was in their pocket? There is no such thing as a free lunch, so I swallowed hard and paid for everything myself.

The last few months before leaving are now a blur. Visas and permits, designing and writing for the website, preparing and kitting out the car, first aid, medicine, money, maps, cameras, power supplies, back-ups, gadgets, fancy shoes and the eternal search for the perfect coats – the list got longer, not shorter. Jack had started university and had teething troubles, then exams. I wanted him to help but he had his own list. Researching the trip and planning everything well into the night, on top of getting up every day before five in the morning to do the daily radio show, meant I was less than useful for anything else. And now I have no idea how I compartmentalised my life the way I did. But once the list was written …

The plan is to cover as much of the trip by car as possible. We will drive north, jump on a ship for the shortest journey to the nearest foreign port – Dili, in Timor – and go island hopping from Timor through Indonesia and beyond, into Southeast Asia and then across China, the 'stans, Iran, eastern Europe and eventually to London. Simple really. We want to get as far as we can on Day 1, as we need to get to Darwin in four days to catch a ship. Otherwise it is weeks until the next one. That schedule equates to about 1000 kilometres every day, an impossibly tight timeline if you keep the promise to only drive on outback roads in the safety of daylight. During winter there is less daylight to use, so we can't waste any time at all.

The tollway signs and city traffic, twenty-four-hour petrol outlets and crowded subdivisions give way to empty roads and farms and trees. We sleep overnight in a grungy motel on the edge of the highway in Port Augusta in South Australia. Day 1 and we are on schedule. Dawn on Monday sees us on the bitumen, and by office hours we are at the old space base at Woomera so I call Darwin and confirm to the shipping company in Darwin, Perkins, that we are on the way. 'Your ship is cancelled … it is in dry dock in Singapore for repairs …' is the news from Kylie, our contact in Darwin, and is greeted with a numb silence in the desert at our end. I feel at first furious, then frustrated, then resigned and go through the motions of asking about the next ship – a two-week delay. Day 2 and our itinerary is blown to bits, the laptop modem will not work, cruise control on the car is playing up – things do not go to plan.

'Better get used to it,' Jack says and he is right.

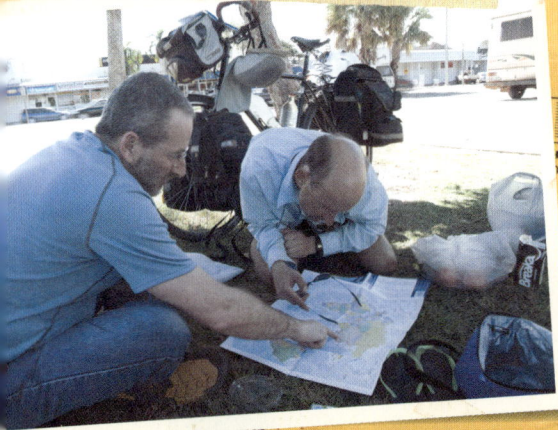

Jeff was eating lunch next to us in Katherine. He had ridden from Barcelona.

Red dirt like nowhere else, Central Australia.

4 | First You Have to Leave Australia

In which we avoid crocodiles, visit sacred caves and rock art and share silly juice. Our delayed trip to Dili is on the MV Kathryn Bay *which we have to board by Wednesday afternoon, July 16. There are worse places to be forced to spend a week than Darwin.*

From Jon on www.MelbourneToLondon.com

Sump Oil Gravy, July 3, 2008

Roadhouse schnitzel with sump oil gravy for dinner yesterday. Territory style. Everything deep fried in batter. Even the batter has batter. Salad – deep fried. Well, almost. Dinner tonight – in Tennant Creek – was Thai beef salad. Thai because it tied me up for about ten minutes chewing each mouthful before I could swallow.

The Stuart Highway is like a giant conveyor belt. Grey nomads towing caravans one after another as far as the eye can see. Having a ball, they are, except the couple arguing in the stopover about whose turn it was to be packing the food away. Why should domestic bliss change just cos you are on the road?

Off we go to Arnhem Land. A phone call or three and we have a permit and a 'cabin' at Oenpelli, now called Gunbalanya, or as it is also spelled, Kunbarllanjnja. You first ask about the river height of the East Alligator River at Cahills Crossing and head off in time to avoid high tide, when the crossing is flooded. So three hours or thereabouts to Jabiru and instead of going south to Kakadu we go northeast on red dust roads into the edge of Arnhem Land.

At the river we stop and watch the fishing – about a dozen people casting optimistically for the elusive barramundi. While we watch them, crocs watch us. One huge Jurassic remnant is a mere 20 metres away from fishermen knee deep in the river. As the tide reaches the crossing and the outflow stops and the inwards flow from the ocean flushes the river, the crocs come alive, snapping and lunging at the fish, sometimes half out of the water. We have seen dolphins herd fish into the shore to feed – this is the croc equivalent. They get a good meal. The fishermen barely budge, such is the hypnotic effect of trying to catch a barra.

One older and more cunning bloke winds in a massive fish, which is greeted with sighs and muttered curses by everyone else. Apparently he does it every day, drawing on all his twenty years-plus experience.

Gunbalanya makes us welcome. We start at the community council and are introduced to Donald, the Native Title holder. We sit for hours with Rammi and Gabriel as they paint at the art centre. Football is our common language, until we grab some food before the supermarket shuts and watch the sunset over the lagoon and adjacent mountains.

Early next morning Donald gives us a quick guided tour of the town before passing us to his 'cousin' Moses, who agrees for the regular fee to take us to the famed rock art. We go to the Dog Dreaming, and then Injalak, site of numerous remarkable rock paintings. The view across the flood plains is straight from a coffee table book: breathtaking.

Several hours of fishing and lost lures confirm my failure as a hunter-gatherer and leave us empty-handed.

Moses tells us to join him for a BBQ at the social club that evening. The entire town attends; only light beer on sale. The community owns and controls the club. Local security and 'night patrol' members wander the lawns, keeping an eye out for trouble. 'Too much silly juice,' warns Moses, using a description of grog that is totally new but makes immediate sense.

Jack always struggles to last more than ten minutes without a ball in his hands. The cheap footy we bought in Alice Springs serves as the perfect ice-breaker in Gunbalanya. Never visit an Aboriginal community without one. It also helps keep us active, and stops our backs from cracking up completely. Jack makes me do sit-ups and stretches every night, a sort of personal trainer on the road. It does me the world of good.

We head back to Darwin and camp out in the spare room of an old friend, Tony

Remmi, an artist from Gunbalanya.

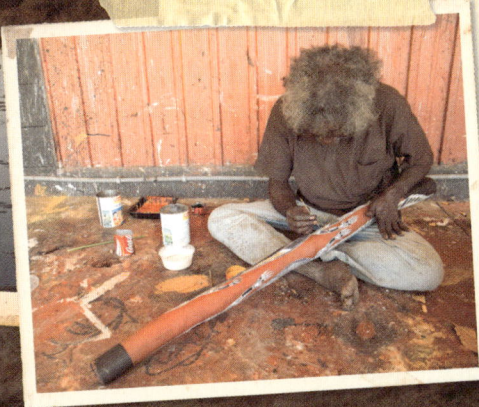

We never planned on any spare time in the NT, but no regrets.

Moses showed us the sites near Gunbalanya, Arnhem Land.

We trekked out here to the Tjaynera Falls with Tony Fitz, jumped off the rocks and swam with turtles.

Fitzgerald. He organises a picnic in Litchfield Park at Tjaynera Falls, even though he is battling cancer (which will sadly claim him within a year). We hang out at Parap market, Mindil beach, visit the Magistrates' Court (always a good free show in any new town anywhere in the world) and get the car serviced. Jack hangs out with Tony's son Gus and they discover a common interest in photography and sit and talk 'f-stops' and Photoshop shortcuts, as well as going for sweaty runs through the mangroves.

Twenty-five years ago, before I started broadcasting with the ABC, I was a lawyer and worked on a complicated and lengthy case with the Public Trustee of the NT, John Flynn. He is as well connected a Territorian as there can be, and he makes us welcome at his new apartment. His wife Kathryn recently died – the MV *Kathryn Bay* on which we will now sail is named in her memory. Peter Hopton from Perkins Shipping and his wife Chris are the other dinner guests and he has much sound advice about Indonesia where he worked and travelled over many years. I am already getting blasé about describing our trip, and gloss over all the gaps in my knowledge and itinerary. I am hoping my confidence bluffs everyone, including Jack. Like all Territorians, they down three glasses to my one, but I long ago stopped worrying about that.

I also find an old friend from my law days, David Allan, is in town, working as a consultant to the review of the Howard government's intervention into remote Aboriginal communities. He tells us many tales of politics interfering in the wellbeing of Indigenous Australians. Dinner with the Review team is a fitting farewell as we prepare to leave for Dili on the MV *Kathryn Bay* the next day. Jack is all ears over dinner as the Indigenous politics heavyweights toss around strategy in their quest for a better outcome for remote communities. The stakes are high and suddenly I wish I was doing something useful in the next six months instead of wandering around scratching a thirty-year-old itch.

It is starting to get serious, this driving to London business.

The writing on our car looks a little ambitious in Arnhem Land.

5 | MV *Kathryn Bay*

In which we intrepidly board our ship, farewell the homeland, survive seasickness, velour cushions, Britney Spears DVDs, deep-fried salads and arrive at Dili Harbour.

Captain Lino always smiles. We are the first passengers ever aboard his huge container ship. The Kathryn Bay and her Filipino crew spend their life chugging backwards and forwards between Darwin – Dili – Singapore – Surabaya – Darwin for Perkins Shipping, containers their payload, not people.

Booking our car as deck cargo from Darwin to Dili was expensive but not logistically difficult. Arranging for us to go on board was almost impossible, sorted at the last minute even after we bought tickets for the daily flight to Dili. Suffice to say, as with so much in life, it is who you know not what you know. We gratefully accept the free ride, the only condition being that we make it clear to anyone who ever asks that this was not a commercial arrangement or one that would be repeated for other travellers. We are the only passengers Perkins have ever taken and we are classified as 'casual crew'.

I drive to the customs gate, excited and expectant, prepared for the third degree from the official. Over thirty years of dreaming and two solid years of planning have led to this moment. Three bored Darwin wharfies, overalls unbuttoned to the navel, barely give me a second glance. A fluoro-vested officer stamps our documents and asks where we are going. 'We are driving to London,' I announce, pausing for effect. I hope for a 'wow' reaction but instead a nonchalant shoulder shrug has to do. Jack laughs at my pretentious effort, delighted at the rebuff. I stare at our Carnet de Passage, the passport for the car. Thirty blank pages – what will fill these empty forms? I imagine my next chat with an Australian customs official when we return and this stapled set of forms will be resplendent with exotic stamps and signatures.

I am convinced our gear will be pilfered as the car sits on the docks. What would we do unloading in Timor without our tools? Our clothes? Our sat phone? Our first-aid and medical kit? It is not that I do not trust Darwin wharfies, but an unlocked car and its contents must present a great temptation. So after endless visits to auto electricians, I have tampered with the fuses for the central locking so that the tailgate stays locked even when the doors are open. That way all our gear behind the cargo barrier is secure, but the car can still be driven around the docks. My paranoia has left me hanging around auto electricians for twice as long as the time the car will be sitting unguarded on the wharf.

Close up, an oceangoing freighter is an imposing sight. Dodging cranes and forklifts, carrying just our day packs and camera bag, we are escorted along the dock, climb over huge cables and ropes and up a steep set of gangplank steps on the steel side of the ship. The decks are littered with machinery, pipes, hoses, cables and crates. A crew member in white overalls greets and lead us through endless corridors and up stairways, almost ladders, into a maze of doors until we clamber into the 'Owner's Cabin'. Green velvet cushions on the bed/couch, fake wood-grain panelled walls, one single bed and a tiny bathroom – this is it, like a caravan. Two portholes look out onto the water and another onto a narrow shaft of light filtering through between a stack of containers barely a metre away. Every crew member we meet is incredibly welcoming, saying how much they are looking forward to having passengers on board. Not only is it a novelty to us, but to them as well.

Australian Immigration officers come aboard, stamp our passports and wish us good luck. Captain Lino tells us to go and meet for dinner in the mess. We have no idea how to get there. Endless sets of narrow stairs, closed doors on every wall: 'Engineer', 'Second Officer', 'First Aid' and the like towards the throbbing heart of the engines and into the dining room. Through a hatch in the wall we can see and smell a kitchen. Two long tables are set with cutlery and plates, maps and charts mingle with noticeboards covering the walls. An enormous television set is showing the latest victory of Filipino boxing champion Manny Pacquiao, whose every bout can be described in minute detail by most of the crew, watching transfixed while

(Name of Shipping Line, Agent, et

Name of Ship	MV Kathryn
Nationality	Singapo

No.	Family Name & Given
1	Balmores. Tranquilino N
2	Rodavia, Mario C.
3	Madrona. Nestor S
4	Lumocso, Eleuterio B.
5	Valeriano Jr., Cecilio
6	Sadoguio, Armando

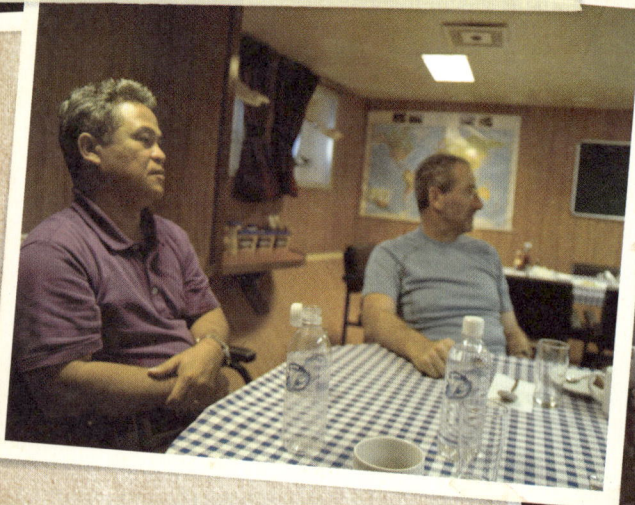

Captain Leno and Jon watching a
Michael Jackson concert after dinner.

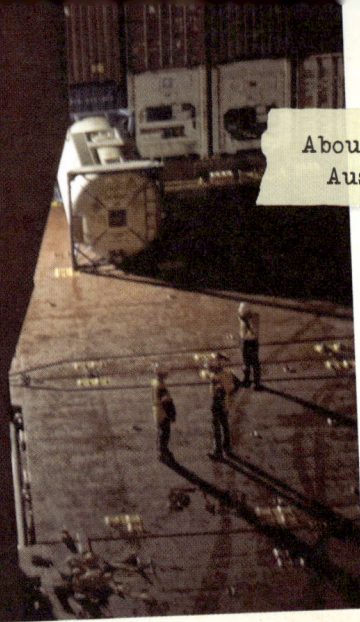

The emergency boat for
all 13 crew plus us...

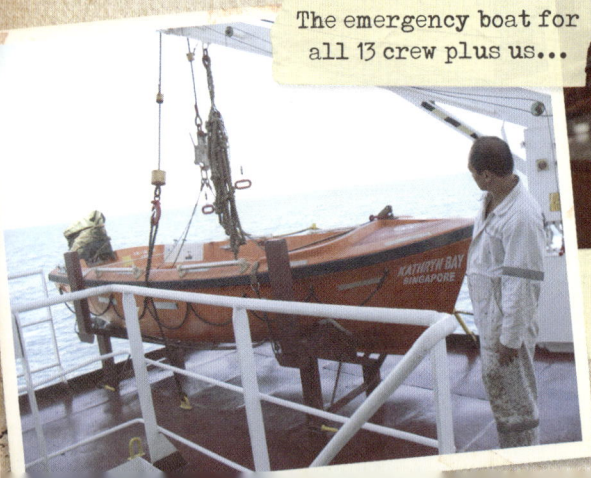

The highlight of the trip for Jon,
seeing the engine of the 100m ship.

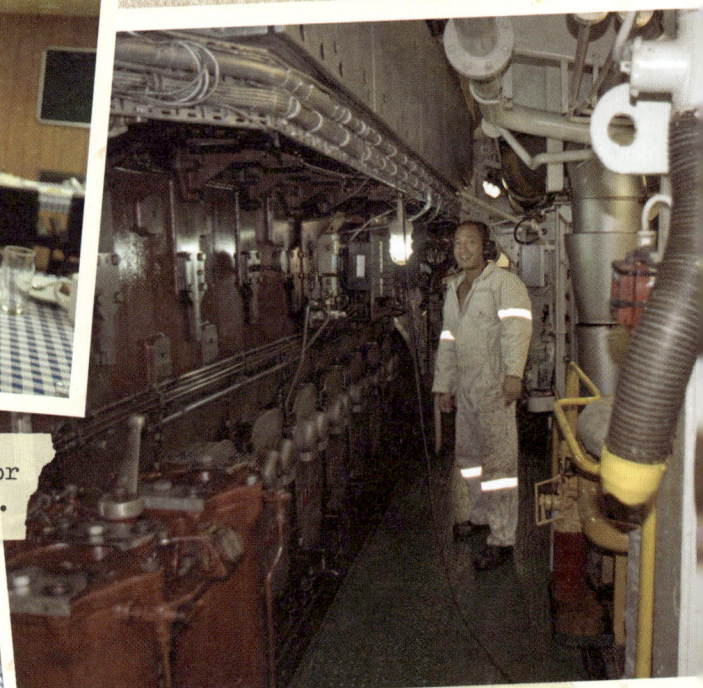

Date and Signature by
M/V
KATHRYN
IMO 91438
OFF NO. 39
CALL SIGN 9

Capt. Tranquilino

CREWLIST

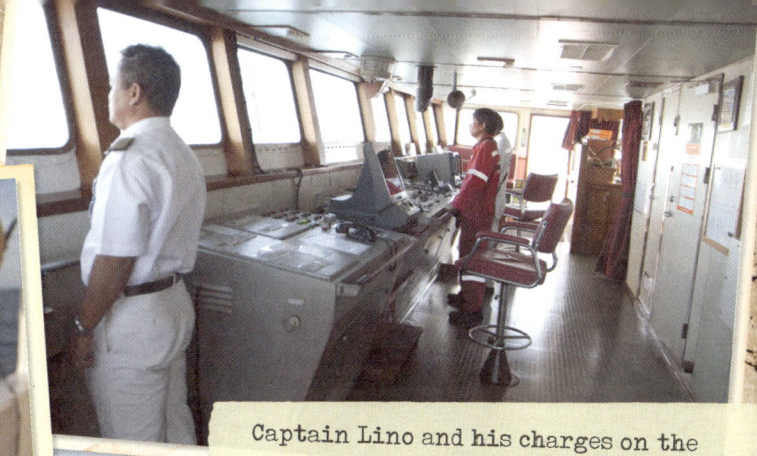

Captain Lino and his charges on the bridge of the Kathryn Bay.

Timor on the horizon.

2nd Eng.	Filipino	
4th Eng.	Filipino	
Bosun	Filipino	05Nov1966 Romblon
		25Feb1974 Cebu
		14Aug1974 Batangas
		04Oct1976 Bago City
		15Aug1981 Capiz
		10Jun1974 Marinduque
		28May1962 Paranaque

From the bridge all you could see was water and the sky meeting at the horizon.

Our arrival in Timor.

they eat. When Manny has finished beating some hapless opponent to a pulp, either Celine Dion or Britney Spears fill the big screen.

Food on the *Kathryn Bay* comes either deep fried or tinned, and boiled cabbage seems part of every meal. No alcohol, just stewed tea in plastic mugs; Worcestershire sauce, mustard and gravy smothering everything and huge servings of every course, including desserts. The officers sit together at one long, plastic tablecloth-covered table, the other is for the rest of the crew. Captain Lino waits until we arrive before eating, his pressed and starched white uniform as spotless after eating as it was before. Only the engineer has any stain or mark on his overalls, which he wears as a badge of honour. Jack and I are so out of place it is comical.

We sleep soundly as they load the containers under floodlights. Around 5 am a knock on the door alerts us that the car is being craned on. It will go on top of the loaded containers, the last thing aboard. I stumble up to the bridge and try to take photos. It is too dark and almost pointless. The harbour pilot arrives, the engines throb louder, the hawsers drop into the water and we start imperceptibly to move. Watching from the bridge as an ocean-going ship leaves dock is an education. So graceful – an enormous lump of steel, moving at snail's pace, silently gathering momentum. Darwin slides away in the dawn light.

I have never left Australia by ship before. I love airports, the sense that something wonderful is about to happen. This time I convince myself we are as daring as Columbus heading to the unknown across the ocean, intrepid beyond belief. Jack seems unmoved, but I swallow hard as Australia disappears. There really is no turning back.

The organisation and effort required to get us this far ambushes me. The trip has taken on a life of its own – or more accurately it has taken over my life. My work at the ABC has meant getting up well before 5 am every day, and it was not unusual over the last six months for me to still be working at midnight, day after day. Countless hours on phones, the internet, endless emails and money being spent beyond anything I had prepared for. The adrenaline has carried me this far – now mixed elation and exhaustion set in and we have only just begun.

As we head into the ocean, the ship starts to roll. The crew laugh at our discomfort. Stories of massive swells, 30-degree pitch and mountainous seas enjoy a new audience. Every crew member asks us about migrating to Australia, usually saying it is for their children's education.

Eleuterio the chief engineer enthusiastically takes me down five sets of ladders into the fumes for a guided tour of the engine room. Earmuffs barely protect me from the roar; spinning steel shafts, cranks and pistons, gear sets and spare bearings, pumps and lagging are everywhere. There are dials and gauges of inexplicable importance; dripping lubricants, copper and brass connections glisten in the dim light. Deep vibration and throbbing penetrates into every part of the vessel and into your body. We shout about lathes and torque settings amid the steam and thudding motion of the biggest engine I have ever seen.

We spend the afternoon reading in the cabin and sitting on the bridge staring out to sea. Jack has lessons in radar and chart navigation. The swell settles into a rhythm, the rise and fall providing a predictable but nauseating roll. At dinnertime, Jack takes one look at the food and runs out the door. He told me he did not quite make it to the tiny toilet in our cabin, but thankfully he cleaned up after himself. He spends the night lying on the cabin floor, quietly moaning. Some herbal ginger seasickness tablets help a bit, allowing intermittent sleep.

Shortly after dawn, there is land on the port side. We have rounded the eastern tip of Timor. Thickly wooded, the island seems almost uninhabited. Occasionally, a building pokes through the treetops. As we approach Dili, another ship appears ahead. It is a drilling survey ship, and makes radio contact. The captain of the *Pacific Titan* asks for advice about procedures at Dili harbour, which he has not visited before. Captain Lino explains that Dili shuts down when the harbour master goes for lunch from noon until two in the afternoon, sometimes later. The *Pacific Titan* captain cannot believe it and expresses his frustration, all the more so when advised that the only large crane at Dili's harbour is broken. A ship already tied up at the only wharf can not finish loading so no new arrivals can get to the dock. All afternoon and evening we sit at anchor in Dili harbour. Through the binoculars we can see people driving around the streets, kids swimming and fishing, construction workers digging and laying concrete until dark.

Next morning it takes one and a half hours to travel the 500 metres from our anchor point to tie up at the wharf. Without tugs, a ballet of rope throwing, winch winding, yelling and radio messaging see the ship inch into the dock, backwards and forwards, propeller thrashing at the sea. Once done, a tense Captain Lino finally smiles and puts his walkie-talkie down, nodding that it is time to go.

We felt spoilt by the luxury of our car.

6 | The World's Newest Nation

Where our adventure really begins: we find luxury amid the poverty, hope within despair and potholes like craters that threaten to swallow us whole. We watch the cockfights, meet a pet monkey that eats baby chickens, narrowly avoid being robbed by a ninja and live like colonial masters for the weekend before heading off to pay tribute at Balibo.

Sensory overload: smells, sounds, sensations we have never known before. Saying goodbye to our new friends on the *MV Kathryn Bay*, we grab our packs, clatter down the endless internal stairs, through the hatch, and clamber over ropes and hoses to get down the gangplank. We step onto the concrete dock, swaying to the motion of the ship despite now being on land. I try to high-five Jack, who is far too cool for such juvenility, spurned for not the first or the last time in my efforts to be in sync with my offspring. I would have embarrassed him less if I had unfurled and planted a flag and made a solemn speech on behalf of the Queen and all who fight beneath her standard.

Desperately trying to keep out of everyone's way until the car is craned ashore, we sway past construction work, tripping amid the chaos and dust as huge forklift tractors balancing containers weave through cement piles and exposed steel. Dili has to be one of the poorest cities on earth. After more than twenty years of Indonesian rule, independence has come at a cost. Despite it being seven years since the Indonesians quit and their scorched earth policy left Dili in ruins, there is still visible evidence of the destruction. Burnt buildings overlook the wharf, the harbour facilities are rudimentary and there are no memorials or plaques to commemorate the massacres that took place right where we stand on the dock as refugees tried to flee the invading Indonesians in 1975. International aid is paying for the rebuilding of the port, and a new wharf is being built around the old one. Temporary buildings and tarpaulins provide work spaces for the dozens of men – no women at all – milling around, fully occupied being spectators. Everyone smokes, cigarettes being the universal currency of Asia.

No one really knows what to do with us – tourists never arrive by ship. There is no arrivals hall, no immigration or customs procedures, no signs whatsoever. A soldier with a machine gun wanders over and, using his gun, points us to a door across the rubble-strewn dock. Two officials soon arrive, neither of them with more than a few words of English. Timor-Leste, as the East Timorese now call their country, has to be the most multi-lingual place on earth – it functions in four languages. Tetum is the native tongue of Timor, but curiously Portuguese has been kept as the official language in a half-hearted attempt to secure more aid from the former colonial masters. Bahasa Indonesia is widely spoken after twenty-five years of military occupation, and then English comes a distant fourth.

We and our passports are scrutinised intensely. We may as well be the first people ever processed by the two young men in military-pattern shirts, denim jeans and leather jackets slouching in plastic chairs behind a broken wooden desk. The empty room is dimly lit by a single naked light bulb dangling perilously from exposed wires. The walls are almost totally bare, with decorative damp stains meeting in the middle, some rising from the floor and others weeping from the leaking ceiling. A government-issue calendar is the only adornment.

We had attempted to arrange visas and a car permit for Timor-Leste from Melbourne and the Honorary Consul, Kevin Bailey, had valiantly tried to assure me all would go smoothly on our arrival. On our behalf he had exchanged about twenty emails with high-ranking people in the government, all replying with assurances that procedures were in place and that someone would look out for us. No one has told that to the two men on duty. And no one knows what to do about a foreign car arriving. Is it being imported? Ought we be made to pay taxes? Is it registered? Insured? I produce emails and papers from my bulging briefcase, but neither of our interlocutors can read English anyway. I try name-dropping the officials who wrote the emails, which seems to have some effect as their scowls are replaced with smiles and laughs.

After some questions that we cannot understand, a mime performance that makes Jack wince and want to slink away in shame, and payment of the US$30 visa fee, we see the stamp pad and rubber stamps emerge from a drawer. Small problem – no ink. A liberal application from a felt pen onto the dry stamp makes a passable job of a visa in each passport, stamps on our carnet for the car, and we are ushered off towards security. We text to Jan: 'Surreal but arrived safely.'

With the entire workforce of Dili dock watching, we lift the bonnet, reconnect the fuses to the central locking, get into our car and drive just ten metres to a boom gate, where two machine gun-toting Timorese soldiers in full battle kit stop us and inspect everything. They open all the car doors and the tailgate, remove three or four bags and start to empty them. I protest as they grab the first-aid kit and rip open a pack of sterile bandages. Eventually bored, they decide we are harmless. This is a pattern to be repeated across twenty more border crossings and countless searches – the facade of security, the veneer of vigilance, and the pretence of policing.

'What do we do now?' I ask Jack as they stop searching – after years of planning, the reality of arriving at our first destination is that we do not have a clue where to go. As we hesitate, a young man astride a motor scooter on the other side of the boom gate calls out in English, and introduces himself. He is Antonio Soares, a local journalist sent to meet and greet us. Our fixer and translator has been waiting on the other side of the boom gate! He cheerfully yells out to follow him as he revs his motor scooter and sets off into the traffic. The boom gate rises, Jack and I look at each other, jump into the car and there we are, merging into the traffic in Dili, the first of twenty foreign countries we will drive through.

Thirty years of dreaming, months of planning, countless hours on the phone, fantasising and staring at maps and guidebooks ... Now here we are, actually doing it at last. I wipe a tear from my eye and the sweat from my brow, swallow hard, whoop a few times and plunge in.

Dili is a crowded town. Jalal Alves Aldeia, the waterfront boulevard, would be three lanes wide if lanes existed, but quickly blends into a labyrinth of smaller streets. Every second vehicle seems to be a United Nations-badged Toyota. Minibuses with people dangling out the doors swerve and weave through the mass of vehicles, scooters darting in and out as cyclists take their chances. There are no rules. Antonio is indistinguishable from zillions of other scooter riders and almost disappears several times. Jack calls out, 'He's over there', as I frantically try to keep up. He takes us along the waterfront, through the main square, around a dusty sports oval and past shops and peeling government buildings into tree-lined streets of older, simple houses. I want to go slowly and take it all in, but Antonio does not ride as if he is guiding a tour.

First impressions of towns can be misleading. Dili had been reduced to rubble by the Indonesians as they left in 1999, anarchy and chaos ushering in a United Nations-led, but unstable, peace. Even years later the legacy of the Indonesian sacking of the colonial central town is still everywhere, burnt-out ruins, potholed roads and blue tarpaulins providing shelter and housing for homeless refugees all around the central cathedral. To remind everyone of the Catholic legacy of the Portuguese, a giant Jesus statue overlooks the town, Rio-style, a beacon for the deeply religious locals. The Pope famously visited in 1989 and a massive statue remembering him had just been officially unveiled on the opposite side of the harbour, where he held Mass. 'This is where the Pope made a mess,' explained a local, or at least that is what I heard. The two religious statues, of Jesus and the Pope, looking across the harbour at each other and blessing the population between, are the two outstanding landmarks of the capital of the world's newest independent nation.

We weave through the shady backstreets, following Antonio's red helmet, until he stops outside a low brick fence on a narrow dirt road, surrounded by houses all hidden behind high walls. The International Centre for Journalism is training young Timorese to create an independent media in this fledgling democracy. Inside, students lounge around smoking and chatting as they do all over the world. There is a hum of industry as dozens of computers whirr and beep on low desks surrounded by broken chairs. Maria-Gabriela Carrascalao greets us as if we are long-lost family. We have never met. Her husband Geoff lives in Melbourne and had emailed me when he heard on the radio that we would be going to Dili. He had assured me his wife would love to host us in Dili and she had honoured his promise. Maria-Gabriela had returned to live in her native Dili after independence, leaving Melbourne where for many years she worked for SBS Radio while in exile during Indonesian rule. Her skills and energy, to say nothing of her intimate knowledge of local family networks and personalities, made her a teacher and mentor of rare ability. She is overwhelming in her hospitality.

The centre is crammed with people, some sitting at computers, others standing around talking, bustle and commotion everywhere. Within minutes, Maria-Gabriela has persuaded us to stay at her home instead of in a hotel, bartering accommodation in exchange for me talking to her students. I do not know what I am supposed to be able to offer them, but she insists and before we even get to see Dili I am talking to an afternoon class. Jack is quickly bored with his father rabbiting on and connects to the internet on a spare computer, downloading music for Antonio, and searching for the football scores from home.

An entire generation of Timorese missed school during the occupation and subsequent war, and Maria-Gabriela explains that her job is to create a culture of independent media and questioning authority that is completely alien to Timorese values. Throughout the Portuguese and then Indonesian era, the clans and tribes that populate the eastern half of the island had been disconnected from decision making. Independence now requires skills that no one has been taught. In the long term it is unsustainable for Timor-Leste to rely on Australians and foreign aid projects to run their country. These students and those at the nearby university are the next generation of leaders, and are hungry for ideas and inspiration. My job is to feed that hunger. I am still swaying from the ship and feel totally inadequate but try to stop too many from falling asleep. Speaking inspirationally through an inexperienced interpreter is a questionable proposition in any circumstances, let alone these ones.

After the class, Maria-Gabriela and Antonio escort us to her home. I have no idea what to expect. I know Dili is one of the poorest places on earth and all around us, as we follow her car, we see ample proof. People are living in makeshift huts, thatched awnings and tarpaulins stretched between poles making extra room. The dirt roads are lined with pedestrians, mostly young men, wandering slowly and apparently aimlessly. Open drains and creeks serve as sewers; chickens, goats and pigs wander across the road. People wash under public taps. The main highway out of town is crowded with vans and minibuses, people spilling out everywhere. As we go further and further, the mass thins. Every corner has people selling cigarettes and two-stroke fuel in soft drink bottles from little makeshift booths, as well as hawkers and touts standing in the middle of the road, selling everything from tissues to batteries. Military helicopters in formation patrol the sky, reminders of the constant state of alert.

Maria-Gabriela has told us she lives on the fringe of town, and it is far less crowded as we turn off the highway. The streets get narrower and we rattle along into a lane between high walls. The houses have become substantial, made of brick and adorned with satellite dishes. Guards and large dogs lounge around iron gates, and we are waved through onto a pebbled drive. Our host lives in a magnificent homestead, bougainvillea tumbling over wide verandas behind which a whitewashed villa beckons with vast gardens, fruit trees and vines all around. Maria-Gabriela shows us through to a huge room with an ensuite western bathroom, decorated like a five-star hotel. We are cocooned from the outside world, and cannot help but feel guilt at the disparity between our accommodation and what we have just driven through. It is something we will never get used to as we are confronted by differing levels of poverty for most of the next six months.

Sunday morning sees breakfast of tropical fruit fresh from the garden – mango, avocado, papaya and sweet bananas – as well as fresh eggs from the chickens. We have coffee brewed from the family's coffee plantations high in the mountains. Here it sells for 50 cents a kilo, in Australia something more like A\$35. Maria-Gabriela introduces us to the house staff, and the family dogs and pet monkey, chained to a tree as punishment for attacking and eating the chickens that freely roam the gardens. We learn the Carrascalao family story. Maria-Gabriela's father was exiled from Portugal to Timor where he served in the colonial administration; many of her siblings occupy senior positions within the government and the parliament. We have stumbled on the Dili elite, the Portuguese establishment.

Antonio arrives and escorts us around Dili for the day. We play at being tourists, visit the market and buy fabrics and woven items from ancient ladies with gums and remaining teeth stained red from betel nut (called 'malus' in Tetum). Tobacco is sold loose, along with a kava-type soporific drink in soft drink bottles. We stop off at the Santa Cruz cemetery, where one of the massacres carried out by the Indonesian military was shown to the world in 1991 after smuggled film of the shootings appeared in Western media. It was a turning point in the struggle for independence.

Antonio is entertaining and good company. His family live in Kupang in Indonesian Timor, but he sees himself as Timorese, not Indonesian. He practises his English on us and volunteers to take us through to Kupang as he is going there for a wedding, leaving the same day we are. The local bus is slow, uncomfortable and expensive compared to our offer.

We cruise around Dili, climb winding hairpin bends on steep dirt roads to visit Dare (pronounced *dah-ray*), high in the hills behind the city for stunning views from the old seminary. Lunch is at one of many cafes lining the beach, and we gobble fresh grilled fish while a New Zealand army crew, mostly made up of huge Maori in full combat kit including bulletproof jackets, patrol around us, talking into helmet microphones and sweeping the road with their guns. It is incongruous, but just six months before there had been an attempt to assassinate the president. Along the harbour front, embassies and official buildings jostle for the water view. The Chinese Government compound is enormous, totally out of proportion to anything else, a symbol of the efforts being made by China to wield influence throughout the Pacific.

After lunch, we ask Antonio to take us to the cockfights. Chris Truman, who runs a local charity, and two Victorian farmers, Roger Haldane and his son Ewan, who are looking to create jobs in agribusiness, are also going. Dili seems to be full of people wanting to help rebuild this tiny nation. The cockfights are the biggest show in town. Hundreds gather in a dusty park, the crowd surrounding a square platform like a boxing ring. Women take no part in the fights, but sell snacks and drink from blankets set on the ground around the perimeter. Dozens of men parade their roosters, stroking the plumage and sharpening lethal razors that attach to the fighters' claws. Occasionally two birds will be teased by being offered up in preparation for battle, but still unarmed and held tightly by their owner, testing them for mettle and pluck. Jack is keen to photograph everyone, but worried he will be abused – or worse – by the crowd. This is a blood sport, so alien to our culture. He discreetly hides his camera, determined to be politically correct and to ask permission from people before snapping their image. He has a Polaroid as well as the digital SLR and starts by impressing a few kids by giving them the instant print. They are mesmerised, and within moments, half the crowd are pleading with him to be in his photos. The cockfight organiser calls him to come into the ring so he can get better shots. The fights begin.

Roosters fighting to the death are a harrowing sight. There is undoubted excitement but it is overlaid with horror as the blood spurts or seeps out of the losing bird, tossed aside gasping its last breath after the match. But what is truly amazing is how a city

The hills around
Maliana, East Timor.

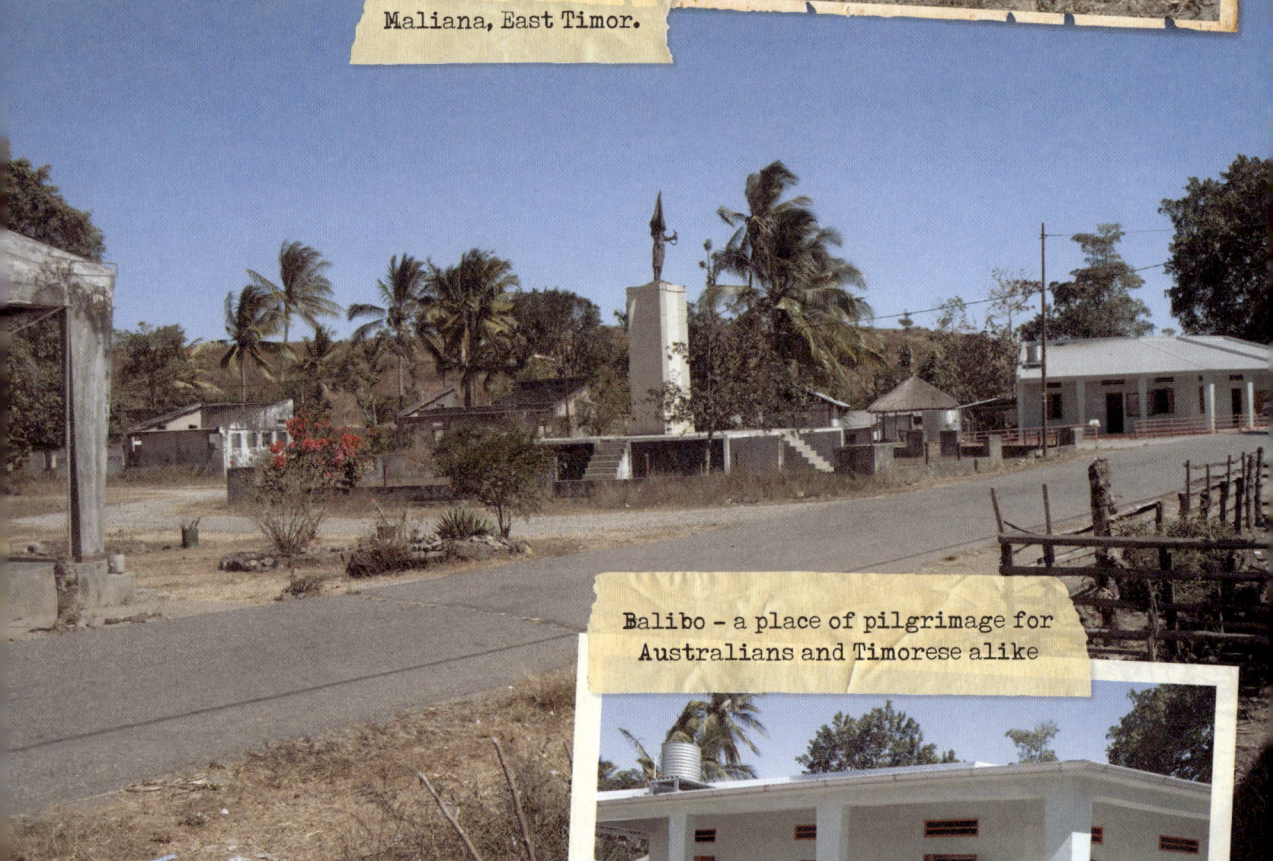

Balibo – a place of pilgrimage for
Australians and Timorese alike

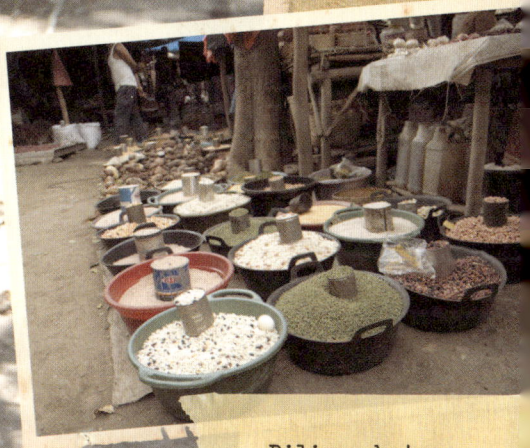

Dili market.

as poor as Dili can suddenly produce hundreds of men gambling with thick bundles of notes over the temperament of a chicken. The amount of currency changing hands is astonishing, the frenzy surrounding it no different to the betting ring at the horse races in Australia. The victory dance of a winning owner contrasts with the steady work of the slaughterman, who beheads the loser and removes the razor from its feet to return to the impoverished owner. Antonio explains that some of the champion birds will have been brought from the mountains where an entire village will pool their money to back their bird in a fight that could last as little as ten seconds, or as long as two minutes. A champion bird can fight all day, make a fortune for its handler and reward its backers richly.

We meet up that evening with Maria-Gabriela, Chris Truman and his guests and have dinner in the centre of town. Only Western aid workers frequent the restaurant. As we leave, Antonio points out a street lined with brothels that service the cashed-up multinational UN force stationed here. Local police arrive and we laugh as the UN vehicles spring into life and frantically scatter in all directions.

Driving back to Maria-Gabriela's home, we slow for the turnoff to her street as a figure looms out of the darkness and nearly gets run over by the car. As we go past I see the glint of moonlight reflected on steel and realise, in a glimpse, that a man with a bandanna covering his face, dressed all in black, is waving a machete at us. If we had stopped, we would have been robbed – or worse. Jack swears – previously an unusual event but one that becomes more frequent as we travel to more and more exotic places. 'Fuck, did you see that ...' is an understatement. My knees are trembling. Back at her house, the gates firmly locked, Maria-Gabriela explains that 'ninjas' regularly try to hold up anyone who passes and that there are burglaries and robberies all the time. The ninja will step in front of the car to force it to stop for a hold-up. Guards and dogs are essential, and 'every now and then there will be a riot. People with very little who see no progress get angry ...' As well as us, she has a house guest who has been in Dili for a few weeks. 'His family were killed in the massacres of '99, they are in the mass graves. Whenever he comes down from the mountains to town he stays with us ...' This sadness is so much a part of their lives. The first of many reminders that Australia is a rare sanctuary from the horrors of everyday violence that dominates so much of the world.

Monday is devoted to the school and nearby university, and Maria-Gabriela has me talking all morning. I meet with the director David Bloss and his wife Jodie, both from Boston. They worked in Georgia in the former USSR before coming to Timor, and Cambodia before that. I am impressed with their altruism. I try to pass on something useful to each group of students, something that has meaning in this chaotic place they live in. But the political climate in Dili is so unlike anything I have experienced, I doubt that the work I do relates to their prospects at all. The concept of questioning a government minister about a decision or a policy, of holding authority to account, using a pen or a microphone not a gun, will take some getting used to. In Timor-Leste everyone knows everybody else, familial ties seem determinative, clan and tribal connections are vital. It is not a meritocracy. The more I see, the more I realise how little I know and understand.

I ask the students about their lives, and what they want most. Peace, education and jobs, in that order, top the list. They are so earnest, and unfailingly polite and attentive, hungry for information and asking plenty of questions, showing that they are soaking it all up. I wish I could stay, or return to train some more.

Dinner that evening is at Maria-Gabriela's sister's house across the road, with three of her siblings and their partners. It is a fabulous home, enormous and new and tastefully decorated. The food is sublime – fish casserole, coconut beef, yam and Portuguese-style desserts. Jack and I get a primer in local politics, hear of some of the skulduggery that goes on much like any town, yet it seems different when so much is at stake here. The people have so little that there is a sense of urgency to politics that simply does not apply in Australia.

Next morning we farewell Maria-Gabriela and as soon as Antonio arrives we head off along the coastal road. The paving quickly gives way to gravel, and the gravel gives way to dirt. There are potholes, ditches, washouts and endless hazards, including trees fallen across the road. We head away from the beaches and into the hills, and as we climb the jungle gets thicker. After hours of twisting roads and travelling at sometimes walking speed, a few rough houses and buildings appear dotted in the jungle. We have arrived in Balibo.

Five young Australians were murdered here by the Indonesian army in late 1975 as they filmed for TV news. At the time Indonesia was publicly denying to the world that they were invading the former Portuguese colony, and the unfortunate Balibo Five had filmed soldiers in Balibo as the Indonesians denied they had crossed the border.

Their deaths have been the subject of endless agitation by family and supporters in Australia, and the house on the main street where they hid and the building across the street where they were shot are now a community centre and a moving memorial to all who died in Timor's troubles. I feel like a pilgrim, and want to teach Jack the entire history of the last days of the Whitlam era on the spot.

It was an appalling episode in Australian foreign policy. The same Timorese who had risked their lives and helped us repel the Japanese in World War II were abandoned by us. Instead we set a premium on appeasing Indonesia in its expansionist push. The Indonesian invasion occurred the day after US President Gerald Ford and Secretary of State Henry Kissinger visited Jakarta and at the very same time as Australia was totally consumed by our own constitutional crisis known as 'The Dismissal'. Liberty and the lives of the Timorese mattered little in comparison to the US strategic interests and Australian politicians' domestic power struggle.

We linger in Balibo for a while, visit the ruins of the colonial Portuguese fort and wander about. There is nothing in the town – no shop, no food, no place to stay – so we continue for an hour or so around the mountain to Maliana, a rice and market town high in the hills. The Hotel Risky, balcony adorned with an NZ flag, is the only place to stay. Some Kiwi police are stationed here, hence the flag. Near the market we buy a stir-fry to eat, and as we wait two heavily armed Australian soldiers walk into the tiny shop on the main street.

'Two dozen Cokes, mate, ta,' says the taller of them to the girl behind the counter, and then turning and seeing us says, 'G'day, how are ya, who are youse with?'

'Hi, we're not with anyone, just looking around,' I reply, as Jack stares at the machine guns, helmets and flak jackets. Antonio shifts uncomfortably in his seat, perhaps a legacy of too many encounters with soldiers in the past. It takes some explanation, but eventually they understand that we are not with an aid agency or any government project. As they relax and begin to chat, we find out they have recently arrived in Timor after seeing service in Iraq. 'I served in the International Zone in Baghdad and we have to wear more gear here than you did there … it sends the wrong message … but we have to follow orders …' As they finish the 'Coke run' and drive off in their armoured Land Rover, two NZ police arrive in short-sleeved shirts, no armour at all, revolvers discreetly holstered, and sit down for a meal. As soon as the diggers are back in their armoured vehicle and gone, the relaxed Kiwis ridicule the army protocols and volunteer that there is no real reason for any military to be in this part of the country, let alone armed to the teeth. The Kiwi cops volunteer that 'higher command' have no concept of the reality of their work and life on the ground.

Next morning we head back over the mountains, along the coast and to the reputedly delicate border with Indonesia. On the Timorese side, the soldiers seem more amused than anything else as we gingerly drive through, and on the Indonesian side the border post is deserted. One civilian clerk, bored and snoozing, makes a phone call to the immigration and customs officer who arrives on a motor scooter half an hour later to check our visas. I am slowly learning how to get things done here, and offer them all a cigarette and then artfully leave the packet on the counter and casually walk away. They stamp us in with barely a second look. So much for border tension between Timor-Leste and Indonesia. We potter along a heavily potholed road to Kupang.

JACK WRITES

Cockfight

The damp smell of poultry and the endless cawing.

The pitter-patter of the bookies scurrying through the crowd before the cocks enter the ring. The clusters of men gathered over a chook all giving advice on which way is best to tie the dagger to the ankle. Which angle is more likely to stab the opposing chicken. The one brave soul listening to everyone's two cents as he holds the chook's legs and a razor-sharp dagger between his teeth. All that bird shit under foot. And the collective stillness of the crowd captivated by the two opposing cock trainers climbing into the sand-floor ring. Their prized roosters clutched to their chests. The trainers staring each other down and the cocks squirming in their arms. All eyes on the ring as the Tetum cries of 'red' split the air. The two cocks are pushed close enough for them to peck at their opponent's neck; close enough to issue a rooster-to-rooster challenge. Their beady eyes bulging violently and full of malicious intent as they are ready to fight. But first, the quick counting and shuffling of all the final bets, the deep-set Timorese eyes flashing over thousands of US dollars. Thousands! Then finally, once all is arranged and ready, what we've all been waiting for – the release of the cocks! Who charge towards one another in the middle of the ring, the sunlight flickering off the metal blades. The crowd bays and jumps as the chickens collide with a spray of feathers and steel and blood. One's injured; maybe he's sliced open from neck to navel and instantly slumped into a heaving heap of blood and hopelessness, or perhaps the fowl has taken a blow at the knee and is severely handicapped and hobbling. He's probably doomed, but for the moment he's alive at least until Round Two and the slim chance of scrambling to victory. The loving trainer hovers beside the battle ready to call 'mercy' and forfeit all the bets for his chicken's life. And if he calls 'mercy' he'll haul the chook to the safety of his chest. There'll be shock and cries of 'cheat', but perhaps the trainer just can't bear to see his precious rooster killed right now. He'll caress the heaving mess of a chicken and edge his way out of the misused boxing ring. Or maybe the trainer will believe in his steed and let the fight continue even when the chicken seems to have no chance.

The inevitable happens and the handicapped cock is sliced apart. The defeated carcass is lifted and thrown to the corner, feathers flying and thick blood spurting across the crowd. And the dejected eyes of the losing trainer fall to the floor, unable to look at the sticky remains of his former beloved. He stands dismal in the middle of the ring, surrounded by the passion and fury, nothing but disappointment falling on his ears. He shuffles his feet uncomfortably.

But the winning trainer! He scoops up his precious chook, careful not to lose a finger on the ankle-dagger, and lifts his little champion bird above his head. The perplexed cock scrambles but he can't escape the trainer's grip. With a grin on his flushed bronze face he holds the rooster before the frenzied crowd and basks in the glory.

Then the next fight gets ready. The crowd jumps on top of one another and crane their necks for a better view of the carnage. More US dollars flash from hand to hand. Chants of 'Red! Red! Red!' building, building, building until only more blood flowing onto the sand floor will suffice. The veins in the normally docile Timorese eyes flash red as their money disappears or doubles with the crash and slash of bird and knife.

After a few fights the organisers noticed me with my camera. They yell something out to me and suddenly the crowd is working as one to push me up into the ring. Hands push and pull me and by the time the next fight starts I am climbing through the ropes of the makeshift stage. An elderly official shakes my hand and points at my camera before unfurling his own collection of little daggers of the kind that are attached to the cocks' ankles. He then points to the fight and motions for me to take pictures. The crowd grows louder and from my new point of view I can clearly see the massive amount of money shuffling its way from hand to hand in the stands. There is a tin roof over the ring, making it very dark for a photo. I bend down to steady the camera for a slower shutter speed. My right knee squelches onto a pile of bird shit and sticky blood. But still, all my photos are too dark: I need to use the flash. A dead bird is thrown next to me. Hot blood squirts across my feet and the bird shudders its last movements. I kneel down again, steady my hand and pop the flash up. Two trainers have their cocks in their arms. One chicken is red, the other white and they are in the pre-fight antagonising, picking and ruffling the feathers of their opponent. I shoot and the centre of the ring lights up. The white chicken pulls back, startled by the light. His trainer covers the scared cock and stares daggers at me, the whites of his eyes gleaming from his bronze skin. He yells at me, his teeth gnashing the words as spit leaps from his mouth. 'No photos!' is all I can make out. I spring to my feet and put two or three bodies between me and his violent hand movements. I looked for the easiest exit, probably straight over the ropes.

I bag my camera and show him my bare hands. The trainer stares, decides I'm not worth it and he retakes his position. The chickens are released in the scuffle, but still the white bird's trainer glares at me. The cocks fight and tumble around the ring for a good fifteen or twenty seconds. They are pounding each other and it is pure chance as to which cock will take the fatal blow. My heart hammers somewhere up near my Adam's apple. I stare at the trainer. He looks up from the fight and his hard eyes bore into mine. His eyes taunt me. I know I'll be in serious trouble if his white cock loses. The crowd roars 'Red! Red! Red!' and I rip my eyes away from the trainer's cold stare and look to the ground, too afraid to watch the fight. Little droplets of dark red spot my sandals and feet. I focus on the crimson specks and I wish for the white chicken to win. Please. Please. Please. Then a victorious bellow rises from the bronze mass swarming around the ring. I look up and the white cock is hobbling away from the fight. Shit. My heart falls. I am in trouble. As I edge towards the ropes, planning my escape, I glance across the ring and there is the red chicken, lying in the sand. An utter mess. I breathe relief. The white cock trainer roars and grabs his winning chook and jumps towards me, yelling and spitting. He stops a foot from my face and roars again, glaring straight into my eyes. The chicken sits confused in his arms, its blood trickling down and dripping from his elbow to the dirt. Spit flies into my face. Then his eyes lose a little of their passion and begin to glow. His big brown body calms and he turns to the organisers and holds an open hand out to them. A wad of US dollars is walloped into it with a sweet *whack* and his fingers close around the prize. He shoots me a glowing wide white smile and his eyes sparkle. The cock shuffles and gives a little '*bgerk!*' and then man and chicken skip out the gate and away into the hysterical screams of hope and despair.

Roosters being antagonised so that they want to fight.

The loser.

7 | Scary Ferry

An ancient car ferry like the ones we promised we would not go on, shared with buffalo and steamrollers, nuns and soldiers, chickens and boom boxes. We learn basic lessons in Indonesian etiquette and culture as we travel between the islands.

Lessons in basic bribery are needed to catch the ancient car ferry that irregularly shuttles between Kupang and Larantuka. Antonio translates as we are told that the ferry is already full, and we will need to wait a week for the next one. I cannot cope with the prospect of losing another week in Kupang after losing two weeks hanging around in Darwin. I can barely stop myself raising my voice, instead letting Antonio negotiate with the ferry manager. He sends subtle hand signals to me to shut my mouth. A discreet payment to the man in charge late in the afternoon sees a truck offloaded and we take its place. Our small bribe is shared between the ferry captain, the harbour master and the truck driver, who is happy to be paid for waiting. I learn the first of many valuable lessons about different ways to get a result in Indonesia.

Deference to Westerners is embarrassing. We are given special treatment without asking for it. We have money, we are white and we speak English. I feel like a colonial master fifty years ago. We are only foreigners; Jack wants to melt into the crowd.

I drive through the congested wharf, overtaking a line of overloaded decrepit trucks, past food sellers and what seems like thousands of people. A narrow ramp leads us into the belly of a rusty, smelly, leaking car ferry as five different wharfies yell and shout things I do not understand. They make me nervous. I stop the car behind a vintage steamroller, just next to a dray laden with massive doe-eyed buffalo. Any space between the cars and trucks is filled with motor scooters and hand carts. Space between the motor scooters and the hand carts is filled with people. Space between the people is filled with chickens. Space between the chickens is filled with parcels. Every available inch of deck is covered with some form of cargo, covered by another layer of cargo.

We make our way up broken rickety steps to the cabin and grab some of the plastic seats, none of which are attached to the floor at the base. Staying upright requires deliberate effort and balance; relaxing risks toppling over. Even when the ferry is full, more people are getting on. When it is overfull, even more people get on. When it is totally overloaded, the second last wave of passengers arrives. As it is about to set off more passengers squeeze in. It reaches saturation. Even if we wanted to get off, it would be impossible. I say nothing to Jack but he senses my discomfort. People are lying on mats and vinyl mattresses and every available square centimetre of floor. Gaps that seemed trivial become room for another person to lie down to sleep. Children bundled into sarongs and *ikat* (local fabric) slings are tucked into nooks and crannies, elderly couples prop themselves against doors, chain-smoking teenagers hang over the railings. We jealously guard our turf.

Our neighbours introduce themselves, mostly using sign language, as Jimmy and Daya. Jimmy has tattoos on his neck, knuckles, and most other available spaces. Daya, his glamorous partner, is decked out in beautiful patterned ikat fabric, with Western clothes as well, finished off with elaborate jewellery. Between the two of them they have three of the latest mobile phones, electronic gadgetry galore. They incessantly play with them, broadcasting their music. They produce an impromptu picnic, lettuce leaves used as spoons, scooping up rice and chicken curry cuddled in sachets of banana leaves. It looks and smells sensational, rendering our Vegemite, rice crackers and bunch of bananas unappetising in comparison.

An elderly ethnic Timorese Catholic nun in an impeccable white wimple majestically straddles three seats, plonking herself down and daring anyone to intrude on her patch. Her massive bum acts like a guard rail. Just outside the door, blocking an exit, a head-high stack of boxes contains one-day-old chickens; their endless cheeping is the soundtrack for the journey to come.

Late arrivals wander the aisles, hopscotching between the mats, searching for a seat or some space to sleep. Eventually, a middle-aged man with fancy sunglasses and a fake gold chain squeezes one seat out from under the nun's bum.

LEMBAR PELAYARAN KUPANG – LARANTUKA LEMBAR PEMAKAI

TIKET TERPADU
PELABUHAN PENYEBERANGAN **GOL. IV. PENUMPANG** KET TERPADU
PELABUHAN PENYEBER.

KUPANG – LARANTUKA **Rp. 1.189.900**

PT. ASDP Indonesia Ferry (Persero)

Golongan IV Penump

Jasa Angkutan **KUPANG – LARANTUK**

Golongan IV Penumpang GOL. IV PENUMPEN

Rp. 839.400, Rb. Kp189.900

BERLAKU SEKALI JALAN

PEMERIN
DIN
RETRIBUSI TEMPAT REKR
PERDA KOTA
Nomor Urut
Nama
Alamat/Kelurahan
Besar Retribusi
Tanggal Pungut
ASLI

The water is the rubbish bin. Anyone with garbage just throws it over the side – empty bags, plastic drink bottles, wrapping, fruit peel, cigarette butts, children's disposable nappies – everything and anything goes into the water. I cannot help judging them by our standards. There are rubbish bins everywhere, but no one uses them. I think of all the money spent and effort invested in 'clean-up' campaigns at home, the littering fines, the tidy town campaigns. Here is a country with a population ten times bigger than Australia, trashing the planet with no second thought or awareness whatsoever. Does it make our efforts at home even more important, or on the other hand irrelevant? A historic appraisal of littering would rationalise this abominable disregard for the environment by pointing out that before plastic packaging, food came in natural wrappings – banana leaves were used to transport food and, years ago, there was nothing wrong with tossing something biodegradable over the side of a boat. But now it is styrofoam and plastic that everyone flings into the sea, and the consequences are bordering on the catastrophic.

Jimmy lights up cigarette after cigarette, despite five no-smoking signs with symbols and words in English and Bahasa Indonesia – *Dilarang Merokak*. It means nothing to him and no one is prepared to tell him either. It will only be a few more years before his gums completely give up their grip on his remaining teeth. He is totally absorbed in playing a game on his computer phone. Daya is engrossed in some equally noisy version of monster shooting on her phone. Then they stop playing their respective games, and, lying on their mats so close that their feet are touching, they video call each other. Much laughter between them. It is going to be a long and noisy night. As the ferry motor rumbles to life the food vendors with their apples, bananas, doughnuts, wafers, cigarettes, lollipops and newspapers rush to the exit, completing sales at bargain prices, even as they jump from the moving boat to the shore.

Daya's computer phone turns into a boom box, broadcasting Indonesian schmaltz pop across the cabin. She sweetly sings along. The girl in the row behind weeps openly as the shore slips from view. Is she leaving her island of Timor for the first time? Will she ever return? Her soldier boyfriend sits rigid and impassive, in starched uniform, displaying badges indicating some elite unit of the Indonesian military. He carries a revolver, gleaming spare bullets clipped on the belt, a dagger on ceremonial cord draped across his hips. He seems embarrassed by his girlfriend and reluctantly, stiffly, offers her slight comfort.

As we leave the island behind and enter open water, picnics break out everywhere. Parcels of food materialise, people exchange snacks amid giggling and singing.

I go downstairs. On the deck below, the scene is even more crowded. Our car has become a picnic table. There are people sitting on every flat surface imaginable. The driver's seat of the steamroller has someone sitting in it, as does the engine cover, and people are even lying arched over the wheels and the roof. It is like Noah's Ark, animals everywhere. Six motor scooters have been squeezed up in a row, and someone is sleeping across the seats as if they are a couch. The buffalo remain calm, the baby chicks content. The smell is magnificent. I would love to join in, but feel like an idiot. I retreat upstairs to my seat, pretending the language barrier is impenetrable. It isn't. I feel guilty for worrying about whether or not our car is secure. People are so friendly. I have insulted them by even thinking they might be thieves. I admonish myself and try to relax.

We are the only Europeans on the ferry. People stare at us, and down below they touch the car, harmlessly poking and prodding. I pray the alarm does not trigger. Jack makes friends with a young man called Calvin, who is on his way home to Bajawa before going on to play tournament soccer in Surabaya. We offer him a lift and he happily barters his services as our guide.

As we hit the open sea, a gentle swell sways the boat like a pendulum. No one seems even the slightest bit perturbed. Hot water is available from a small hatch in the wall, and tea is the perfect balm. Our seasickness tablets work their magic. The night passes, fitful sleep interrupted by noises from the ferry, the people and animals. Jack keeps himself earplugged to the iPod. I have no such luxury. Card-playing young men stay up all night, sipping on soft drinks and coffee. There is no alcohol, Indonesia being a Muslim nation, even though there are many Catholics in the former Portuguese colonies of Flores and Timor-Leste.

At dawn the vague silhouette of a classic conical volcano slowly materialises from the gloom, a perfect triangle in two-dimensional light, slowly revealing its sides and texture as the sunbeams create shadows. A wisp of smoke drifts skywards, grey turning to green as the sunrays illuminate jungle and rainforest, covering their flanks all the way to the top. Any number of small islands, some barely rocky outcrops, others showing signs of settlements, glide past us, peppering the sea and creating neighbourhoods out of disconnected pinnacles from submerged mountains.

The ferry slowly docks at Larantuka shortly after dawn. It is a tiny port town, a handful of nondescript tin shacks surrounding the jetty. Low cloud-topped hills overshadow the bay. The jetty is barely wider than the car with no fencing on either side and is at least 200 metres long. It is packed with people, motorcycles, hand carts and animals. Our car was last on the ferry, so we are required to be first off and have to reverse out. Even before the ramp has clanged onto the concrete of the jetty, passengers are leaping across the gap to beat the crush. Crew members start shouting and yelling at me to hurry as I anxiously reverse up the ferry ramp. Out of either of my mirrors, all I can see is the crowd and the water below. Out the back window it looks as if I am driving straight into the crowd, but the crew are shouting at me and making motions with their hands, telling me to drive backwards regardless. I am convinced I will run someone over or drive off the jetty into the water. To add extra difficulty, there is a 90-degree dogleg in the middle of the jetty with no extra space for turning. I go backwards at walking speed, spinning like a top in the driver's seat, leaning as far as I can side to side, trying to look out both mirrors and windows at once. Jack is walking behind the car yelling in English, Calvin yelling in Indonesian, trying to guide me. Jack is smiling, enjoying the moment. I sweat like a pig. The crowd parts to let us through.

As I reverse onto terra firma, I notice my left leg is shaking. I park the car, jump out and my knees almost give way beneath me. Welcome to Flores.

Sunrise on the Kelimutu volcano in Flores.

JACK WRITES

8 | Kelimutu Sunrise

The island of Flores is so breathtakingly wild and alive that it's no wonder the locals are devoutly religious.

It'd be easy to believe in God when surrounded by such beauty. Common sense would imply that a skilled artist had crafted the powerful landscape. The east of the island sparkles. Cordial green rainforest and heavy old-growth trees groan under the weight of vines that pour down to the road. The canopies of the ancient enormous trees are lost in the mystical deep green of raw jungle. The misshapen road passes along cliffs that plummet to bubbling streams and when the banana and palm trees part there are gasping views that make your heart beat large inside your chest: views down crevices, along streams and past people's homes and histories; views along rice fields that show generations of hard work; views across jungles, towards honest villages made insignificant by menacing magical volcanoes smoking high into the baby blue sky.

And in each village a sweet banana smell hangs in the air like humidity. The children jump and wave and scream, 'Hello, *bule!* (foreigner)' The adults look on from their shabby huts, initially suspicious but lightning fast at summing us up and then grinning so warmly that you feel it hit you. After a while your own cheeks are hurting from smiling so much.

And far away, on the other side of the island, the sun slowly sinks, the remaining drips of sunlight skip off the waves as the night eases its way across from one horizon to the other. The shade darkens to shadows and the sand grows cold to touch. The sky, now black, glitters with millions of worlds that tease us with their distant secrets, but to the locals, the stars and the secrets are just another impossible part of this elaborate masterpiece.

Overnight in the village at the foot of the Kelimutu craters, we find a room in a guesthouse and discover a teacher from Jack's high school in the adjoining room, trekking through the islands with her husband. Rising before dawn we hike to the volcano's summit, marvelling at the three different coloured lakes in each of the three volcanic cones. Different clay and rock creates an amazing effect – aquamarine blue in one, offset with brown and a deeper dark green in each of the other two. At sunrise the golden glow reflects off the water and we all meditate and worship the rising sun.

9 | Dragons – Flores, Indonesia

In which Jack sneezes endlessly, Jon panics, shoes disappear, boats drift and dragons lurk.

Jack sneezing wakes me up. The air-conditioning has been on all night and he has caught a cold. An explosive sneezer, Jack has the endearing capacity to sneeze to the point of exhaustion. After he collapses he mops up inelegantly.

'Can I have your hanky?' has to be the single most repeated sentence between us for the entire six months of the trip, along with 'Can I have some money?' and 'Is it safe to go in yet?' referring to the toilet. Five months later, as we arrive in France, I buy Jack a pack of twenty beautiful cotton hankies as a not-too-subtle farewell memento of the trip. He leaves them behind in a hotel.

The room we are staying in has a magnificent view out over the harbour of Labuanbajo, at the very western tip of the island of Flores. From a small tiled terrace, where tropical mango, pineapple and watermelon are obligingly delivered, sweeter than any you have tasted, we look out to the water over jagged rooftops. Last night, we bumped into a neighbour from Melbourne who had recognised our filthy car. Rod and his wife Rinski have been regular visitors to the islands for years and over dinner tell us about the Muslim, Hindu and Catholic tensions that beset these communities. We watch the sunset over the water, a strip of golden carpet threading across the bay to meet the sinking sun. Boats bobbing at anchor dot the waterfront, large and small, ancient and modern, motor and sail. As darkness falls, tiny points of light scatter across the blackness as the outrigger boats cast nets for night fishing.

The kids in Labuanbajo, get a real kick out of playing with the tourists who come to see the Komodo dragons.

This morning, Augustin from our hotel has arranged with a local fisherman to take us to visit the famous dragons at the Komodo National Park. For the impoverished locals, the tourists are a more reliable catch than the fish. The dragons, capable of eating a human, but usually satisfied just with buffalo and lesser species, are a day trip away to the west. I step out onto the terrace and find only one of my sandals on the mat outside. My sandals are not just basic footwear – they are fancy, expensive, ergonomic, cushioned, stop-cord, adjustable, you-beaut, hamburger-with-the-lot, all-singing, all-dancing sandals that have not been off my feet since we left home. One sandal alone is not a lot of use.

Trying to be politically correct, and despite Flores being a Catholic island in this Muslim country, I had left my shoes at the door overnight. I search everywhere without success. I go downstairs to the office and ask Augustin if anyone might have seen my missing sandal. The three young boys sitting around with him in the office burst out laughing. 'The dog, he like shoes … no leave outside,' he explains. We all start to look around in corners and under furniture for the missing sandal. It is nowhere. I offer a cash reward for the missing shoe. The impact of this generosity is immediate and small boys arrive from everywhere and spread out searching for the now very valuable item. But we have to meet our boat, so I go to the shops to look for something for my feet.

The general store is a cluttered space selling everything from taps and tools to clothes and crockery. Five or six young Indonesians rush around yelling and laughing, serving the locals. I point to my feet and mime shoes, and am pointed towards slip-on sandals, all too small, more suited to local feet. I take the biggest pair and go to the counter to pay the boss. A middle-aged ethnic Chinese woman who has been shouting orders the whole time at her own hard-working staff suddenly speaks to me in fluent English. I count out my notes, apologising that some of the rupiah are torn. 'Dirty people, dirty money,' she says dismissively.

I reflect on her perception of the hierarchy of race as I wander back down the dusty main street past the cafes, bars and building sites. To her mind, she can confide in a European her disdain for the locals. We are, she thinks, united in our superiority, and all I can think is how unhappy she must be living in a community where she feels such contempt for her neighbours and even her own staff. Back at the guest house we grab some water, fruit, hats, cameras and swimwear and head down towards the wharf.

The passageway between Jalal Yos Sudarso, the main street, and the rock wall is barely 100 paces but each step is a revelation. The ramshackle timber and tin buildings are built high, sitting on a foundation of tall poles embedded in the tidal beach. We slide along an open gutter, mud and sewage squelching through our toes, winding along underneath the houses, clothes and sarongs flapping in our faces greasy from being washed in grimy water. The clotheslines of knotted string are propped up by broken poles. A partially clad elderly woman is squatting on some stairs, a small boy standing one step higher, leaning down and picking through her hair. It reminds me of monkeys in the zoo picking through each other's fur – he does not have a comb or a brush, but is picking out some bugs. Tiny chickens run everywhere in the mud. Plastic bottles and litter carpet the slime.

Our boat is waiting at the other end of a long rock wall. My new cheap sandals are too small and are already starting to give me a blister. Jack is still sneezing, eyes streaming, muttering under his breath. It is shaping up to be a terrific day. These dragons better be good.

There are six or seven boats tied up alongside each other, waiting for tourists making the trip to Rinca Island. We have been warned to be careful of unseaworthy boats without lifejackets or any safety equipment. I cast my eye over the fleet, wondering which of these wooden fishing boats will be ours. They all remind me of pictures I have seen of boatloads of refugees arriving off Australia's northern shores in rickety vessels chartered for the one-way trip by people smugglers. The leaky boats are notorious for sinking en route. Our voyage is a whole lot shorter, but I am a coward and risk averse.

The sailor we haggled with the evening before is standing astride the smallest of all the boats. Sayus waves to us, a huge smile splitting his cheeks. He helps us on board, and as I poke my head into the cabin to satisfy myself about the lifejackets and safety equipment, I am overwhelmed by fumes and the sight of rust and splitting wooden planks. There are no lifejackets, no radio. A thirteen- or fourteen-year-old boy is the only other crew member and Sayus might be in his early twenties. We settle onto the bench seat with sparse matting covers under a plastic sunshade as we slip away from the jetty, weaving between the boats and dozens of small islands, each lush and green, but most uninhabited. I compare our tiny dilapidated tub with the bigger, more elaborate tourist boats, fitted out with deckchairs and striped awnings. You get what you pay for, although I have spent my whole life trying to prove the opposite.

Jack goes to sleep in the shade, still feeling lousy. I want someone to talk to, a companion for the hours on the boat as we putt-putt across the water. He just sleeps. We are barely half an hour away from the town when the engine dies – for the first time. I watch anxiously as Sayus fiddles with the fuel pump, a lit cigarette dangling from his lips as he grabs a jerry can and pours three or four litres of fuel into the plastic bottle rigged up with rubber hose that imitates a fuel tank. He primes the pump, spins the flywheel and off we go again.

The second time we break down, he cleans the gauze filter with his shirt tail, the engine fires and we clatter and wheeze across the water ... until the third breakdown. Now we are a long way from shore and there is a slight swell. No matter what Sayus attempts, this time the engine will not restart. We drift. His tool kit consists of one enormous adjustable spanner, a hammer, a broken screwdriver and a dirty rag. We keep drifting. There is no radio and neither of our crew speaks any English. I start to mentally calculate the distance to the nearest island, wondering whether we will be able to swim that far. Jack pretends to keep snoozing on the deck, trying to stop his endless sneezing. I weigh up whether to save the cameras or Jack. I try to offer some help to Sayus but he waves his cigarette at me and keeps hitting the fuel pump with his spanner. I would do the same, but harder. We drift some more.

Another tourist boat, noticing we are drifting, pulls alongside. Coincidentally, Valentina and Marko, two Slovenians we met at the Kelimutu volcano several days ago, are aboard. I try to explain to Sayus that we want to join the bigger safer boat. Instead, one of the crew from the bigger boat jumps aboard our boat, another huge adjustable wrench in his hand. The fuel hoses are all taken apart, flushed, reassembled, and after much shouting, cursing and hitting, our boat motor splutters back to life. The two boats separate and we head off again. Jack goes back to sleep.

After another hour, we arrive at the Rinca Island jetty. The volcanic terrain is stunning, the forest coming down all the way to the water's edge. The clarity of the sea is startling – you can see to the bottom even where the warm water is very deep. We clamber along the jetty and are shown into a small hut where two uniformed rangers collect an entrance fee of about A$20 each. This is a World Heritage site, and clearly great care is being taken to preserve the habitat of these huge monitor lizards. About a thousand Komodo dragons still live on Rinca Island, and several people

Two metres of Komodo Dragon.

The massive tide at Labuanbajo on Flores leaves a film of water across the bay.

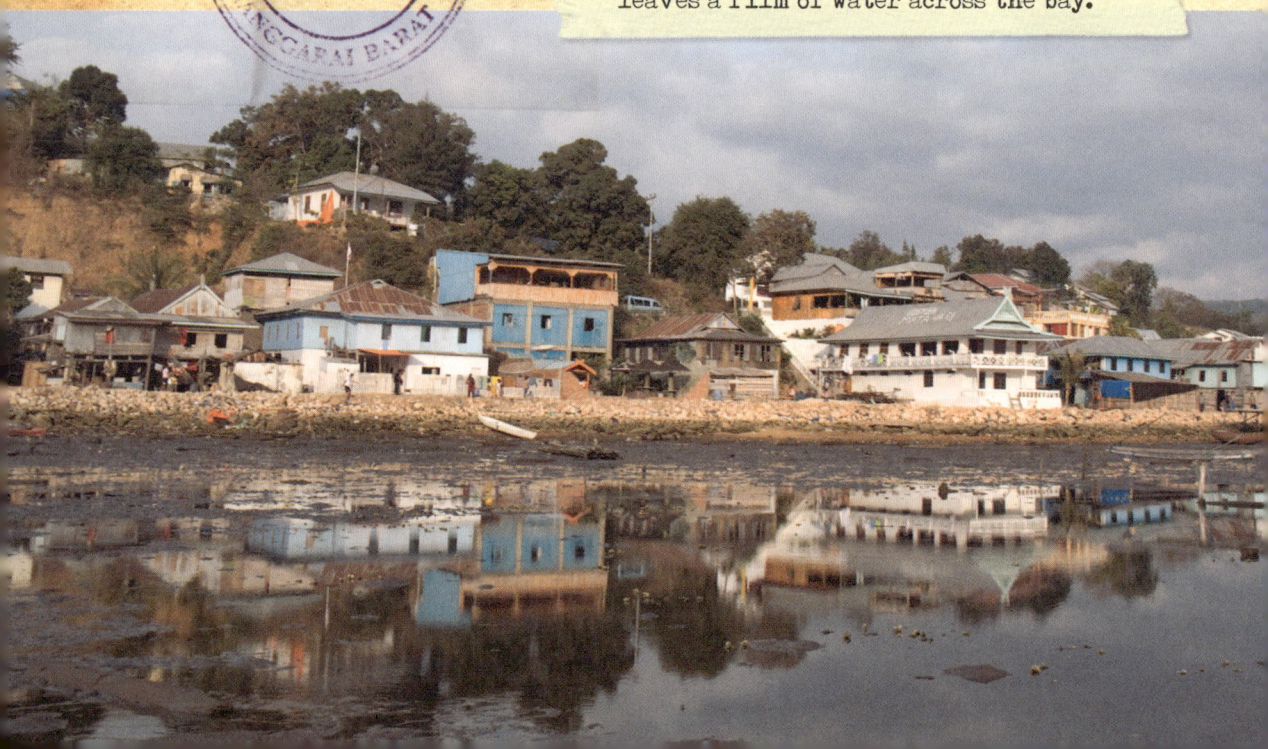

have said it is a much better place to get close to these amazing creatures than nearby Komodo Island itself.

We start our walk at the Loh Buaya camp, and our guide, carrying a stout stick as tall as himself, gives us a potted history and obligingly answers our questions. As we wander through the huts, we turn a corner and enter a clearing and barely two metres away is a dragon as big as me. The guide tells us it is a male. Ten minutes' walk into the jungle is a slightly smaller female digging a burrow to lay her eggs. Her forked tongue slips in and out of her mouth, eyes never leaving us, as she keeps digging with her powerful clawed rear legs. Along the path, a larger male is slowly walking on all fours, looking arthritic with his exaggerated gait. I pray Jack does not startle the killer with a sneezing spasm. The guide explains that if they want to chase prey, they run on their rear legs and are incredibly fast over a short distance. There is something magical about seeing wild animals in their natural surrounds, totally untroubled by camera-clicking interruptions from tourists. They could kill us if they chose, and I suspect the guide's stick would be useless if the dragon wanted to attack.

Walking around the island for some hours we also see stunning butterflies, birds, monkeys, bush turkeys, wild horses and boar. I take off my stupid plastic slip-ons and walk barefoot, blisters bleeding and stinging. But we do not see all the animals on

Our first opportunity to give away stuffed koalas and kangaroos.

1 AUG 200

-TN/R-I/M

jung

nodo

Berdasarkan Peraturan Pemerintah RI
Nomor   : 59 Tahun 1998
Tanggal   : 5 Mei 1998

Model : DKWA No. 1

offer – the buffalo are hiding. There is a bungalow where you can stay, and it would be an absolutely stunning thing to do, but we are just on a day trip, and eventually return stumbling to our boat, wondering whether it will make it back to Labuanbajo.

Snorkelling at a tiny protected cove, the volcanic peak jutting through the foliage, Jack still feels poorly and I am disappointed with the coral, which is mostly dead, and there are very few fish to look at. We head back to Labuanbajo, and as we walk towards the car parked outside the hotel, I sense something is wrong. It takes a few moments for the penny to drop – the car has been washed. It had been accumulating red dust from Arnhem Land, dirt in the mountains of Timor-Leste, mud from the road to Kupang and even more on Flores in the 6000 kilometres and four weeks since we left home. We were seriously considering not washing it all the way to London, but Augustin has foiled our plan. His driver is mesmerised by my truck, so we go for a spin and I let him take the wheel. He giggles like a kid with a new toy, and we go together to get fuel. He asks me, 'This car, mister – how big? How much? You must be very rich man, sir,' and I suppose by their standards I am. I lie about how much the car is worth as I am ashamed at the wealth gap between us. Even at a quarter of the true cost they are amazed.

My missing sandal has been found and I gladly pay the reward. On reflection, I cannot help noticing that the sandal does not seem to have been chewed at all and now I am sure many tourists volunteer generous rewards as the local kids, not the dogs, scam them for fun and profit.

The ferry trip between Flores and Sumbawa is long and slow, but far less confronting than our first car ferry experience in Indonesia. Sumbawa provides cultural opposites to Flores: Muslim, not Catholic, orderly and quiet after the chaos and tourism associated with Komodo dragons and Flores. And then to Lombok and Bali – beautiful but the regular tourist trail. Sanur in Bali reminds me of Noosa in Queensland. Kim and Diane from Melbourne make us utterly and luxuriously welcome in their home in Sanur and the kite-flying competition that weekend reminds us that culture on Bali is not just arranged for the tourists.

10 | The Missing Link

In which our travellers survive a greedy wild elephant and poisoning from exhaust fumes in Jakarta, but fail to bribe a ferry-master or cheer up an accused drug trafficker in Singapore.

We are stuck. I am convinced there has to be a way of getting the car from Sumatra across the Straits of Malaka to Malaysia, avoiding Singapore. I refuse to accept the absence of a ferry service – it must be somewhere. It isn't. So why not just go through Singapore? Singapore waterfront paperwork is notoriously tiresome and it is an expensive Western-style city. I am quite happy not to go there. My last visit was when I was sent by the ABC in December 2005 for the unpleasant task of reporting the execution of an Australian convicted of smuggling drugs. Unhappy memories await.

The distance between the northern coast of Sumatra and the western coast of Malaysia is minimal – maybe 100ks. In the months before leaving, I find information for motorbike tourers about chartering local fishermen to take their bikes across. Four-wheel drives are not quite as easy to move as motorbikes, although it seems logical that there be a link. I am naive enough to believe in logic. If the world was run sensibly, there would be a high-speed car ferry just in case someone wanted to go that way while they were trying to drive around the world. A sleepless night surfing the internet for clues reveals a press release announcing a new ferry service between Dumai and Malaka, but the information is several years old and I cannot find any other reference to it, let alone a timetable. I send emails to everyone under the sun, and even try making phone calls from Melbourne to the local tourism office in Padang

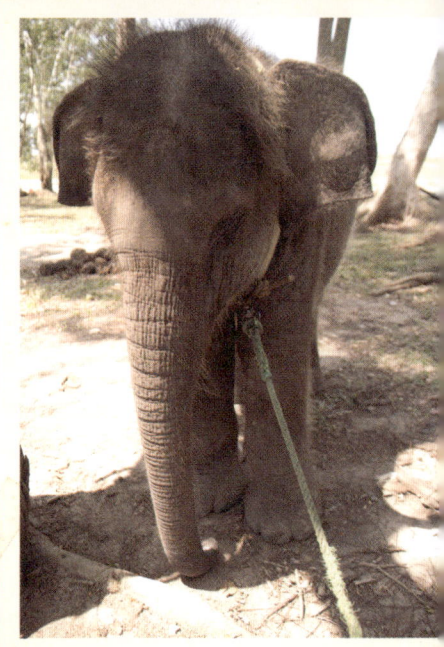

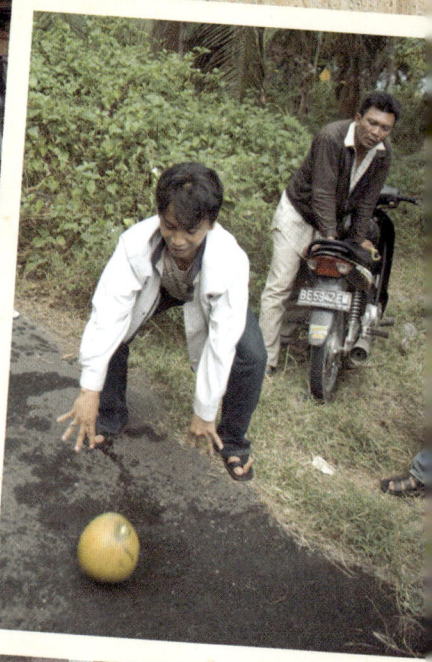

but no one speaks good English and it becomes clear I am wasting time and money. Frustrated, I abandon the search, and decide it is one of those many things that will have to be sorted on the road. It nags away at me as 'the missing link' in our trip.

As we drive through Surabaya and then Semarang on Java's industrial northern coast, we trust in fate and make only vague inquiries about getting the car across the notorious pirate-infested stretch of water between Indonesia and Malaysia. In between endless analysis of his cricket team's batting and bowling strength and how to reorganise the hockey team line-up to make the finals, Jack asks from time to time how we are going to conquer this small challenge. I remain calm, always authoritative and in control. 'How the hell would I know, stop hassling me, there must be something' was typical. Arriving in Jakarta, I decide the riddle must be solved.

In sport, 'white line fever' is where a normally civil person turns into a maniac when they cross the line to go out onto the field to play. 'White centre line fever' is a term that should be used to denote a normally placid driver who becomes demonic when confronted with Javanese drivers who show no regard for road rules. Without going into detail, I am not proud of what I did, but it worked and we got to the capital.

Jakarta is a shockingly polluted, gridlocked sprawl of a mere nine million people. For six weeks we had been travelling in small towns or countryside, and it overwhelms us to be back in a bursting smelly metropolis. It takes hours to get anywhere. Our intention when approaching any city is to promise to stay overnight nearby, never enter a big city at peak hour and certainly not late in our day, or when tired, busting for a pee or impatient. So we arrive in Jakarta late on Tuesday, fed up and frustrated, busting for a pee and desperate to find somewhere to stay. Our huge off-road-equipped 4x4 with bullbar, driving lights and antenna that seemed so appropriate in the Northern Territory now seems utterly incongruous amidst the tiny cars, scooters and bicycles of an Asian city. The traffic is impenetrable, the weather threatening, road signs inadequate and inevitably Jack cannot make sense of the map. 'Do you know where we are?' and 'Is this the right road?' are answered with 'I don't know' and 'This might be the way down here', followed by 'Might be? *Might be?* What do you mean, "Might be" … you either know where we are or you don't.'

I know I'm being grumpy and mean, but for the driver in a strange town few things combine worse than juggling the traffic, unfamiliar road etiquette, bad lights, and near misses galore, and all with a bladder threatening to explode. A navigator – or as we tagged it, a NAG-ivator – who is regularly lost, relying on skeletal Lonely Planet maps and threatening to throw the book out the window does not help things. When it is your son, and you see too much of yourself in his every action, it is worse.

'Give me the map.'

'What difference will that make, it hasn't got this road on it, it is crap, I hate Lonely Planet, I want to kill them …' before a startled cry, 'That monument, that's where we are, quick, turn back, go the other way, down that street instead … oh, shit – it is one way.' We always kissed and made up afterwards.

Our inexpensive tourist hotel offers a business centre. We ask the staff to phone ASDP, the ferry company, and Pelni, the shipping line, and ask in Indonesian about their schedules. The ferry company website has collapsed, the phone numbers do not connect. A totally wasted hour is spent trying to contact them, failing entirely. How hard can it be to find the phone numbers of the country's biggest businesses and a major infrastructure provider at that? But no one could. A restorative fish curry served on banana leaves heals the wounds, one glass of wine each costing as much as all the food. Back in our room, I mistake the prayer rug for a bathroom mat. The arrow on the ceiling of every room in a Muslim country, pointing to Mecca, reminds me that the place caters for Muslims and the nice thick bit of carpet is not to keep my toes warm on the tiled floor of the loo.

Wednesday is spent driving around Tanjung Priok Harbour, asking everyone we meet if there is a car ferry service to Malaysia – to Melaka or even Klang or Georgetown, even though they are miles further north. No one knows of anything like what we want. Ferocious-looking security guards nursing machine guns to protect the vital shipping industry from terrorists wave us through with barely a second glance. Yet again, white guys with flash cars are clearly special: colonial cringe alive and well in Indonesia. Or is it the line of Arabic script on the side of the car, saying 'Driving Melbourne to London' which makes us look special in a nation where not many can read Arabic but everyone recognises it as the calligraphy of the Koran? The same words are there in English and Chinese, but in Indonesia, the world's most populous Muslim nation, it is good to connect to Arabic.

A very helpful chainsmoker in an elaborate uniform suggestive of high rank, but who is actually in charge of three parking bays at the customs office, tells me to go to Pelni, the government ferry company. Throughout Indonesia we realise the more elaborate a uniform, the lesser the duties attached are likely to be. A gold-braided lanyard and sash is provided to every street-crossing supervisor and parking-bay attendant as if they are a field marshal or an admiral.

At Pelni I go into a dingy office where a cluster of business-suited middle-aged men seem busy on ancient computers. They are surprised to see me, and two quickly minimise the computer card games they are deeply involved with. Another is picking his nails with a penknife, a fourth reading the newspapers. They are all smoking. No one seems to do any work. I am deferentially ushered into the next room to see Mr Fresno, who is in charge of the ferry service to Palau Batam, a tiny Indonesian island just twenty minutes off the coast of Singapore. He sits behind an enormous desk adorned with an ancient typewriter, speaks little English, but explains that even after we get to Batam, our car will still need a shipping container for the final tiny hop over to Singapore, and that will take as long and cost as much as containerising it from Jakarta. There is no roll on, roll off ferry anywhere to Malaysia or Singapore. He elaborates that, as it is peak season, his ferry cannot take us until next week. I try to offer Mr Fresno a 'special fee' to get us to Batam on this week's ferry, but he shifts in his seat with embarrassment and laughs ostentatiously in refusal. I ought to have asked for his mobile number and called later to offer the bribe more discreetly when no one else was present – I have failed, again. I am a poor student of Asian bribing techniques. Jack says he would have done a better job of it. Another mistake.

Mr Fresno recommends we see a freight company nearby and sends us to see Miss Adelaide. It takes about an hour in the fumes and traffic to find her office even though it is only a few kilometres from the wharf. Our Bahasa Indonesian is inadequate for directions and very few people speak any English. We get lost several times, stuck on one-way streets and at no-turn intersections. The traffic is suffocating and my frustration is rising proportionately. I do several illegal U-turns across four or even five lanes of oncoming trucks and buses and get cautioned by a stern policeman, who wears a surgical mask while directing traffic. It is steaming hot and Jack is complaining that he is choking on fumes and is also bored. This is not going well. How can it be that our entire journey is jeopardised by this tiniest link in the chain? Can it really be so hard? If we take two weeks to get from Jakarta to Singapore, we will have to drive from there straight through to the China border to meet our nonnegotiable deadline with the China guides. It will ruin the Southeast Asian part of the trip – two weeks in Jakarta and Singapore instead of two weeks in the jungles of Cambodia and Laos. Not our idea of a good time.

Miss Adelaide, when we find her, is a middle-aged ethnic Chinese business woman of great charm. She speaks perfect English and has adopted the name of the city in South Australia where she lived for her school years. She offers a soothing cup of tea and a comfortable chair. I explain our plight. She is one of those people who assure you that everything will be all right – but refuses to say how much 'all right' will cost. She makes some phone calls and confirms there is no car ferry from Sumatra to Malaysia, that we must go via Singapore and that she will arrange everything for us. Reassured, we retreat to the shops. Retail therapy – fake Calvin Klein underpants and fancy brand T-shirts for $3.

The next day, we get a text from Miss Adelaide. The quote to containerise the car to Singapore is ridiculous. We could charter a ship for less. Sensing our desperation she has sought to take advantage of it. I become determined not to ship the car via Singapore, just to spite her and everyone else who is making things difficult, as if I can somehow conjure a non-existent service out of thin air by my anger. Jack tries to calm me down, but I am in a vengeful and spiteful frame of mind. We spread the maps out on the bed in our hotel and calculate our options. Jack hates Jakarta, the smog makes him ill, and I am less than enthralled. We decide to leave no matter what and go to Sumatra to see what we can find. If we drive a few days to Padang in central Sumatra we can see what is on offer once we are there. In a huff we take the freeway west and then the regular ferry for the twenty minute trip across the narrow straits from Java to Sumatra.

The change is immediate and refreshing. Sumatra is green, Java was grey. Jakarta was polluted, Sumatra is clean and rural. City people were aggressive, busy and pushy. Sumatra seems universally populated by gentle welcoming folk who want to help us. We like the vibe in the first large town, Bandar Lampung, and decide immediately to stay. The sight of a bustling container port encourages me to try again. Jan calls from home and while we explain our dilemma she trawls the internet afresh, and calls Indonesian travel companies. We drive past a travel agency with English signs outside. We go in and are welcomed by English-speaking Dolly. She spends half an hour on the phone, calling Dumai and Medan. She checks and rechecks for a car

There's always important work to do on Jakarta's docks.

ferry service. None exists. She offers to arrange for us to get to Singapore by train and ferry if we transport the car by ship.

Jan calls back to tell us she has spoken to three travel companies in Medan and Dumai and no one knows of any car ferry to Malaysia at all. I reluctantly admit defeat – but still kid myself that if we were to just go to Dumai we could surely find someone who would ship us across. Jack asks about the pirates – what if we end up being robbed of everything we own, all because I am pig-headed and refuse to believe what everyone is telling me? He lectures me about various character flaws that are becoming evident and I mutter quietly in unconvincing defence. Who said this father–son bonding was such a great idea? Tail between my legs, I retreat to our hotel. Simply using the tourist brochure I ring a freight company that advertises its services. An English-speaking clerk puts me through to a Mr Seno who comes to see us within an hour. He promptly quotes a fraction of the amount Miss Adelaide wanted, and promises the car will be in Singapore within a week. Missing link found.

We have three days before the ship leaves, and get to wander around Bandar Lampung and tour southern Sumatra. One evening I drive the car into a gaping pothole on the side of the road while parking. Our unstoppable beast sinks to its chassis, wheels spinning in thin air. Ten young men appear from cafes and together we pick the car up and lift it from the hole. I liberally distribute cigarettes by the packet, exhausting our supply of bribes. We eat at the street stalls – satays and fish curries and deep-fried dumplings galore – and we play badminton with Rizar and Almet, two very patient waiters, indulging me and encouraging Jack, who plays each shot like it is squash … but at least he hits the shuttle more often than not, which is more than can be said for his father.

Our first day trip is to Way Kambas Elephant Sanctuary, reputedly famous for soccer-playing elephants rescued from the forestry industry and rehabilitated for tourism. Driving several hours along a densely wooded highway, through villages of subsistence farms, banana plantations, tropical fruit orchards and commercial flower growing, we inhale deeply the perfumed jungle air. The terrain is lush and fertile. Down a long dirt road is a clearing with several picnic shelters and a car park adjoining a wire enclosure. Two large elephants with children riding on little seats are being led in circles by a trainer holding a small stick. Surrounded by the thick jungle, the chained elephants seem incredibly sad, plodding in dusty circles and tugging at tufts of grass as they wait for another payload of squealing infants. We have no appetite for this, and cannot believe that we have come all this way to see the famous elephants, only to discover such a tawdry display. Wandering around the back of the huts is a baby elephant no taller than our shoulders, chained to a tree. It is a sullen but still cute creature, frightened by the few people milling around. It is a bit of fun to pat it, but Jack wants to kidnap it, to unchain the beast and set it free in the jungle.

Hoping to salvage some adventure from the day, we plunge into the forest and within fifteen minutes of driving down a mud road, we find a massive bull elephant, tusks gleaming, munching on the foliage. He looks at us as we look at him. We take photos from the car, then Jack gets out for a better perspective. The elephant wanders over, Jack scouting behind for a good angle. I think it a good idea to offer the elephant a banana from the bunch on the back seat. It isn't. In a flash I am pinned in my seat by an enormous, wiry, pulsing, wrinkly trunk, the pink moist snout on its tip elastically roving around inside the car sniffing for more bananas. The elephant's head is up against the car window, one eye staring into mine through the open window frame. It dawns on me that this huge wild animal could tip the car over just by leaning on it, that the comical trunk is solid muscle and we are a long way from any help. I stuff a banana into the trunk tip which immediately curls towards the mouth, banana gone in a flash. I can smell the elephant's breath and see into its mouth. I yell to Jack to get into the car instead of taking photos, and keep offering bananas one at a time to an increasingly greedy pachyderm. Jack wants to get a better shot of what looks likely to become my last moments, prized photos of his idiotic father being crushed by a wild elephant. He ignores my slowly panicked calls for escape. I feed the beast the last banana. The elephant does not know there are no more. It presses its trunk deeper into the car, sniffing the gearstick, the heater controls and all the switches, leaving a trail of elephant dribble. I am grasping the trunk, overwhelmed with its power and the futility of trying to wrestle it. Jack calls out that he has got a really good shot and we can go now. The animal turns to look at him and takes its trunk out of the window. Jack suddenly realises the animal is moving towards him. He sprints around the front of the car and as I start to move off he rips the door open and jumps in as the car gathers speed. Once well away from the elephant we burst out laughing. We have been monumentally stupid.

Leaving the elephant park we stop at the roadside stalls at the ranger's hut to restock our banana supply. A uniformed guide approaches us and within a few minutes, and with the payment of a special fee, a boom gate is lifted, and a new guide joins us as we head off to see the rare endangered Sumatran rhino, of which it is thought fewer than 300 survive. As we drive through the jungle, through an elaborate set of locked gates and barricades designed to deter poachers, magnificent birds and monkeys bound out of the way. Thirty or so Sumatran tigers still live here, but never announce themselves to tourists. Arriving at the Sumatran Rhino Sanctuary we are greeted in English by the head vet who tells us he welcomes Australians because he works closely with the Perth zoo in Western Australia. He is in charge of a captive breeding programme here deep in the jungle, where five rhinos live in large enclosures of several acres in the rainforest while getting veterinary care and special diets. They have recently bred the first Sumatran rhino born in captivity and hope that they can save these magnificent animals from extinction. They get no money from the government, only from overseas philanthropists, and their work is itself now endangered.

Back in Bandar Lampung, we fill daypacks with bare essentials and deliver the laden car to the port, and with much fanfare and fuss it is lashed down inside a shipping container and trucked off to the ship. The paperwork takes hours; most of it spent looking for an officer with enough authority or confidence to apply the stamp to our carnet. We have lunch with Mr Seno and his assistant, and discuss

It seemed a good idea at the time.

worldly affairs including democracy and religion. He is a devout Muslim but wants to blend Islam with modernity. He worries about the way Westerners portray Islam as a violent religion and he despairs about corruption. 'It has been our way for thirty years,' he says and explains that now everyone is very determined to change.

Now we have to get to Singapore. The train station is at the opposite end of the town to our hotel, and it takes three visits and much sign language to secure our seats on the overnight train to Palembang. We join the crushing throng to get aboard and jostle and wrestle along with everyone else for our supposedly reserved seats. Everyone is sipping milky coffee through a straw from clear plastic bags. We buy take-away parcels of dumplings and bananas. The train rattles through the night and somehow we arrive after dawn at the port city of Palembang, another minor city of only two million people, from where a high-speed ferry goes to Palau Batam.

Palembang offers almost nothing historic, having been all but destroyed in battles between the Dutch and the Indonesians. We wander around the markets and visit the museums until Jack is approached by a group of three university-age girls who flirt openly with him, pretending to practise their English. Yaya is the best English speaker, and within minutes of chatting she explains that she wants to study in Australia and invites Jack to go fishing with her brother – she insists he uses bananas as bait. Jack declines. We eat at Palapa, the best *Ikan Bakar* (Indonesian tapas) in the world, and marvel at the waiter carrying sixteen plates on one arm as he serves the freshest, most diverse and appealing meal we have had in ages. Sardines, chicken in curry

Jon: It's getting a bit close!
Jack: Hang on, just one more photo...

sauce, pickled tomatoes, onions, chillied eggs, prawn pancakes, fried fish, fritters, beef coconut curry, spinach, tofu in coconut milk, the obligatory rice … it is the Rolls Royce of Padang dining.

The ferry from Palembang to Batam takes all the next day. It is an overcrowded smelly noisy thing, our seats hard up against the engine and as uncomfortable as possible. The trip seems to take forever, winding through swamps and low mangroves, occasional villages with houses suspended over the river to break the monotony. We both finish the books we carry and remain utterly bored. As the sun sets, we arrive at Batam and everyone tries to get off the ferry at once. It is a mad crush in the dark. We struggle ashore and look for the connecting boat to Singapore. There are no signs, no ticket offices, no information counters at all but eventually a taxi driver tells us the last ferry for Singapore leaves in ten minutes from another harbour on the opposite side of the tiny island, a ten-minute taxi ride away. We get there with moments to spare.

The Singapore influence is immediate. We go from a Third World tub to a modern, clean, quiet and punctual service in a blink. It is a shock. No one throws rubbish on the floor – no one sits on the floor. No one spits, no one fights to get on or off. The Singapore ferry terminal is like a shopping mall. I already miss the Indonesian chaos. Everything instantly costs five times more than it has for the last two months.

Singapore is slick and Western, orderly and officious. I spend two entire days waiting in queues, filling in forms, paying the minimum three months insurance for the car (even though it would be on the road in Singapore for about two hours) and securing a freeway pass for an exorbitant amount. I meet a French couple driving around the world. They have just been told their vehicle is illegal in Singapore, and will need to go by truck to the Malaysia border, because it is left-hand drive and equipped with a gas-fuelled stove. They have already spent two days negotiating with the Singaporeans – my paperwork is progressing swiftly compared to theirs. I torture the clerk at the Land Transport Office, appropriately named Austin, according to his badge, who insists that it is not possible to process my freeway pass in less than two days … I offer to sleep on the floor of the office until he issues me with the electronic pass, without which we face arrest and possibly execution. Magically it can be done after all.

We indulge in breakfast at Raffles Hotel. A genuine five-star colonial relic, we stick out like sore thumbs. We eat as much as is humanly possible and I feel like Mr Creosote in the Monty Python sketch, who explodes when he eats 'just a wafer-thin mint … only a tiny, little, thin one'. Smoked salmon, porridge, omelette, cheeses, poached fruit, fruit bread, patisserie, tropical fruits … and straight-laced business people and wealthy retired tourists all being thoroughly dignified around us. Jack decides to souvenir a spoon, and is shattered when he uncovers it later to find it does not have Raffles engraved on it – he took the wrong one.

One incident in Singapore illustrates the culture of this city-state amply. We are waiting at a busy intersection just near the start of a toll road. There are massive overhead gantries that illuminate scrolling traffic alert messages for drivers. It is one minute before eight at night, and a luxury car is stopped in the middle of the road under the gantry for no obvious reason. It is blocking the traffic, as if broken down. As the clock changes to eight o'clock, the car moves off onto the toll road, and the traffic flows again. The man beside us at the crossing explains that after eight there is no charge to use the road, but before eight it costs fifty cents. The driver of this expensive car has just saved fifty cents. 'In Singapore everything is about money,' our companion sighs.

We have one more day to wait for the car and we meet up with an ABC Television colleague stuck in Singapore for the worst possible reason. Peter Lloyd is a famous foreign correspondent who is on bail in Singapore after being arrested. He is awaiting trial on drug trafficking charges that could see him in goal for a very long time or sentenced to a caning by the rattan. He has been in the headlines in Australia and Singapore, and I offer to take him out for lunch to cheer him up. We spend hours eating and talking; he is charming and very interested in Jack and our trip, eager for company. After a while he tells us about his arrest and explains how he came to use recreational drugs – as a form of self-medication after years of reporting traumatic events around Asia. He had been sent by the ABC to terrorist bombings, plane crashes, the tsunami … and never with any debriefing or a proper holiday. His marriage had ended and he had found comfort in the gay party scene. He is terrified about going back into gaol and tells us about the few days he was in custody before getting bail, where as a gay man he was singled out for extra humiliation by the guards. I hope we have cheered him up, even if only for a day. He is later sentenced to ten months' prison after pleading guilty to lesser charges than the trafficking allegations that always seemed fanciful, and is granted early release in June 2009.

The Beijing Olympics closing ceremony is on TV. We have been keeping a close eye on the Games – not just the sport, but the security – and hoping each day passes without incident. Our permit to drive along the Silk Road through China depends on the Games progressing without major terrorism problems, particularly in Tibet or the Muslim western province of Xinjiang. Our tour company NAVO forewarned us that the authorities are very sensitive about foreigners being in any of the rebellious regions, and we still do not know which way we will go. A report of a bomb exploding in Kashgar outside an army base just days before the opening ceremony had spooked us, but the closing ceremony seems to be a triumph for China and we keep our fingers crossed. The Paralympics now need to go smoothly, the Chinese Government having told NAVO that we are not allowed to cross the border until that too has finished without major incident. The Olympics coverage throughout Indonesia has focused exclusively on badminton – and anything less than a gold medal is greeted with open disbelief. I cannot recall ever seeing anything about badminton on Australian TV in any Olympics. Every country goes overboard on its own heroes.

Next morning, at the docks, I get a special photo ID card before I am allowed to enter the secure zone, then watch the container being opened, drive my car off the wharf and through the traffic to the hotel. Unbelievably, from here we will drive overland the whole way to Europe – the next water obstacle will be the Dardanelles in Turkey, to cross from the continent of Asia to Europe, hopefully around early December. We leave Singapore without looking back.

Rice drying on the road —
what else are roads for?

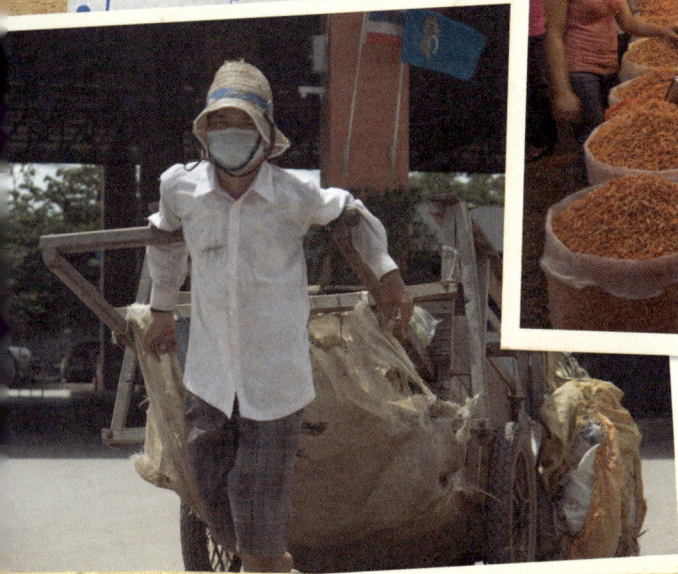

Thai market stalls —
delicious and cheap.

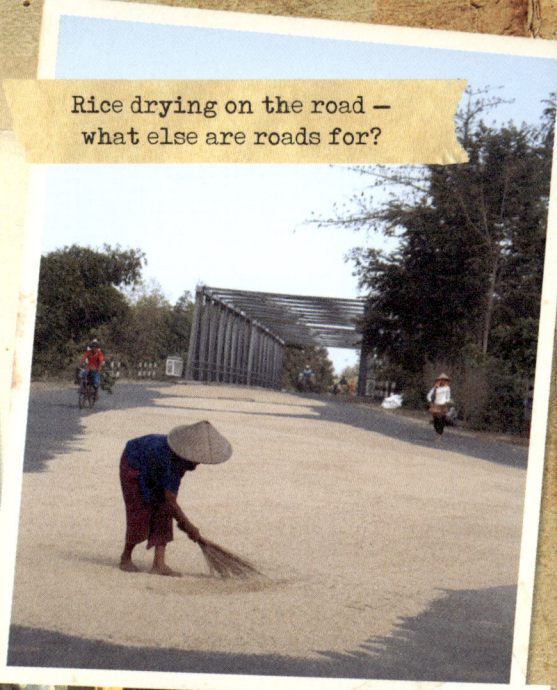

The border crossings process trucks, cars,
busses ... And hand carts. Thai — Cambodia border.

ยินดีต้อนรับสู่ประเทศไทย
WELCOME TO THAILAND

ONE DA
SOKHA HOTEL C
Date of entry :   2/9
Date of expiry :   2/9/
Nationality :   Q09
This portion to be kept by visitor and shown [...]
NON-TRA[...]

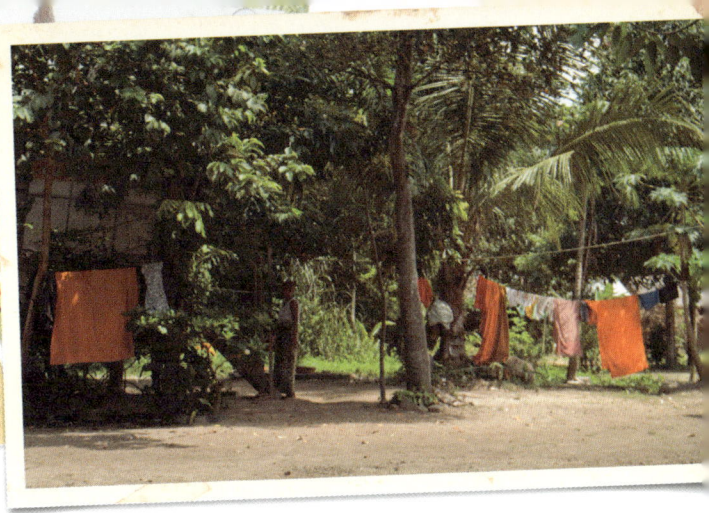

11 | Plastic Chairs

In which we race through beautiful places in order to get to plain ones; get swept away in an anti-government protest in Bangkok; choose a gay brothel as a hotel; and suffer from an overdose of Buddhas. In Cambodia, the Killing Fields remind us that we are condemned to repeat the mistakes of the past if we do not learn our own history.

We drive straight through Malaysia and Thailand. Not that we want to, but we have to. There is less than four weeks before we must rendezvous with our guide at the Laos–China border, and four entire countries to get through. Where best to spend it? Jack raves about the delights of the Laotian jungle and Phnom Penh. He visited both just six months before with friends. 'Why would you spend time hanging out in some shit hotel in a city instead of the mountains, like at Nong Khiaw on the river? We might even meet travellers instead of tourists …' I detect a dose of serious travel snobbery; probably my fault and influence, if I dare confess the truth.

But he is right – what are we doing and why are we doing it? There is not much point in getting here and spending too much of our time hanging out in Western-style shopping malls, stocked with the same consumer goods and branded clothing as we could find at home. This is not a shopping expedition. We want to see and smell and eat the experiences we could not have at home, visit the places that show us how people whose lives are not imitations of TV sitcoms or Hollywood romances might live. How can we grow our experiences and challenge our view of the world?

At the opposite end of the spectrum we are not seeking bragging rights for being the most audacious or the most extreme either. Our trip need not be compared to whatever other people are choosing to do. We know it is a folly, a fantasy, an itch being scratched.

My laptop has died. Did it cook in the heat of the shipping container? It is like a limb has been severed. Despite rejoicing at being away from work I am still connecting to the internet most days, checking the news at home and wherever we are. I am struggling to disconnect, until the laptop does it for me. After a few days offline we stop for a night or two in Bangkok to repair the infernal machine, and, as soon as we arrive, find ourselves lost in the teeming traffic and gridlock caused by anti-government protests. There are people everywhere with coloured scarves around their heads, crowds chanting all around us. Thailand has been in the grip of a seemingly insoluble constitutional crisis for months and it is erupting onto the streets. We barely move for half an hour, eventually rescued when a sympathetic activist with a megaphone takes pity on us and directs us out of the demonstration and towards where a hotel may be. For just the briefest of moments I think like an ABC staffer and consider reporting back on what we see. Then I recover my senses, remind myself I am on leave and disconnect from the world of work. Jack is pickpocketed at Jatujak market, a massive assembly of 10,000 stalls and 20,000 thieves, and loses his cherished diary and sunglasses, both from the same pocket – the only things that get stolen in our entire trip. But of all the crap that could be taken, it has to be his notepad, full of sketches and memories and jottings. He just might have been seen wiping away a tear.

Thailand is full of contrast. The beach resorts are legendary and rightfully attract tourists from all over the world. Away from the beaches, it is grimy and much bespoiled. Bangkok is a jungle as dense as anything found in the wilds of Sumatra. You have to love a country where even the petrol station has a shrine to honour ancestors. Everyone who walks past any of the frequent street shrines clasps their palms together in front of their lips as a sign of respect, bowing to their forebears. But the worship of the god of retail overwhelms any other religion, and Bangkok reminds me of Sodom and Gomorrah.

Bangkok, September 1, 2008

Indonesia is behind us. So is Singapore and Malaysia and tomorrow Thailand will be a memory. After five glorious weeks in the Indonesian archipelago that were nothing short of life-changing we have fallen behind our mythical itinerary. Sadly, we had to sprint through Malaysia's rainforests and southern Thailand's beaches to get to Bangkok (to eat ourselves stupid). Something had to give. Travel is always a frustrating compromise within yourself and on this occasion the stomach won. Bangkok is a mesmerisingly chaotic jumble that demands visitors peek around that next corner, walk into that marketplace and eat that smoking, juicy satay sitting on a banana leaf next to an open BBQ. The tangle of freeways and monorail lines that clouds the city gives us mere humans walking beneath the sense of constantly being cooped up and surrounded. The sun beats down through the smog making me regret my recent lack of exercise.

Tomorrow we are off to Cambodia. Dad's computer is broken so we have very limited (and expensive!) internet access.

We get lost on the way north on the frenzy that is Bangkok's freeways, eventually hiring a taxi to lead us out of town; we make good time to the Cambodian border, whizzing past the endless topiary elephants that adorn the freeway. As we try to clear customs and immigration an officious man with gold epaulettes rejects our carnet and yells rudely, 'TCM4, you need TCM4,' and refuses to tell me what a TCM4 is. He says, 'You go back to Sadao,' which is over 1200 kilometres south, back at the Malaysian border. I try charm, bribes, pleading … everything. I ask if someone else can process our papers, but there is no one with more gold on their shoulders and this officer seems to be in charge. We are stuck. Jack reverts to his typical strategy of kicking his football around while I stew. I try hard not to look angry, and to remember that in Asia it is vital neither to lose face nor to insist on a solution where anyone else loses face. This level of discipline tests me to the limit – my natural tendency is to be assertive and impatient. After some hours of walking around the border post looking for someone who can speak English, I find a more senior officer and eventually an interpreter, explain our plight, and he asks me, 'How long you return to Thailand?' I tell him that we are not coming back – we are on a one-way trip to London. He immediately laughs and in a flash stamps our passports and carnet and tells us to go. I ask the interpreter what just happened. He explains that they thought we had a hire car that we were taking from Thailand into Cambodia and back again. We gratefully cross through the boom gate.

Thailand is right-hand drive. Cambodia is left-hand drive. No man's land is both. For about 200 metres no one knows which side of the road to drive on. The paved freeway stops and dirt and mud take over. Thai orderliness surrenders to anarchy. The Cambodian government provides a strip of dirt pretending to be a road and then what you do with it is entirely up to you.

East towards Siem Riep it is one endless construction site, culverts, ditches and every few hundred metres bridges in various stages of disrepair, washouts and open drains slowing our progress to a crawl. Someone in this district of Cambodia has been very creative with an oxy torch. Ten-year-old Camrys have had their roofs surgically removed, making for open-top no-door cars. To stop the chassis collapsing and the entire car bending banana-style, an LPG bottle has been welded across each door pillar as a brace. I try desperately to photograph these contraptions hooning along with seats removed, drivers sitting on plastic garden chairs, but fail each time. It is an engineering miracle and a safety nightmare. But these are people who have bigger worries to face than road-worthiness tests.

Jack remembers reading something about the plastic chair being the most ubiquitous symbol of Western influence in the world. I say it is Coca-Cola, omnipresent and iconic, and we try to figure out what comes first – supply or demand. Do people in dirt-poor countries want plastic chairs? Is there something wrong with what they have sat on for thousands of years that is corrected by the arrival of the plastic chair? Does it change the way they live once the plastic chair is there? Mysteries unanswered as we barrel along the dirt and mud roads of Cambodia.

Siem Riep is the tourist town where hotels service Angkor Wat, the twelfth-century World Heritage temple complex that draws visitors from around the world. We select a hotel, squabble over Jack's navigating and map reading, ignore the Western-style chains and monoliths on the highway and discover a pleasant back-street affair with a central leafy courtyard and prices we can manage. A wander through town for dinner is our first encounter since Darwin with backpackers and wall-to-wall internet cafes, dodgy dope dealers and the shocking sight of an orchestra of amputees playing traditional stringed instruments. Each busker is missing one or more limbs, a legacy of the land mines and the ruination of war that has so devastated this country. Dozens

Another day on the road in Cambodia.

Home-made and hand-cranked — the
artificial leg explains the engineering.

of puffy, unattractive middle-aged Western men strut the streets with gorgeous young local girls on their arms. It is tempting to be judgmental and to assume the worst about these often incongruous couples, but many seem happy and the equation cuts both ways. What do we really know about other people's lives?

Our hotel, however, turns out to be something more than we planned for. Sitting in the cool of the courtyard with a beer and the laptop to update the blog, I am struck by the imbalance of gender in the guests. It all makes sense when a chatty Australian man at the next table finishes his drink and calls the waiter for what I expect to be the bill. Instead, he slips his hand into the young staffer's shirt, caresses his stomach and then arm in arm they go up the stairs. Jack is in our room, playing with his camera and finessing photos on his computer. I wonder if it even matters that the menu extends beyond snacks and drinks and whether I even need to tell him what I have seen. How worldly is my nineteen-year-old son? Am I kidding myself? I race into the room and tell all.

The news reports that the demonstrations in Bangkok have turned ugly, and there has been a death and more than forty injuries in the same crowd we were stuck in a day before. When I tell Jack he flippantly says he wishes we were still there as 'I have never been somewhere in an emergency ...'

Angkor Wat is the Asian Vatican, on a scale with Pompeii. It overwhelms with its sheer size and richness. It is sacrilege to only spend one day exploring, but that is what we do. The sculptural friezes, the bas-reliefs and murals, the intricate detail in the story-telling reinforce my ignorance of the intersection of the Hindu and Buddhist traditions. Temples vary from the magnificently restored to the ruined, some swallowed by the jungle, vines twisting and eating the stones, swallowing them python-like after squeezing the life out of them. Each temple tells its story and has a role to play, in this vast complex that spreads out like a city through the fields and foliage. Incalculable hours by unimaginable numbers of craftsmen are responsible over years for carving these pieces, all painstakingly worked by hand with primitive tools. Watching some of the restoration work going ahead with modern tools reinforces how amazingly difficult and painstaking it must have been to make these buildings with whatever was available centuries ago. The more we see, the less we know.

But the lasting impressions are not just the structures and their layers of meaning, but the people whose livelihood depends on the tourists. The complex is Cambodia's biggest drawcard, and tourism the main cash cow for the nation's economy. A whole family's income depends on who we buy a bottle of water from. Children miss school day in and day out so they can tout, selling postcards and souvenirs. The tip we pay our tuk-tuk driver is an irrelevance in our ordered world but sustenance in his. Some tourists complain about being hassled to buy trinkets and fake antiques all over the world, but what we spend is small change in our world and everything to them. Regard it as an indirect tax on travel – if you go somewhere exotic, then just accept that the overall cost includes passing some of your money around to the locals.

That evening, I do one of my regular radio chats, this time to ABC Radio's Trevor Chappell. Trev asks, 'Does being in such a religious country make you think more about God?' It is a point of regular debate with Jack, and I detect that he is developing a fashionable regard for Buddhism. He seems respectful of Buddhists' ritual – much more so than any other religion. I am a thoroughly lapsed Jew, no doubt to the chagrin of my parents. Jan is a lapsed Catholic and Jack and Nigel have been brought up to have respect for all religion but have never attended any religious ceremonies. It is a puzzle to me that Buddhism is regarded as the fad religion of choice for people disillusioned with the conventional offerings, and is promoted as a peaceful school of worship. Yet here the ground is soaked in blood from centuries of religious battles and slaughter, conveniently overlooked by the Hollywood version. I tell Trev that we do talk about religion, but more in confusion than certainty. The reality is that we argue about it constantly. Is it Jack testing the boundaries, developing a worthwhile curiosity as well as finding out what his father does not know? Is he set to join the Hare Krishna? Scientology? What is the difference between them all anyway? Is a sect just a new religion? And how is a cult different? What sets some apart as respectable and others as disreputable? He has been reading Hemingway and now starts Kerouac; those choices reflected in our discussions. It is to become a recurring theme for the rest of the trip. Hours and hours in the car are filled with these often circular debates.

It is only a few hours' drive on to Phnom Penh. Thirty years ago the fanatical Khmer Rouge staged their revolution and slaughtered a generation of thinkers, teachers, writers and anyone else who posed a threat to their regime. The anarchy that followed the collapse of their rule is still being sorted out, and the capital city is a frenzied mass of still-displaced Cambodians and hordes of foreign aid agencies and their workers. We stay with some French friends, the Mouzards, Jack's second

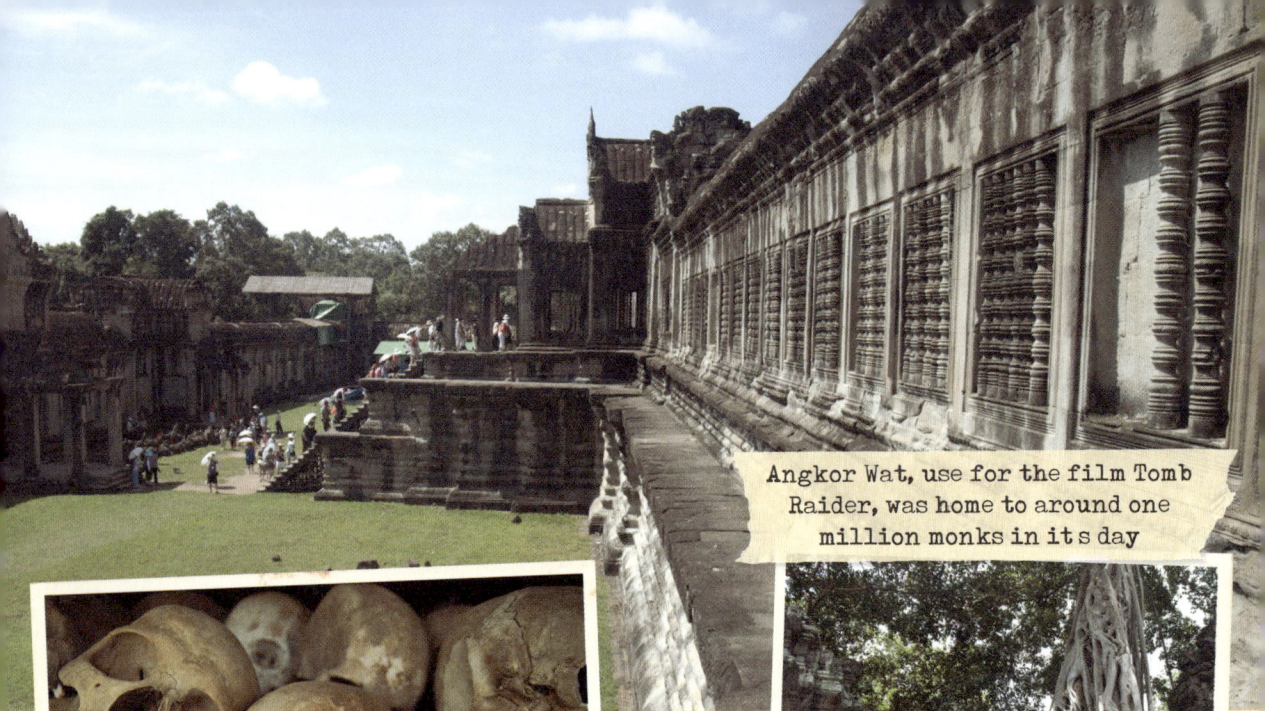

Angkor Wat, use for the film Tomb Raider, was home to around one million monks in its day

The Killing Fields in Phnom Penh are a chilling memorial to the generation murdered by Pol Pot's regime.

family who he lived with in Nantes when on student exchange. Their son Theo later came to live with us, and Theo and Jack have remained firm friends. Alain, Isabelle and young Antoine are living in the Cambodian capital working in a French-funded hospital and escaping what they fear will be an unpleasant time in France under President Sarkozy. They live in a mansion, tended by several staff. Alain explains that their house is owned by a woman who defied the Khmer Rouge and squatted here as the regime collapsed. With her family she just grabbed houses abandoned by families who had perished. There is one renowned landlord who apparently grabbed around a hundred houses in the central city that way. There was no rule of law, no authority at all. So the bourgeoisie slaughtered by the Khmer Rouge have, over time, been replicated. Seeing Jack interact with his 'other' parents is invigorating, but I struggle to understand the rapid colloquial French, including Jack's, let alone say what I want the way I want to say it. For someone who makes a living out of talking it is a frustrating reality check.

Phnom Penh is like the Wild West. Urchins search for scraps in the street as a brand new cream Bentley glides past. Who can afford the Porsche Cayenne 4x4, the big new latest model BMW, Mercedes and Audis roaming around? Slums ring the central districts, an elephant walks down the main street, the Mekong River tumbles through. We visit the Killing Fields, immortalised in the Hollywood film of the same name, now a memorial park encompassing the mass graves, exposed human bones, piles of teeth, remnant clothing and tributes to the dead, weeping at the enormity of the horror there revealed. The Tuol Sleng Museum at the old high school, used as a prison and torture centre, is nauseating but essential visiting. Graphic displays reveal the horror of the fanatical communist Khmer generals. Twenty thousand prisoners were sent there, seven people survived to tell of the horrors within. Their testimony will be crucial in the looming war crimes trials, thirty years after the regime lost power.

Cambodia also serves up an introduction to the world of international aid agencies. Since we left Australia Jack has been talking of one day working in the Third World. So many of his generation think globally and express an interest in human rights. We spend a day with Chanel and Cam, two Australian charity workers living in Phnom Penh. Chanel works for a Swiss charity called Hagar that assists trafficked women and their children. They show us around the refuge. The forty or fifty women with their children would be on the street if not for this Christian aid organisation. Chanel seems slightly uncomfortable when I ask if prayers and religion are an intrinsic part of their operation. Is it missionary work disguised as a refuge for trafficked women? She assures us there is no insistence on joining the prayer groups. Her husband Cam was working for World Vision, but has just that day purchased a cafe that employs young survivors of trauma and trains them in hospitality. Then the next day, at the junction of the Mekong with the Sekong River at Stung Treng, we meet Alex, the manager of the TonLe Guesthouse. Operating as a training venture, local school leavers working here are learning how to cook, clean and wait on tables in order to make them employable in tourism.

Alex tells how he was a high-powered IT guru in Switzerland who found himself on holiday in Thailand when the 2004 tsunami hit. He volunteered his computer skills and established a database for identifying bodies and matching retrieved passports and other found possessions. As Jack sits enthralled, Alex tells how he felt useful here and his life back in Switzerland lost meaning. He has been volunteering his services in several different Asian countries ever since, with some low-key funding from Swiss companies he used to work with. He has been drawn to Cambodia to get involved with the rebuilding of a society ravaged by genocide. Because of the Khmer Rouge, an entire generation of Cambodians was lost, and with them their culture – that is what a cultural revolution is about. Alex is now expanding his guest house to embrace a new project: retrieving lost local recipes and food, finding scraps of information to piece together the puzzle of what ingredients people used and how food was cooked before the genocide. There is so much to do to make Cambodia sustainable again after thirty years of horror.

From Jon on www.MelbourneToLondon.com

Phnom Penh, September 8, 2008

The world made a promise after the enormity of the Holocaust was revealed at the end of World War II. We promised it would not happen again. But it did. We failed.

Visiting Phnom Penh is a charming but also chilling experience. While soaking up the French-influenced ambience, it is simply impossible to ignore the all-too-recent horrors of the Khmer

Rouge. The Killing Fields and the S-21 Tuol Sleng Genocide Museum are compelling places to visit. The Killing Fields Memorial is an eight-storey high stupa filled with skulls encased in glass. Mass graves dot the fields, disconcertingly close to ordinary local farms. Likewise, the old high school used as a torture centre by Pol Pot and his ghouls is slap bang in the middle of the suburbs, blocks of flats abutting. The neighbours MUST have known what was happening at this grisly location, where as many as 20,000 people were tortured and killed as the Khmer Rouge purged the nation of a generation of intellectuals, professionals, free thinkers – anyone they thought may be a threat to their regime.

But Cambodia is a lot more than just a gruesome horror show. Welcoming, friendly and fun, it is also home to zillions of NGOs, organisations trying to help Cambodia get things back in order. We visit two: a refuge for trafficked women run by HAGAR, and TonLe, a guesthouse in Stung Treng where local kids are trained in tourism. Both do wonderful work with not enough money and depend on overseas (mainly Swiss) donations.

Now we have crossed the Mekong River in Laos and head for the mountains.

The jungle border,
Cambodia and Laos.

12 | BBQ Dog

In which our intrepid heroes dodge avian flu, encounter smugglers, float through a mountain, choke and gag at BBQ dog and join the search for unexploded landmines in the jungle.

From Jack on www.MelbourneToLondon.com

One Day at a Time, September 12, 2008

Day by day, city by city, country by country, we realise how large and complex the world is. We realise how ridiculous it is to try and traverse more than half of it in a meagre six months. We realise that the car is a very small place to spend that time. We realise that we've got a long journey ahead of us.

Never again will I chuckle about how 'it's a small world . . .' It really isn't.

We have now come more than 13,000 kilometres through eight countries. We arrived in Laos less than a week ago. We came up from Cambodia, and within only a few kilometres of the border the cows were fatter, the people were stockier, and the roads were flatter. We plodded up to Central Laos passing straw-hut villages and every now and then the provincial riverside towns, their streets lined with romantic, decaying French colonial buildings.

A sleepy, bare-chested man is sitting at an outside table under the shade of the only tree, drowsily rubbing his eyes. He has a woven ikat sarong on, nothing else. A bowl of porridge-like breakfast sits in front of him, half eaten. He looks at us as if we are intruding – which we undoubtedly are.

'*Subaydii*,' we chorus in greeting, waving passports at him because this undressed man is the only Laotian guard securing the border between Cambodia and Laos. He grunts in official reply.

'Five dollar, my stamp, five dollar,' he says, and will not say another word. I make theatrical protests at this extortion; he equally theatrically shuts his rubber stamp pad and starts to turn away. I instantly find the required US$5.

'Five dollar and five dollar,' he says, pointing to each of us. The price has just doubled. I produce the carnet, and haggle for three stamps for the price of two.

We had moments earlier arrived at the border crossing at Dong Kalaw, a shingle shack on the single-lane road, adjacent to a wobbly boom gate, where the Cambodian officials had a small deck under cover, their 'office' just a tiny cubby with a bed and a stool. A flag flopped outside, the bent pole of the boom blocking the path of the occasional car or truck that came through. We were early, and it was as though we had ambushed the guards. They laughed heartily at us, stamped our passports and carnet without hesitation and waved and smiled as we passed through.

We drove through no man's land, maybe 500 metres. Yet again I told Jack to take his feet off the dashboard, to sit up in his seat, turn off the music, to look as if he is not a threat to national security. I am convinced we will be detained one day and charged with the offence of an overt display of teenage attitude. He sighed the resigned pout of the ever-put-upon adult-child, worldly beyond his years but still a father's son. It has been ten weeks since we left home – two months of 24-hour-a-day cohabitation and travel within the confines of either the car or a small room. We have not shouted at each other or had any real arguments … yet. But the tensions are building and I feel he is indulging me. He weighs heavily the injustice of being trapped on an exotic trip with his father of all people!

I need not have worried – no arrest this time as it became clear that security will not be a concern here. The jungle has been cleared, the vegetation stripped back to trimmed grass as we approached a second gate where we had to stop. Off to the side we found a damp wooden hut with a military Jeep parked beside it and the undressed border guard yawning and rubbing his eyes.

He does not look into the car, or check the contents. No one has searched the car or shown the slightest interest in our luggage since we got off the ship at the docks in Dili. We have crossed six borders without being searched at all. Passports endorsed, we get back in the car, and as we prepare to drive on, I suddenly decide I want a photo of this charming example of Laotian officialdom. Jack thinks I am crazy, refuses despite his duties as trip photographer and begs me to leave the official alone.

'Go and take his photo.'

'No, it's not a good shot, and the light is lousy,' he replies.

'Stuff the light, it's a great shot. Can you go and snap it and stop wasting time?'

'If you want it, you take it; I'm not,' asserts the official photographer.

So I return, cradling the camera.

'Five dollars, photo,' I offer, thinking that as we've just found out the immigration officer is for sale, it is just a matter of price and that he'll know a bargain when he sees one.

'No, no, no ... NO!' he yells, starting to rise from his seat, still undressed, his pot belly wobbling as his midriff clears the bench top. Again, Jack proves to be a more astute judge than I am – but it was worth a try.

The border region boasts two of Laos' prime tourist attractions, the Irrawaddy dolphins and the 4000 Islands on the Mekong River. We pause for long enough to decide it looks too touristy and press ahead. Another mistake.

The terrain throughout Cambodia was totally flat, no hills or anything resembling a mountain anywhere. Cambodia is like Holland with rice paddies. But within an hour of crossing into Laos, the road starts to wind through woody hills. The jungle presses in on us, birdlife reappears and families of monkeys stare curiously from the side of the road. Buffalo seem to wallow in every creek and ditch, and any hut or village we drive through looks well endowed with chickens and goats. Laos is poor but not as poor as Cambodia. Some houses are even made of brick, roofs of iron instead of thatch. Electricity works, taps produce water when turned on. Thailand is just to the west, across the river, and the Second Friendship Bridge has recently opened, making road travel between poor Laos and rich Thailand an easy trip. The ferries that until recently ploughed across the Mekong sit rotting and abandoned on the riverbanks at Savannakhet.

We head north searching for the turn-off to an exotic river that flows through a mountain. Lonely Planet describes 'a river disappearing at the edge of a monolithic limestone mountain and running seven kilometres through a pitch-black, winding

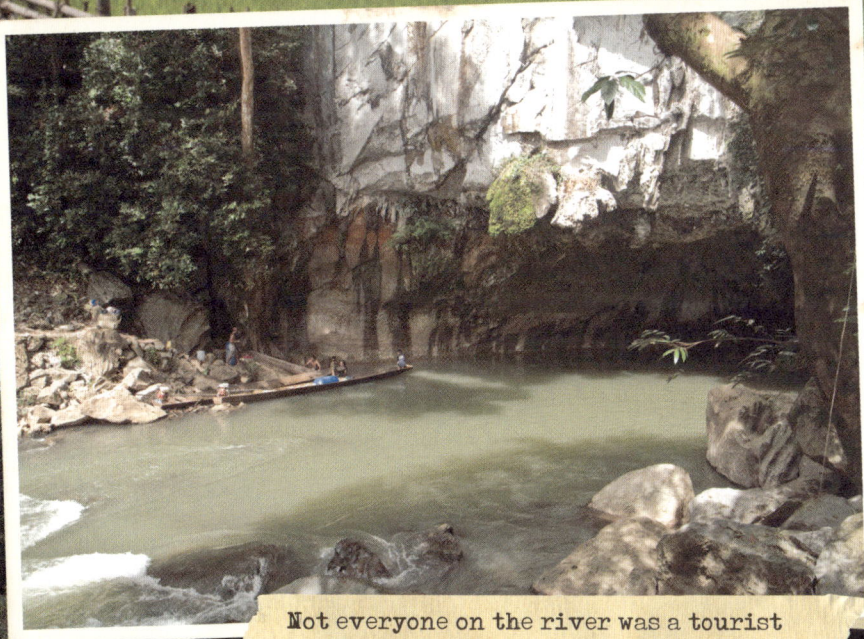

Not everyone on the river was a tourist
— smugglers taking petrol through
theTong Lo Cave into Vietnam.

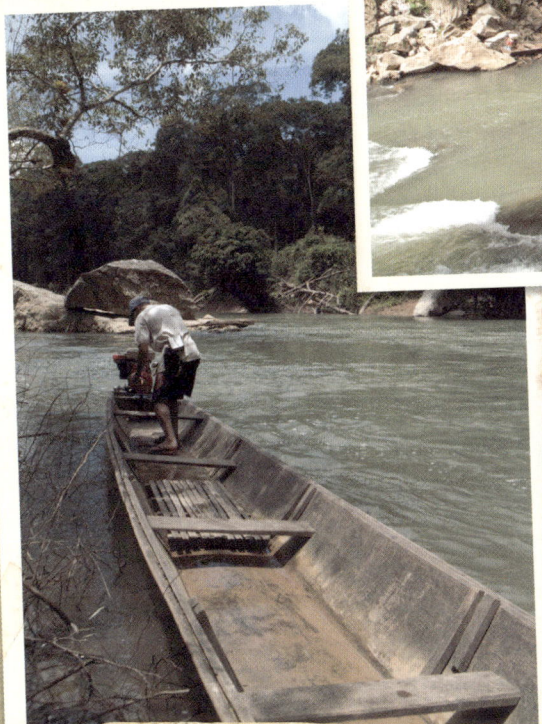

Attaching an outboard motor
for a cruise through the
Tong Lo Cave, Northern Laos.

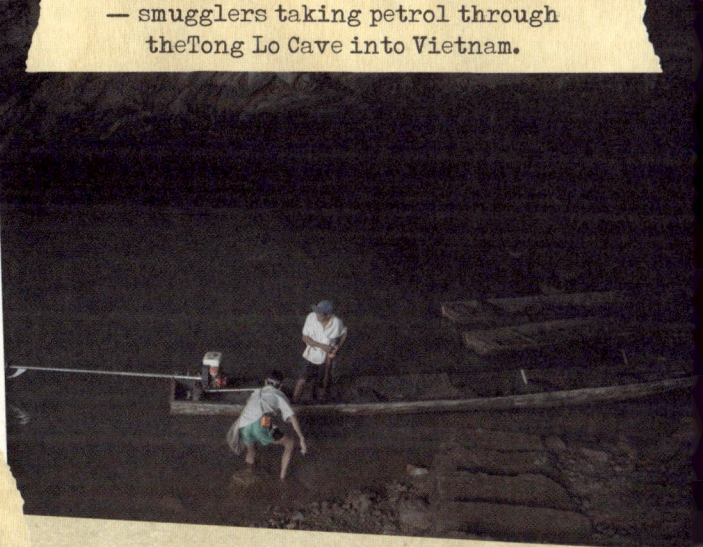

cave ...' Jack volunteers to find it. 'Come on, Dad,' he pleads, 'let's do stuff. I'm sick of sitting in the car and driving.' I am too, but it is not because I lack the adventure gene. It has been an incredible slog to get here, and until we got past Phnom Penh I was always wondering if we would actually make it. The pre-paid deposit of thousands of dollars sent to the China tour company NAVO means I'm still anxious about meeting that deadline. So much depends on it, so much can still go wrong – as my head hits the pillow each night I run through how far we have to go and how long we have to get there, allowing for the inevitable problems. When will the car break down? What if we are robbed? When will we lose our passports? What if beri-beri or bubonic plague strikes us down? When will a dinosaur step out of the jungle and rip our heads off? Anything could still happen, and as it turns out it nearly does. But more on bird flu later.

Hoping to indulge my jaded son, we follow a rutted muddy road through rice paddies over endless bridges still under construction, almost impassable, driving according to the compass and the map. There are no signs or road markings anywhere and we end up at a dead end amidst a village of houses on stilts, pigs and chickens running beneath, and one small sign in English, 'Bed Food' – they must be expecting tourists! Are we in the right place, a village called Ban Kong Lor? Two young boys spy us, engage in animated one-way conversation in Laotian and escort us across the mud to a riverbank. Three or four skinny wooden longboats with longshaft motors clamped to the back are bobbing in the brown water beside the buffaloes. We ask in sign language about the caves and enthusiastic nods and quick negotiation secures a ride. The boatman straps a torch to his head, we wobble aboard the leaky vessel and off we go. In just two minutes we get to the mouth of what seems to be just a large wide cave ... except the river is flowing from it, water cascading out like a giant bath spout. We pass some small rapids and continue on inside the cave. The light fades and only the headtorch pierces the pitch black. The beam cuts through, and for an hour we putter along the river inside the mountain, stalactites, stalagmites and sensational rock formations, sandbanks and little beaches breaking the journey. The glimmer of reflected light from the water onto the cave ceiling makes a lightshow that technology cannot replicate – a haunting beauty combining with the utter silence whenever the motor is off reminding us of our tiny existence in the face of nature so raw.

The leaky dugout is precariously balanced, threatening to tip up on any sudden movement. The water is black, usually deep but occasionally we scrape the bottom as we go through shale and pebble rapids. It is so dark you cannot see your own hand in front of your face. The opposite end of the cave is nearly into Vietnam, and the river serves as a popular route for smugglers. The return journey, downstream, is fast and smoother, drifting with the current, until we emerge into sunlight back where we started.

Blinking rapidly as we exit the cave, we follow the 'Bed Food' sign down a path through a rice paddy. A collection of huts welcomes us, but not a soul is to be seen. We wander around, and are eventually greeted by a tall man in traditional woven ikat, and I try to explain we are looking for somewhere to stay. Using the phrase book and mangling the language I try to say, 'Room, meals, how much?' His reply is in perfect Australian English! Yoi had lived in Crows Nest in Sydney as a refugee after escaping the war and went to Chatswood High School. His brother had been sent to Australia on a Colombo Plan scholarship and Yoi, escaping the communists and a re-education camp, had joined him there. He is as surprised at our arrival at Sala Hin Boun as we are to find him.

We are the only tourists to arrive for weeks, and we sit on the veranda and talk all night while his staff cook fresh, delicious chicken and fish. We learn local history, religion and of Laotian nationalism. 'We never forget that Laos was the empirical power in Southeast Asia for hundreds of years until the seventeenth century. Now we are poor relations to the Thais, but we have not forgotten – although we know it will not happen again.' He explains how Thailand has ridden a wave of modernity by so closely aligning with the USA, but 'the Thais just work all the time, we are a much more relaxed people'. Cambodia ten years ago was 'like Rambo – machine guns everywhere and warlords still defiant. Progress now is slow but there are things happening. UNCTAD [the UN Development Agency] is the problem – they pour billions into the economy, inflation is 13 per cent and locals cannot afford anything.'

Jack asks Yoi what he misses about living in Australia. 'I miss the TV shows, and the newspaper ... here I earn one-tenth of what I did in Australia but I have probably added fifteen years to my life and I am happy. We worry now about China, the sleeping dragon ... it is unstoppable. We are wary – they have too much influence and they sell everything cheap here just like in Australia.'

Next morning, Yoi leads the way as we walk down the path to Pone Nyang, the adjacent village, and watch a woman introduced as Ka-In weaving on her wooden loom, tucked in amongst the stilts propping up her home. He translates as we offer to buy the traditional black, white and red patterned fabrics, the little wooden battens still attached. Her husband, excited at so many dollars appearing, rushes inside and brings out a bag with more woven cloth in it. We buy the lot – it does not get more authentic, to buy direct from the weaver rather than at the markets. I curb my haggling instincts, wary of taking advantage in such an unequal transaction.

We could stop off with Yoi for weeks. He is the perfect host: gentle, spiritual and unobtrusive but engaging and knowledgeable when you do connect. The river slurps and bubbles alongside the armchairs, birds and goats interrupting the tranquillity. Yoi's guest house, Sala Hin Boun, has all the simple pleasures of a remote location combined with basic Western amenities, nestled beneath limestone mountains, jungle on one side and village life on the other. As the bridges on the new road will soon be finished, many more tourists will be able to access the caves and Yoi may be busier than he ever wanted. But if we stop here to relax there will be no margin for error or breakdown or illness on the way to China – we have to keep moving. Better to be close to the border with a few days to spare than to miss the deadline for our crossing.

Passing through the Laotian capital Vientiane we catch up with a friend from Melbourne who is working as a consultant to the United Nations. Cathy warns us that there is an outbreak of bird flu in northern Laos and she has heard that the roads are closed to all traffic near the China border. This is exactly what we do not want to hear: quarantine rules can prevent us from getting through to China and will stop our trip right there. No amount of planning and preparation can avoid something like this – quarantine rules are not negotiable. We have ten days to get to the border, plenty of time for a small flu outbreak to become a big one or on the other hand for it to be eradicated. Which way will it go?

Taking advantage of a big Toyota dealership in Vientiane I hoist the car into the air and get underneath with the mechanics to check everything. Amazingly, nothing needs fixing at all, despite the punishing rough roads and the relentless progress we have been making. The mechanics all stop work and crowd around, fascinated by the gadgets on

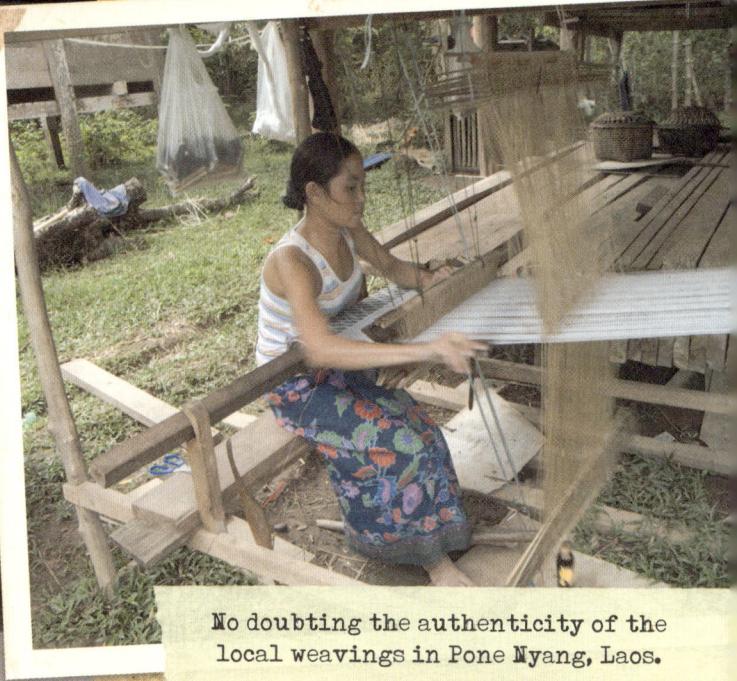

No doubting the authenticity of the local weavings in Pone Nyang, Laos.

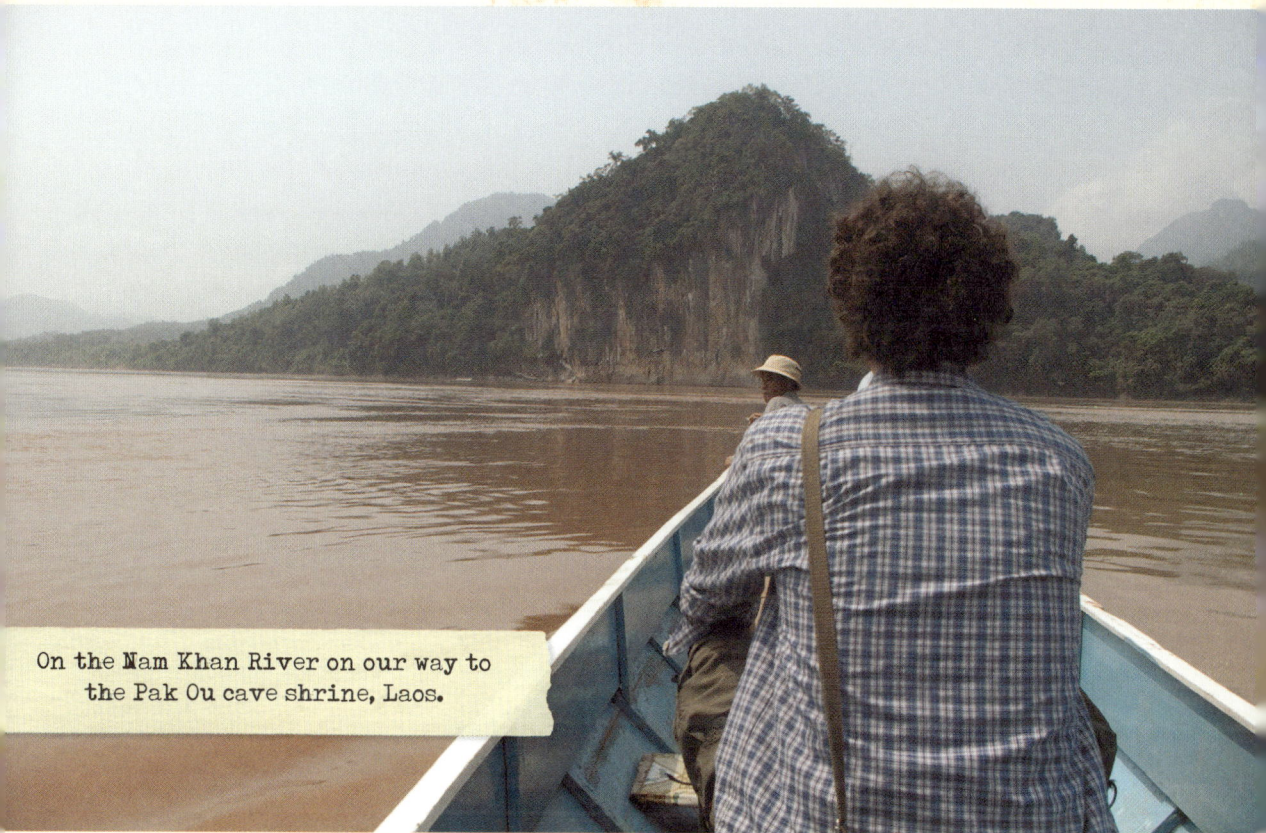

On the Nam Khan River on our way to the Pak Ou cave shrine, Laos.

our car. They have never seen dual batteries, an intake snorkel or a built-in compressor, let alone diff lockers. They climb in and under the car, prodding and poking, giggling the whole time. I insist on doing some of the work myself which astonishes them and breaks all the workshop rules.

A text message from Nigel reminds us of the world left behind. 'Any chance you can get me tickets to the grand final if St Kilda make it next week …' is the closest thing to a football score we have had for ages. Incongruous is not the word to describe being reminded of left-behind priorities thousands of kilometres away. What matters there is not even on the radar here.

We head north from Vientiane along continuously winding roads to the backpacker haven of Van Vieng, and Jack declines the opportunity to go river tubing with pasty, drunk, tattooed English and American tourists, but I do fall in love with a baby goat at our small riverside hotel. Can you house-train kid goats? Is there anything so cute? I ponder my chances of stealing this little pet and tucking it into the back seat for the rest of the trip. When it tries to eat my shoe I reconsider. I wonder if Jack would be having a wild old time if not for his burned-out father being here to drag him down. It is backpacker paradise: bars and parties everywhere. Van Vieng is also remarkable for celebrating the American sitcom *Friends*. The town has adopted the dated cheesy TV show as some sort of anthem. In open-air bar after cafe after restaurant there are loud televisions continuously showing episodes of *Friends* in a ritual that no doubt has its origins in ancient backpacker times. There must be twenty or more of these copy-cat establishments, and no shortage of stoned or drunk Westerners lolling around on couches and day-beds soaking it all up, hour after hour, bar after bar. Why *Friends*? We could not find out, but there is a PhD in it for someone.

Watching a group of locals kicking their rattan ball around, like a hackysack but in bamboo, I am mesmerised by their agility. One bloke upends himself with an over-the-head scissor kick in their game, a cross between volleyball and soccer. Despite my urging, Jack will not join in.

North of Van Vieng is the World Heritage town of Luang Prabang. We confront our inner tourist for a few days, wandering the markets and fielding questions from inquisitive Englishmen asking if we will sell them our car when we get to London. There is an endless conversation with Jack about the extent to which we are tourists or travellers, or something else again. Is it a distinction of any significance, or just a plaything for bored middle-class wankers, exploring the limits of their own snobbery?

I drool over King Savang Vatthana's mid-1960s Citroen DS Prestige in the Royal Palace garage, wondering how to distract the guards for long enough to open the bonnet and check underneath. Jack deserts me. He seems bewitched by the backpacker climate, drawn away from me by the prospect of company closer to his age and interests. I feel abandoned, begrudgingly accepting my fate. It reminds me of travelling with my parents when I was a teenager, walking three steps behind, self-consciously pretending that I had no connection with anyone so embarrassing. I fancy myself better company than I actually am, and feel tragic, lonely and bereft. Much as he no doubt wants someone other than me to talk to, it cuts both ways. I am not 100 per cent satisfied with him as my sole conversation partner either, but do not want to hurt his feelings by saying so. As a personal trainer though he is a great success, our creaking backs holding up owing to the occasionally comical exercise regime we go through most nights in our hotel room. I shall never erase the vision of Jack in poor-fitting fake Calvin Kleins doing sit-ups on the floor.

Tamarind Restaurant, established by Melbourne woman Caroline Gaylard with her Laotian husband, Joy Ngeuamboupha, becomes a sanctuary and we make gluttons of ourselves on fish in banana leaf with mango and lemongrass and similar delicacies. Jack becomes addicted to sticky rice. I plot a way to come back sometime for their all-day cooking classes which seem like a great idea. We watch the ritual dawn procession of orange-robed monks being provided with offerings, locals lining the streets, food containers at the ready, bowing as they put small portions into each monk's bowl as the procession passes.

Heading north, the people and places change. Road signs, where they exist at all, are in both Laotian and Chinese. The Chinese are paying for infrastructure as they gradually colonise the north of Laos, chequebooks buying access but not popularity with the locals. People's faces are broader with higher cheekbones, and men in particular are noticeably taller. Everyone's skin is darker and women as a rule now have incredibly long, shiny black hair. We see an occasional plump person – a novelty until now – and a trickle of tourists. Roadside stalls offer a display of snakes and scorpions in glass bottles marinating in supposedly medicinal home brew, the alcohol negating the toxicity of the venom. The young girl selling these concoctions can speak just enough English to recite parrot-fashion 'good for lungs', 'good for man things' and 'good for heart' as we examine the cobra and huge spider pickled in lao-lao, the local rice whisky.

At Nong Khiaw, on the banks of the Nam Ou River, our host is fascinated by the car. We are the only people staying in Chan's guesthouse, and we sit on the deck next to the kitchen overlooking the river and talk as his wife cooks chicken pho. I take him for a drive, and after a few minutes offer him the driver's seat. He is overwhelmed, toots the horn to all and sundry, giggling and waving to the villagers. A Ferrari would not have pleased him more; he has never driven with an automatic gearbox and cannot stop marvelling at the comfort and power.

Just out of town is a white jeep parked on the jungle's edge. Three men are unloading equipment, and Chan explains they are searching for land mines and bombs from the war. We ask if we can go with them. They think we are crazy, and they might be right. It is thirty-five years since the 'American War' ended, but such was the intensity of the secret undeclared bombing by the USA that they are still at risk from what is called UXO, unexploded ordnance. I read somewhere that Laos is the most heavily bombed country in the world per capita. And the Americans have not bothered to clear up their mess. We go with the UXO crew back to their base, look at their shrapnel souvenirs and marvel at how stoic people can be under such hardship. Again I struggle to explain to Jack exactly how the world sat by and did nothing to protect innocent civilians from the impact of such a rotten war. Both Cambodia and Laos scream at our collective conscience, the dead deserving a better response than anything we have provided so far.

We head to the Pak Hon complex of caves used as a refuge and command centre in the war, and I notice a small fire out of the corner of my eye, with a charred corpse smouldering. It is a middle-size dog, bloated belly and paws stiffly pointing to the sky, teeth gleaming through the smoke. The two men tending to the BBQ are delighted that we stop and as we step over the bowl of fresh foamy blood left from the throat-slitting execution, they lift the animal from the logs, beckoning us to follow. They sharpen two long curved knives and hack off the ears, feet, tail, head and then butcher the animal, putting various delicacies aside as they work. They are flattered that we pay so much attention, offering us better angles for our photos, pausing in their methodical work to ensure we do not miss a shot. I am nauseated at first, but

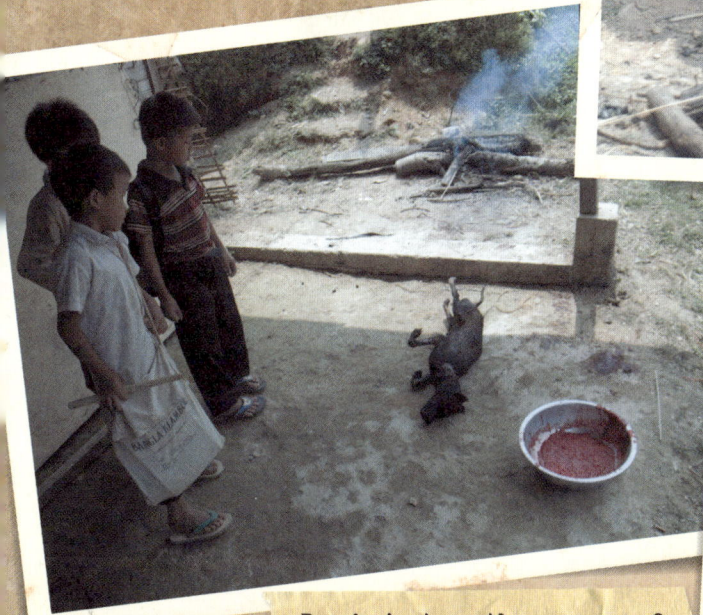

Dog is just another source of cheap protein in Laos.

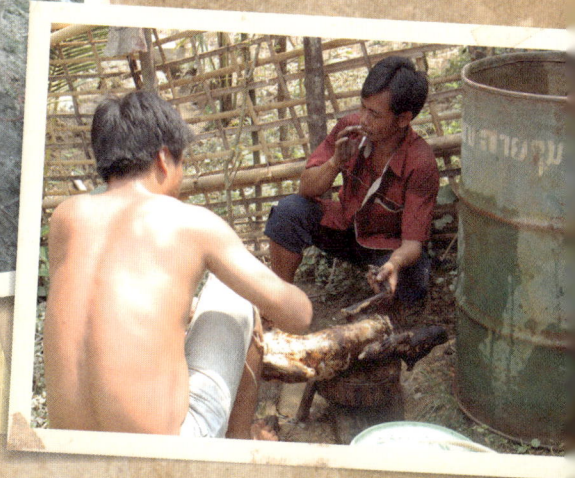

a strange fascination compels me to look inside a dog, to see it being dismembered. It is a creature about the same size as our Bess at home, which makes things harder. But these people feel no compunction at all in eating an animal that in our culture is regarded as special. What is the difference between a dog and a sheep? Or a goat? Or a cow? Or chickens? We had chickens for a while, running around the garden. They had names, yet we ate chicken, although not our own pets. We have an adorable house-trained pet rabbit, but I have eaten rabbit so why the squeamishness? At an intellectual level I can rationalise it all, but it is still confronting to see it, smell it, touch it.

The best dog cuts end up in plastic bags, and we repair to our car breathless and speechless. I drink about a litre of water without pausing, Jack admits his knees are shaking. We toss around our emotions, questioning our own values but are still sentimental about dogs, rational or not. Jack chuckles over the prospect of posting some dog BBQ photos on our website, as a sequel to his controversial post about watching the cockfights in Dili. Some 180 people responded to his photo essay, many upset with him for saying that he found the fight to the death 'exciting'. Imagine what they will say if he admits to being fascinated by the butchering and cooking of a puppy? We are tempted just to make the point – you cannot go to remote places and then complain that the people are not like everyone at home. You may as well just stay where you are.

We drive off the main road, heading north into the jungle, and within an hour are stopped at another roadblock. There are several men at the boomgate with breathing masks and spray packs. It is an ominous sight. They speak to us in Lao, and I smile and shrug my shoulders. They talk to each other, then gesture to wind up the window and start spraying the car tyres and around the wheel arches. The boom gate is lifted and we drive away. So much for the threat of avian flu and the complete ban on any cars going north. Our car does look official – it is white, a Toyota, and has a big aerial on the front. There is almost no other traffic at all, so it is quite possible that there is a ban on anyone driving north but we have been allowed through. Our logo and stickers on the side mean that the car could pass as belonging to an NGO or even be a UN vehicle and to someone illiterate in their own language and unfamiliar with the English/Chinese/Arabic lettering we have on our car, we just appear to be important. It works in our favour many times, but I suspect most significantly here. Our rendezvous at the Chinese border in a few days might actually happen.

I celebrate my birthday at a swish guesthouse called The Boat Landing. Jack has bought me a Tom Waits CD and kept it hidden as a surprise. I happily spend the day spreading out our maps, plotting our course through Central Asia and then lash out and buy myself a birthday present in the market. At a small backstreet tailor, under a glass counter along with the zips and buttons, I see two magnificent Mong-Sin tribe antique swords – genuine, not fake. They are remarkably different to anything we have seen, with elaborate and intricate handwork on the hilt and the scabbard. They disappear into the back of the car, hidden from scrutiny. The next day we drive the two or three hours through the rainforest and the chaotic border town and to the border with China.

Jon doing his best to ask directions,
and failing miserably.

The snakes are added to lao-lao rice whisky to improve male **virility**.

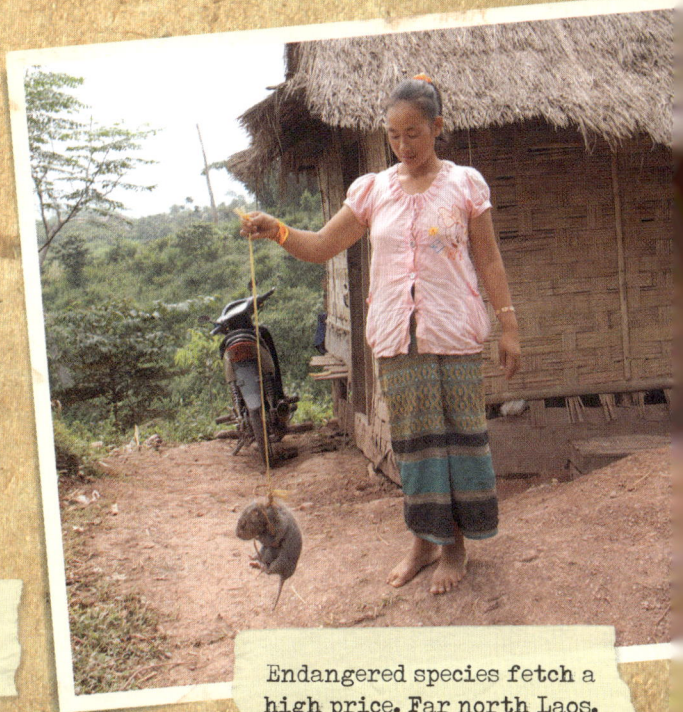

Endangered species fetch a high price. Far north Laos.

13 | Chinese Checkers

Wherein we explain the arcane world of Chinese bureaucracy and permits and how to achieve the impossible. But you can still get stuck ...

The *Rough Guide* says: 'Driving a car across China is an appealing idea but an experience currently forbidden to foreign tourists ...'

The *Lonely Planet* guide says: 'Don't even bother. Driving around China is impossible unless you have a residency permit ...'

Trailblazers' *The Silk Roads* says: 'It is impossible for standard foreign visitors to take a car into China.'

Australia's leading travel agency specialising in China travel emailed: 'It is not possible to take a foreign car or for a foreign driver to drive a car in China, we are sorry we cannot help you ...'

Countless hours of trawling on the internet at different China travel sites confirmed the advice that foreigners are not allowed to take cars into China.

They are all wrong. You can ... but you have to really want to. And you have to be very persistent.

In typical stubborn fashion I looked for a way around these supposed prohibitions. In early 2008, I emailed the Chinese government tour company CITS and, describing our preferred route, asked if it was possible. They advised that we could drive across China if we joined a group and accepted the services of an official guide sitting in the car and touring with us at all times. We would need permits from each provincial government along the way, Chinese registration for our car, insurance, security clearances, a Chinese driver's licence for each of us and we had to pay all expenses for the guide including hotel rooms and all food. Once we agreed to these conditions, they quoted a staggering A$26,000 for one month. A flurry of emails saw the price halved. It was still far more than I could afford. But the Silk Road beckoned. The more I looked into it the more I wanted to do it.

Staying up one night chasing internet link after link, hour after hour, I chanced upon a website devoted to the launch of a fancy European make of 4x4. They had mounted an expedition from Germany to Beijing to demonstrate how tough their new car was. In the 'thank you' section they mentioned NAVO as their Chinese tour guides. I looked at NAVO's website and exchanged emails. They told me they cater for groups from Europe, travelling west to east entering China from Russia or Mongolia. They had never had an inquiry from Australia, had never before collected anyone from the southern borders and only dealt with groups of two or more cars. Over several emails in which they told me to look for a companion car in order to create a group, I cheekily suggested that we could be a group if that was required – a group of one. Laughably, the reply came through that my joke satisfied the bureaucrats. No mention was ever made of my work in the media. I had been forewarned that journalists requiring visas for China at any time, let alone the Olympics year, and also while Tibet was in turmoil, would find procedures much more complicated.

Endless negotiations and haggling saw NAVO quote about a quarter the original price from CITS, and the paperwork began. They needed 100 days to get all the permits. The local government of every province had to approve our route. Central security in Beijing had to vet our application. The army had to check our intended schedule to ensure it did not threaten national security! They finally contracted to escort us from the Laos border, to Chengdu, north to Xián, then west across the Silk Road to Kashgar and on to Kyrgyzstan. We would be in China from September 1 for the entire month. I sent a deposit, copies of car registration, insurance, they even required photos of the car taken from each side and front and rear ... endless documents. But it seemed we were going to be able to drive through China after all. The dominoes were falling into place. What was the fuss about?

And then it became complicated.

A terrible earthquake in Chengdu in mid-May meant major changes to our route were forced upon us. We adapted readily. In June, just as we were about to leave home, the very week I was finishing work, a thousand loose threads needing tying, Jack was doing university exams, stress levels through the roof – another email hit the inbox. A very embarrassed Tracy from NAVO passed on the news that because of the 2008 Olympic Games in Beijing our permit had been totally refused, on security grounds. The government was determined that nothing would mar their showpiece games, and no foreigners were allowed independent travel. She apologised and wrote that they had never had a permit refused before, and offered a full refund of our deposit. I sat and stared at the screen, unable to believe what I was seeing. The bags were half packed, our ship and flights from Darwin to Dili were booked, visas had been stamped … this was a disaster. We were leaving in four days. I felt sick. If we could not drive across China, we would have to go from somewhere in Southeast Asia to somewhere in India instead, and as Pakistan was politically unstable, we might have to ship out from Mumbai to maybe Cairo or Turkey. The very purpose of the trip would collapse. Overland to England … but by sea … not quite the trip I wanted.

A furious round-robin of emails followed, continuing even as we were on the road. What if we agreed to wait until the Olympics were over before we entered China? After checking with Beijing, Tracy replied we would have to wait until even the Paralympics were finished, and if anything 'bad' happened we would be refused permission entirely. And even then we would not be allowed to go along the Silk Road, but only to enter China from Laos and exit to Mongolia. But at least we were making progress.

If we went into China twenty-one days later than expected, could we still get across China, through the 'stans and into Europe in time for Christmas in Paris? I did a quick recalculation … it was doable but regrettable. It meant we were gambling on the early snows not closing the mountain passes in central Asia or Siberia if we had to go that way, and the extra time taken in Asia was at the expense of having to rush through the 'stans. We tentatively agreed, and asked if we could reapply for the Silk Road option after the Olympics. We raced to the map shop and bought guidebooks and maps for Mongolia, Russia – and India – to cover all eventualities.

As we drove from home, we still had no approved route nor even permits for entry to China. Negotiating the Indonesian islands, I was emailing back and forth, endlessly negotiating, haranguing and arguing through cyberspace. The knot in my stomach was tightening. As we made our way through Malaysia and Thailand, even into Cambodia and Laos, we were still not sure that our eventual entry date and time would stick.

Not until it happened could we be sure we would be allowed across the border. While coping with soaring tropical temperatures in Cambodia, we were looking anxiously at the weather forecasts for Bishkek and Almaty to see whether the snows had started and if the mountain passes remained open. Even if we got to Mongolia and the weather turned, we could be stuck, forced to abandon our car and the trip. We could be marooned in Mongolia: unable to go west because of the weather, unable to return south without multiple entry permits for China and without permits to drive through Russia. The whole thing was a huge gamble.

中华人民共和国签证
CHINESE VISA

签证种类
CATEGORY   L
请于此前入境
ENTER BEFORE 30SEP2
签发日期
ISSUE DATE 30

ZHONG

2008

驶许可
g Permits

瑞克 芬尼

型 C1
in China
99-22至 2008-10-15
to
当与所持境外机动车驾驶证
使用。
permits should be used with the
chinese translation.

临

云K0037

Another day on the road, another crazy hazard, Yunnan, China.

14 | China for Beginners

In which we negotiate the border, survive a snake attack, a tourist trap, Chinese driving etiquette, get bogged, learn Tracy's life plan, observe the ritual of the tea ceremony, and Jack befriends a blind orphan girl.

No man's land between Laos and China extends for a few kilometres of winding potholed road through lush rainforest. A few ramshackle thatched huts and small plots of cultivated land interrupt the dense foliage. As we round a bend, the greenery gives way to an enormous concrete triumphal arch, still covered in builders' scaffolding, grandly spanning the road. Brand-new concrete terraced shops three storeys high line the tarmac, which has been transformed from a dirt track into a four-lane bitumen highway. A more incongruous sight you would struggle to find – it is as if a Hollywood film set has been dropped into the mountainous pass. A boom gate guarded by three soldiers, standing stiffly to attention despite the heat, signals that we are about to enter China. There is not a single other vehicle on the road travelling in either direction. I wonder aloud if this is a pantomime performance put on entirely for our benefit. Was there a hidden camera that detected our approach a few minutes ago and they have all sprung to life to impress us? I tell Jack to sit up in his seat, to turn off the music, to take his feet off the dashboard and put his shoes on. I am nervous and half expecting to be told to go away. Several travellers have warned us about Chinese border checks, seizure of guidebooks and laptops, satellite phones being confiscated and eternal searches for contraband or politically sensitive materials. I am prepared for an argument, determined not to lose any of our gear. The golden rule is never argue with the man with the machine gun. But what if they have discovered I work in the media and have disguised my profession? All paperwork for China had me declaring myself by my former occupation of lawyer rather than journalist or broadcaster – it just seemed less complicated and more likely to avoid problems. I have no media or ABC accreditation or ID with me, and have even removed the ABC tags from the work laptop they have lent me. I have rationalised the deceit by telling myself I am on leave, I am on a private trip with Jack, only reporting back for colour pieces instead of anything that could be regarded as proper journalism. Who do I think I am kidding? I could be thrown out of half the countries we want to go through.

The boom gate lifts, the soldier waves us to a parking bay, all tidy and concrete and kerbs and flowers neatly arranged, almost in defiance of the surrounding jungle. The run-down Laotian side of the border suddenly seems a world away as the soldier uses his machine-gun to gesture to us to get out of the car.

We walk into a glass and steel office and greet the guards with our typical bravado. 'Ni Hao,' I attempt, trying to break the ice. As will happen throughout China, no one in a uniform will readily smile. No relaxed easygoing banter, it is all formidably official and proper.

The infrastructure is totally out of proportion to the setting. There are dozens of shops, but no customers. There are customs brokers standing around but no trucks. A cluster of women follow our every move, waving bundles of notes at us trying to get us to change money with them. There are soldiers and police and immigration and quarantine and customs inspectors … but no tourists, buses or trucks. No one speaks a word of English.

A young woman runs over to us and introduces herself as Tracy, our guide. After hundreds of emails exchanged over half a year, it is a relief that this meeting has come to fruition. She has been waiting for us and immediately gives me a birthday present. I open the package as we say hello, and greet a fluffy panda stuffed toy with magnetic paws. Tracy is from Chengdu, the home of the giant pandas. He is instantly installed in the car, clasping the grab handle behind my seat, looking over my shoulder for the rest of our trip. Tracy starts negotiating with the authorities on our behalf. It takes more than an hour to get the proper stamps on the various papers, Tracy tearing from desk to desk while we kick the football around. In that time not one other vehicle crosses through this immense border post in either direction. The investment required for this elaborate infrastructure is clearly justified by something other than human traffic. It is more a signal of Chinese power and modernity than anything else, an attention-seeking gesture but one that frustratingly almost no one will ever see. China is building roads, power supplies and infrastructure throughout the region as gifts and goodwill gestures to poorer nations as far away as Timor-Leste. Soft power, diplomatic favours, influence peddling – call it whatever you like.

Finally, without even a cursory search of our luggage, we are allowed to drive off … into China! We climb back into the car – Jack relegated to the back seat now as Tracy guides from the front, but I still try to offer a high-five. Of course he duds me – desperate to impress. As we cover our first kilometre on smooth Chinese highway, I am elated – we have finally done what we were told could not be done. I swallow hard and send Jan a text message of jubilation.

We drive towards Mengla, through a deep gorge lush with jungle, over a suspension bridge crossing a fast-flowing river. It is odd to be told what to do and where to go – for three months we have got used to not knowing what is around the next corner, driving from maps and guidebooks, asking for directions and making it up as we go. Now we have someone with us who tells me where to turn, someone who makes decisions and I am reduced to being a follower. I am not happy – there is no discussion, she just says, 'Now we go down to this road and we stop at the town there.' Jack is exuberant that he is no longer under pressure to navigate, able to snooze, read or look out the window without hassle. I am irritated, my inner control freak confronted by the intruder, and worse, one I am paying top dollar for!

Parking by the side of the road, we cross the bridge and hike for about an hour into the thick trees, the path barely wide enough for two to walk side by side. After an hour, the valley offers up the occasional hut, some animal shelters made from bamboo and rough fences of poles strung together with wire. We wander through the mud into a village of simple timber homes, wary eyes scrutinising us as much as we do them. Tracy introduces herself and explains our visit; wary hostility is immediately replaced with cups of tea and a tomato-like fruit fresh from the vine offered up with smiles. We are invited to stay for dinner, welcomed into the dirt floor huts and treated like special guests. Again, those with least in life are the most generous hosts imaginable. Back on the path, chatting as we head back towards the car, Tracy shrieks and Jack catapults himself into the air as a snake objects to being disturbed by lashing at his leg. His reflex reaction avoids disaster, but for hours we talk about what we would have done, what we should have done, what we might have done and whether our first-aid training months ago in Melbourne would have kicked in if he had been bitten. A more remote place for a medical emergency you would be hard pressed to find.

Our next stop is at a cafe for what Tracy says is a cup of tea, but from the other side of the world Jan has arranged a birthday cake, a massive, bright yellow, mock cream and sponge creation with a marshmallow and chocolate mouse on top. I am overwhelmed by the realisation that Jan has been conspiring with Tracy to surprise me, but between three of us we struggle to make more than a slight dent in it. Still wiping crumbs from our chins, we go to the motor registration office where over several hours we sign paperwork not knowing what it says, the car is safety inspected and the 'Provisional Driving Permit' and foreign vehicle registration are issued. Officials in various uniforms shout orders and instructions at me as I reluctantly let them test the brakes and steering on the Toyota. A Chinese temporary number plate – 'K 00378' – is eventually handed over and then we explore the town of Mengla.

First impressions are everything. We see two car crashes in three minutes, apparently drunk drivers weaving across the streets, totally out of control. Tracy locates an ATM, I celebrate that it accepts my card and we won't be running out of money, and then we wander around the shops, where people are milling around well into the night. We are starving and find a small restaurant where the kitchen is also the dining area. Our fish is lifted from a tub of water, hit on the head with a cleaver and butterflied in a flash. Garlic, ginger, coriander and chilli are all chopped together into a paste, stuffed inside the fish and the whole thing grilled on coals and served in moments. Together with pork crackling with a tomato-style salsa, beef stew, rice and steamed greens, we eat a feast for our first night in China, all for about A$10 for three of us in total. It seems so exotic, but as time passes we learn that freshly killed is the norm in off-the-beaten-track China and no one would consider eating all sorts of animals any other way. Home-style restaurants are typical, the middle-aged woman running a kitchen much as she would at home. The cooking is not tucked away in a back room, but in front of you and even with you if you want to take an active role.

As we spend a few days heading along the rough mountain roads along the Burma border, lined with stunning terraced rice fields, rubber trees and tea plantations, we visit towns where the children gawp and stare at Europeans. In Mongman, small boys, maybe eight years old, play at battered pool tables, cigarettes dangling from their broken teeth. The town is so remote there is no school. The children work on their parents' farms, or at the market, as they always have for as long as anyone can remember. We are treated warily, until Tracy explains what we are doing, whereupon people smile and joke about us to each other, inviting us to share their table and the food upon it. A dentist is working in the main street, the patient's chair brightly lit in the window of his surgery so passers-by can see how things are done. Privacy Chinese-style … no concept of personal space.

In the massive car park of the famous Tropical Plant Botanic Gardens we are greeted by a family of Chinese Melbourne residents whose kids go to the same high school as Jack. The kids recognise him and the parents recognise me and make a fuss. I am nervous about being outed as a journalist, astonished that in our first few days in China we bump into people from home. Tracy asks how it is that these Chinese-speaking Australians told her that they knew me because I was 'on the radio' back in Melbourne when I had declared my occupation to the officials and to her as a lawyer. I fudge the answer, saying I talk about the law on the radio – all true but not the entire truth. If I confide in her, is she under an obligation to inform the security officials who made such a fuss about our permits in the first place? Is it better to stay quiet or to confess? What will happen if they find out?

The gardens also mean the first of many encounters with 'ethnic minority' women – always women – elaborately costumed and Disney-fied, escorting tourists through the site, around endless fountains and man-made waterfalls on electric carts with megaphones loudly declaiming the various features. These guides are dolled up in bright synthetic versions of traditional garb, fake jewellery, decorations and hats, cutesy smiles and typical tour guide chatter. The botanic exhibits are exquisite – plants that wave and respond when you sing to them, variants on Venus flytrap plants, waterlilies the size of elephants – all stunningly laid out and presented in this remote corner of China.

We head off high into the mountains, negotiating a road so thick in mud from construction that our car struggles to get through. Buses and trucks – even tractors

– are bogged, stuck in the mire, impassable sludge made worse by recent rain. Heavy logging leading to deforestation has created landslides and the logging trucks have ruined the roads. We slide and slip at walking pace. I silently curse our guide, convinced that our trip will end here as rocks crash into the suspension and bang the undertray and drivetrain protective plates. We take four hours to cover barely 40 kilometres, using full four-wheel drive. One waterlogged intersection is totally blocked by a bogged bus, the driver frantically digging to remove mud and rocks to clear a passage. We are stuck behind, wedged between mud walls of farms in a narrow laneway, so we pitch in and help with the digging, but the passengers and villagers watch passively, refusing to get their hands dirty. Thirty people stand around watching one man working. None of them feels any need or apparent desire to help. Collectivism or generations of centralised decision-making stripping people of initiative … or do we read too much into it? Once we three pitch in to help, a few others do too and eventually, with wheels spinning and engine roaring, the bus slides through and we too can get away.

Highways alternate between cobbled passages as ancient as a Roman road, to super freeways and tunnels that slice grandly through mountains. Driver behaviour is appalling – U-turns on the freeway without any warning, pedestrians crossing right in front of speeding cars, tractors at farm speed wandering alongside speeding buses. A jeep without lights stops in the middle of an unlit tunnel and the passengers step out into the traffic, cars swerving, skidding and braking in every direction. There are police and roadblocks bristling with army that require regular paperwork checks, passports and permits carefully scrutinised, but we never see those same police enforcing the road rules.

Our first choice of hotel that night in Ninger refuses us a room – they are not allowed to take foreigners. As we eat, Tracy tells us more about herself. 'My parents' generation, they wanted just three things in life … a bicycle, a radio and a fridge. My generation, we want a motorbike, a mobile phone, and an apartment. This is the new China.' She is twenty-five, and determined to soon be married. The man she marries must provide an apartment, as he will not be deserving of her if he has not achieved that goal. She saves RMB500 (A$100) a month invested into the stockmarket, as she has been taught that if she sticks to that disciplined regime, then by the time she turns fifty she will be able to stop work. 'I am so proud of

Even the trainee monk joins
the game of pool near the
China-Burma border town Mongman.

Our introduction to Chinese roads - near the
Burmese border. Miles and miles of deep mud with
huge rocks invisible beneath.

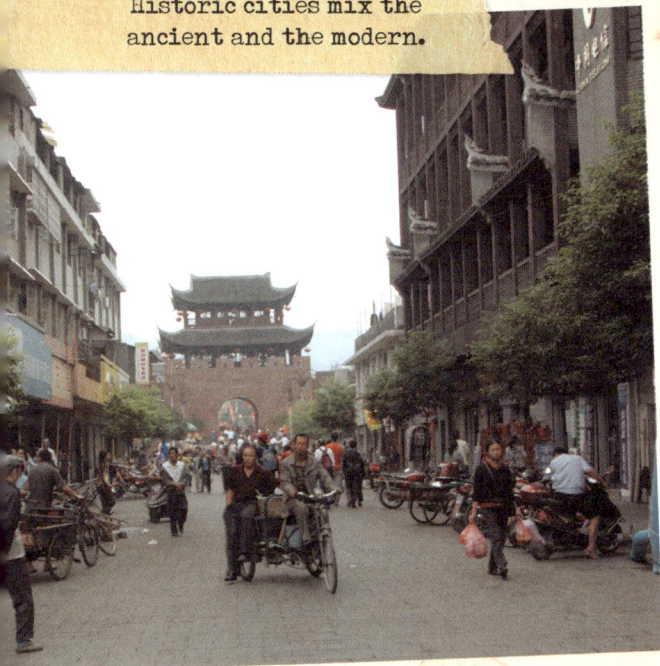
Historic cities mix the ancient and the modern.

Traditionally-clothed women, posing for the tourists.

China. We are not like Japan where people just work all the time and have no life. My parents worked all the time but now as we become more rich we can enjoy life more than they did.'

Massive trucks laden with coal block the roads as they crawl along at irritatingly slow speed. Typically overloaded and belching filthy thick black diesel fumes, they infuriate and frustrate faster vehicles on narrow winding roads and freeways alike. Over breakfast – kerbside noodles and porridge – Tracy seeks directions from the driver of one of these huge blue monster trucks. I get her to negotiate a deal – the driver can take our exotic right-hand-drive, relatively luxurious car for a spin if he will let me drive his truck around the block. He slaps his thigh with laughter, welcomes me as I climb up and into the rough cabin, and we crunch and crawl our way around a few blocks of town.

As I climb down Jack has fallen in love – he is in earnest conversation with a toddler, a tiny wide-eyed girl just walking and staggering as she trips from chair to table at the roadside breakfast stall. There is something amazing about the little girl's eyes – they are huge and unblinking, and it hits me that she is blind. The girl's mother readily explains that her daughter has an eye disease and she is losing her sight – they cannot afford even the trip to the hospital in Kunming, let alone pay for the treatment she needs. She weeps, sobbing into her apron, embarrassed. I get Tracy to ask how we can help, and we learn that the mother, herself divorced, has adopted this little girl who was abandoned at birth. Girls are unwanted in one-baby China. As we talk, we are plied with tea, sweet corn and biscuits. In the back of the car we have a stash of fluffy toy koalas, and I dig one out. Jack squeezes the soft toy into the toddler's arms and I self-consciously press a bundle of notes into her mother's apron pocket to assuage my guilt. We spend more each time we refuel the car than it will cost to save this little girl's sight. I spent just as much on two antique swords in Laos, static objects that will one day hang on the wall at home. Which is the better use of my money?

We drive away with tears in our eyes, moved by the plight of a total stranger. Jack mutters something about injustice and feeling powerless and useless as we grapple with our conscience. Tracy says nothing at first, then, 'It is so sad.' What difference does one little girl's eyesight make? There are thousands like her, I tell myself; we cannot go through life feeling guilty about what we have, just because others are stuck with a worse lot in life. Overwhelming us, though, is the deep acceptance that we are so lucky to be who and what we are compared to so many others on this planet. Jack threatens to hit me if I utter, 'We are the luckiest of the luckiest', just one more time but it has never lost its relevance for me.

Dinner is pigs' ears, pig intestines, pork dumplings and salty broth with pork. Pork and pig in every imaginable variation. Hotel rooms are rented as 'single', 'double' 'triple' and 'o'clock'. We ask Tracy about the last of these and she blushes before explaining how unmarried couples can take a room by the hour. How sensible.

The fish are char-grilled laden with spices in one of Xian's night markets.

JACK WRITES

15 | Lijiang Hotpot

As an intrepid devotee of Anthony Bourdain, Jack overdoses on chilli and leaves Jon wondering how he will explain to Jan their son's demise from an excess of hotpot.

After a few careful bites the heat hit. The pang jumped on my tongue and, stupid for a stronger hit, I doused the next mouthfuls in the liquid chilli. I was instantly gone, instantly in love.

The spices throbbed through my blood, along my veins and into my limbs that became so numb I couldn't control my hands. I was tingling all over and snot leaked from deep inside my nose. Sweat violently pushed out of my pores in a useless attempt to cool my body down. I wiped my face at every bite but it made no difference. My ears closed down, shutting out the din of the restaurant and with each inward breath of thick steamy air my numbed tongue, gums and throat stung. I continued stuffing my steaming face with more red hot chilli paste until my knees shook like a dosed junkie and my head throbbed. My teeth vibrated, surely about to explode out of my mouth. My eyes pushed at the tight confines of their sockets. My heart thumped. Time passed slow.

Then there was Dad looking into my eyes the way parents do when they're trying to work out if their kids are stoned. I couldn't hear but he was motioning for me to slow down. I just grunted or nodded and slurped another piece. My throat burned for relief. I poured some water down, but my next outward breath just reignited the fire scorching its way along my tongue and tonsils.

A few people from other tables giggled at the white kid with strange hair moaning and groaning in both pain and ecstasy.

The hotpot in the centre of the table continued to spit liquid fire out like a volcano. The oily steam was clouding my face. The morsels of beef had thinned, the rice had almost disappeared and the rich broth was evaporating fast.

I picked one last mushroom up with my chopsticks, carefully lifting it above the hotpot and holding it there. The gleaming droplets of stock flowed to the edge of the mushroom before tinkling lightly into the stock with a *drip drop*. I ushered my prized possession into my bowl and mixed it with my handful of red and green chilli and dirty spices. A gluggy film of slippery pepper paste now coated the mushroom. My hand was shaking uncontrollably and starting to cramp. I brought the mushroom to my mouth slowly and carefully with intent, my bowl following close behind to catch any mishap. My eyes stared at my hand, willing it to steady. A waft of chilli sprinted up my nose and attacked my upper throat, then my eyes. Tears rolled down my cheeks. My face recoiled just as my mushroom got close enough to hear the sizzling oils still cooking on the inside of it, and my hand gave in to painful cramps and relinquished its already precarious hold on the vegetable. The chopsticks opened and the mushroom slipped down and plonked into the messy bowl of chilli paste and herbs gripped in my left hand. I breathed out and the hot air from my lungs reignited the blaze on my tongue. The nerves sprung to life and made my eyes burn stronger. Snot dripped down, following the mushroom into the bowl sitting in my limp left hand.

I muttered something about needing fresh air and stumbled and rolled my way outside, tripping over stools in my drugged lurch. I stood in the cool breeze, my arms spread and mouth open. The wind flowed through my scorched airways and freshened my damp, clammy body.

They say Chinese food is addictive.

16 | Tiger Leaping Gorge

Our two adventurers risk life and limb – and heart attack for the elder – on a slippery cliff in the rain, stumble on bonsai heaven, ponder Chinese toilet etiquette, invent the Chopstick Olympics and visit a restaurant where dog is the specialty, freshly barbecued or smoked, whichever you prefer.

It is pouring rain the day we drive to one of southern China's most spectacular attractions. We plan to hike for the day to, through and across Tiger Leaping Gorge, a gash in the mountains where a river cuts like a knife dissecting the topography of swooping cliffs and raging torrents, so narrow at one point that legend has it a tiger leapt across the gap above the raging river. We are in the closest thing to wilderness that China can offer – near the Burma border, in mountains spared development and sparsely populated, not even subjected to intensive farming. The buses taking tourists – almost all of them young Chinese from the coastal cities – along the winding passage to the start of the trail are barely slowed by the conditions. Blind corners and steep ascents inspire Chinese bus drivers, for whom the mere presence of any other vehicles on the road provokes outrageous behaviour behind the wheel. There is no other possible explanation for their deliberate efforts to eradicate the challenge posed by our car sharing 'their' tarmac.

We snake our way up the hills in the fog, past the bus depot and modern visitors' centre. Free from the constraints of group tourism we simply drive past the car park and continue up the mountain. A low natural rock tunnel prevents any buses from going further, but we fit through and venture to where most tourists cannot go. Tracy

reads a sign in Chinese warning about hazardous roads, tries to persuade me to stop but the idea of walking further than we need to in soaking rain does not appeal. What is Chinese for 'drowned rat'? And would it cause offence? Do they eat them?

The slippery road is full of potholes and loose gravel, the rutted surface heavily washed out and in some places as narrow as our car, mirrors scraping the rocks on the uphill side and the edges of our tyres just clearing the unfenced edge of a sheer drop to the Yangzi River below on the other. Several times, Jack gets out and walks ahead to guide me through, making sure we have clearance before chancing the track. Waterfalls created by the heavy rain punctuate steep valleys, filling pools for the occasional mountain pony. Way up the gorge we find a guesthouse and take advantage of the slight widening of the road to park our car without blocking the narrow passage. At this lookout, serious hikers are mingling with day-trippers, shouting and laughing if they have jubilantly come up the hill, checking bootlaces and water bottles if they are heading down.

Jack and I have a small disagreement about his choice of footwear. Having equipped him at great expense and fuss with a flash pair of solid hiking shoes, it seemed to the father to be the perfect opportunity to make use of them. If not here, then where? If not now, then when? What sensible person would not want strong, waterproof, purpose-designed hiking shoes for a trek up and down wet, greasy, mud tracks? And why would thin-soled sleek runners be better? Jack wants to prove the point that the fancy, expensive, purpose-designed hiking shoes were a waste of money, that he ought not have been forced into buying them and that he would be just as happy in his sneakers. Just another day on the road …

The walking trail to the river starts at a rickety stone cottage, watched over by a diminutive, toothless, elderly woman in peasant blue coveralls, complete with Chairman Mao cap, who collects a fee from each tourist, recompense for her family, who over

Chinese safety regulations keep everything shipshape at Tiger Leaping Gorge.

Tracy and Jack with our guide at Tiger Leaping Gorge – that drop goes straight down into the rapids below.

the years have literally carved out and maintained the walking track along the gorge. A bargain whatever the price, and we descend a treacherous vertical trail, which cuts through rock and mud and bushes that drench us as we brush against them. Several people die each year underestimating the danger of the gorge. Layer after layer of clothing is peeled off despite the cold, until we finally make it down to a crowded rock jutting out into the river midstream, affording a photo opportunity that every single person wants to share at the same moment. A human traffic jam on a slippery rock in the middle of a raging flooded river is the result, before we retire to a tiny ledge where an enterprising local makes a fortune selling drinks and chocolate bars. How they get them here is anyone's guess.

The ascent is almost enough to do me in. Jack and Tracy laugh as I sweat and groan and drag myself up rusty steel ladders hammered into the rock ledges and endless sets of steps made from rocks that wobble as you climb. Don't look up, don't look down. Any equivalent in Australia or any similarly litigious society would be replete with guardrails, barriers, warning signs and disclaimers. None exist here. My glasses fog up in the rain, conveniently creating an excuse for frequent stops that serve to let me get my breath back while pretending to defog and clear lenses. As we get near the top again the rain stops and the clouds clear for long enough to offer a superb view down the valley – grassy slopes giving way to sheer cliffs as far as we can see. Tracy confirms the guidebook rumour that the government is considering damming the river, which will flood the gorge and in a few years obliterate the entire tourism industry generated by the natural beauty of this special place. Along with so much else in China I cannot understand how anyone could get things so wrong. Reminiscent of the Franklin Dam debate in Tasmania, it is hard to imagine people power having the same impact in China. It must not be allowed to happen, but then again it is not a democracy, and dissent and activism are not rewarding pastimes for ordinary Chinese.

We try to engage in discussions about the environment with Tracy on many occasions. She accepts the need for China to change, proudly defending their record of progress on solar and wind power, and dogmatically calling smog 'fog' whenever we complain, choking and rubbing our eyes from pollution. Throughout the provinces, overladen coal trucks belch exhaust fumes while delivering loads of lumps of heating fuel for villages where there is nothing else to help people through freezing winters, and river after river is dry and exhausted from irrigation and hydro schemes that deny any natural flow.

Groundwater supplies are dwindling in provinces that have relied upon it for years. But progress and industry are far and away the priorities of everyone in China: 'We just want what you already have', we are told on several occasions.

How can a tourist get past the official party line, standard propaganda? We spend days driving through countryside, Tracy sitting with her maps and guidebooks in the front passenger seat describing the area where we are, the local food, the culture and customs, while we absorb it all and stare out the windows. She recounts an idealised world of ethnic harmony, heroic industry, poverty eradication programmes and the like, even as we see untold poverty and ghastly pollution. Jack occasionally tries to cross-examine her, seeking an insight into Chinese thinking through our hard-working guide. She is always our go-between – whenever we meet anyone, it is Tracy's version of that encounter that we get to hear. Charming as she is, it grates to have to live China via a guide. We realise it would not be possible to find our way around without someone – navigating and negotiating without fluent Chinese is unimaginable, China being impenetrable unlike every other country in our twenty-nation odyssey. But everything is translated by her, every conversation mediated through her, an officially approved filter. She never loses her cool, is utterly professional and charming, always energetic and the perfect travel companion. But is she required to deliver the government line on any topic, or is it that Tracy is just a very proud and patriotic Chinese? Or are we blunt and rude? Is it a classic clash of Australian larrikin spirit rubbing up against the Chinese etiquette of never losing face and never upsetting a guest? Australians are amongst the least blindly patriotic peoples on earth, readily mocking our own failings and sending up our national heroes and political leaders. No one we meet would dare do that in China.

After Kunming we head east. The Huangguoshu Waterfall is the biggest waterfall in Asia, over 100 metres wide and nearly 80 metres high, and the famous water curtain cave boasts a trail behind the waterfall itself, like in a Phantom comic. Looking out from behind, through the cascade, onto the pond and dazzling rainbows makes the drenching worthwhile. We join the throng of exclusively Chinese tourists and find we are nearly as great an attraction as the waterfall. The first dozen or so people asking us to pose for a photo are a novelty, but then it becomes tiresome and eventually plain annoying. It seems every school-age child and teenager wants to say 'Hello, mister, how are you?', souvenir a photo of two wandering Australians and then run giggling to their friends and parents to report that they have spoken English. Tracy has taught us the Chinese for 'Australia' and we will say '*Or-da-leeya jen*' and save her the explanation time and time again. Here too the ethnic minority dress-up party is in full swing, affording any tourist the chance of donning colourful recreations of what might have once been the signature of the local tribes, as reinterpreted by a Chinese Walt Disney.

Crowds in China are somehow different to crowds at home. I cannot easily explain how a crowd is different, but there is little regard for personal space or privacy in China and we seem always surrounded. No one goes out of their way to intrude, but also no one goes to any effort to make space. It is just how things are: that you will be up close to someone all the time, part of a wave of humans moving this way and that like a tide. Coughing, spitting, hacking and nose clearing are taken to new heights and Western sensitivities about bumping into people seem quaint.

Adjoining the waterfall park we stumble on a massive bonsai collection, a vast and magnificent maze of potted trees and miniature forests numbering literally hundreds and hundreds of examples. It is the Tianxiangqiao Bonsai Stone Forest, not mentioned in any of our guidebooks and just an accidental find. Jack has been a bonsai connoisseur for several years, tending half-a-dozen small trees at home. He goes into a trance; ancient trees of every botanical type stretching in every direction as far as we can see. There are maples and cedars and figs and rare species that must be hundreds of years old, many of them bonsai but still metres tall. He wanders amongst them, marvelling at the sculptured forms and the tortured branches, and chooses a favourite to pose with for a photo. Tracy finds a gardener and seeks details, and they talk bonsai for a while. Then Jack asks the gardener to select the best tree of all, the most pure and clear expression of the philosophy of bonsai. Astonishingly, the gardener selects the exact same tree as Jack. They congratulate each other on their refined taste and appreciation of all things bonsai.

Going to a public toilet in any Chinese town is a confronting experience for anyone from the West. In Dali I walk into a low-ceilinged building, hoping that I have the male side of the entrance. The signs are all in Mandarin, so I watch to see who else is going in or coming out. Inside, the walls are tiled in white from floor to ceiling all around. There are neither partitions nor cubicles; it is open plan. There are no urinals or toilet bowls, just a wide gutter in the concrete floor along one wall with a steady trickle of water running along. Opposite there are a series of holes in the floor, not even porcelain floor pans as expected. There is a man squatting in front of me, smoking as he does his business. He smiles and greets me in Chinese which I cannot respond to. I hope he does not think me rude or inappropriate, but the stench is overpowering and there are several piles of unflushed droppings sitting in mounds waiting to be hosed away. There are taps at regular intervals for washing your bottom and hands, no paper or anything else for wiping. I have never had to crap in public before, and no amount of rationalising will overcome my discomfort at adapting the habits of a lifetime. I retreat, deciding that maybe it is not such an urgent call after all – I can wait.

I want to buy Jan a mah-jong set. I haunt the tourist and fake antique shops looking for something a little different to the pretend ivory tablets in plastic boxes that adorn every second stall. I scour the markets in Dali, Lijiang, Kunming, Xián and later Pingyao and wherever else we go. They are universally run by elderly women who are asleep until you walk in and who spring instantly to life, solar calculators at the ready. I find endless variations on the theme, dusty musty shops crammed full of fake antique knives, swords and muskets, carvings, brass statues, tapestry, coins, clothing, old locks, cameras, Mao's Little Red Books, army badges, Buddha statues, opium pipes, jade, old compasses, fake fob watches, abacuses, early books written on what look like ice-cream sticks held together with cotton thread, lacquer boxes of every description, calligraphy scrolls, bangles and earrings copying the style of every ethnic group, lamps, clocks, pedestals and those red frilly dangly things that hang off lanterns but look really good on car mirrors. Prices collapse with a little haggling – as much as 60 per cent or 70 per cent if you work harder. But can I find a decent mah-jong set? No one has what I want. They are either real ivory and out of my league or so plastic they are indescribably tacky. I suspect Tracy thinks I am mad, or just driven, but wherever we go I seek out the perfect mah-jong set. Eventually, almost giving up, I settle for a leather-bound box with small drawers each fitting a tray of tiles made from bone and bamboo. I can hear Tracy's sigh of relief – the quest is over. Imagine my horror when the week after returning home to Melbourne I see a near identical set for sale in our local shops … although for much more than I paid in China!

I become addicted to a pomegranate-flavoured icy pole. It is hard to find, but has a distinctive wrapper featuring the giant Chinese basketballer Yao Ming, famous for advancing to a successful career in the USA basketball competition. I cannot remember ever eating pomegranate in my life, but this cheap water ice is so refreshing and delicious that I search freezers wherever we go, seeking them out. Since it is October and no longer hot, stocks are hard to find, and I wonder what the shopkeepers think of the slightly agitated, middle-aged, bearded, overweight Westerner rifling through their freezers like a bag lady going through the rubbish bins. Jack is again horrified, Tracy bemused. Later in western China in Xinjiang province, I am doubly rewarded when we find street stalls in markets and towns run by sun-dried men in white pill-box hats crushing fresh pomegranates into juice for a trifling sum of money.

Although we are eating well, Tracy constantly finds more exotic foods for us to sample. We have told her we want to eat local, never in Western hotels nor restaurants where tourists go. We've said we want to eat anything and everything. Jack is reading the New York gastronomic adventurer Anthony Bourdain as we travel, and embraces his mantra of eating all the weird stuff wherever you are. We sample bugs, eel, black skin chicken, tree bark mixed into a type of omelette, every imaginable form of pork and pig, from ears to cheeks to intestines to crackling pancakes, dozens of freshly killed fish cooked in every way imaginable, chickens' feet, drunken chicken, searing hotpots, mutton, kebabs in the Muslim towns, dozens of different species of mushrooms, sprouts, beans and pulses, yams, tofu, porridges, corn broth, duck's blood sausage, dumplings galore and proper Peking duck, including the soup at the end made from the carcass. As we get north, a Muslim breakfast food based around a crepe, with an egg broken into it and chilli and pickled vegetables, captures Jack's affections and he insists on searching for it wherever we go.

Ritual plays a large part, and hours are spent in Yunnan watching the tea ceremony that goes with Puer tea in its various incarnations. Jack becomes a tea purist, and I am seldom without my little clear double-walled thermos, a few fresh leaves of Puer tea in the bottom and fresh hot water topping it up all day. Tracy constantly explains how whatever we are eating is good for some part of the anatomy – we start to tease her after a while, jumping in before she can say anything when we eat: 'it is good for the blood', 'this food good for skin and hair' or 'good for the teeth' becomes common. For our part, we introduce her to Vegemite. She gags on first sampling it, and politely tells us it is delicious but does not eat more than a crumb, hiding the uneaten portion of her cracker in her hand until she can dispose of it discreetly. We offer her Vegemite every day, noting the different excuses she comes up with for saying 'no'. She is far too polite to ever admit it is not to her liking.

We invent the Chopstick Olympics. Jack is quick to adapt his Melbourne Chinatown chopstick technique under tutelage, but I am less adept and he lords it over me at every meal. He challenges me to several events – speed lifting and maximum weight come first. How heavy an item can you lift and for how long? How quickly can you shift a pile of peanuts from one plate to the next, without dropping a single nut? Basketball is tossing leftover bits of bone into the empty bowls on the other side of the table, sprints are how quickly you can eat a bowl of rice down to the last grain, and the most appalling of all, a combined skills test where the two of us fight over a single dumpling on a plate, a cross between fencing and wrestling. Porridge with corn is half slurped and half moved by chopstick, leading to a slurping event. Football rules are adapted and accuracy in placement and splashless eating deserve reward. There is an opposite event – who can make the most mess on the table – spitting out bone and gristle, dribbling sauce and spilling food in a wide arc around your bowl becoming a contest in itself. Tracy covers her mouth laughing – or is it that she cannot believe we are so badly behaved?

Restaurants are often where we get to chat to locals. Tracy is tireless in explaining where we are from and what we are doing. Other diners as well as staff are universally friendly, laughing, shaking our hands and making us feel welcome in their towns and villages. Children are sent to practise their few stock English phrases, sometimes to show us their homework. Only once, in Kunming, are we greeted with suspicion, bordering on hostility. A government-owned noodle and breakfast cafe is sparse, cold and poorly run. The staff refuse to provide tea or hot water and the food is lousy. Tracy explains, 'It is run by government, the people do not care, they have a job anyway ...'

The local specialty in Tongren is dog. Each restaurant has illuminated signs identifying their signature dishes, featuring happy Labradors, tails wagging enticingly. Tracy hesitatingly offers us the chance to try dog, and once inside the proprietor proudly assembles a selection on a tray. Jack goes a little pale, I sample two different types, one grilled and one boiled. The whole carcass of a small animal, tail cheekily intact and curling up from the body, is spread out, thinly sliced, on the serving dish, unremarkable for the locals. It tastes like any other boiled meat, too tough and dry for my liking. The grilled meat is much easier to digest although still not pleasant. Or am I aware of what I am eating and unable to disconnect my affection for our pets from what is on offer?

They'd make tasty dress-up masks.

Lunch that day included fried tree bark (bottom right).

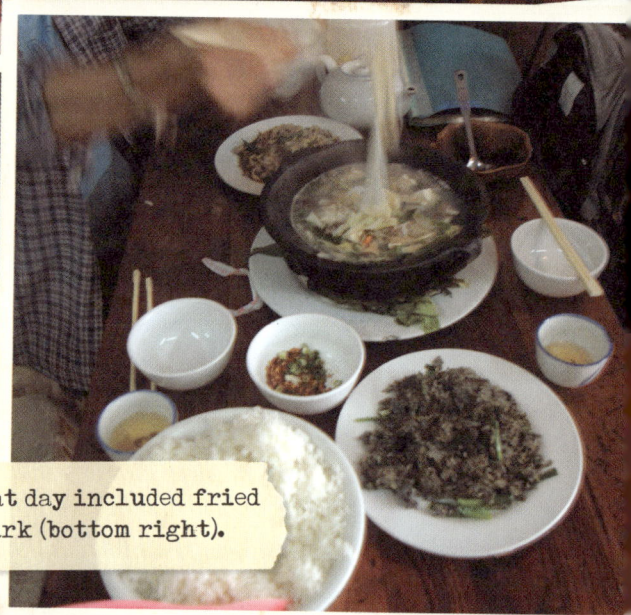

There's nothing you can't eat in China.

Freshly skinned bamboo
rat for lunch.

Chinese breakfast ... dumplings with
noodles — or noodles with dumplings.

The cat is safe from the pot, but
their canine friends are not.

What would I say if I did not know what was being served? A few nights later we park the car in a hotel courtyard, a large guard dog tied up nearby. Jack befriends and pats the dog and we reminisce about Bess back home. Next morning as we prepare to leave, the cook is cutting up the unfortunate animal's carcass outside the kitchen door and another anxious-looking mutt is chained in exactly the same spot.

We haunt the vibrant night markets most evenings, eating in open-air cafes on streets wherever possible. In larger towns and cities the food choice on the street is staggering, naked bulbs dangling from scaffolds and dimly lit kitchens steaming and smoking away for a lively trade late into the night. Buckets and tubs contain live fish, yabbie-like critters, chickens, pheasants, crabs and sometimes exotica like bamboo rats and other unidentifiable furry creatures that are butchered on demand. Menus do not exist, pointing and haggling preferred instead. A fish once selected will be weighed, whacked on the head and slit open for grilling in less time than it takes to read this description. Coals and flames are coaxed into life, boys of school age in little white caps bustle around, everyone yelling and chattering into mobile phones even in the remote villages. Beer is equal favourite with whisky, and of course tea is always served. Whole racks of greens and vegetables, bins of sauces ready to be ladled, stock and broth bubbling in cauldrons, all makes for quick, uncomplicated dining. Skewers of chicken, pork, prawn, mutton, mince, fish, skin on, skin off, fat on, fat off, kidneys, vegetables of every description … it seems endless choices have to be made.

In the street market I get a lesson in stir-frying on an open fire by the portly Lui Cheng Chan, a matronly figure commanding a stall as small as a phone booth that feeds dozens of people with delicious and fresh wok-cooked dishes. She shows me how to regulate the gas with my foot while tossing small fish like whitebait around the wok with a huge spatula in one hand, while keeping chilli, bean sprouts and green vegetables flowing in the correct order into the mix with the other. A crowd gathers, people laughing at me as she scowls and admonishes me for my failings as a cook. Sharing some fun achieves more than any team of diplomats.

As often as not when we return to our parked car there will be some explaining required for a small gathering attracted by this strange vehicle. The engine intake snorkel attracts many inquiries: what is it, why is it there? The map of our route on the doors either side gets well worn with fingers tracing our progress, marvelling at how far we have come and how we are going to get the rest of the way. No one ever travels much, familiarity with the world beyond their neighbourhood restricted to what they have seen on TV. Everyone knows kangaroos; no one knows anything else about Australia at all.

Several times we ask Tracy about Chinese politics. She nominates President Hu Jintao as the person in the world she most admires, and is quite anxious when we ask her about the massacre at Tiananmen Square. She learned about what happened from her uncle, not at school or university, where nothing is taught about it at all. She believes the students were lighting fires and creating danger, and the army had to act – but the government went too far in tackling the problem. 'Now we have a good government – before they were bad. Human rights is a big challenge for China – as we get rich we want things to be like America. The people in Taiwan must become part of China, like Hong Kong; we do many good things for them, like in Tibet. None of them are grateful for all that China has done. We have made their lives much better and they are still not happy. We give them money and hospitals and schools – they were always starving with the Dalai Lama and now they have food and roads – life is much better for them now. Minority people all over China are better off than they used to be.'

Ironically, these discussions come as we are refused permission to drive west from Xián to Datong. The Chinese showcase space shuttle launch is never mentioned, but we hear that no foreigners are allowed within the entire province of Gansu near the space base. Our alternative prescribed route is north to Mongolia, then we will have to somehow travel west either through Russia and Kazakhstan or back into Xinjiang from Mongolia. Every day I nag Tracy to try to get a second China entry approved, to allow us to cross Mongolia and join the Silk Road near Urumqi, for the drive to Kashgar, and then thru the 'stans and Iran to Turkey. There are security issues here too, as there has been a bomb attack in Kashgar attributed to Muslim separatists seeking an Uyghur homeland in Xinjiang. The longer the delay, the greater the chance we will be blocked by snow on the Torugart Pass, which each year becomes snowbound and impassable at exactly the time we will want to cross. She finally tells me as we arrive in Xián that permits can be secured for this second China leg, but it will be difficult and expensive as they need to find a local guide for us.

The sole border crossing between China and western Mongolia, at Takeshiken, is forbidden for foreigners, only local trucks and traders are permitted to cross. I am anxious to make sure we will be granted permits to get through if we go that way, because the alternatives through Russia and Siberia need visas and permits that will take ages to get if we are to chase that route instead. I am in touch with a travel specialist back in Melbourne, Brent McCunn, who emails me daily the almost-insurmountable hurdles we will encounter if we try to get into Russia without Russian visas already in our passports. He advises that we will need to stop in the Mongolian capital Ulaan Baatar and post our passports back to Australia. Russia will only issue visas at the embassy in the country of residence. A two- or three-week delay in Mongolia will mean we will have to go hell for leather and drive non-stop across Russia to get to Paris to meet Jan in mid-December as promised. It might just be doable but it will be robbing the trip of any fun, very stressful and a race. And we *must* make Paris on time – my marriage depends upon it.

Meanwhile, Jan gets the first quarterly phone bill covering the time since we left home. It is not good news, and much as we need to keep talking, mobile roaming is the most expensive way of doing it. Skype only works where there is a fast internet connection, so we either talk on mobiles or not at all. I think these calls are all worthwhile, but I am not looking at the bank balance and she is. My attitude is that the budget is already a work of loose fiction – we may as well just forget about it and plunge on and sort the mess out afterwards. That I can even think like that shows how relaxed and disconnected I have become in three months away – and more than half our trip time gone. Because of the global financial crisis, the exchange rate has collapsed as we travel, our dollar now worth nearly 30 per cent less than when we started. There is nothing we can do about it, except keep going.

We are **not the only crazies** driving through China

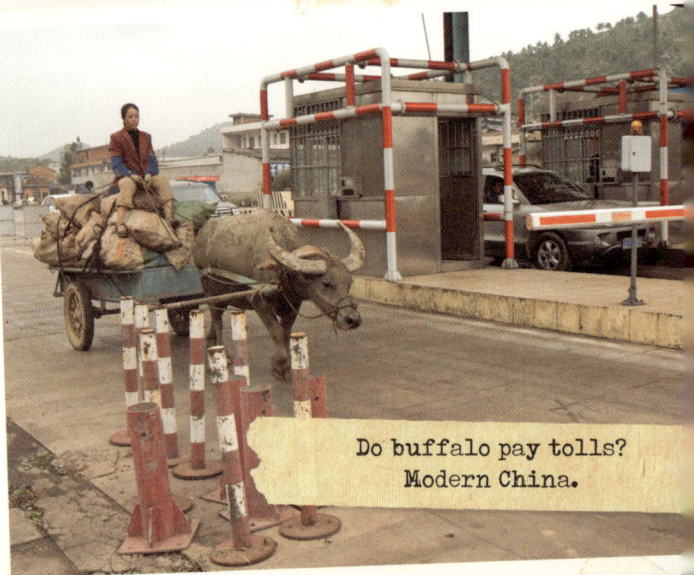

Do buffalo pay tolls? Modern China.

Another day of impenetrable traffic – on the road, China.

17 | Chinese Medicine Makes Us Sick

We meet another car load of Overlanders, explain how knives and forks work, sleep on beds of brick in Pingyao, defy gravity in Datong, take snake liver pills and race to the Mongolia border, all the while not having a clue if we can get any further than that. Will we be stuck in Mongolia forever?

Jack seems heartily sick of me. He never laughs at my jokes, won't indulge me in conversation anymore, argues readily about trifles, begrudgingly kicks the football, spending his time instead endlessly cropping and finessing photos on the laptop. I wonder if he is fretting over the girlfriend he left behind, from whom he has not heard in a while. Maybe he is tired of our trip. Perhaps he is homesick? Am I kidding myself – we have been together twenty-four hours a day for nearly four months and it is hardly surprising that the novelty is wearing off. I would not mind another source of conversation too. I am grumpy, tired and stressed about our next leg of the journey. Nothing is going right – all our plans have turned to *merde* and I am starting to entertain the notion that we might be stuck. What then? Abandon the car? Store it? Fly out? Fail? I seize a moment to try to sort it out with Jack – I have enough to worry about without a war on another front. I am lonely too – I miss Jan more than words can describe; our frequent phone calls make things even worse, not better. I had hoped she would meet us somewhere in Asia, or in China, or anywhere really. Maybe Tashkent, if we ever get there?

I am no stranger to confrontation. All my professional life, as a litigation lawyer, then in legal aid, and on the radio, I have dealt with conflict daily, often of the most intense kind. To challenge a politician, a premier or a prime minister, to cross-examine a police commissioner or a business leader requires a certain self-belief and confidence; maybe an arrogance but certainly a self-belief. Radio is a performance, a daily display for three and a half hours in front of hundreds of thousands of people without a script or rehearsal. It equips you well for pretty much anything that life can throw at you – but not a grumpy son. I hop from foot to foot, try to make small talk, to chat about football or cricket or anything except what I really want to deal with. It makes things worse. Finally, I ask, 'Is there something wrong? Let's clear the air – what's the matter?'

He tells me he is sick of having a guide in the car, tired of being told where we have to go, what to do. We were free to duck and weave before we got to China – we had three months of pretty much going wherever we wanted to, whenever we wanted to, however we wanted to. The need to accommodate our guide, to follow a strict itinerary and to fit in with her notion of what we ought to be doing, has robbed us of the spontaneity, which he tells me he is missing. We no longer pore over and scrutinise the maps, guess at intersections, make sign language with locals and stumble our way through cities and towns. We have become dependent on someone, instead of independent; captive instead of self-reliant. It is disempowering. He felt important before – we were a team, the two of us. Now he is sitting in the back seat, reduced to spectating. He gives me a hug – I cry. Again and again I am overwhelmed with the growth and maturity I see developing in front of my eyes in Jack. His capacity to see things the way I cannot and do not is astonishing. His photos and interweaving of what he reads with where we are is a delight, if occasionally contrived. Steinbeck and the terracotta warriors? I don't think so. As much as I miss Jan and Nigel I am compensated by spending this time with Jack. I console him that we will soon be in Mongolia, where we will again be making our own way. I feel euphoric that the problem is something other than me.

In several industrial centres we drive along roads where the manhole covers on the sewers have been stolen. From crap to scrap, those steel discs. There are gaping holes in the roads, no warnings or barricades, no witches hats nor orange flags – just huge gaps in the tarmac, enough to snap the front end of the car if we drop in. It would be comical if it was not so dangerous, and everyone weaves around the traps with no regard for safety. Highways are clogged with coal trucks, convoys of filthy, overloaded, crawling monsters with massive queues of traffic stuck behind. We prefer the tollways, even though the fees are often steep and, over the huge distances we want to cover, the cost is mounting formidably. We spend thousands of RMB on tolls, and because the steering wheel is on the wrong side for China the toll booth operators are invariably confounded to find a passenger paying, not the driver.

Tollroads are usually owned and operated by the local council, sometimes collecting a fee for only a few kilometres before you start again with a new toll to another gate and a different uniformed collector. Some tollways measure the fee with scanning technology, photographing the numberplate as you go through a boom gate and calculating the fee at the end of their stretch. As our Victorian numberplate is not recognised by their software, and our temporary China plate is on the sun visor, we always hold up the queue and confuse the attendant.

The pollution as we head northeast is appalling, the rivers grimy and the air foul. We notice the people are more aggressive, the pace of life is faster, the towns are even more crowded. If it is possible for driver behaviour to get any worse, it does. We see buffalo carts ambling along in the fast lane, cars abandoned in the middle of lanes where they've crashed, overturned trucks with cargo spilling off across the road, a duck herder walking a flock of several hundred waddlers down the freeway with a long bamboo pole to keep them from wandering. A broken-down bus is stopped on the road with its motor out on the bitumen, dismantled and being rebuilt: two men are up to their elbows in oil and grease, spanners flying, parts spread out around them as if the freeway is their workshop. A small tent propped on the crash barriers made from blankets must be their shelter at night, a fire keeping their supply of tea hot and no doubt providing dinner as well.

The Yangtze River is enormous, wider and with more water in it than any river we have seen in China. The main bridge is a phenomenal structure, an engineering marvel, seemingly suspended in the air by magic. As we cross, and Tracy tells us the formal history of the river, we both yell out 'Where's Ping?' and then we have to tell her about the children's book of the little duck that lives on the river. Without hesitation we agree to call the car 'Ping' and enjoy the nostalgia of the moment.

In an industrial town near Xiangfan, we stop to eat and a middle-aged woman approaches Tracy to chat. She is offering to sell us some embroidery, inviting us to her home to choose from her collection of old fabrics that she knows tourists like. She says she used to have a shop, but now just sells from home. She hops into Ping and we weave through the backstreets and up steep hills to a grimy apartment building. We climb many flights of stairs and she waves us into a tiny flat, plastic covers on all the furnishings and neat displays of family photos and knick-knacks. In her bedroom she opens a cupboard stuffed full with piles of superb old embroidered bedspreads, tablecloths, cushion covers, gowns and skirts, baby jackets, hats and scarves. They are uniformly stunning, elaborately gilded and tasselled, and she explains the ethnic connections and history of each one. She is a historian as well as collector, and nothing is cheap – but it is not tourist tat, it is the genuine thing. I am torn, wanting to grab a tub full and spend lots of money, but we have just handed Tracy thousands to cover the deposit for the permits for Kashgar so I choose only three small, choice pieces and thank her for the opportunity. She offers us tea and fruit, and seems about to prepare a whole meal as we take our leave. Nowhere else in China has someone been so forward, so pushy. I take it as an indication of our proximity to Beijing, Xian and other big tourist cities.

As we make our way north, NAVO have another guide heading south working with an English family driving from the UK to Singapore, having crossed Russia and Mongolia already. The two NAVO guides contrive a rendezvous. They are furiously texting, trying to work out where our paths will cross. As we round a bend, we see their Citroen hatchback with a trailer, and we meet the delightful Dwight and Tessie and their kids Loong and Lewis. Loong, also called Dee, is the same age as Jack; Lewis is about six years old. Bizarrely, they left their home near London the exact same day we left Melbourne, heading towards Tessie's family home in Singapore. Dee and Jack swap books, yarns and no doubt complaints about daggy parents. The two guides, Queenie and Tracy, head off for a debrief.

Dwight shows off his ingenious homemade trailer, and boasts of spending only GBP300 to buy their car, which impressively has just kept on keeping on for their whole trip. He is one of those engaging pragmatic stoics who delight in doing things cheap and tough and dispensing with trimmings. They all complain about how crowded their car is, but Dwight sees it as a virtue. 'I reckon some people overcook this thing,' he says, clearly regarding Ping, our four-wheel drive, as excessive for just the two of us. I shrug with indifference, having decided right from the start that I was not compromising on ABS, airbags, reliability and comfort. We share a quick meal, talking fifteen to the dozen, lapping up new conversation partners for the first time in ages. After posing for photos we drive off in opposite directions, and I immediately regret not suggesting that we spend the night in their company. They seem wonderful people, full of wise advice and experiences, and Jack craves company his own age. Another mistake.

North of Xian we eat spicy fish, fried peanuts and broccoli in a tiny backstreet hole-in-the-wall place where the woman cooking tells us, 'I have seen Westerners before … once … when I was in the fields and they went past in a bus and took photos, but I have never met any or spoken to them …' She calls her kids to come out and look at us and they watch us eat. Tracy translates when she asks, 'If you are not used to chopsticks, how else do you eat?' She has never heard of knives and forks, has no concept of other ways of living. 'How sad,' I remark to Jack, 'that the first Europeans these children meet are us, and what terrible impressions they must have of the entire breed just from this one encounter. What an onerous responsibility, what a burden.' He tells me, again, that I am an idiot.

In Linshi, the Lu-Yuan Hotel has also not seen Westerners before. Mr Li Wei Hua, the manager, makes a huge fuss, asking if we agree to having our photo taken with him in the morning. We agree, thinking nothing of it. Next day, the entire staff, more than thirty people, are lined up on the marble steps to the main street, a professional photographer with tripod and camera at the ready waiting for us to come downstairs. They are all in their uniforms, and after the group shots we are asked to wait while every individual staff member has their photo taken with us, laughing and giggling and preening the whole time.

Pingyao is an intact historic Imperial walled town, in Shanxi province. There are two adjoining provinces called Shanxi and Shaanxi, the difference between the sound of the two a matter of such fine intonation that our ears cannot make it out. Tracy gives up trying to point out the difference in pitch that distinguishes the two. We have learned a smattering of Chinese – we can say 'hello', 'thank you', 'we are from Australia', and Jack can count to ten, although I can only make it to six. He is quick to pick up some more, as he has been wherever we have gone. He teases me mercilessly, reciting basic phrases in Tetum, Bahasa Indonesia, Malay, Thai, Khmer and Lao and challenging me to remember which is which. Mandarin is so subtle a language, though, with pitch as important as pronunciation. It proves to be a higher hurdle and invokes great respect for any Westerner who manages to learn it.

Tracy knows that Kevin Rudd speaks fluent Mandarin as she has told us he has been featured on Chinese TV.

We park as required on Pingyao's outskirts, it being a fully pedestrianised town. Wandering the streets with a daypack, exploring the alleyways, we find lodgings in a typical courtyard guesthouse run by Wu Lee Ping, who includes breakfast as part of the package. The street frontage of her building is used for shops, the home and guest rooms up a cobbled pathway behind. No one else is staying there. Each room opens onto the central courtyard and is large but freezing. The beds are platforms of brick with just a thin mattress, a small fire warms water that flows through pipes in the bricks beneath, and although it should be utterly uncomfortable, somehow it works. We wander the town, admire the shrines and temples, the cobbled streets and intact architecture, the museum and the endless tourist shops. Away from the main streets, lined wall to wall with fake antiques and tea shops, the citizens of Pingyao seem to just go about their business, happy to smile and wave and continue on as if they are not living in a functioning museum. Next morning the Wu children wolf their breakfast as we rise, and trundle off to school with their plastic backpacks, leaving Mum to make us noodles and egg as her husband rises, washes and brushes his teeth under the single central tap in the kitchen courtyard.

I negotiate to buy some final souvenirs from China. Walking around a dozen shops, I check prices and haggle to try to get a feel for the range I ought to aim for. I want some small swords and daggers representing the different ethnic traditions, to add to a collection I have assembled from all over the world over many years. I pick out what I have decided is the best, engage in an elaborate and theatrical process, part with my money and am humiliated in the very next street to be offered an identical sheath and sword for two thirds of the price I just paid. My pride dented, we retreat to the new town and look for a pharmacy. Tracy has a cold and I have a sniffle too. We buy some medicine that is based on snake liver and are assured it will do wonders for my cough, sinus and throat. Within a day I am covered in red spots, and my cold gets worse.

Each day we are getting closer to our Mongolian border crossing. We do not know where and how we will get to Europe from there. All we know is that we will go north until Ulaan Baatar and then go west! Viewed in its simplest possible form, that is what we have been doing since the day we left home – north until Mongolia, then turn left. I want to connect to the Silk Road, or more accurately one of the Silk

Roads, as there are multiple routes. My dream has always been to stick to it as closely as we can – sadly the Chinese authorities do not seem to take my dream into account. I drive Jack nuts workshopping the options with him, sometimes several times a day. He stays nonchalant and relaxed and trusts me to sort it out, but I do not trust myself and wish he would get more involved in order to at least humour me in my stress. We are still negotiating on multiple fronts: how to get from western Mongolia through the mountains where foreigners are not allowed; if we get to the border and are refused permission to cross, is there the fallback option of permission to go into Russian Siberia to the north? We still have not sorted out how we can get out the other side of Central Asia and through to Europe. I am every day chasing Russian and Iranian visas as well as the Chinese authorities over re-entry to western China and also trying to understand the bizarre and rigid visa requirements for Kazakhstan, Kyrgyzstan, Uzbekistan and Turkmenistan.

There are two mountain passes west out of Kashgar, the Torugart Pass being my preferred route, but as it's higher it might be snowbound. Lonely Planet *China* says, 'From June to September it is theoretically possible to cross the dramatic 3752m Torugart Pass on a rough road from Kashgar to Bishkek', and we are already into October before we even start to cross Mongolia. We are one month and several thousand kilometres late. It will be November when we get there and what will the weather be doing by then? Tracy insists that the security officials demand to know which pass we plan to use, but I want to choose when we are closer, depending on the snow. She says the permits cannot be issued unless and until we choose. I gamble on the lower altitude pass, the less snow-prone pass, that goes from Kashgar due west to Osh, through Irkeshtam into Kyrgyzstan. It is an almost critical error, but I do not appreciate the significance until later. Casual decisions taken one day can have consequences much later that betray you.

The last two days in China include visits to the Yingxian wooden pagoda, a 70-metre wooden tower nearly 1000 years old, the Yungang Caves complex at Datong and the Hengshan Hanging Monastery. The caves are more accurately described as a kilometre-long wall of Buddha statues carved into and out of the cliffs, dating back to 400AD, and it is one of the most famous sites in China. There are fifty-one caves with hundreds of separate statues, and the evolution in style can be seen from the oldest to the newest. It is a shrine of great holy significance for Buddhists, set

If an architect
suggested it today...

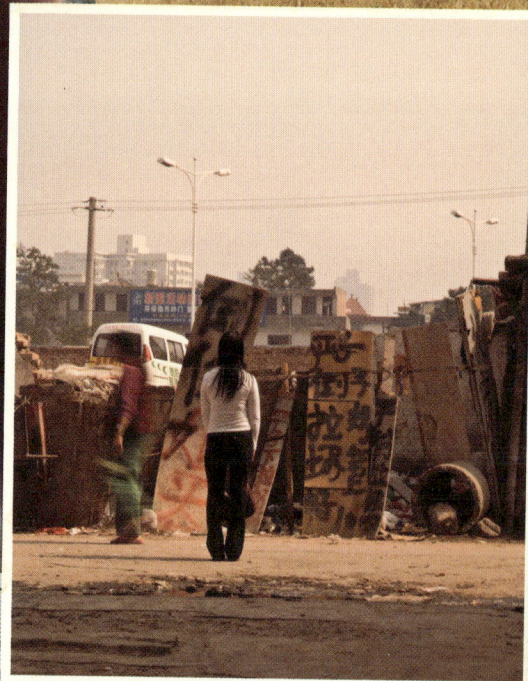

The Hanging Monastery is held up by
wooden structural beams embedded deep
into the cliff-face.

世界一绝

悬空寺，位于山西省浑源县城
491年），迄今已有一千五百多年

整座寺院面对恒山，背倚翠屏，上载危崖，下临深谷，楼阁悬空，结构巧可。

飞虹；隔峡遥望，似壁间雕嵌。全寺共有殿阁四十间，利用力学原理半插横梁为基，巧借岩石暗托，
　　　　　　　　　　　　　　　　虚实相生。寺内共有铜、铁、石、泥佛像八十余尊，其中

Nostalgic Pingyao, from the buildings to the people. Mercifully, not yet modernized.

The massive army of terracotta warriors, Xian.

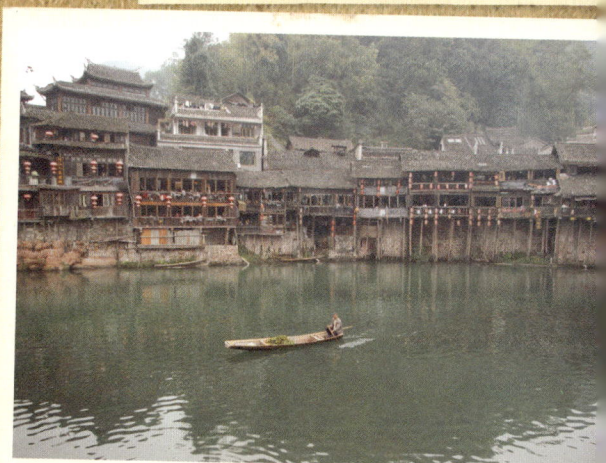

Fenhuang looks scenic and peaceful from the river, but the streets are overridden with tourists.

in a tranquil garden, but all around is the grimy, barren, industrial reality of this part of China. Each cave has its own history, as well as the important story of the discovery in modern times of these relics, lost for generations. Great care is now being taken to preserve them, and to explain their story. The guidebooks are all in Chinese, and Tracy tries to translate as we walk, but it is an impossible task and we give up and just wander and photograph the statues as objects of beauty and undoubted significance.

The landscape has changed – there is nothing green any more and the mud walls and stark, almost lunar, surrounds are a hint of what lies to our north. The Hanging Monastery is breathtaking, clinging high up a sheer cliff wall above what used to be the flood level of the Heng River below. It seems suspended in midair, but in reality it is supported by beams that cantilever out from the cliffs and prop up the foundations, as well as rickety poles poking up from ledges well below. It is a shrine for Buddhism, Taoism and Confucianism, magnificently preserved, and clambering around the gnarled wooden stairs and exposed balconies reinforces admiration for engineers and builders who put it all together years ago with primitive and rudimentary tools, yet it has lasted through the centuries. I ask Jack, 'What is there that we have built in our times that will ever stand the test of time like these buildings do?' We struggle to come up with more than a few examples of anything lasting, endearing or significant of our era.

At one of our last dinners in China, we ask Tracy if she is a communist. 'Oh, no, no one in China is communist,' she laughs. 'The government is, but the Chinese people like business, they like money … we are not truly communist but the government is and that is best.' She asks our advice about investing in the stock market, which she has been doing for some time. It is starting to wobble, the Wall Street rumblings of a few weeks before are reaching China, and she is nervous. I have never bought shares and feel a fraud dispensing any advice whatsoever about Chinese shares, so I decline, which she sees as a sure sign that I know something that I do not want to tell her. She persists, assuming that if we can afford to do a trip like this, and because I am a lawyer, and a customer of her company, then I must be terribly wealthy and therefore wise on all things to do with business and investing. If only she knew the truth.

The stock market collapse seems a curious event, so disconnected from what we are doing and how we are seeing the world. I am suddenly sorry not to be at work, where this would be the biggest story for years. I am missing out on the very thing we hang out for. The daily news cycle can be a slog, but when big things happen that is when it is most fun being on the radio. I log on to internet sites across the globe trying to get a handle on the meltdown of the global capital system and wonder whether the US election will act as a circuit breaker in a few weeks' time.

Heading north, into the Chinese province called Inner Mongolia, flying along all day at 140 kilometres per hour, Ping is literally the only vehicle as far as we can see in any direction on a six-lane superhighway. Hour upon hour of nothingness, a hint of what is to come in Mongolia. The Great Wall of China is marked on the map as crossing the freeway, but we go well past where it is supposed to be and notice nothing. I turn around, puzzled that it seems missing. This is, after all, the greatest man-made object on earth. We backtrack, and find that the Great Wall is not so great, amounting here to little more than a subdued line of dirt mounds stretching across the plain. The famous and iconic stone watchtowers and battlements of the tourist strip near Beijing do not continue west, instead crumbling dirt piles two metres high barely suggestive of greater glory are all that remain. The freeway respectfully tunnels underneath.

We arrive finally at the border at Erinhot in Inner Mongolia, a frontier town if ever there was one. The Gobi Desert starts on the China side, flat earth and sparse vegetation, stones and rocks instead of fields and trees. Mud walls replace brick for the few structures that dot the horizon, and as we drive into town brand-new bronze life-size sculptures of dinosaurs roam the roadside verge. They are a striking and creative welcome to an otherwise featureless plain. The town is a maze of new and still under construction concrete towers, with cranes and scaffolding everywhere. There seems to be no reason for any of this construction – there is no commerce, no market, barely any life but for the construction. We find a five-star hotel that is totally empty and offers rooms at the price we have paid for vastly inferior places further south. The staff fuss over us, excited to have something to do. The lift is on the outside of the building in a glass shaft, totally incongruous on the edge of the desert. Central planning and political considerations, not the free market, have driven this development, much like we saw on the border with Laos at the exact opposite end of China thousands of kilometres south and a month before.

Never did I imagine I would drive across the Gobi desert, but now we cross into Mongolia.

JACK WRITES

18 | Mongolia Ramblings

The More I See ...

Part 1: The Gobi

The asphalt road long ago faded into sand, now tyre tracks darting off every which way. The Gobi Desert resplendent in the background. Emptiness expanding on barren plains. The Trans-Siberian train line on the left, a row of bare telephone poles on the right.

We bumped along for hours over rock, sand and clumps of desert grass. There were real tumbleweeds, almost as big as the tyres, blowing along in the wind and getting caught up in scrags of tree and brush until a gust came along and released them, letting them continue bumping and jerking along, free as the desert breeze in the emptiness.

After a while we came across some desert camels with two humps. They just stood and stared at us while we stood and stared back. They munched at dry grass.

And as we pushed on through the desert my mind was lost. We stopped for a piss and I saw our lonely footprints in the dirt, the twin trails of our footsteps so insignificant in the face of the emptiness of the steppes. How much of this desert, if any of it, had never been graced by a foot – human or beast? Did a clump of dirt exist that had never been upturned by the soles of an animal? Since the beginning of eternity? If not, how many dirt particles or atoms had never been in contact with anything but more dirt? And air ... How much of the air that we were breathing had been inside someone else's lungs? I wanted to know whose air I had had inside me and whose lungs my air had been inside. I imagine in the city we must exchange a lot of air. In those big offices and apartment blocks, we must all be sharing and exchanging our air, but out here in the middle of nowhere, were these particles of air that I was sniffling in completely fresh, raw and virgin? Untouched and untarnished by anyone else? I took a deep breath and jumped back in the car.

We came across some men working on a road and we stopped and asked directions. We were well lost and they couldn't read our English map so it took a while to work out where we were and where we wanted to go. They pointed us to a distant valley and on as far as we could see. We started Ping and left as they chuckled to themselves, joking around and probably muttering about another bunch of Western wankers winding through the wilderness of their world.

We arrived in a small town 400 kilometres from Ulaan Baatar. Dusk turned the rims of the sky pink and the shadows had all but disappeared from the sand. We found a crumbling hotel, had something deliciously greasy and oily to eat, and flopped into bed, worn-out and craving sleep.

Part 2: Ulaan Baatar

The next day we arrived in Ulaan Baatar after lunch, having bounced and bumped our way past snow-sprinkled hills and through ger (Mongolian tent) suburbs.

Draped in cold white light, the capital city was a bleak array of Soviet-era apartment blocks, droopy grey trees and grim faces refusing to crack the smallest smile. The locals were dressed in heavy jackets which protected them from the stinging wind. Their faces were dry and their eyes bitter. The rich women clicked along in high heels and furry coats with wrap-around sunglasses sitting on their cheeks. Some of the girls were beautiful, so dolled up and cute-nosed with their long shiny hair. But the ugly women were chunky. Stocky with round faces; broad and dry cheeks, wide noses and small beady eyes that bore right through you. They pushed past with sharp elbows and strong hands that didn't give a damn about you and your culture of courtesies and politeness.

We had a bite down a side-street where we were served heavy steamed buns and cabbage by a couple of heavy women. Their faces were flushed and pasty after years of being beaten by the biting wind. They grunted and bustled, ducked under the board that served as both a counter and as a divider between the kitchen and dining room, grabbed more plates to run about with and did all this in the candlelight during one of the day's several blackouts. The food sat bloated in my stomach.

On the way back to where we were staying we passed a little antique shop. Inside it was dim like only a musty antique shop can be, and in that dusty murk the fat antique seller sat eating greasy dumplings out of a plastic container. He sucked them loudly before eating them, letting the oil of the dumplings ooze down his arm and drip into his yak-milk tea.

We left the shop and I put my finger on a feeling I'd had for a long time. I was a visitor in a zoo, or in some kind of amusement park. I'd bought my ticket, I'd brought my camera and here I was to be entertained and intrigued by the animals. I felt an invisible cage around it all, I felt invisible bars between us and them. Their shy eyes stared out from the enclosures, looking at us with fear, unable to understand why we wanted to stand there and for some weird reason watch what they were doing, watch their everyday actions. Why we would come all this way and stand there and watch living breathing humans doing nothing more than live, work and walk the streets?

This had been eating at my subconscious for a long time and slowly making its way through to the surface. To be honest, I'd been uncomfortable with the unequal relationship between the tourist and the local since our visit to Arnhem Land. And now I had it in words, a solid form, and I felt a bit sick.

Part 3: Back to the Gobi

We scooted out of Ulaan Baatar as quickly as possible. And still in the back of my mind the discomfort remained, and would remain in varying degrees of relevance, for the rest of the trip.

We started out west and barrelled off the main highway with a solitary sign pointing across the desert. The car grew smaller and smaller as we cannoned deeper and deeper into the desert. I sat in awe, pondering my insignificance in all of history and musing over our disproportionate perspective of ourselves in all of time. The realisation that we were but a speck of dust on a granule of sand in the history of earth seemed so obvious and depressingly and harrowingly clear. Triumphs and glories, troubles and worries, nations and empires, everything was so out of proportion. This land had only been known as Mongolia for a few decades, and before that it was the part of USSR, and before that it was a nation of constantly changing boundaries run by long-haired warlords, and going back further it was for centuries and centuries nothing more than some land on which nomads roamed without borders. The current physical and political restraints were only a blip in the timeline of this place. One day soon it will change, and then it will change again and it will just keep on changing forever. At each of those changes the incumbent people will acknowledge this land and it's updated borders. With no recognition of history's lessons, the land is nothing more than just that – the land – and the borders are only mental barriers, a human creation made to try and put ownership on something that cannot be owned. No one owns the land.

We stopped at the peak of a hill and gulped at the vast area between us and the area where our eyes could no longer make out the finer details of the desert. On the other side there was nothing but more vastness.

It was one massive moment where you have to stop and stare and look around and ask if the world could really be an accident. Even the harmonious twinkle and shimmer of the sun off the sand? And the eerie piercing breeze sweeping the steppes that make your skin swoon and prickle and tickle. Could that really be an accident of atoms colliding?

I napped and forgot where I was. When I woke up to the cold blue sky I tried to get my head around where on earth we were. I sat glued to the windowsill absorbing every thump and rumble of the wheels, completely separated from anything else happening outside of this horizon-to-horizon sphere. And now that my head wasn't distracted by the rest of the world I saw that it was just the confronting cold sun and sky, the rocks and dirt and steppes.

Little field mice sprang out of their holey homes and scuttled for safety. Every now and then a cheeky fox would bound along with its plume-like tail waving. Out in the desert, lonesome footprints were sunk in the dirt as the rims of the earth turned purple tinged with pink. There was no one and nothing as far as the eye could see or the ear could hear. And the sun danced in the sand to the deafening hum of silence.

19 | Welcome to Mongolia

The Gobi Desert, Bactrian camels, yaks, foxes, abandoned Soviet Air Force bases, no roads through the desert, inedible food, and the ugliest city in the world. Welcome to Mongolia.

From Jon on www.MelbourneToLondon.com

Harsh people, harsh terrain

Snow. Coats. Hats. Steam. Heating. Soups. Stews. Mutton. Greatcoats. Fur hats. Boots with turned-up toes. But stilettos too! Yurts. Gers. Trucks. Dust in the desert. Tracks in the desert. No road signs. At all. Nothing, nil, nix. Just follow someone else's tyre marks and see where they go. Keep the Trans-Siberian Railway line to your left. Or your right. But do not lose sight of it.

Crossing the border takes hours. Queuing on the Chinese side, waiting while documents are processed by official after official, our car checked and checked again to make sure the same engine is in it as was there when we entered … it just goes on and on. Little bits of paper are handed from booth to booth, checkpoint after checkpoint, interrupted for an hour when the electricity fails and then the computers will not reboot. Either side of us on the concrete access road are Mongolian jeeps loaded with shopping. Most of these Russian-made relics refuse to start when the key is turned, needing pushing, jump-starting or elaborate tinkering under the bonnet before kicking into life. They are all falling apart, lights dangling from wires, windscreens smashed, windows replaced with plastic, exhausts broken and belching smoke and noise. One car is even being towed through the border crossing on a rope. Ping, our flash white Toyota, looks totally out of place. No one has any regard for queuing etiquette. If the line moves and you are not ready, three cars will fight to squeeze into your spot. Police and soldiers are moving up and down the line, the Chinese authorities checking every car for contraband and weapons. The Mongolians are all swarthy, windburned and wearing massive fur-lined felt or leather jackets. Tracy has been racing around finessing our clearance – then suddenly it is done and a soldier yells at us to go. We hug Tracy and wave goodbye, turn around and drive through massive steel gates into Mongolia.

It is instant bedlam. There is a small ramshackle gatehouse with a uniformed official sitting behind a glass window. The window is open just wide enough to slide a passport through. There are twenty people crushed around the window, all shouting and pushing and waving their papers. No queue. Every few minutes he selects someone's passport at random and, puffing on his cigarette, slowly scrutinises the pages and the owner in turn. He then gradually transcribes details with a pencil into a ledger book, pausing frequently, apparently exhausted from the effort. When done, he stretches, slides the processed passport through the crack in the window and takes another. People arrive at a greater rate than they are being processed. I lock the car and we join the throng, squeezing and elbowing like everyone else until we get our turn. It is a good-natured throng, but it is every man for himself, no favours given. There are no women. Our visas were purchased the day before with a speedy issue fee at the consul in Erinhot. The fee is basically a tax on Westerners who do not want to wait a week for their visa, supplemented by a little extra bribery to get the one-hour turnaround instead of half a day. We are stared at and talked about, no doubt, but eventually allowed past passport control and sent to customs.

If the passport control area was bedlam, customs is hell. The building is two storeys, freezing cold, partitioned offices everywhere and no obvious system or signs. Women in uniform wander around collecting documents at random. There is no queue, no windows or gates, no offices to go to. Someone takes pity on me and points me towards one officer who speaks a smattering of English. She takes our passports and the carnet for the car and goes upstairs. After waiting for about an hour, everyone goes to lunch, but there is no sign of our documents. Jack has given up and in disgust has gone to read, enthroned in Ping with his iPod. There is no food or drink that I can find and I am starting to get angry and frustrated. We have been in queues most of the day and are not progressing at all.

Another hour passes and an English-speaking officer asks me why I am waiting and takes me upstairs looking for the officer who took our papers. There is a maze of rooms all populated by half-a-dozen people sitting talking to each other with mountains of documents piled on their desks. No one is processing anything. We find the woman who took our papers, slurping noodles with a man who has serious braid on his epaulettes. An exchange between the three of them ends with our carnet and passport being returned to me, and with a wave of his hand the senior customs man says one word in English: 'Go.' I do not need to be told twice.

The Mongolian side of the border town Zamyn-Uud is even more bleak than the Chinese. We change money and buy some bread, little hamburger-style pancakes and some juice for a late lunch. We drive off through the shanty town's streets, and then the road just stops. At the side of the last building in the street, the gravel ends and there is nothing in front of us except low grass and rolling hills, telephone poles stretching into the distance the only feature on the landscape. No path, no track, no signs, nothing but wheel ruts in several directions fanning across the slopes. We follow one set and end up in a railyard, so backtrack and start again on the next-most-worn set of ruts. The map shows the railway line – the Trans-Siberian – is always to the east of the supposed road, so using the telephone poles and the railway as guides we choose the rutted track between them. We bounce along, laughing and enjoying being together in the front seat again.

The trail splits regularly, some tracks crossing the railway line while others continue under the powerlines. We stumble on construction crews bulldozing and grading a proper road – must remember to come back in a few years and enjoy the drive with a road beneath the wheels. As the iPod keeps us amused, we pass Bactrian camels, their distinctive double hump sometimes full and standing proud, or limp, curling over as a sign of distress or thirst. Goats and sheep make an occasional appearance, no doubt belonging to someone, but no one we can see. We rejoice in driving with the windows down, the air cool but clean and a delight after the smog of China. The fine chalk-like dust that soon covers everything is a small price to pay. The potholes are shocking, the track broken and difficult. Jack drives, allowing me a rest for the first time in ages. He was spooked by the terrible traffic hazards in China and it seemed unsafe to expect him to cope. But here there is no traffic, no hazards, nothing to go wrong except going too fast when the road drops away. It is relaxing to navigate and have a chance to goof off looking out the window. We are instantly happier.

Our topics of conversation have changed. As we left home and raced across Australia, Jack was very much still talking about school, university and sporting triumphs and disasters. Now we have long discussions about how Australia has changed, even in my lifetime, about the global financial crisis, it's all grist to the mill. But we still relive every cricket match he has ever played in, every victory his hockey team has enjoyed, every record set in the laneway cricket that he and his mates have created.

We overnight in Saynshand, the first town after the border. It is a dump. There is a small square of broken pavings, weeds protruding, dressed on each flank by nondescript, Soviet-style, square two- and three-storey buildings. They are all closed. There are a few young men milling around outside our hotel, where the cash machine and its yellow neon light seem to be the town's main attraction. On a hill overlooking the highway is a memorial to Mongolian military might, consisting of a freshly painted but ancient Soviet tank, barrel protruding to the sky, signifying some faint memories of once guarding the mountain pass. Our hotel boasts a restaurant and we have a European menu for the first time in months – schnitzel for dinner, with tinned sauerkraut, greasy chips, a fried egg and lukewarm tea. We are only 220 kilometres from China but in culinary terms we are light years away already.

In the morning the guard ignores our requests to open the gates to the carpark until we pay a hefty tip. We have 400 kilometres to get to Ulaan Baatar, across the steppes, and the only feature on the way of any note is at the halfway mark, an abandoned Soviet air force base at Choyr. The first hint of the old base is when the dirt and dust greets a paved road, the tarmac being a legacy of the Russians and their need to get to and from this spot, their most remote military location, the furthest reach of the old empire. Exploring and photographing this eerie ghost town seems fun until we are chased and menaced by a local seeking money. We proffer a fraction of what he demands for the 'photo fee' but he smiles as soon as the notes are handed over and walks off content. There is a Russian air force MIG fighter jet on a pedestal, stripped of anything that can be unbolted but still pointing to the heavens as if ready to be scrambled against the Chinese in a moment. The hangars and buildings have been stripped to their concrete and steel shells, scavengers still working to extract anything whatsoever that can be used. The runways and bunkers are intact, and in the more remote corners the heavy double doors remain shut, barbed wire protecting them, hiding who knows what from scrutiny; it is all quite untouched, hinting that a truckload of the USSR's finest could magically appear around a corner if the Cold War were to restart.

Some 200 kilometres of flat, boring, straight road takes us to the outskirts of UB, Mongolia's chaotic capital. Trolley buses bounce around, traffic jams are a shock and we get lost looking for somewhere to stay. It is an unattractive city, half-a-dozen modern skyscrapers seemingly dropped in amongst Soviet-era square featureless blocks, frontages not even facing the street. Owing to the extreme weather, there are no shopfronts, no pavements, nor windows. Every aspect of life is tucked indoors, away from passing observation. Mud alternates as a road surface with potholed concrete, and police prey on drivers at random, extracting bribes for imaginary offences. The hotel staff counsel me to garage Ping, the first time in our whole trip that someone has said it is not safe to leave the car on the street overnight. A sign in the foyer reads:

Hotel Rules
Dynamite, drugs, inflammables and poisons, all radioactive material prohibited
All kinds of arms and weapons prohibited to bring into hotel
Singing, drinking, bringing girls into hotel prohibited

Dinner is greasy dumplings from plastic bowls in a backstreet cafe and then we wrap up warmly in clothes we have not seen since we packed them at home three and a half months ago. Every cafe and most shops have some sort of picture of Genghis Khan on the wall, the national hero depicted either embroidered in gaudy gold and silver, in beaten pewter bas reliefs or just painted in noble profile. He is usually on horseback, occasionally just a bust, ranging from fierce to statesmanlike, always defiant, eyes always blazing. He is a constant reminder of their glorious past, which must offer little comfort to the family camping on the bare concrete shell of the second floor of a construction site – no walls, just scaffolding and framework. A naked light bulb swings from an extension cord that runs from the next building.

Our few days in UB are spent queuing at the Chinese Embassy for visas, queuing at the Russian Embassy to be refused visas, trying to find the Kazakhstan Embassy only to learn that even if you can find it, they do not issue visas unless you have a letter of invitation. We still have not been approved to re-enter China for the Silk Road and I decide we must prepare Plan B – via Russia and Kazakhstan. At the Russian Embassy there is a queue at the external gate, then a queue to get from within the compound into the foyer, then a queue to get to the counter, then a queue to speak to the consular staff. Helen from Cambria in England is in front of us in this nightmare, and leaves in tears after waiting all day. She is booked to fly home via Moscow but has just been refused the transit visa she needs. She has purchased online a non-refundable airfare and train ticket, but they do not care. They tell her she should not have bought the ticket without getting the visa first. She argues that a travel agent told her she would not get a visa until she had a valid ticket. She is stuck. Confronted with the inflexibility of Soviet bureaucracy, it takes little time to be told we will not be allowed a transit visa for Russia unless and until we have the approval for the next country we visit. Kazakh visas are only issued with a letter of introduction, and we will have to find and visit their embassy, wait for their visa, then revisit the Russians. I am despairing at the unutterable frustration of it all, but just as we grapple with the finessing of the Kazakh visas, I get a text from Tracy confirming that we are approved to go through Xinjiang after all. It is a huge relief – the Silk Road beckons at last.

The next day we spend exploring the fabulous market and the few museums. At the Victims of Political Persecution Memorial Museum we learn of the Stalin-era Russian terror of Mongolians that claimed tens of thousands of victims in a prolonged occupation that the world has by and large overlooked. An entire generation of educated Mongolians was eliminated or sent to Siberian labour camps; nearly 30,000 are known to have perished and the Mongolians are keen not to let the Russians forget. Yet again I am overwhelmed with sadness – the blood keeps oozing out of the ground wherever we go.

The imperious Gandan Khiid monastery reminds me of a synagogue. The priests sit on cushions in front of the assembled boys, who are either chanting in a trance-like melody or clowning around and not paying attention at all. Middle-ranking clergy are supervising the younger scholars, sometimes flamboyantly rearranging

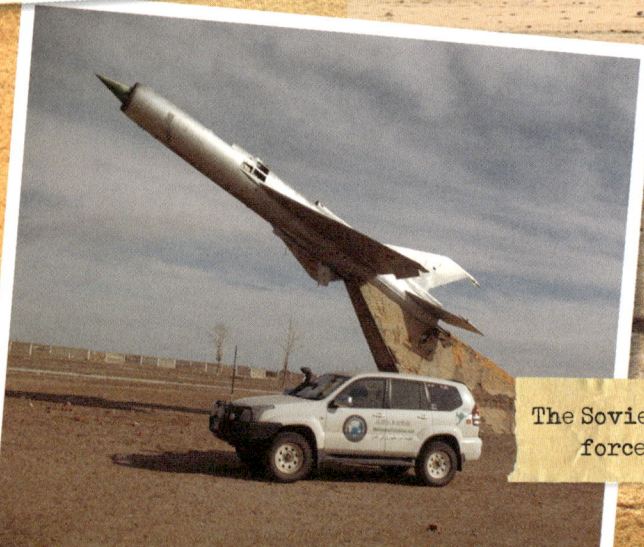

The Soviets just abandoned an entire air force base in Southern Mongolia.

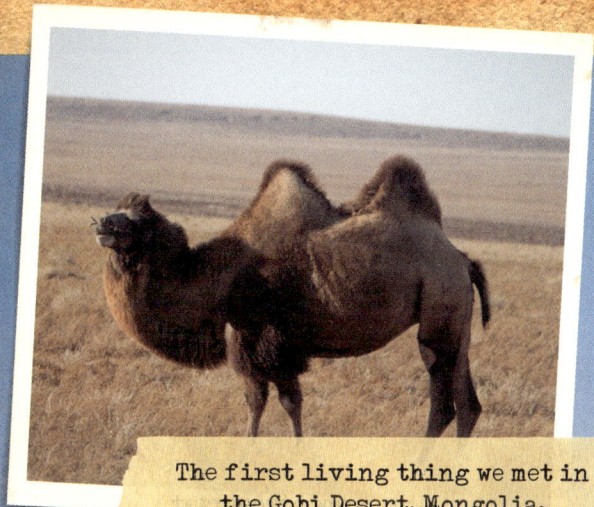
The first living thing we met in
the Gobi Desert, Mongolia.

He **thought** we were exotic...

their golden scarves in exactly the way the rabbi would rearrange his tallis or prayer shawl when I was studying for my bar mitzvah. Elderly pilgrims, universally women, bow-legged and weighed down with thick dressing-gown-style cloaks and curled-toe shoes, run their fingers over prayer wheels and holy relics, mesmerised by their devotions. Jack renews his interest in Buddhism, but I find shamans more interesting, a more ancient and just as puzzling set of superstitions and silly rules and irrational practices that mean whatever you want them to.

UB, as it is known, is the closest to a Western city we have seen since Bangkok. But the contrasts between the old and new overwhelm. Soviet-era architecture, public buildings with broken windows, smoky stovepipes, muddy surrounds, smashed concrete … juxtaposed with skyscrapers under construction with reflective glass and chrome, Porsche four-wheel drives and Hummers. Some of the buildings could be going up or maybe they are coming down? It is hard to tell. We struggle to find fresh fruit or vegetables, and the food is all so greasy! Little crescents of pastry with boiled mutton that spurt fountains of fat as you bite into them. Stew. Sauerkraut. Mince steaks. We try Korean …

Another bizarre travel coincidence happens while we are sitting in our hotel one afternoon, taking a break from the freezing cold while we wait for the Chinese to process our passports. There is an unexpected knock on the door, and a middle-aged European woman, looking up the corridor, holds a bottle of water out to me. In English she says, 'Here it is,' then turns to look at me, and says, 'Sorry, wrong room … oh, it's Jon Faine …' Carol and Martin are staying in the next room. I play veterans hockey with Martin. They are in transit with a group tour on the Trans-Siberian Railway from Moscow heading to Beijing. We join them for dinner, and it is bizarre to bump into people with whom we can have a conversation, let alone the first Australians we have seen for a long time.

The power keeps going out, half an hour at a time and no obvious pattern to it. The hotel staff shrug their arms and apologise and issue candles. I ask for help choosing our route west, studying the maps, and half-a-dozen people, including other guests, assemble and stare. They all confess to never having been west and have no idea what the roads will be like or even if there will be places to stay. As I go around the block to load up with diesel, a policeman waves me over with his illuminated orange baton and demands my licence. 'You drinking,' he says, when he identifies me as a foreigner. The standoff lasts half an hour, until he realises I am in no hurry and am not offering a bribe to get away.

I set up office in our hotel room and, over the course of an entire day of study, with the internet on the laptop, some helpful emails from other travellers and the guidebooks open around me like a Talmudic scholar, I work out that if we can get to Urumqi in China we can there apply for the visa to get into Kyrgyzstan. In the capital Bishkek is an Uzbekistan embassy. If we get that visa, we will get to Tashkent where we can collect our Iranian visa, if it is ever approved. Once we have that, we are entitled to apply for the elusive transit visa to cross Turkmenistan. The jigsaw puzzle is starting to fall into place. We might, just might, get across Central Asia and the Silk Road after all.

Exultant at my diligence and exhausted by the complexity, I rejoice and hug Jack with excitement. 'Whatever,' he says and goes back to editing photos on the laptop. More bonding, eh?

20 | Diarrhoea and Near Disaster in the Desert

Diarrhoea strikes Jon in the middle of the night in sub-zero temperatures, Jack takes advantage of the opportunity to enjoy fish stew and yak butter tea, our last ration of Weet-Bix has weevils ... and the whole expedition nearly comes unstuck.

It is two o'clock in the morning. It is minus 10 degrees. I am lying, wide-eyed, in my sleeping bag on a bed made of unforgiving hardwood. There is no mattress. A shabby blanket beneath me, draped over the wooden planks, is my only comfort. The single bed is designed for a small child. If I roll sideways, I fall off. The damp walls are plastered with a shiny, ghastly pink shade of paint. Jack is asleep on an identical bed in the same room. He is gently snuffling. Sleep evades me, as my stomach is churning. Something I have eaten has made me so bloated that I am threatening to explode. Our unheated room adjoins a corridor, which leads in one direction to a locked door and, in the other direction, to the living room in the house. Asleep in that room are our hosts, a charming Mongolian couple, who have hit the jackpot with paid guests out of the tourist season. Their 'guesthouse' is the only building as far as the eye can see.

We have arrived here from UB, and the road out of the capital was, in typical Mongolian fashion, a mess of snarled anarchic traffic, intersections without signs, level crossings without gates, and dead-end streets. As the so-called city buildings made way for small homes and yurts, we optimistically charted our course westwards. We wanted to arrive at a picturesque lake called Oglii Nuur. According to our trusty map, it was about 300 kilometres away. The intermittently reliable guidebook described Oglii Nuur as a lake where 'you can swim and fish and a logical camping spot if travelling between' the capital and Western Mongolia. Typical for Mongolia, we discovered at least three different ways to spell the name of our destination, adding to the confusion. But no matter how we pronounced the name to locals, they looked quizzically at us when we sought directions.

Within twenty minutes of leaving Ulaan Baatar, we were lost. After several U-turns and much laughter, as we pointed to the map and mimed directions, we eventually were directed away from the only paved road onto a track, defying common sense. Surely the main road west from the Mongolian capital would at least be navigable? But then, common sense is not common in Mongolia.

Jack started playing with the iPod, endlessly changing the music and driving me nuts. Whose idea was it to let him control the music?

The rutted dirt road was barely wide enough for two cars to pass. The verge of the road was treacherous and sharp rocks would rip our tyres to ribbons if we were nudged there at speed. On either side, on the horizon, steep bare mountains presented a haunting landscape. In the distance, the peaks were covered in snow. The completely featureless foreground was occasionally interrupted by a nomadic herdsman, typically riding a yak pulling a crude wooden cart laden with a collapsible yurt – the family's main possession. The cattle, goats, yaks, dogs, donkeys and horses were their collective wealth. Traditional clothing, mostly felt, protects them from the elements, making them look just as their ancestors would have 500 years ago. Harsh people for a harsh terrain.

After hours of teeth-jarring bumps and shallow river crossings we arrived at a town called Dashinchilen, where we looked for lunch. Buildings slowly emerged from the horizon, low humble structures, often with antennae or satellite dishes protruding from the roof. Typically, an oil tank perched above scaffolding indicate the availability of some fuel. Uninviting closed doors did not deter us from looking for food. We saw several men trying to fix a jeep. One man was standing inside the engine compartment, his feet alongside the motor, his head touching the underside of the bonnet. Using our Mongolian phrase book, we asked if anyone sold food or if there was a restaurant. The man and his companion looked at us quizzically and only when we smiled and laughed did they respond. Our attempts at Mongolian probably had us asking where to find a surf shop. I embarrassed Jack – yet again – by miming hunger, putting my hand to my mouth as if eating. They pointed at a closed blue door on an adjoining wall and judging by their stares we might as well have been Martians emerging from a UFO.

Wandering over, I opened the door and bent down to fit through. Inside were Formica tables, plastic chairs and a shoulder-high hatch in a wall, covered by a plastic flap. We stood, quietly waiting, for a few minutes and nothing happened. I lifted the plastic. On the other side, three women were making dumplings, oblivious to our presence. '*Sain Bainuu*,' I said, 'hello' in Mongolian, to a collective giggle. By pointing at the dumplings, and holding up six fingers, we ordered our lunch. I asked for '*Lefton tay*' for a teabag just as I had been taught in Ulaan Baatar.

Smug and satisfied, expecting a feast, we settled back in the plastic chairs. It was freezing outside and only slightly warmer inside. As our fingers thawed out, the woman pushed plastic plates through the flap. The dumplings arrived, steamy and smelling delicious. I picked one up, took an exultant bite, and sprayed the table with greasy fat which spurted out like an exploding pimple. From inside the soggy crust, a lump of boiled gristle dripped into my lap. I nearly choked. Reaching for the tea, I saw it was a milky, lukewarm, filmy concoction. I ate three dumplings, casings only, and left the fat. We paid, wriggled out the door, jumped in the car and no doubt left the Mongolian cooks wondering why we only ate the dumpling dough, unimpressed with the Mongolian custom to offer the prized piece of fat to the honoured guest.

Still hungry, we were determined to try to get the 150ks to Tsetserleg. It didn't seem far on the map, but the road deteriorated even more. The potholes got closer together, even sometimes overlapping; the craters and ditches almost connected with each other. There were no signs or directions whatsoever. Sometimes, a wobbly row of telephone poles suggested that there might be a town over the horizon. A yurt in the middle of nowhere had fierce dogs around it, a motorbike outside and a young girl staring warily as we approached. She ran to get her father, who greeted me with an embrace and pushed me into his home. Without a word he poured a mug of steaming yak milk tea, but could not read the map nor communicate directions in any way. We shook hands and said goodbye. Jack said we should stop and stay there, but I wanted to press on. The compass said that sooner or later we simply had to bump into the lake. There were no recognisable features from horizon to horizon. No trees, no structures, no sign of human intervention at all.

As the odometer ticked over we reached the notional distance to our destination.

A crater-like depression slowly appeared. The light was fading. We began to think we might be spending our first night sleeping in Ping. Two small lights pierced the gloom, glowing from a house with a small, low fence made of rocks. We drove over and two large dogs fiercely barked their welcome and came to greet us. We had been warned about Mongolian dogs. It is apparently a risky business to get out of your car until someone controls them. We stopped the car and waited until a squat lady emerged, a scarf tied around her head, an apron across her ample waist and hips. She had the typical leather and felt boots that came to just below her knee, making her look a bit like a fairground doll. At last she smiled, and we waved. We hoped we were looking friendly. She chained the dogs up, and we descended from the car to mime with hands and tilted head that we were looking for somewhere to sleep, and with fingers towards an open mouth that we also would like to eat. She was rapidly speaking in Mongolian, but nodding her head in the universal sign of agreement. I took some money from my wallet and offered it; she took one note of 10,000 togrog and held two fingers up to indicate she wanted T20,000. We haggled and agreed to T12,000 (equivalent to A$30). We grabbed our sleeping bags and went inside her home, praying that they had good food.

A similarly middle-aged man was warming his hands by a fire and we were made welcome in their cosy hut. With our Mongolian phrase book we attempted to converse, but we were so hopeless at pronouncing words it was comical and futile. Much laughing, smiling, nodding and miming. Showing them the phrase book was pointless as it seemed they could not read. I had been feeling lousy and now felt quite sick, and realised that I sat rapidly fading. We sat in front of a tiny, flickering black-and-white TV perched atop a wooden crate, powered by a 12-volt car battery. I devoured a cup of tea, insisting that the greasy yak's milk be left out. A younger man appeared and with very few words of English explained he was Massar, the son of the owners, whose names were Adai and Bur.

Adai asked if we would like fish for dinner. Jack agreed readily on both of our behalves. I was shaking and pale. Adai collected two fish from a keep on the side of the lake, about 250 metres from the hut, still dripping and flapping, a variety of catfish, and in a moment they were skinned and tossed into a cast-iron pot on an open fire along with freshly peeled potatoes, some herbs and carrots. The fish stew made for what at any other time would have been a delicious meal, but I was totally unable

Gobi Nomads. Notice the
wheels on the carts.

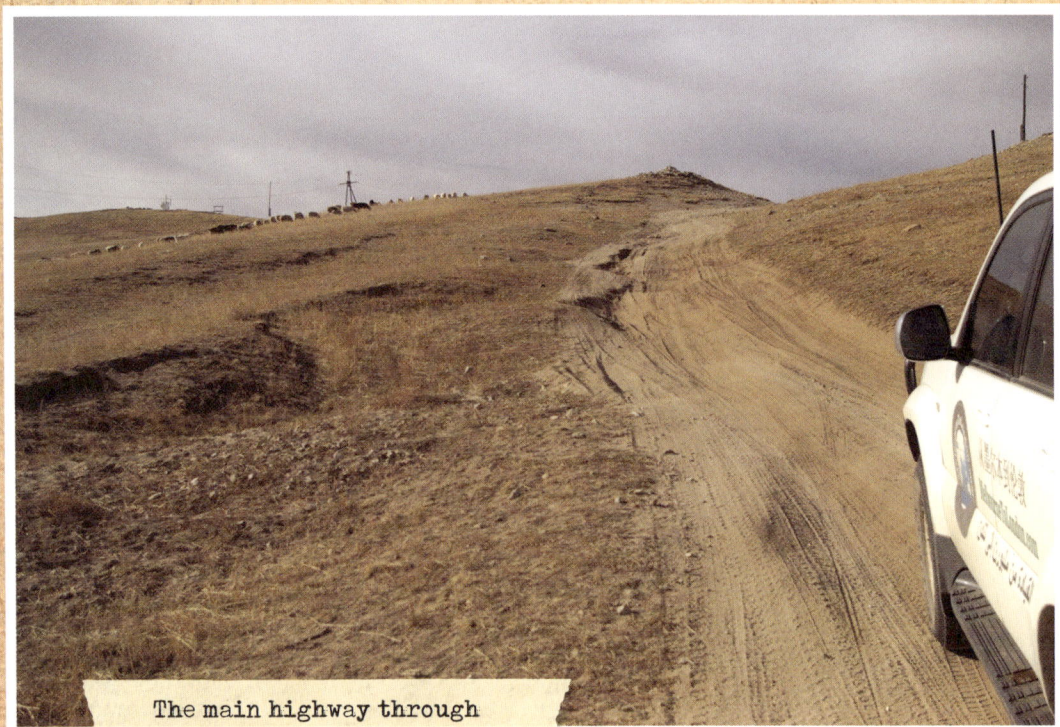

The main highway through
the Gobi Desert.

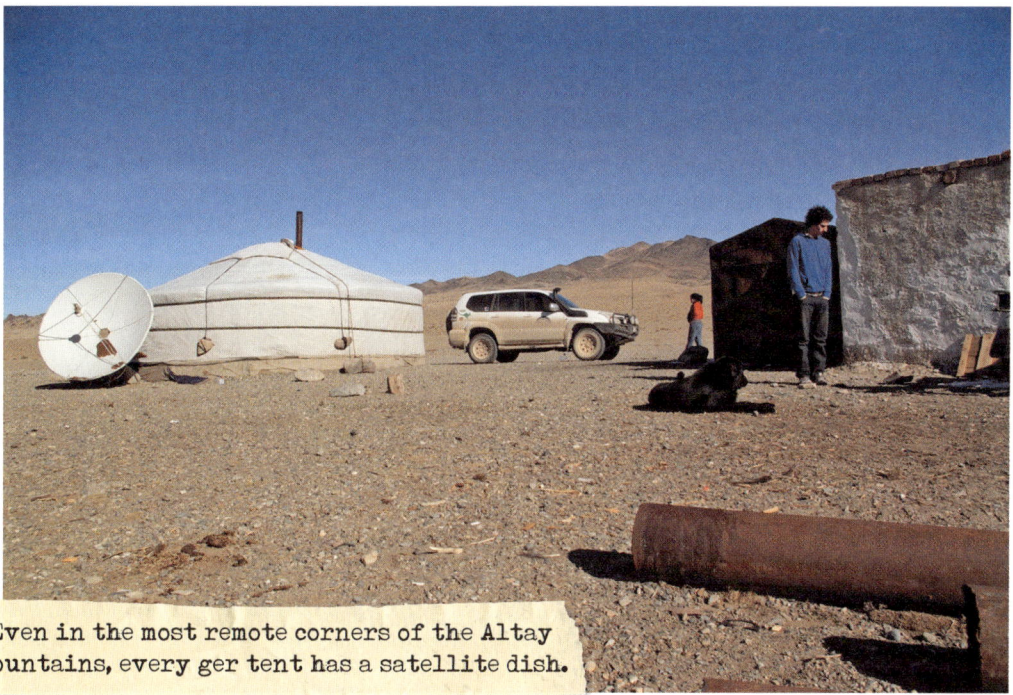

Even in the most remote corners of the Altay Mountains, every ger tent has a satellite dish.

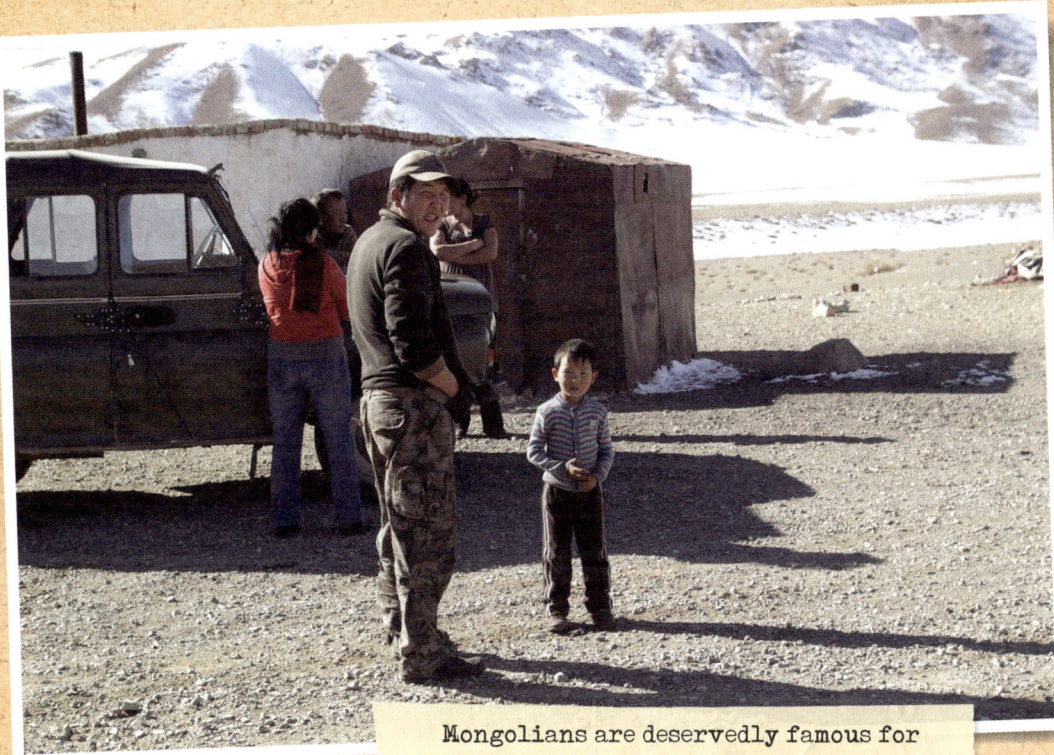

Mongolians are deservedly famous for their friendliness and hospitality.

to eat anything. Jack wolfed it down, eating for two. The small television, fed by the inevitable satellite dish outside, was the centre of attention and clearly their pride and joy. It sat like an altar in their main room. The programmes were incoherent quiz shows and music competitions. Collapsing, I retreated to the bedroom.

Incapable of sleep, I tossed and turned until about three in the morning. Jack snores gently. My stomach feels like it is going to erupt. I count the timing of the spasms the way I imagine a woman in labour measures contractions. I am sweating despite the sub-zero temperature. I calculate how long it will be before morning and whether I will last the distance. The alternative is to run the gauntlet of the snow and dogs, as well as waking Adai, Massar and Bur. In order to get to the front door, I have to climb out of my sleeping bag, creep across the room, straddle the water pipe, which crosses the hall at knee height on its way to the kitchen, open the squeaky door to the main room, skirt the large bed and couch used by our hosts and their son, go through the kitchen, out another squeaky door and a front gate to get past the dogs. Then there is the gate in the external perimeter fence, and finally in the snow and dark a dash across 150 metres to the outside drop toilet. Each movement of my legs risks complete loss of control and the real prospect of an unspeakable explosion.

Another seismic shift in my bowels helps me make my mind up. Waiting is no longer an option. I grab the torch, our precious supply of toilet paper, and decide to make a dash for it.

I trip over the water pipe hurdle and stub my toe on the bed where Massar sleeps, smile wanly as Adai wakes, nod, fumble the door lock, curse the gate, growl back at the dogs and stumble into the snow.

As I waddle to the tin outhouse, barely containing the rebellious contents of my stomach, I find the toilet door has a padlock. It is almost the last straw. My torch casts enough light to see the glint of metal and I spy a key on a string. It won't go into the lock. After an eternal struggle, the padlock clicks open and I avoid near catastrophe by some acrobatic moves worthy of an Olympian. I gasp with relief, and automatically relaxing every muscle from the incredible strain I let go of my torch, just grabbing the string as it heads into the unimaginable depths below.

Relieved like I never have been in my life, I reassemble my bits and stumble in the snow and dark back to my sleeping bag. After what seems like ten minutes of sleep, we are woken by our hosts offering us breakfast. Oblivious to the night-long drama,

Jack happily drinks the yak-milk tea. I prefer hot water with sugar. Some bread is all I can keep down but Jack enjoys a hearty porridge. We pack our sleeping bags away, and as I prepare to clamber through the main house towards the car, Adai points me to the opposite end of the corridor, and shows me the door to the outside, which I thought was locked but just needed a firm shove to open. I need not have lain in agony all night in fear of waking the house – there was an escape route, but too late do I learn of it. We shake hands, take photos, and fire up the car. Jack takes to the wheel and after seeking directions we wave goodbye and head off across the plains.

If I never visit Oglii Nuur again, I will not be missing much. How these people eke out a living, I have no idea, but they are friendly, welcoming and seemed content with their lot in life.

We drive through wild hills for several hours and stop Ping beside a semi-frozen creek for lunch – gourmet Vegemite and tuna on stale crackers. I fuel up the camping stove, boil bottled water and make tea with teabags that have remained unopened in the back of the car for three and a half months since Australia. Eagles and hawks circle above us. Little field mice emerge from burrows to stare. Jack discovers a packet of Weet-Bix and is shattered to discover weevils in it. We feed the weevils and Weet-Bix to the mice and move on. Our picnic on the side of the creek is one of the best meals we will have in Mongolia.

Can we find Tsetserleg? Along the way we dodge Bactrian camels, wild horses, goats and sheep. Each hill involves negotiating washed-out ruts deep enough to swallow a tyre. Loose rocks and gravel leave the wheels sometimes spinning. A bushy-tailed fox – or is it a snow leopard? – jumps from the roadside and, panicked by the car, races ahead of us for 200 metres. We apologise to him for trespassing on his turf.

The outskirts of Tsetserleg, a town described by Lonely Planet as Mongolia's prettiest *amag* (provincial capital), do not fill us with promise. High timber fences hide whatever lies behind, creating long alleyways of nothing but blank walls of wooden planks. Kids zip around on smoky, noisy two-stroke motor scooters. Dogs lie in the middle of the road, refusing to move. Most of the buildings are collapsing and there are people butchering a sheep on a sheet of cardboard by the side of the road.

After finding somewhere to stay Jack insists I make the effort to go for a walk. I am dog-tired, but I agree we need exercise, so we clamber up a steep hill, broken concrete steps leading to what seems to be the local museum. It is closed for renovations but the doors are wide open. There are workmen digging and laying new paths and plastering the walls. It seems a beautiful and historic single-storey building, low to the ground, rendered walls, but laid out as a large square with a substantial central courtyard. The sloped shingle roof has huge gaping holes in it. The builders encourage us to wander in and explore at leisure. The exhibits are scattered around the courtyard, some covered and some not. There are sad moth-eaten stuffed tigers, yaks and snow leopards. An ancient timber cart is missing side planks and the wooden wheels are split and broken. Display cases with broken glass still have pottery and fossil exhibits, but no labels or markings.

There is a temple behind the museum, with a three-storey-high pagoda-like spire, but it has been vandalised, its windows smashed, and is all but collapsing. Although it is of great historic significance the roof has fallen in and no one seems to have taken any interest in arresting its collapse.

We walk a little further. A giant golden Buddha statue sits atop a hill and overlooks the town. We climb several hundred steps to reach it and join the locals in walking around the base three times. It is the meeting point for the young of Tsetserleg, boys and girls in mostly Western jeans and shirts, coats with collars up-turned against the wind. Next to Buddha is a huge brass bell, sitting under a stupa. It has no clapper; instead a large wooden pole hangs next to it from two ropes. A hefty push makes the bell sound, a low vibrant glorious dong that reverberates across the valley to the whole town. On the other side of Buddha are prayer wheels, huge man-size drums on vertical axles. The young women push the handles that make them revolve, walking in circles with the prayer wheels. The girls seem to be here to pray, but the young men to prey. Some of the local boys are drunk, loud and unruly. The girls are universally quiet, deferential and even reverent.

The next morning, we seek directions but no one has a clue how to get to Bayankhongor. According to the map, it is 230ks through the Hangayn Nuruu National Park, and the road a mere track. No one we find has ever been there. No one has ever been anywhere but here.

Tsetserleg Market is our last stop before we head out of town. It is a low building with triple glass and wooden doors to keep out the weather. Wide concrete paths wind between stalls selling yak butter, cheese and dripping. Butchered goats and sheep hang from hooks, severed heads sitting on cardboard platters, tongues poking out.

Mountains of tinned food and plastic packets of rice, noodles and cruskets complete the array. There is nothing green and no fruit. The only vegetables are potatoes and onions. Some greasy, flyblown sausages break the monotony. Out the back, shipping containers form a square and are converted to clothes and car parts shops. We buy several bottles of water and drive away.

It takes four hours to cover the first 100 kilometres. The road is invisible, and we navigate due south with the compass. We traverse countless creeks and a few actual rivers, water halfway up the doors in the bigger ones. We crawl through gravel on riverbanks, slipping and inching forward looking for safe passage. Herds of wild yak and camels stare as we pass. Eagles soar above. Tiny little ferret or chipmunk-type critters race away from our path as we approach. There are almost no trees anywhere. We see no people or other cars. For lunch we open a tin of sardines and spread Vegemite on crackers. We have no idea if we are on the right track, but there is no other to choose. As we descend a rutted muddy pass, an incongruous modern concrete bridge crosses the next river – we must be on the right road, as there would not be a new bridge built on a lesser crossing.

The map shows that a monastery ought be on our road about 30ks from Bayankhongor. We see only the roadside shrines built to the shaman gods on the tallest peak of every mountain range. Every passer-by adds another rock to the cairn, called an *ovoo* and some blue ribbon or fabric as well to appease the spirits and worship the sky. Tall poles are usually protruding from the middle, and as the rocks threaten to bury the top of one pole a new one is added. Tradition demands that we walk clockwise three times around the shrine, to bring luck for travellers. We don't, inviting the displeasure of our ancestors and their spirits. Is this our biggest mistake?

As the odometer ticks over 250ks since we left Tsetserleg, and I start to voice fears that we are lost, a smudge on the horizon becomes buildings which become Bayankhongor. As we drive past a school and some apartments, we merge onto a potholed street with several low square buildings surrounded by people. A tall Soviet-era statue of an unknown statesman or general adorns a square and as we get out of the car we realise the crowd is in fact an all-in brawl involving about a dozen men wildly belting each other. One man is on the ground being kicked as another throws haymakers, two more wrestle each other until they fall. They are all stumbling drunk. We keep a respectful distance, mesmerised by the unusual sight of a real fight, not the Hollywood version. A police van arrives, then another police car. Three policemen and a few passers-by stop the fighting, line them all up against a wall, and one individual is escorted away. The remaining ten or so are all comically bundled into the police van, where they have to squeeze in and even sit on each other's knees to fit. Just minutes before, they were belting each other; now they are laughing as they cram into the tiny van.

A large woman in Western-branded Gore-Tex strikes up a conversation. She is an American Peace Corp volunteer, and has been living in Bayankhongor for two months. Leslie is from Vermont, recently married and has been sent with her new husband to teach English for two years. She recommends a place to stay and somewhere to eat as we chat about life in Mongolia. We give her a lift home as she tells us that it is typical for volunteers to become very jaded as they approach the end of their term, but as she is just beginning hers she is full of beans, learning Mongolian and making friends. It is such a novelty to meet someone we can talk to; I am annoyed when she does not invite us in for a meal.

We retreat to our guesthouse and find the cafe Leslie told us about for dinner. Astonishingly, the cook trained in New Zealand and we wolf down a schnitzel with vegetables, a solid pub-style meal in a hut on the edge of the Gobi desert. Back in the hotel, our room is above a restaurant that seems to be the karaoke centre of Bayankhongor, but I am so tired I fall asleep despite the wafting notes of Mongol pop drifting up the stairs.

It is 400ks to the next town, called Altay on the map and Altai in the guidebook. It is the capital of the Altay province. The road is marked on the map as a major highway. They lie again. We head out of Bayankhongor the next day as it starts to snow. Within a few hours I am sure we are lost. The map shows a major fork in the road at the 145k mark. We have gone well past it but not seen anything that could pass as a fork in what pretends to be the road. We keep going, as the snow gets thicker on the ground. We soon are on a plain that extends to the horizon, snow covered as far as we can see. The road must be under the white blanket somewhere, but there is no sign whatsoever showing us where it is. We slowly pick our way across, thumping and crashing into invisible potholes and ditches. Ping is occasionally airborne, as I impatiently drive too fast for the conditions. The steering wheel sometimes points in a different direction to the wheels, as if something has broken. I climb under the car with a torch, terrified that our worst nightmare has happened – the car breaks in the middle of nowhere. I cannot see anything wrong – but I cannot see most of the linkages and struts anyway as they are covered in mud and ice, and the longer we stay still the more piles up around us. Driving gingerly, we move on, my neck and back tensing and cramping and my knuckles tight on the wheel. I watch the gauges and warning lights just waiting for bad news. At this rate of progress, we will be sleeping in the car or driving all night to get to Altai.

The road gets slippery. The temperature readout says minus 7. Sometimes we travel at walking pace. Frozen rivers are a trap – the weight of the car could break the ice and we cannot tell how deep the water is beneath. We just have to keep going, taking our chances. Our mood shifts from fear to frustration to wonder at the beauty of the landscape. The Gobi Desert covered in snow. To the south, out the left-side windows, the mountain peaks form an impenetrable barrier. To the north, it is flat plains as far as we can see. Somewhere to the west, in front, ought to be our destination. We plough on and on for hours.

Late in the day we climb a slight rise and on the other side is a collection of huts and shacks that must be a monastery marked on the map. Jack wants to stop here for the night – I want to press on to Altai. He accuses me of lacking a spirit of adventure. I plead the need to find somewhere that offers the prospect of actually sleeping. He says he is sick of 'doing it easy' and says, 'What sort of adventure is it if we stay in hotels all the time and drive around in the flashest car this road has ever seen?' I tell him to pull his head in, point out I am not a backpacker and he replies by turning up the music and not talking for the next hour.

It gets dark and is snowing. We cannot see anything out the windows, the wipers working furiously to clear just the area of the windscreen they swipe for the time it takes to sweep the glass. Everything is obscured. Ping slides and spins as we keep driving, all six lights blazing. As we pass the 350k mark there is a minivan stopped on the side of the road. The driver waves us down and asks something in Mongolian. We shrug, and he mimes that he has run out of fuel. We do not carry a jerry can – 180 litres of diesel is enough without needing ten more sloshing around the back of the car. In sign language we offer him a lift to collect some, but he tries to explain that there is already help on the way. The poor passengers are freezing, sitting in the dark waiting to be rescued. We offer to take a few, but they all decline.

Tsetserleg, like a scene from
One Day In The Life of Ivan Denisovich.

In the snow, the road all but disappears – Western Gobi Desert.

Billiards – an all-weather sport in Western Mongolia.

					МАГ БУЯНТ ЗОЧИД БУУДАЛ								
						Үйлчилсэн хугацаа						Хөлс	
				Эхэлсэн			Дууссан					Нэг бүгд хоногийн	
Овог нэр	Зэрэг	№	Сар	Өдөр	Цаг	Өдөр	Сар	Бүгд		Нэг бүгд хоногийн			
1	2	3	4	5	6	7	8	9	10	11
Мухт		28	10							

Within an hour, we see lights in the gloom. As we approach Altai, nodding oil donkey pumps are dotted across a valley. Power station chimneys belch out smoke, silhouetted against the dim electric light. These towns are like a scene from *One Day in the Life of Ivan Denisovich* set in Siberia. Grim does not describe it.

We drive around asking directions and eventually find the only guesthouse. The forecourt is as icy as a skating rink. Our room is freezing cold, damp and mouldy. Water drips down the inside of the window glass. Peeling floral wallpaper hides electric wires that sometimes poke their bare ends out of cracks and crevices. Unattached power points break up the pattern. Laminated cupboards are delaminating. The chipboard swells from the damp, and disintegrates when touched. The bathroom smells of urine and the water is icy. We grab a plate of gruel at a cafe and, despite the surrounds, I sleep like a baby.

Late that night, still worried about the steering, I check international time zones and make a phone call back to the specialist four-wheel-drive garage in Melbourne that sorted our car. David chuckles when he takes a call from Mongolia – 'I have been waiting for this call …' – listens attentively, asks a few questions and tells me not to worry.

In the morning, the temperature is minus 13. We scrape Ping's windows to clear the ice and snow, and astonishingly the motor fires straight up. We buy fuel and head west for the mountain pass that will get us towards the border town of Bulgan. Everything is snowbound. We do not have snow chains for the tyres and for the first time in the whole trip I doubt we will be able to just go wherever we need. We skirt the mountain range, looking for any sign of a road or trail through the valleys and peaks. There is none. Our tyre tracks are the only ones in the snow. We do not see another vehicle on the road all day. We have no choice but to keep travelling. If the snow is this deep on the plains, how will we get across the mountains? Several times we divert down furrows that might become the mountain pass, but each time the track peters out, going nowhere. I try to sound like I know what I am doing, not wanting Jack to doubt his father's wisdom for trying this route. I sense he is not fooled by my attempts at cheery humour, and I can tell he is getting worried. The map tells lies again with little red lines on the paper that do not exist. We will have to go several hundred kilometres past where we need to be to find out how to cross the mountains to China.

As we keep driving, eating from our rations, the snow thins and then disappears.

A collection of huts must be a town marked on the map as Darvi: five low garage or hangar-type buildings and a water tower, the only other feature a weather-beaten billiard table outside the cafe, the green felt covered in snow. The sole sign of life is a squat cafe where hot dumplings are available from the surprised but friendly women inside. By the time we leave, a small crowd has materialised. How they survive is a mystery.

The terrain changes dramatically. An occasional house flanks the gravel strip and animals are corralled into poorly fenced muddy farmyards. Barely another car uses the road, dust plumes appearing on the horizon well before any vehicle can be seen. On a long barren stretch, we are waved down by two patient people and offer a ride to a hitchhiking teen, farewelled with a hug by his father, entrusting him to strangers. We cannot communicate with each other, other than saying 'Hovd', the name of the next town, but Jack plays some music on the iPod and with sign language and laughs and smiles they find some understanding. I speed up and soon we are making good time towards Hovd on a long straight stretch of good gravel road.

We pass a huge lake, bare and grey in pre-winter late October. I am distracted by the scenery and not concentrating, driving too fast for the loose surface, and I misjudge a sweeping left-hand bend. As I realise my mistake, it is too late to brake and we slide and swing across the gravel, fishtailing around a corner. Ping violently swerves and bucks, climbs the steep roadside verge on the left, then mounts the loose rubble on the right, nearly rolling. Jack swears, I mutter and our hitchhiker laughs as if it is all part of the fun. If there had been any other cars on the road, or if I had swung the steering wheel the wrong way … My knees are weak and I break out in a sweat. It is the first time we have nearly come to grief in the whole trip, and caused entirely by my bad driving. I am wracked with guilt, hoping Jack has not lost confidence in me, berating myself for my arrogance and complacency.

I pull over, jump out and inspect the car for damage. Only a mudflap has broken off from the impact as we sideswiped the mound of roadside gravel. A close call. I slow down, concentrate more, and we cruise toward Hovd. The road slowly improves, stone huts become small houses, then apartments, and as a few trees and a river pop up we roll into the local capital, complete with main square, petrol stations and official buildings. But somewhere in the Mongolian wilderness lies a left-side rear mudflap for a Toyota Prado.

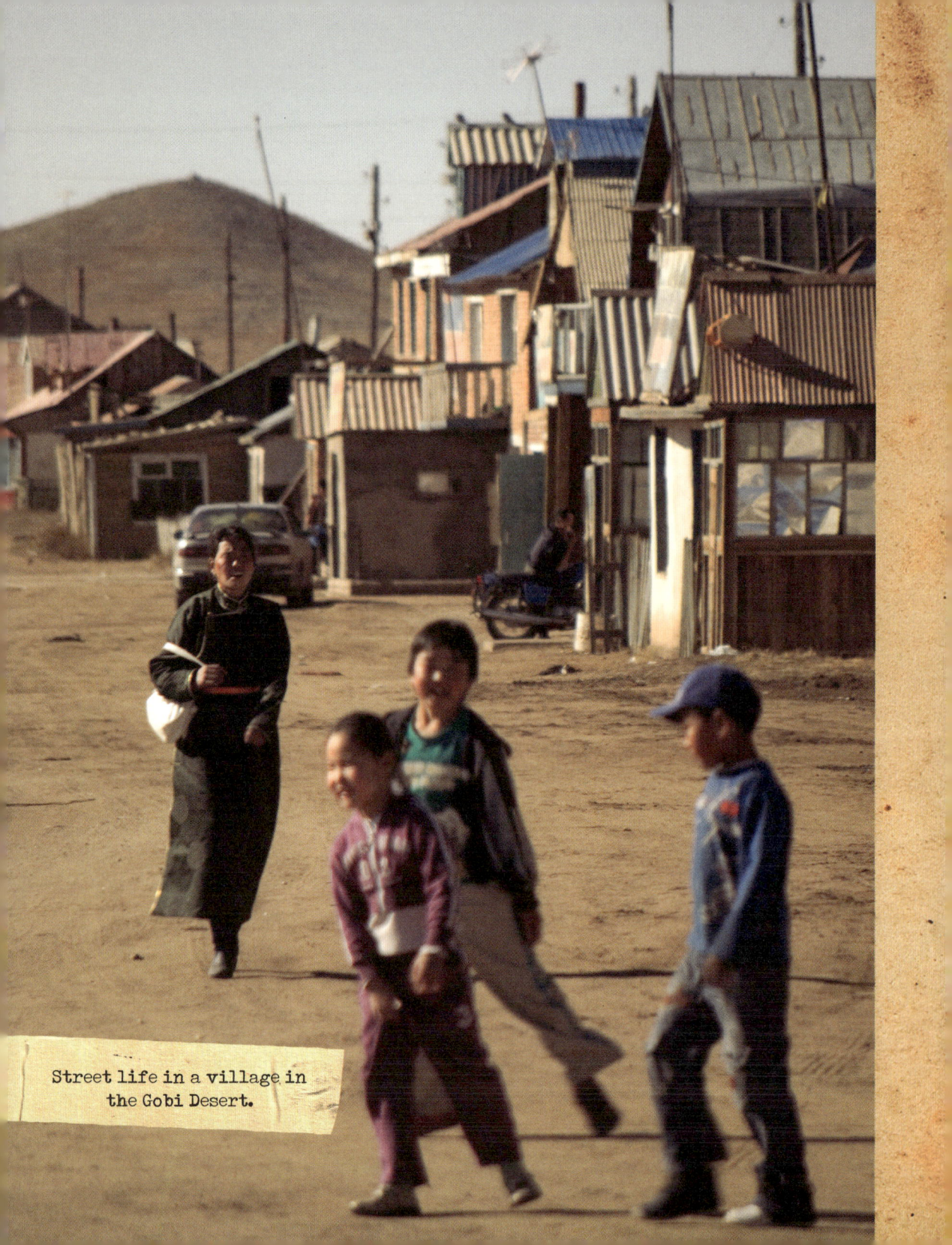

Street life in a village in the Gobi Desert.

21 | Yurts, Yaks, Yoghurt and Yucky Food

Can it get any more remote? Explore the Altai mountains, drive for ten hours, climb 3000 metres, traverse 280 kilometres of dirt and mud road, encounter just two cars and one truck – crashed and on its side – the only other vehicles seen all day.

I will not pretend that I am enjoying Mongolia. It is a great disappointment. Images of wild open plains, friendly shepherds, welcoming yurts and exotic traditions have not measured up. Instead these are tough people from a tough environment, surviving on next to nothing with next to nothing. I cannot eat most of the food and cannot find a point of entry or engagement with the people. For months moving throughout Southeast Asia and across China, everywhere we have been, some connection has been possible. Shared values, mutual respect, etiquette, manners, familiarity with culture – all that seems missing in Mongolia.

It is the wrong season, and the weather makes it harder. The facilities that nourish tourists are closed, the streets devoid of activity, the countryside forbidding. The guidebooks say that there is a flourishing wilderness tourism industry growing throughout remote corners of Mongolia, but we do not find it. Perhaps it is geared to package tours, groups in particular, or maybe we are just blind or not making enough effort, or are we too far off the beaten track.

Driving through Mongolia is not made easier by the bizarre practice of giving places in different provinces identical names, and spelling place names differently from region to region. There are multiple towns with the same name, sometimes even near each other, but in different government regions. Asking for directions from a shepherd or a nomad becomes comical when they point in two directions at once as you ask for 'Altai', trying to clarify in Mongolian whether you want Altai in Govi or Altai in Hovd. Hovd will be spelled 'Khovd' on some maps and so on. Locals no doubt have no difficulty with this system, as they can resolve ambiguity easily. We could not. Pride demanded we try to get through without a guide, and we were exultant after China to be guideless, but with hindsight it would have made much more sense and transformed our experience completely. Another mistake.

Crossing the tundra, there is nothing but snow as far as we can see. To the south and west, the mountains create a forbidding barrier. To the north and east there are flat rolling plains, white all the way to the horizon. We talk aimlessly about life back at home – what will Europe be like, what would Jan be having for dinner, where will Jack's friends be going out to tonight, who was keen on which girl before which friend hooked up with her instead – all the big topics in the world.

Jack takes the wheel and a speck grows into a person as we slip and slide through the fields, eventually materialising as an elderly woman walking across the plain, tall stick in hand. She must be miles from anywhere or anything that we can see, no buildings, no yurts, no anything. But there she is, steadily just walking across the Gobi Desert, calf deep in snow. We stop to say hello, see if she wants a lift, and to check if Hovd is in the direction we are driving. She acknowledges us, points towards the hills but keeps her head down and mutters barely another murmur.

Hovd is in the far west of Mongolia. It is ethnically as much Kazakh as Mongol, the commercial centre of this region, and one of the larger towns on the road that continues to the Russian border 300 kilometres northwest. Our destination, the Chinese border crossing near Bulgan, is in the opposite direction, to the southwest, along lines marked on the map as the lowest grade of road, fragile red lines across the mountains that snake like spare threads over the now dog-eared and worn chart. I keep staring, hoping something becomes clearer, but it never does. We have been given a fixed date to cross the border, and if we do not get there on time we will risk being turned away by the Chinese, whose obsession with paperwork we have already experienced. To make it this far, and be sent back, would be unthinkable, as well as the small problem that we have no other way out of Mongolia, and I become totally determined and focused on getting to Bulgan in plenty of time to keep our rendezvous.

The snowbound roads frighten me, and I imagine Ping sitting in a deep drift in a remote gully, wheels spinning uselessly as days drift by and our deadline passes. Snow chains seemed a waste of money and space back in Melbourne when I equipped the car. I wish I had listened to my father who said to take them, when I recited the list of all the other gear snugly tucked into the tubs that creak and groan in the back every time we jump another bump.

Hovd turns out to be the friendliest place in Mongolia. Is it that Kazakhs are more hospitable than Mongols? Wandering this unremarkable town, people smile and greet us, a welcome contrast to UB or anywhere else in Mongolia. Our hotel is the best we have seen in ages, warm and boasting hot water and a Western toilet. Dinner is Chinese takeaway, complete with fried egg on top just like when I was a kid.

I am stressing about how we cross the mountains. The hotel staff speak no English so I plan to go to the police the next morning to see if they can suggest how we get to Bulgan. Lonely Planet says, 'The southern road through the spine of the Mongol Altai Muruu, one of the most remote roads in the country, is the back door into Khovd … the mosquito infested Mongolian-Chinese border post sees many petrol tankers but is closed to foreign travellers.' Jack goes downstairs late in the evening to get some clothes from the car and notices a group of English speakers in the cafe. In an extraordinary stroke of pure luck we have stumbled on the weekly English language club of Hovd, run by two American Peace Corps workers. I offer to pay whatever it takes for someone to guide us through the mountains, and within an hour we are introduced to Marima Khaumen. She works as a tour guide in the summer and a Russian teacher at the high school in winter. She arranges to take a day off the next morning and assures me she knows how to guide us through the Altai Mountains. Exhilarated to sleep in a proper bed and flushed with optimism at finding a guide, we sleep properly for the first time since leaving UB.

Early the next day we refuel, sort out Marima's babysitting arrangements and head into the hills. Marima teaches us some Mongolian and Russian as we slowly wind our way through rough tracks going higher and higher up into the peaks. The trail winds through valleys and over rock ledges, past streams and waterfalls from snowmelt. As we get higher the sparse greenery gets thinner, eventually giving way to just rocks and dirt. Lunch is beside a river, on a patch of flat ground: water boiled on our little spirit stove for tea and tinned sardines. Cows grazing nearby seem unfussed by us and untended by any obvious owners.

Marima gives us instruction in Mongolian culture, religion and Kazakh pride. The province is home to sixteen ethnic groups, including the Zahchin, Durvud, Oold, Uriankhai, Chandman, and Torgud, as well as Mongols. I am astonished that such fragments of ancient clans still exist and have distinct strands to them. She describes them as tribes. The famous throat singers of Torgud are from this province, which she claims is the original throat singing, copied by the neighbouring and more famous Tuva Russian throat singers. She has been instrumental in establishing a thriving craft centre where the women of the region are keeping needlework and embroidery traditions alive. Upon cue she produces beautiful needlework from her bag, including a huge Tuskiiz, an embroidered dowry cloth that hangs as decoration on the wall when a couple marry. I obligingly purchase it for what she asks, a ridiculously low amount.

Driving for hours on terrible roads takes us further and higher through the Altai offering occasional views through the clouds. At last the snow clears and as dusk looms she tells us we have many more hours to go. I have tried to avoid driving at night wherever possible, and mostly successfully, but here there is no choice whatsoever. As the light fades, we round a sharp bend and confront a huge rock in the middle of the road. I slam on the brakes, wrestle the wheel and manage to swing Ping to avoid the front suspension and steering being ripped out, but the rear passenger side wheel catches the edge of the rock and the immediate rasping noise tells the story. The tyre is flat and the wheel rim buckled, totally ruined. In record time Jack applies what he has learned and we whip the car up and change wheels. Our first puncture after four months and 22,000 kilometres of rugged driving. Remarkable.

Minutes later, as the track winds along the river bed, we are confronted by a huge but ancient crane truck that has rolled over, blocking the way, smashed and immovable. It has rolled off the steep embankment while trying to get around the corner, and now is blocking the road. The driver and a companion have lit a fire and are astonished to see us. They speak in animated conversation with Marima, explaining that they are stuck until another heavy truck can come and lift them back on their wheels. Ironically, they are the local crane which picks up other smashed trucks. They have no food or water, so we give them what we can and drive around their stricken machine by going down the bank, along the river bed and back up again where we can.

Continuing in the dark, we get stuck in a gorge where there is no exit at all. The

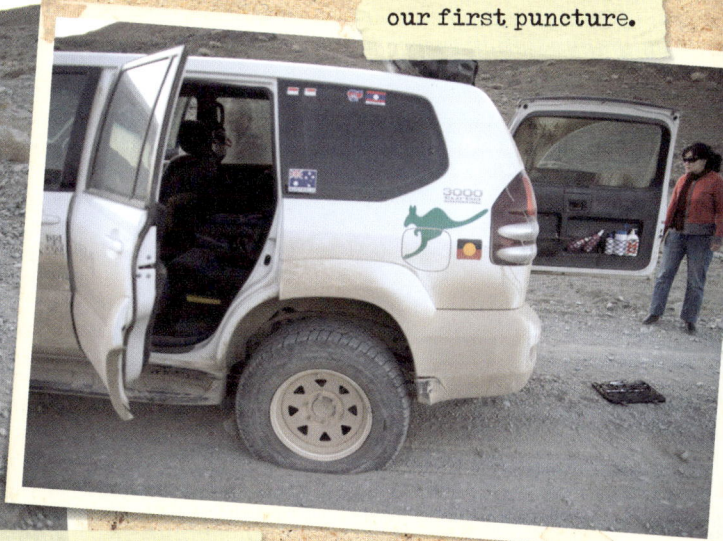

We got this far before our first puncture.

With the sunlight fading from the Mongolian desert sky — a massive, sharp rock in the middle of the road was just what we wanted.

Our passage was blocked — the crane needed to lift this truck was on this truck itself.

road leads to high cliffs on one side, gulleys and ravines on the other. We beat a retreat. Another pass outside the settlement of Uuyench also has us backtracking for ages when we're caught in a maze of walls and fences, the pitch-black impenetrable night making it impossible to detect anything resembling a road or even a path. Our spotlights cut a swathe through the black, sweeping and swooping across the hills, but we just guess where to go and guess badly as often as not.

Bulgan is reached well into the night. A tree-lined main street is home to dark official buildings and the sole hotel has two horses tied up outside like a Wild West bar room. If there is such a thing as negative stars, this hotel has them. No running water nor power and they have no food at all. The rooms are damp and the beds bare boards. The toilet is a drop job at the back of the car park. There is no heating, needless to say, and there is frost on the ground already. But we are delighted. Marima has got us through.

Next morning, Friday, our appointed day to go into China, we take Marima into the main square so she can look for a car heading back to Hovd to give her a lift. The entire town consists of a post office, a bank, two or three shops selling car parts or basic foods, and a school. Most people move around by donkey or horse, a few battered Russian jeeps being used by officials or drivers moving between towns. Marima quickly finds someone she knows who is heading back through the pass, and we thank her and go back to our hotel, waiting for a message from the new Chinese guide that NAVO have hired, confirming that we can cross the border. We fiddle with the car, kick the football and wait.

Nothing could have surprised me more than someone saying, 'G'day, how ya doin'?' Jill Howe has wandered along to check out the foreigners she heard were in town. She has been living in Bulgan for five years, volunteering at the primary school. She is a born-again Christian from Sydney, without any organisational backing whatsoever, and cheerfully admits to having had a rough life. 'This is my way of saying thank you to the Lord for keeping me alive,' she tells us as we chat. She is curious to know what we are doing in her neck of the woods, and we explain our trip to her and that we are supposed to be crossing the border into China. 'I have been trying to get across there for years; they refuse, even when you have a visa,' she replies, sending shivers down my spine.

We are invited to her yurt, and suddenly Bulgan is not looking so harsh. She lives on the outskirts of town, her yurt cheerfully decorated with a mix of Western and Eastern furniture, dominated by large velvet Jesus wall hangings. She introduces us to her neighbour who runs the car repair shop we have seen in the main square. They shower us with hospitality, invite us in for tea and biscuits and introduce us as honoured guests to their children. Jill offers to put us up if we are stuck and promises lamb stew for dinner. We now want to stay, but until meeting her have been furiously texting the NAVO agent in Urumqi demanding that they keep to the agreed schedule. Our guide is apparently 600ks away in Urumqi, not expected until Monday. Just as I am about to send a text saying we have changed our minds and we will stop the night in Bulgan and accept Jill's hospitality, a message hits the phone telling us to go directly to the border crossing as all is in place for our passage. Jill's neighbour sells us some bolts to reattach our front splash guard that has shaken loose and we head off to China. Another mistake.

If border crossings have been tedious and tiresome before, they pale into insignificance compared to this ordeal. We first are made to show documents and pay a fee to even drive on the access road to get to the border, and then ten minutes later we stop at a strip of barbed spikes protruding as tyre traps from the road. Next we are made to buy a ticket to get into no man's land, are passport checked by Mongolian security five times, luggage and Ping searched twice more by separate personnel over about 100 metres of pavement, before being made to park beside the boom gate for two hours. After sitting patiently for most of the afternoon, with no food or drink, a senior officer with a walkie-talkie and good English explains that the Chinese will not permit us to cross. I text urgently to our agent in Urumqi. An hour later the Mongolian officer in charge gets into our car and tells me to drive through no man's land as far as the Chinese barbed wire fence. He then gets out and has a meeting across the boom gate with a senior Chinese official, much hand waving and shouting and gesticulating under the machine guns. We are then told to go back to Mongolia, where we queue up and have our visas for Mongolia stamped 'Departed'. There is now no going back. We drive again across no man's land, this time through the compulsory quarantine wash, and at the China gate Jack is told to get out and follow a soldier into the huge new building that houses their border control. I am left in the car and told to drive to an inspection pit, then a charming young officer called Alexander goes through our luggage and opens every bag. He sees the laptop

Bulgan main street.

Bored Bulgan teenagers, the same all over the world.

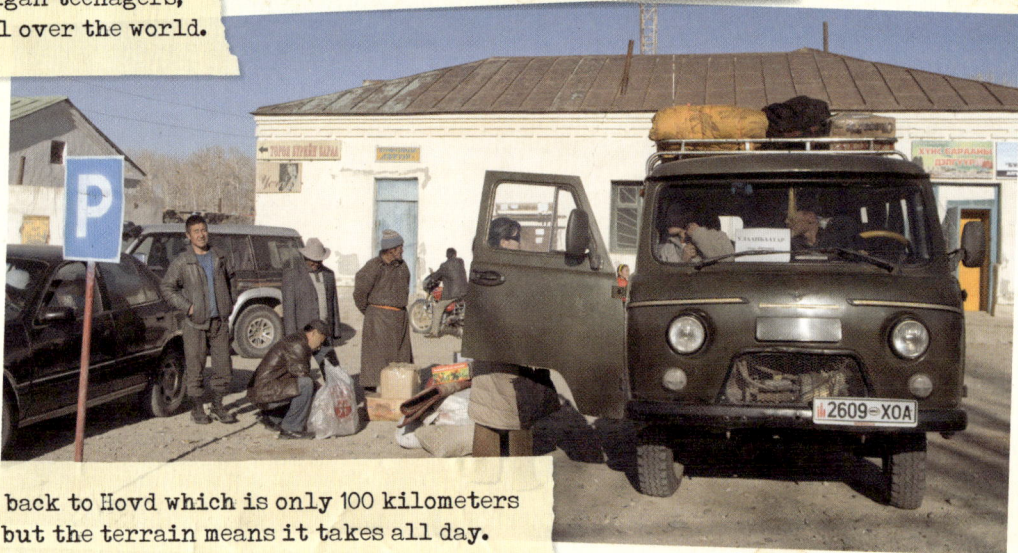
The bus back to Hovd which is only 100 kilometers away but the terrain means it takes all day.

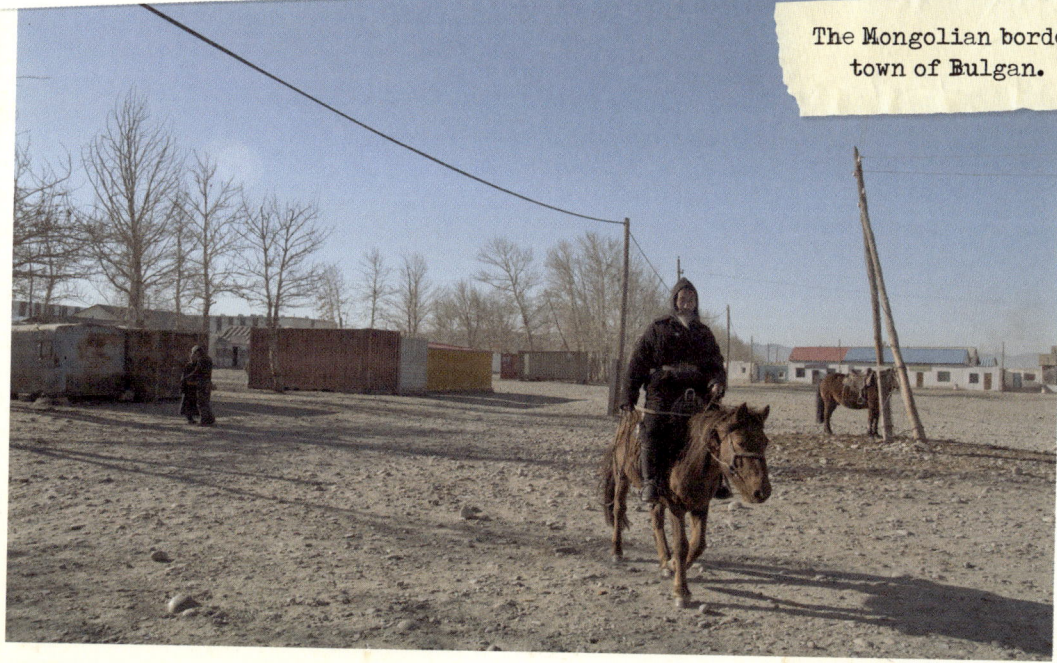

The Mongolian border town of Bulgan.

and asks what is in it. I am required to turn it on and he inspects all the photo files. We sit in the car for half an hour looking at photos of Indonesia, Cambodia, Laos and China. He gets very excited with photos of Kunming and Tiger Leaping Gorge which he has never been to, then eventually gets bored and allows me to pack it away and to enter the building. Although we are kept apart, I can see Jack through glass partitions across the building. He is sitting in a room with about ten police and soldiers. He looks worried.

I am required to deal with quarantine, customs, passport control, security, motor registration and who knows what else. No one speaks much English, Alexander being the most fluent. He is clearly outranked by a much older and very aggressive officer who is refusing to let us go, for reasons no one can explain to me. This standoff goes for ages, until there is no one else at the border except us. I contemplate volunteering a bribe, but there are always three or four soldiers around and no opportunity for a discreet exchange with the boss. It is getting dark and the entire building is clearly set to close. Every single soldier and policeman and quarantine and customs and immigration official is standing around shouting, sometimes at us and usually at each other. It is getting ugly. They all want to go back to their barracks but we are clearly a problem. There is something irregular about one of the documents emailed to me by NAVO that I printed in Ulaan Baatar. Eventually my phone rings. The tour boss David from Urumqi explains they want an original document, not a copy printed off an email, to clear our car into China. We are allowed in, but Ping is not. He tells us to ask for a local customs broker called Bejik who is supposed to be here, and to let Bejik sort it out. I am exhausted, angry, irritated and worried.

The soldiers reunite me with Jack. This is progress, I feel. Bejik is brought into the room. She is a young Mongolian who also speaks Chinese, but not English. She smiles a lot and clearly charms the soldiers. My phone rings again, and David explains that he has negotiated a solution to the impasse. We will go with Bejik in our car to the next town, where Ping will be impounded until the document defect is fixed. We should go with Bejik and she will look after us. I am thoroughly fed up, happy to agree to anything if it means we get out of the border post and get something to eat, and suddenly as I hand my phone back to the man in charge, everyone is cheering and laughing.

22 | The Brothel

Jon introduces Jack to a brothel, the wild frontier trading post of Takeshiken in Xinjiang reveals its charms, and we meet our new guide who cannot tell left from right in either Chinese or English.

I have never been to a brothel until Takeshiken, and I hope it is the last.

It is dark by the time we are allowed to leave the border post. The chief soldier tells us we are strictly to stay with the soldiers and Bejik, and we must not go off on our own. There are no lights on the road and it is pitch black. There are potholes, ditches and roadworks. The only instruction I have been given is to follow the minibus in front, but the soldier is driving so fast I cannot keep up with him and drive safely at the same time. So I fall further and further behind. Our guide, Bejik, seems unperturbed.

We wind through rocky outcrops, with only an occasional light bulb illuminating primitive buildings on either side of the road. After twenty minutes we are suddenly on a wide, smooth, new road, which after only a few more turns reveals a bustling trading outpost. Welcome to Takeshiken.

The town is laid out on a perfect grid. The paved but unguttered streets are lined with simple single-storey shops, wide unpaved and muddy forecourts crammed with pallets and trucks loading and unloading even in the night. Young men and boys are playing billiards on outdoor billiard tables, all smoking as if their lives depended upon it. Huge trucks, overloaded with boxes, ropes holding their precariously balanced loads, are preparing to go back over the mountains. Bejik directs me past the town, along a road flanked by a low whitewashed stone wall, and tries to explain that we have to park Ping in an enormous empty compound. We are saluted by a quizzical guard as we take the bare essentials, lock the car and bundle into a minibus.

The minibus hurtles down through the blackness, and we negotiate the crowded streets. Any attempt at asking where we are being taken is futile as no one speaks English and no one can understand a word we are saying. I mime that we are hungry and Bejik laughs and nods her head. The minibus pulls up outside the only building that is more than one storey high, which also has neon lights at the front. It seems to be a hotel and we go inside double glass doors to a reception desk. Bejik explains something in Chinese and we are shown up a flight of stairs and down a gloomy corridor to a tiny filthy chamber with a broken toilet, cigarette butts on the floor and two dirty single beds. The room is overheated and reeks of cigarette smoke. We put our things down, double-lock the door and go back to the lobby. Several loud and drunk Chinese men have arrived at the same time as we are leaving and the penny drops as half-a-dozen heavily made-up giggling girls in miniskirts and ridiculous high heels emerge from a side room to greet them. Will Jan ever forgive me for corrupting her baby boy? Will Jan ever forgive me for this whole crazy trip?

Bejik takes us around the streets looking for some food. Along the way we are joined by a Mongolian policewoman, Pil-chen, who speaks a little English and explains that we are going to a restaurant run by Bejik's sister. As we walk through the streets, every single person stops and stares, points at us, laughs, calls out and seems amazed. Every few minutes, someone speaks to Bejik or Pil-chen, and we hear the word 'ordaliya' in the answer. We laugh too. We finally make it to the restaurant, which has three plastic tables inside. Bejik's sister cooks some mushrooms and dumplings and food has never tasted so good. I do not care if I never eat Mongolian food again. Ever.

Next morning I go downstairs looking for the communal bathroom. There is a glass door and a dim unlit corridor which has several rooms off to one side. Each room has a hot tub and a massage bench, as well as a toilet and shower. The hot tubs have cold water in them with a thin scum floating across the top. There are cigarette butts all over the slimy, wet, slippery floor. It is unmentionably disgusting. I find some soap, which is caked with hair and unidentifiable putrid contaminant. I wash myself and escape as quickly as possible. I go back upstairs and break the news to Jack.

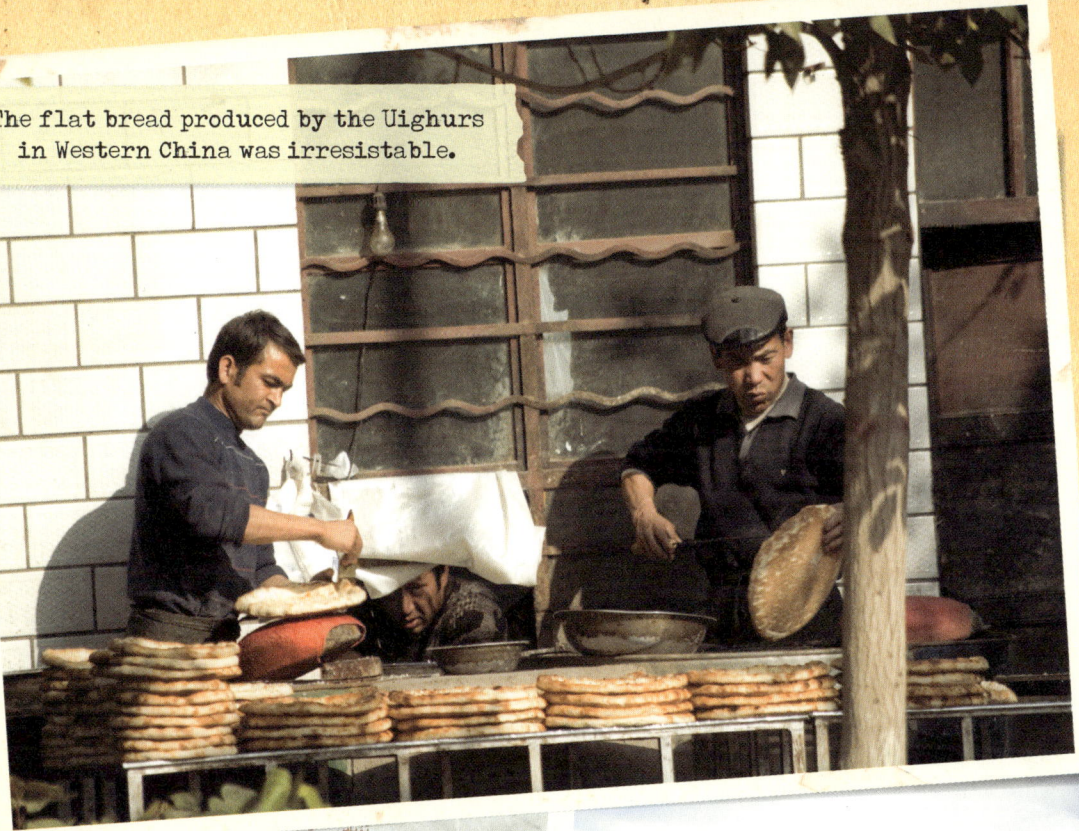

The flat bread produced by the Uighurs in Western China was irresistable.

Allah and Mao — perpetual tension.

Despite my warnings, he decides to risk a shower. We both regret it afterwards. I feel dirtier after the shower than before.

We go downstairs and there is no one at the reception desk. I am worried about just wandering the streets after being told at the border we must not go out alone. I foolishly look for someone to help us, and find three women in skimpy underwear sitting on the couch doing their nails. They smile, giggle, and one jumps to her feet and sashays towards me. I start talking rapidly and embarrassingly in English, and they just laugh more. I hope I make it clear that my intentions are anything other than business but can feel my ears burning. I escape back to the lobby, and we do up our coats and step outside. Bejik had last night showed us where her shop is, so we walk across the road and find her there.

She sells women's clothes and coats, shampoos, hairbrushes and clips. She takes us back to her sister's shop for some breakfast. The streets are deserted. It is freezing cold, and there is nobody out. Light snow has fallen giving everything a beautiful clean cover. We have dumplings and rice porridge for breakfast and Chinese tea. I do not want to leave the restaurant – it is warm, the food is better than edible, and there is nothing else to do anyway.

Eventually, as the sun rises, some of the other shops show some life. Wherever we are we draw a crowd. People are amazed to see Europeans. It is apparent that some of them have never seen people like us before. One Kazakh man engages in an animated conversation about us with Bejik for some time. He is taller than me, broad shouldered and swarthy, with gold teeth, and a round fluffy woollen hat. He has an enormous ancient blue truck, dangerously overloaded, onto which even more is being lashed while we talk. In the cabin, a large round woman, her head covered in a decorative scarf, stares out the window, but does not join in the conversation. He is so excited to meet us. I do my kangaroo hop routine as Jack, again, rolls his eyes. The man roars with laughter. He slaps me on the back, and we part best friends.

Jack buys a soccer ball from a shop bursting with clutter. Upon closer examination, we discover it is not round, and when kicked it loops and bumps unevenly along the street. I buy some elastic cord so I can fix the tripod carrier in the back of the car that rattled loose in Mongolia. I feel a great sense of achievement from conducting even this simple transaction in mime.

Every corner sports a billiard table, weathered and battered after years of exposure to the elements. We stop to play. There are four or five tables set up on the forecourt of a larger cafe. It seems to be the only recreation available. Half-a-dozen young men are standing around, as they do anywhere in the world, potting balls and talking nonsense. We play one game and then I leave Jack to play with the locals. They have not one word in common language. As I wander across the street, past a vacant block, I notice a peasant woman squatting down, lifting her skirt, and going to the toilet in full view of everybody walking past. No one except me seems to think there is anything unusual about this. I cannot believe what I've just seen; such immodesty is alien to any culture that I have ever experienced.

We walk the streets for some hours and see pretty much everything there is to see in Takeshiken. There are shops selling machinery, bearings, trolleys, car parts, bicycles, motor scooters, pumps, generators, toys, furniture, clothes, shoes, bathroom equipment, glass, processed and packaged and tinned food, building materials, tools … everything imaginable. There are people buying and selling out on the street, and inside every building. There are trucks, overloaded, groaning and creaking even as they stand still. There are soldiers, policemen, customs officers, people who look Chinese, Mongolian, Kazakh, Russian, Kyrgyz, Uzbek, Arab, Pakistani, Tajik, Turkmen and everything in between. It is a genuine frontier trading post, complete with the local equivalent of cowboys.

In mid-afternoon our new guide arrives. His English name is also Jack and he speaks excellent English. Immediately I feel a flood of relief. I realise how tense I have been and how helpless I have felt for the last few days. He seems incredibly energetic and authoritative and assures us straightaway that the next day, Sunday, he expects to be able to complete the paperwork and we will head off to Urumqi. I want to kiss him to celebrate. I send Jan a text in celebration and as the tension lifts I realise how utterly miserable I have been.

Four chairs, no waiting – Kashgar Sunday market.

23 | The Silk Road at Last

Wherein our adventurers finally make it to the fabled Silk Road, only to find it is a shitty highway like any other cutting through a desert and nothing romantic or historic at all. Still, it is exhilarating to get there and the places the bitumen takes us to are surreal and meet expectations.

A bottle of whisky to the customs chief, the original customs documents and a refundable fee of US$750 get Ping out of gaol on Sunday morning. NAVO ought to have prepaid the bond, so Guide Jack and his boss insist that the money will be returned to me in Urumqi in cash if I could please just pay it now. I have a stash of US dollar bills hidden in the car for exactly this contingency and am almost pleased to be able to use the money, feeling simultaneously smug at being vindicated at tucking so much away, but wary of a con.

We are on our way – the Silk Road at last. We have plenty of time – a week to cover the 600 kilometres to Urumqi, apply for visas for Kyrgyzstan and then travel the 1400 kilometres to Kashgar in time for the fabled Sunday market. Then, over the Torugart Pass and into the 'stans; Bob's your uncle, we are home and hosed. What could be easier than that?

Our new guide is in some ways the opposite of Tracy. She was measured, he is restless. She was careful about what she said, he is chatty and garrulous. But like Tracy he is sporty and energetic, and keen to learn how to master the tricky Aussie rules football we kick around. Fatally, though, he does not know his left from his right. There are several qualities that are desirable in a professional tour guide – and surely this is one of them. At every intersection, as we seek directions, he will say 'left' and then 'no, I mean right' or 'no, the other way', usually just as it is too late to safely correct. After a few cursed detours, including a very long one on a freeway, we agree he will point instead, and he admits that it is not a language issue – he does the same thing in Chinese as in English.

The main exit from Takeshiken is a sealed military access road and as we descend from the Altai Mountains we can travel at speed for the first time since getting into Mongolia. Ping positively flies through hundreds of kilometres of bland land, heading south to Urumqi through the Junggar Basin, barren and flat featureless plains.

Urumqi is a big city, skyscrapers, traffic jams, a heady and giddy splash of neon signs on the edge of the Taklimakan Desert. The central city is a thriving metropolis with bars and shops and lots of flash cars. Ping is smothered in dust and grime from the Gobi inside and out. Our big four-wheel drive sits uneasily on the narrow streets, attracting attention wherever it is parked. We gobble up a hotpot with tender chicken, lamb and steamed green vegetables, the best meal we have eaten in weeks.

Our time in Urumqi is spent between the Kyrgyz embassy, Toyota, the post office and the Chinese Customs Bureau. Ping is thoroughly checked after the battering of Mongolia. Only the CD player has jammed, nothing else needs fixing – astonishingly – and the buckled wheel is hammered out by a roadside repairer for about A$10. With hindsight, I now understand why all Mongolian cars are so battered and in such disrepair. Not only are the people incredibly poor, but the roads are simply the worst around. It is amazing that anything keeps going for long under those conditions.

Jan has sent an emergency rations parcel to the central post office. Three different departments claim to know nothing about it until I say '*Ordaliya*', whereupon it is instantly found and handed over. We are revived by Sao biscuits, Vegemite, Outback Critters, a Phantom comic for Jack, a classic car magazine and *The Economist* for me, as well as fur clippings from Bess the dog and Bert our pet rabbit. Guide Jack latches onto an *Australian Women's Weekly* and curiously asks if he can have it, about which there is no argument. I choke an emotional tear or two at the thought of Jan lovingly putting all this together and then with our friend Marcia trekking off to our local post office to send it to a rendezvous on the other side of the world. Realising how miserable I was sounding in our endless phone calls, she has made

We visit the parental home of our Xinjiang guide, Jack Ho.

Outside the mosque in Kashgar, this man watched everyone coming and going and only moved for prayer.

me want to magically transport myself, in a Dr Who TARDIS, to be home right then and there. Jack teases me about being homesick. I do not mind.

A visit to the Kyrgyz Consul requires first finding someone who knows where it is – it has moved and there are no maps or phone directories at all – and then once found payment of a 'special fee'. I am slow, but getting to understand how things work in this part of the world.

Wandering the streets and markets of Urumqi gives us our first glimpse of the Muslim Chinese Uyghur people. They are an underclass, the original inhabitants of this territory but now overwhelmed by Han Chinese migration from the east. For decades it has been Communist Party policy to settle millions of poor farmers from the overpopulated east to this frontier, for strategic as well as cultural reasons. Not without its share of controversy, this policy has been bitterly opposed by Uyghurs, and just a few months after our visit riots claim an unknown number of lives as a Tibet-style civil uprising threatens local order. There is little evidence of this tension as we wander the streets, admiring the modernity after Mongolia.

Our final errand in Urumqi is to persuade the security and customs officials to alter our exit papers from the Osh road to the Torugart Pass. There are two roads west from Kashgar, and a month ago back in Xian with Tracy I had foolishly and in a rush nominated what looked the easier crossing, to Osh. It seemed a good idea as it was less prone to snow, and en route to Tashkent. But back when I had made that choice I had not understood that only in Bishkek, the Kyrgyz capital, could we secure the obligatory visa for onward travel to Uzbekistan. If we go to Osh we will have to detour more than 500 kilometres all across Kyrgyzstan to go to Bishkek anyway – effectively travelling two sides of a very large Kyrgyz triangle. The Torugart Pass is not yet snowbound, so we want to swap. This poses a massive problem and hours are spent in a bland office building sitting around watching Guide Jack and his boss David finessing, flattering, cajoling and maybe bribing the officials to reissue the papers to identify our exit from China as through the Torugart Pass instead of Osh. I would have much preferred to wander the streets of Urumqi with my son, but it gave him precious exploring time on his own.

Waiting for visas means we have time for a visit to the oasis of Turpan, a couple of hours to our east, on the edge of the Taklimakan Desert, a fruit-growing centre, easily the most charming place we have seen in ages. We pass massive wind farms, boasting literally hundreds of towers and more being erected as we pass, and acres of red chilli spread out on tarpaulins drying in the sun. Turpan boasts soaring mosaic-covered mosques and minarets, stunning Muslim architecture, huge dried fruit and nut stalls offering twenty or thirty varieties of dates, figs, raisin, muscatel, walnuts, cashews, and almonds, and trucks by the side of the road, selling melons the size of cannonballs. We dine on kebabs and pilaff and wonder to each other how Xinjiang is regarded as China. The Uyghur people are so different to the Han majority, as different as we are. Most men display beards, sometimes long, wispy, straggly strands that extend halfway down their chests. Typically, cheeks will be clean-shaven, the beard growing from the chin alone. Their skin is almost mummified from exposure to the sun; their strong Arab influence is evident, with cheekbone structures and noses more Roman than Asian. Pillbox hats denote piety, something akin to the ritual for Jews to cover their heads in recognition of a higher being. The women cover their hair but not their faces, vibrant-coloured skirts and spangly jumpers confounding the Islamic dress codes of the Middle East.

Guide Jack takes us to some farms where he knows the families and we sample fruit and dried raisins, our hosts refusing payment until we buy a bagful of nuts, apricots, figs and an assortment of other fruits from the staggering choice of sultanas, muscatels and huge juicy black raisins. Garlic the size of apples, fresh and aromatic, not the shrivelled, exhausted specimens we see at home, changes my attitude forever to the moist bulbs. Visits to the Thousand Buddha Caves, the ruins of the vast ancient city of Gaochang and 2000-year-old tombs and crypts called 'tells', intact with embalmed mummies, complete our tourist circuit.

Gaochang was the seat of an empire that ruled over vast lands and peoples and was but one of the bridges between east and west, long before any modern contact. Donkey-drawn carts potter along the trails amongst vast ruins, spreading as far as the eye can see. China has so many rich stories, so vast a past, so many mentally exhausting experiences – it is hardly surprising that here is another lost world to explore. Intact murals of ducks being hunted, of mathematics and the measurements of the stars and the seasons, well before anything in Europe of that kind, shows the vital role the Silk Road traders had in exchanging ideas between Islam and China thousands of years ago. This is how knowledge spread between the East and the West.

After returning to Urumqi and collecting our new Kyrgyz visas, Guide Jack suggests we detour on the way to Kashgar and visit his parents. The Silk Road, subject of so much reading and romanticism, beckons. I am not sure what to expect, having spent hours looking at early black-and-white photos of Sir Aurel Stein and reading of his various expeditions. Will it bear any resemblance to the winding dusty road offering mystery and undiscovered treasure at every turn? Are we about to stumble on a lost caravanserai, unchanged for millennia, laden with exotic spices and merchandise exchanged between Occident and Orient? We are soon flying down a new sealed expressway, the only features being regular concrete culverts to channel the winter rains. No camel trains, nomads or tent cities. Every few hours a small assembly of drab huts around a petrol station appears, no spices or silk in evidence at all. To the north, out the right-side window, are the low canyons and yellow-soiled gullies of the bare Tian Shan Mountains; to the south the endless empty grey expanse of the Taklimakan Desert.

From Urumqi to Korla, we speed through the desert, only diverting to stop off near Korla at Toksum for tea and fruit at the mud adobe house of our guide's parents. They greet us with great hospitality in their basic home, tea served in the shady courtyard surrounded by farming paraphernalia, the only sign of modernity being the ubiquitous satellite dish. Guide Jack's parents came west in the 70s, accepting the offer of free land for Han Chinese prepared to settle in the Muslim western province. What is now regarded as controversial, bordering on ethnic cleansing, was then described as opening and settling the new frontier. The Han Chinese quarter in their village is well apart from the Uyghurs, the small produce market separating them. Guide Jack's father, unwell with heart disease, was a cotton farmer with a small acreage adjoining their home. He wears a fading Mao suit, blue coveralls and the typical peaked cap, slippers betraying his age. Guide Jack's mother, wrapped in an apron, fusses over our tea and fruit plates like a house-proud homemaker anywhere in the world. Seeing our gadget-happy guide sitting with his Gore-Tex North Face jacket, Salomon hiking boots and iPod on a low wooden block against a donkey cart – adobe mud walls around us – is a snapshot of modern China, the tension between the new and the old, from illiterate to electronic in one generation.

Oilfields appear as we move on towards Kuqa, nodding donkey pumps dotting the desert, weird steel and concrete barriers like soccer goals framing the road, preventing oversize vehicles from entering the lucrative ground. We only just squeeze

Garlic like we
have never seen.

Shoe repairs while you wait.
Nothing is wasted.

Medicinal lizards.

Mutual fascination, Kashgar.

through, folding the mirrors in to fit past these massive pillars designed to prevent smugglers from getting to the reserves. The only roadside stalls are selling huge pink watermelons, stacked up in small mountains and incredibly cheap. How these are farmed is a mystery, there being no visible water whatsoever. Guide Jack explains that groundwater supplies are tapped for the melon industry, and when we ask what happens when that runs out, he says, 'It never has before, why will it now?', the exact same answer Tracy gave us a month before and thousands of kilometres to the east when we posed the same obvious question.

Hour after hour Ping sails through the desert. The Silk Road traders must have taken months to cover what we do in a day. It is a common misconception that a camel train would trek the whole Silk Road from the Mediterranean to Xian or Shanghai. But in fact spices and silks would pass baton-like on a relay across the Silk Road, with local caravans moving backward and forward across their turf but never going further afield. Today locals still do not travel far beyond their own patch. Most people we meet, not just here but from Southeast Asia onwards, do not know much about life beyond their own province, their own valley, their own group. Paradoxically they believe it is not safe to go beyond their known boundaries, even though no one has done it. Where does this universal fear of the unknown spring from? Baseless suspicion of anything foreign, anything different makes for paranoia and xenophobia. One of our lofty ambitions on this trip was to 'dispel fear' which is all well and good as a slogan, but the reality is that fear drives most emotion, and through history the earth oozes blood to prove it. Although we are greeted with great hospitality throughout our journey, we are constantly warned of the perils of venturing to the next province, country or ethnic enclave. 'You are safe here, but there are thieves when you get to …' was an often-heard warning.

The Silk Road extends into the haze, a black ribbon in the desert, tumbleweeds rolling across in the wind. Sand encroaches on the bitumen, disguising the edges of the tarmac. Hour after hour, we drive across hundreds and hundreds of kilometres of nothing. I remark on the parallels with central Australia – if we were driving on the other side of the road and the occasional sign was not in Chinese you could blink and not know the difference. As we head west towards Aksu, our last stop before Kashgar, trees appear, poplars in long rows, lining the road and offering shade to irrigation trenches that have sprung up around the town, a majority Uyghur community. The people are no more Chinese than I am. Their Turkic ethnic origins distinguish them from any of the more than fifty major Chinese ethnicities so lauded in the East. They are indistinguishable from their Middle Eastern cousins in looks, and could easily pass muster thousands of miles and several countries to the west, or in Afghanistan to the south. The men wear bright pillbox hats, embroidered or braided in gold or silver, or otherwise furry beehive-shaped lambskins that look like tea cosies. Women are veiled, their hair covered at least in part if not fully, but their faces uncovered in the Turkish or moderate Islamic fashion. Their welcoming smiles and open hospitality is a treat.

Aksu boasts a thriving market: pomegranate juicers, leather workers, ghastly velour and fleece clothes, knives and tools on offer, and of course the medicine man, where a crowd gathers around Jack as he photographs the remedies and cures on offer, ranging from antlers to dried lizards, animal skulls and teeth and powders of every imaginable, and some unimaginable, description. Two live lizards, tethered to each other, are hopping around the groundsheet of the medicine man's stall, and barely has Jack paused to take stock before a prankster launches them into the bird's nest of dreadlocks that his hair has become, to the great hilarity of the gathered crowd. It is just as well we cannot understand their commentary.

Between Aksu and Kashgar, for hundreds of kilometres, the road is lined with cotton fields and factories. The season is just drawing to an end, the pickers have nearly finished and the procession of tractors tugging huge caged trailers overloaded to the sky with crisp white cotton balls makes a continuous chain along the road. Cotton is blowing around like snow, and paupers chase the loose fluff around even on the freeway verge to try to make some money. The tractors form queues at factory gates, massive belching smokestacks betraying the industry behind the high walls. 'This is where underpants come from,' I announce, citing Joe Bennett's bestseller, a Kiwi author who visited Xinjiang to try to research the economics of underpants. It is unbelievable that anyone can make a living out here, let alone that these cotton smudges end up in chain stores all over the world, processed and dyed and trimmed and overlocked and wrapped in plastic for next to nothing. Again the environmental degradation seems no one's concern – the dry rivers, the exhausted soil and the sky soiled with emissions belching from trucks, tractors, generators and cotton factories. What will they do when the groundwater runs out? What will happen if global

Kashgar's old magical laneways are being replaced with controversial new buildings.

Markets in Xinjiang are full of the smell of fresh bread.

Hand production is still highly valued in Kashgar and Xinjiang, Western China.

warming reduces the snow melt from the mountains to the north? How will these people survive?

Kashgar's outskirts are the same as any other city, but the ancient centre is breathtaking. This is what I have been looking forward to since the day I started planning the whole trip. Kashgar is at the epicentre of this expedition, in a way, the drive to here being the first part of our journey and the drive from here the remainder. It is the magical mythical city of the Silk Road, the most famous market city in the world, the focal point of thousands of years of intercontinental trading. The legendary Sunday market is reputed to be the market to end all markets, the greatest trading place on earth, the crossroads of civilisations and cultures. If you cannot get something at Kashgar market, it is said, it cannot be got anywhere at all. I am looking forward to putting this to the test. As we see signs of the city and I pinch myself that I am finally here, a lump forms in my throat. This is the itch I have been scratching: not the first time nor the last that it all seems surreal.

We lodge in the former Russian Embassy, now a hotel, but still retaining the extraordinary plaster decorations and gilded wall and ceiling adornments befitting the last players in 'The Great Game', the name given over hundreds of years to the battle for colonial supremacy over this part of the world. Empires from the East and the West – for hundreds of years it was England and Russia – have fought over this intersection of interests, England having vested great importance in controlling Afghanistan and Turkistan, as the area was once called and once again may be. We debate the folly of the Afghan War currently under way, the futility of trying now to do what the USSR spectacularly failed to do as have others before them. Just to our south the roads go to Pakistan over the Karakoram Highway, into the Pamir Mountains and beyond. To the southwest the Afghani militias have been making a mockery of modern fighting armies and do so again, shifting alliances and tribal rivalries leaving the American-led anti-Al Qaeda alliance wondering how they will ever extricate themselves.

The gaudiness of the Russian decoration of our hotel is matched by comfort but the whole place is run down and no doubt but a shadow of its past glory. Guide Jack is called back to Urumqi for what he tells us is his last booking for the season. Before we drop him off at the station, he introduces us to Abdul, who will take us to the fabled Sunday market and then up the Torugart Pass to the Kyrgyzstan border on

Monday. Guide Jack is totally spooked by the global financial crisis, has lost money in the stock market crash and does not know where his next pay is to come from. We are sad to see him go – he has been fun and worked hard to show us his patch.

The old city walls are barely discernible, hidden behind apartment buildings and nondescript Chinese government apartment blocks. Once within the fold of the Uyghur old city centre, it is literally like stepping back in time. The buildings and people seem barely touched by modernity. Craftsmen are squatting on the street hammering copper, soldering tin, turning wood, sharpening knives on foot treadles and always munching on peanuts, sipping tea or coffee, or smoking cigarettes. Rickety, elaborately carved and crenullated wooden balconies fold around the wobbly walls of two- or three-storeyed houses and shops. Sometimes the wooden beams supporting upper-floor rooms join on either side of an alley, creating a tunnel under the floorboards. Cobbled lanes wind chaotically between the brick and mud walls, sometimes ending abruptly in a massive gate to someone's house. Donkeys vie with electric scooters to weave a path delivering the necessities of life to every nook and cranny. The smells of animal droppings mixed with fire and food awaken the sinus.

The bustle of commerce and community life sweeps us along, and we spend hours just wandering the alleyways. We are adopted by a local English teacher, Anwer, who, after several cups of tea, asks us to make some time for his students to practise their English. He introduces us to Ajim the jeweller and Mohammed, a perfume seller, and they show us around for the rest of the day. Mohammed, in his early twenties, has a stall on two portable tables by the door to the old central mosque. He stocks sweet-smelling waters and fake French perfume but in all the hours we spend sitting at the gate with him over two days he never sells anything. He is charming and funny, delighted to practise his English with someone his own age. Ajim and his brothers have several stalls in the bazaar selling flash fake watches and gold and silver necklaces, bangles and earrings, clearly prosperous and thriving, unlike the perfumer.

The massive covered bazaar extends forever: huge carpet stalls, musical instruments, entire alleys of coats and jeans, shoes, gold jewellery and watches, and of course household goods and electronics. The food section is mouth-watering, spices displayed in overflowing sacks, lined up in swollen rows ten deep like the tips of coloured pencils in a case. Dried dates, raisins and glazed fruit, pickled vegetables, fresh bread, grains and pulses – the range is better than we have seen in a month, since Xián. It is unbelievable that impoverished and undernourished Mongolia is only a few days' drive behind us. Butchers are working in a far corner, skinning cattle, chopping limbs and heads and carcasses into popular cuts, responding on the spot to the wishes of shoppers. Fishmongers display live catfish and yabby-like crustaceans, pumps bubbling water into tubs to keep them alive. The entire market is a city within a city and has a restless energy, a life of its own.

Abdul is waiting for us early on Sunday morning and we head off to the new site of the famous Sunday animal market. Traders congregate from all around, Kashgar being the central point for Uyghurs, Tajiks, Turkmen, Uzbeks, Kyrgyzs, Kazakhs, Pamirs, Pakistanis, Afghans – even Chinese – and whoever else is passing through, including Australians! The Chinese authorities have recently relocated the market, and are in the process of demolishing the old city entirely. It ought to be an international scandal; heritage buildings gorgeous in their design and execution, historic in their entirety, full of character, are being bulldozed and replaced with modern concrete and glass nothingness. The Chinese argue that they want to provide more modern and cleaner housing for Uyghurs, but every local we meet and talk to says they want sewers and electricity without demolishing the historic heart of Kashgar. The month before we arrived a jewel of a building in the very middle of the old city, a former palace hundreds of years old, was demolished to be replaced with a new school, a needed but inappropriately placed facility. The politically active amongst the Uyghurs argue that the demolition is a deliberate programme by Beijing to dilute Muslim culture and force assimilation of Uyghurs. The Chinese Government argue they will replace the crumbling buildings with a reproduction historic quarter – but if our observations of other Chinese tourist precincts are anything to judge by, it will be a Disney version and a pale imitation of what is already there.

The animal market is overwhelming. Bactrian camels, ponies, donkeys, buffalo, goats, sheep – all lined up and on display, having their teeth and hoofs and various orifices inspected. The bird market has pigeons, ducks, geese, chickens and zillions of varieties of delicate colourful songbirds displayed for breeding and food. The grain market, the vegetable market, the leather goods and harnesses, tools, trinkets … it is exhausting. A line of barbers shaving in the open air is tempting, but I decide to wait for something other than a dodgy cut-throat razor. Throughout the vast acres of the market are dumpling and kebab stalls steamed and smoked, peanut brittle stalls, squashed tight against fig, date and raisin sellers, and everywhere fresh garlic traders, juice makers, intestines sellers, eggs of every bird and size and colour, butchers and samosa makers, corn and cabbages, hats and scarves, spruikers and hawkers, all creating a kaleidoscope of the senses.

Abdul our local guide is charming, generous in his time and full of information. Lunch of pilaff and kebabs is taken horizontally outside the market, sipping tea, lounging on day beds, munching the warm soft round naan bread that comes direct from the furnaces. We both decline the goat's head soup, discovering our threshold for disgusting food. Talking, sitting and taking photos, our conversation turns to worldly affairs. The US election is just a few days away, but while Abdul knows who George W. Bush is he has never heard of Barack Obama and does not know there is an election looming. He cannot see how it matters in his world who the President of the United States is, although his knowledge of the outside world extends to a basic understanding of the Middle East and solidarity with Palestinian Muslims. Jack observes we are probably closer to Beirut than Beijing.

'China is like a worried father,' Abdul tells us, 'always looking out for the safety of his children, making sure nothing will hurt them, but now everything is different, the young people, they want a totally different life from the old people. My kids are going to Chinese school, not Uyghur, but they learn Uyghur at home, and English at school. But the internet, yes it is everywhere – but the government control what you can view.' Abdul knows nothing about Australia except kangaroos. We are used to that quirk by now.

Wandering the streets of old Kashgar, sampling the kebabs and soft, warm, doughy bread, munching on nuts and dried fruit, Jack starts rhapsodising about the feast he is planning when we meet Jan in Paris for Christmas. For the first time in months, I am confident that it will happen – that we can get from Kashgar, across the mountains, through the 'stans, into Iran and through Turkey in six weeks to keep my solemn promise to meet our deadline, our destination and my wife.

24 | The Torugart Pass

Deep snow, thick ice, dense fog, crashed trucks blocking the road, a wheel change for a puncture in no man's land, a hitchhiking machine gun-toting Kyrgyz soldier … welcome to the Torugart Pass.

Kashgar's old city boasts buildings of many vintages, mud, brick and timber. But our hotel in Kashgar has a history of its own to tell, a story that could overshadow many of its occupants over the years. The former embassy of Russia is now the Seman Hotel, and among the other guests enjoying its otherworldly charms is a car load of elderly English travellers, straight out of central casting, who are heading over the Torugart Pass the same day as us. Like characters from the movie *Tea with Mussolini* they are an incongruous sight. Their Chinese guide has taken them around the Taklimakan Desert in a loop, across the North Silk Road via Urumqi and Turpan and then all the way around to Dunhuang and back to Kashgar via the southern Silk Road. Their four-wheel drive and Ping head off up the mountain in loose convoy and we sit with them at the modern Chinese border post for more than an hour, waiting to be processed. One moustachioed, overweight, balding man, seventy years old or thereabouts, agitated and anxious at the delay, starts shouting at the Chinese soldiers, berating them in clipped military tones, telling them in loud English that only we understand that they are lazy, corrupt and inept. His superior attitude and attempts at colonial authority are somewhat undermined by his unzipped trouser fly, but blissfully unaware he rants and rages until placated by one of his companions. She chain-smokes a cigarette through a long holder, a filter like I have not seen in years and Jack has never encountered at all. She is a marvellous woman, tiny but very fit and active for what must also have been nearly seventy years on the planet. She tells us, 'I lived in Pah-kiss-tarn for years after the war, it was always like this, they're all hopeless you know …' and continues on like a miniature Joan Plowright, regaling us with tales of the Karakoram Highway in the 1950s. Marvellous really.

Abdul clearly knows the border control system much better than their guide and helps them get their papers sorted after a preposterous delay. We manage to stay ahead of a busload of Chinese heading over the mountain, every piece of their luggage being X-rayed and scrutinised. The bus is forbidden for foreigners, but popular with smugglers. A snappy salute from the final soldier, who even clicks his heels for me, and we jump into Ping and are off. I ask Abdul why we had such trouble getting through. 'Because you did not have your China numberplate,' he explains. I tell him it's in the glove box and he looks incredulously at me. 'Why you did not tell me?' he says. 'Because you did not ask,' I answer, laughing because the officious Chinese bureaucracy and security has been exposed as just a silly game, so easy was it to circumvent without trying. The road climbed steeply, sweeping through ravines and around narrow ledges, snow gradually welcoming us as we bump along to the higher slopes of the treacherous 3752-metre-high pass.

Lonely Planet warns: 'Torugart is one of Asia's most unpredictable border posts. Even the most painstaking arrangements can be thwarted by logistical gridlock on the Chinese side or by unpredictable border closures, eg for holidays, snow or heaven knows what else … The trucks accumulate in huge tailbacks at both sides for 500m or more …'

Tailback indeed. High up in the mountains the single lane narrow road is totally blocked by massive semi-trailers, some with mechanical failure, others stopped by frozen diesel, the rest unable to get past. We seem stuck. Facing a choice between spending hours – even days – blocked in by inert trucks, and conferring with Abdul and Jack, I drive Ping off the road down a steep embankment and along a creek bed running roughly parallel, picking a track through the rocks, mud and snow for half a kilometre. It was worth having a low range gearbox after all. The Chinese driver with our English companions follows, sticking to our wheel ruts, rejoining the road for the next boom gate where documents are again all checked. Abdul thinks it great fun, Jack seems slightly worried.

As we climb the steep winding road higher towards the summit, the snow is thicker,

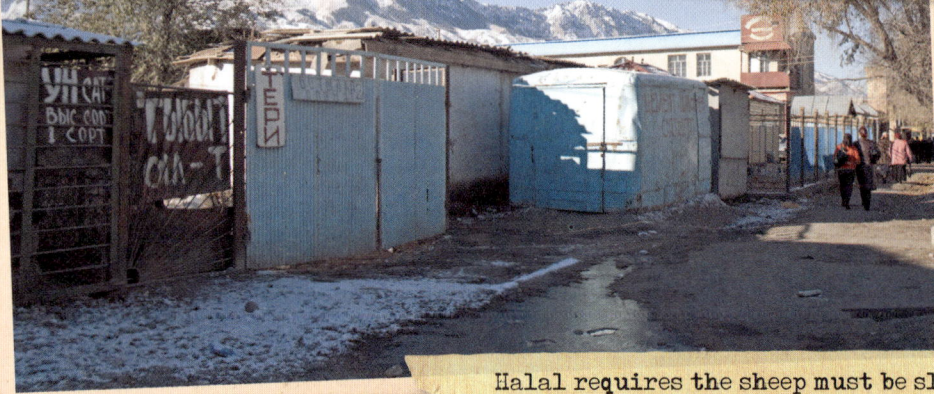

Halal requires the sheep must be slaughtered several hours before being butchered — the truck driver will want to cook one sheep upon arriving at market.

Bottles of honey for sale.

Kyrgyzstan's petrol station.

A truck stop on the Torugart Pass, Kyrgyzstan.

Our first morning in Central Asia, Kyrgyzstan.

the road becomes slippery, the cloud closes in and tragically the view – reputedly stunning – disappears. In thick snow at the top, the road breasts the mountain top and widens to embrace a tiny windswept soldier's hut where we endure one last document check, and as we say our farewell to Abdul we are waved through an imposing set of barbed wire and steel gates, first by Chinese soldiers in fur hats and huge greatcoats, then Kyrgyz soldiers who seem utterly uninterested in checking anything. The car load of Poms have to swap cars, carry their bags in the blizzard across the 100-metre fenced area, and jump into a minibus waiting for them. The Chinese 4x4 turns around, collects Abdul and goes straight back down the pass. We drive off, Jack exuberant to be back in the front seat, waving and expecting to see our English friends along the way down the 60 kilometres of militarised no man's land and beyond to the Kyrgyz town of Naryn.

The road on the Kyrgyz side immediately gets even worse. There is an impolite tussle for road space with ancient Soviet trucks belching clouds of filthy exhaust, split flat windscreens almost smothered in ice and snow, tiny wipers furiously and ineffectually sweeping a minute clear arc as their detached lights, like snail eyes on stalks, mounted high on shaky mudguards, hardly pierce the snowstorm. Most of them are crawling along with massive chains across their huge wheels, crunching into the ice at barely walking pace. A trail can just be found through the rocks and ditches, and I am again wishing that we had snow chains. What was I thinking?

About thirty minutes down the mountain, still in knee-deep snow, the gloom reveals a cluster of low, spot-lit hangars surrounded by imposing high fences. The road seems to go directly to a huge roller door which opens slowly as we approach. Inside is a concrete inspection pit, floodlit and otherwise bare. We stop, assuming correctly that someone will eventually appear. A burly, fur-hat-wearing soldier complete with machine gun emerges from the side, grunts a greeting, pokes his head through the window for a quick look around, says, '*Zdrastvuitya*, *Salaam*, pay-pahs pliz,' takes our passports and carnet and disappears for only a few minutes, returns and jumps into the back seat, greeting us with a handshake and then gesturing to me to drive away, shoving the documents back at the same time. He points down the road and we emerge from the protective space of the hangar back into the snowstorm. It is still the middle of the day but dark, and visibility is limited. We get halfway across the fenced compound and our passenger says, 'Stop, no go,' and gets out, trundles into what looks like an ancient railway carriage sitting in the snow, and a few minutes later comes back out carrying a large electric heater, still in its box, made in China and no doubt extracted from a helpful truckdriver. He gets back into Ping, smiles this time and says 'Go', pointing down the road.

Our escort ensures smooth passage through the next boom gate and we descend from the summit, skirting a massive barbed-wire double electric fence, just like in WWII prison camp movies, that stretches as far as we can see. We try to engage in conversation, 'Kyrgyzstan good?' 'Yes, Kyrgyzstan very good.' Jack at his charming multilingual best tries hard but the few words of Russian we learned from Marima in Mongolia are soon exhausted and sign language takes over. About half an hour down the mountain, snow still thick on the ground but mercifully no longer falling, we approach a three-storey barracks and our guest points toward the surrounding security fence. He jumps out as we get to the gate, says, '*Spaseeba*, *Rakhmat*, *Spaseeba*', in thanks several times and some other Russian we cannot understand and waves us off towards a featureless horizon.

There is no sign of the minibus loaded with elderly Poms, which seems odd given our various delays. We keep driving slowly, across open, empty, snowbound, rocky plains, a plateau in the mountains. In summer it must be spectacular, in winter it is just plain scary. Visibility gets better – we can see 100 metres along the barbed wire and electric fence as we slowly descend, no man's land continuing forever. I relax enough to agree to some music – Jack goes straight to his favourites and we hear the same twenty songs he has played to death for the last few months. I petition for changes – he reminds me of our deal, he is in charge of music. Another checkpoint, another gate, this time guarded by a burly alpine-camouflaged soldier who carries a machine-gun strapped to his back but a pink jumpsuited toddler in his arms. He waves cheerily to us to stop, introduces his daughter and asks for papers. I jump out and dig through our luggage for a fluffy koala and he stamps our passports and waves us off with a cheer. Jack holds up his camera and asks 'Photo?' but the soldier scowls and says, '*Nyet*, no, *nyet*, *da svidanya*,' and off we go.

The snowbound road continues snaking through the gorges and rocky pass. Moments after the soldier has waved us through his gate a loud rhythmic banging from the rear signals another puncture. The temperature gauge says minus 13. I groan, but Jack is quickly out of Ping to first take a photo and then is wrestling with the bags to get to the wheel brace and carjack. Together we perform a world-record four-wheel-drive tyre change in the snow, knuckles seizing and breath fogging up. When I reach down to get the wheel nuts to bolt them back onto the axle studs, they are stuck, frozen solid to the ground and I have to hit them free with the wheel brace to dislodge them. Even though we are quick to change the wheel, it seems odd that there is no sign of the Poms in their minibus catching up to us.

There are very few buildings, but as we descend and clear the final checkpoint out of no man's land, several low brick and rock houses lie crumbled and battered, detritus from a terrible earthquake that struck here just a month before. Seventy-five people died and the nearby town of Nura, a little further south near the Afghanistan–China–Kyrgyzstan intersection, was all but destroyed. But the road here seems unaffected and we cannot see any other evidence of the recent damage. Some more railway carriage buildings – low huts with bowed iron roofs, chimneys protruding and always painted a pale blue – appear cheery in the gloom.

Winding our way down the mountain, the only other living creatures we see for more than an hour are a herdsman on horseback with his hairy goats and shaggy sheep well protected from the wind, his woolly hat barely protecting his weather-beaten face, a massive sheepskin coat doubling his bulk to keep warm. We wave but get no response. It is a relief to be unescorted again and we are able to talk to each other in the car without Abdul or Guide Jack with us; the volume for the iPod goes up a few notches. Driving unescorted and relying on our own instincts and judgement is far better than being bossed around by any guide. The trade-off is that we do not know where we are going or what we might be missing.

Our Kyrgyz target for the day is Naryn, according to our map a fairly straight 190 kilometres from the summit. It is 210 kilometres of hairpin bends from Kashgar up to the summit, so it is exactly 400 kilometres that we want to cover in the day. Although we left Kashgar shortly after dawn, it is twilight as we get to Naryn and bone-tired and hungry we drive around this pretty town straddling a fast-running river, looking for the only place to stay, called the Celestial Guesthouse. Nothing is lit, the hotel seems not to be where the map says it is, and all we can find is closed gates and high walls wherever we go. We try asking people when we see anyone but no one speaks a word of English, no one recognises the name, and we literally drive around in circles getting angry with each other because there is no one else to get angry with instead. The third time I drive along a narrow driveway that ends in a huge steel fence I spy a small faded sign saying 'Celestial', not in Cyrillic but in Roman letters high up above a door. It is exactly where the map shows it to be, but we have missed it each time. We tumble in and are greeted by an English-speaking receptionist who tells us they are expecting a bus full of tourists from China and she thinks they have no spare rooms. With some gentle persuasion they open an extra room and offer dinner as well. We think we might wait for the Poms but hunger gets the better of us. In the dining room is a young Russian-speaking American, Kerry, from New York, who tells us she is working for Save The Children, having previously been a Peace Corps volunteer in Turkmenistan. Her stories of travelling around the region are a quick education as we sit and drink bottomless cups of tea. As we go to bed the Poms have still not arrived and I am worried. They are not young people and we have been mightily impressed with their pluck to even embark on an adventure of this scale in this climate.

Banging and shouting wakes us at about one in the morning, as our Kashgar Poms finally make it. At breakfast next morning, exhausted, they recount how the minibus waiting for them on the Torugart summit had failed to start. Apparently the driver was sitting there for so long that he worried he would run out of diesel if he kept the engine running, so he turned it off. He flattened the battery by running the heater, and then the fuel froze in the lines so they had to get a truck to tow them down the mountain. The tow rope broke three times, the big Chinese-passengers-only bus that operates between Kashgar and Bishkek had a smash with a truck and blocked the road and altogether they had a torrid time. We were so lucky to miss it all.

Our punctured tyre, pierced by a bullet-shaped piece of pipe, is repaired in Naryn at a primitive garage by the riverbank. Locals arrive every few minutes with banged-up old Russian Gaz 4x4s and ancient Volgas, Ladas and Moskvitchs. Some fifteen-year-old Audis seem out of keeping, and an occasional clapped out BMW or Mercedes denotes high status. There is a thriving trade importing second-hand German cars to Central Asia … this is where old Audis come to die. The town boasts a small market and we change money and stock up on dried fruit and bread, wander about looking for anything worth seeing, realise there is not much and strike off again towards Bishkek. More ice and snow, more rough roads, more boom gates and a hitchhiker who can tell us his name is Maxi but nothing else are the highlights of our first day in the former Soviet states. Around the stunning picture-postcard Lake Issyk-Kul, ramshackle stalls sell smoked and dried fish, trout-sized, salty but served for lunch soaked into a soup-like broth with dumplings and hard dry dark bread. Mansions line the lake, but all are closed for winter. Lake Issyk-Kul is a summer resort and spa town, wealthy Russian and oil-boom Kazakhs seek out its mountain waters in the warmer months. In early winter there are no signs of life whatsoever. A picnic on the pebbled shores, more tinned sardines and a stone-skipping competition prepare us for the final drive over another, but lower, mountain pass into Bishkek.

25 | Why the Soviets Ran Away

'Can I live in Oss-tray-a? You help me?' Welcome to the former Soviet republics, the 'stans, where everyone wants to leave and life is better anywhere but here.

'I help you, you help me,' says Lilia the Russian travel agent in Bishkek who can arrange visas for Uzbekistan. A letter of introduction is required, issued through Tashkent, and she has forewarned us it will take at least a week, sometimes ten days. 'Im-poss-eebull,' she answers when I say we need it in two days. We quickly learn that anything is possible; it just costs more depending on how impossible it is. She warns that sometimes, for no reason, a visa is refused, and quotes a remarkable amount of money, which with minimal ritual haggling is nearly halved, but also wants a kangaroo in payment. I promise to find one. Aleksander is a tall, earnest young Russian man in the agency who does some of our paperwork and grills me about Australian immigration. 'Is it true woman can go to Australia but not man?' he asks. It takes a few minutes but eventually the penny drops that he knows about Russian brides and is looking at websites targeting women and thinks that it is the Australian Government that recruits these girls. From his perspective, the government is in charge of everything and it takes quite some explaining to get across the idea that recruiting brides is not an official activity of our government.

The divide between Russians and Kyrgyz is clear as we wander around the city. Leafy tree-lined streets with filthy vintage trolley buses are laid out in a neat grid, as this city has none of the ancient history of Kashgar or other Silk Road cities. It is of recent invention, less than 100 years old and originally the creation of the Soviet

The two sides of Central Asian society; Russians and locals.

Uzbek bread is not the tastiest we ate, but it is the most colourful.

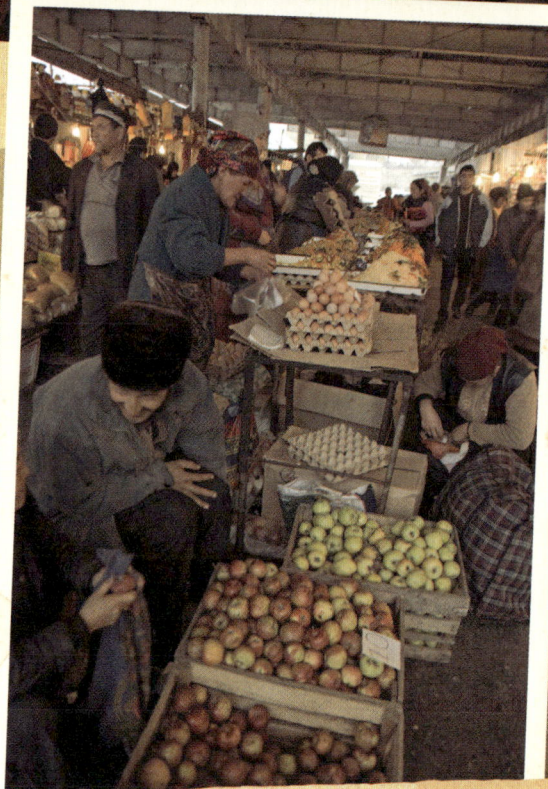

Kyrgyz apples, small and dry just like the country.

empire, for whom a fort and military base in their far-flung corner, keeping an eye on China, was a strategic necessity. The welfare of the ethnic Kyrgyz never featured as a priority in their plans, and Stalin drew boundaries through the 'stans to mix the ethnic groups, to assimilate them into Mother Russia, to break up ethnic loyalty and enclaves. A Russian elite established supremacy in local affairs, the remnants and descendants of which still maintain a stranglehold on the local economy despite comprising only 10 per cent of the population. Upon the collapse of the USSR in 1991 each republic seized control of its own affairs, amidst chaotic and sometimes bloody scenes. As recently as 2005 the 'Tulip Revolution' had brought instability to this city and the surrounding countryside.

No one smiles much in Bishkek. We again get caught spending ages trying to secure visas for Uzbekistan, but manage to exhaust the tourism options of the city in-between. It does not take long. The main market is disappointing, the shops nondescript, the antiques fake but the beggars genuine and the surplus Russian military equipment tempting but too bulky. Endless displays of mobile phones and electronic gadgetry are the main concession to modernity. Babushka dolls – more accurately called matryoshka nesting dolls – are tempting but we hold off for later. Hummers and flash new European luxury four-wheel drives zoom around with darkened windows, testimony to the rumours of organised crime and racketeers running the place. A fairground shooting gallery with slug guns is a hit with Jack who has never fired a gun in his life. John Howard's reaction to Port Arthur having robbed him of his share of fairground stuffed toys, he makes up for it here. It is the most fun you can have in Bishkek.

Tellingly, when we ask Lilia and Aleksander for advice about the roads south through the Ferghana Valley and then west into Uzbekistan, they have never been there and show little interest in ever doing so. Their travel agency work consists entirely of getting cheap fares for those leaving. The countryside is Muslim heartland, Kyrgyz peasant populated and, despite being born and bred in Bishkek, it is like foreign soil to the educated, city-focused Russian Orthodox.

We sit up all night and watch the US election result on cable TV and I cry as McCain and Obama make two of the best political speeches you could ever hope to hear. I try to impress upon Jack what a historic occasion this is – he quite rightly tells me to stop being so soppy and patronising, but I start talking about where Jan and I were when we heard about the Berlin Wall coming down and he seems placated. We celebrate Obama's election with pancakes and a slap-up Western breakfast – the best since Raffles Hotel in Singapore three months earlier.

We get out of Bishkek as soon as the visa for Uzbekistan is in our passports. No mention can be made of the ABC or my media work – as the guidebooks put it, 'It remains next to impossible for a foreign journalist to get a visa into Uzbekistan.' I look everywhere for a plastic or toy kangaroo for Lilia as promised, and just as I give up there is a poster of one on a wall, advertising what I think is some washing powder. I peel it off and together with chocolates and cash I keep my promise.

The road south starts gently through orchards and fields, but quickly deteriorates as we climb a muddy ascent towards the Tyuz-Ashuu Pass – at 3586 metres one of the highest road passes in the world (for comparison the Mont Blanc tunnel between Italy and Switzerland is only 1380 metres altitude). We go through a very long tunnel and on the other side the road is totally snowbound. The view is said to be stunning – one of the best vistas in central Asia – but we can barely see the car in front. Most cars and trucks have snow chains; we drive in full four-wheel drive and stay safe, but chains would have been better. Cars are sliding and skating everywhere – the Kyrgyz response to snow is to go faster and to sweep through the bends as if the car is on skis. We see several crashes and spend half an hour helping to dig a bride and groom in an old Audi from a deep drift they have slid into. Why does anyone drive fast in these conditions? Why don't they put their lights on? Why are they so reckless? We plough on, through massive unpopulated ravines and valleys, the cloud and fog clearing but the snow getting heavier.

After dark, on a deserted road in pitch black and blinding snow we despair at finding anywhere to sleep. We move along at walking pace, snowflakes dancing and drifting like a veil in our blazing spotlights, revealing just enough to make out the edge of the bitumen and the ditch. My shoulders and neck are seizing up from the strain, Jack trying hard to jolly me along. I am bone tired, we have nothing to eat. Will this be our first night sleeping in Ping? A house beside the road has a bare light bulb in a window and after a pathetic charades attempt at putting food into my mouth and a pillow under my head, a young man offers to jump into the car and takes us further up the road to a guesthouse. A freezing room and cold water shower, goulash soup and the promise of bread and tea for breakfast are a godsend before we attempt the violent and troubled Ferghana Valley and the border to Uzbekistan tomorrow.

26 | Love Thy Neighbour, Not

You can make the man with the Kalashnikov laugh, but it don't mean a thing.

There are two crossings from Kyrgyzstan to Uzbekistan. Only one is open to foreigners. We try to cross at the other. We have nothing to lose – it is a 300-kilometre shortcut if we can get through, saving an entire day. The Kyrgyz soldiers laugh and tell me it is futile as I request to cross their side of a heavily fortified no man's land, but obligingly agree to slide the crash barriers aside and lift the boom gate and off we go. The barren 100-metre stretch of land at Kochkor-Ata includes a smashed concrete bridge over a small river and that is where we are stopped by the Uzbek soldiers. A friendly man in a helmet and flak jacket and huge machine gun wanders across to see what on earth we think we are doing. Jack tells me I am an idiot, but I jump out of Ping and show him our Uzbekistan visa and the carnet, hoping it looks official enough to bluff our way through. He reaches for a walkie-talkie and chats a few minutes then takes the documents and walks off to the guardroom. Fifteen minutes later he comes back, shakes his head, '*Nyet*, no, go,' and with a wave of his hand that is all he will say.

I naively thought that all the former Russian republics were on friendly terms, co-operating as they did by forming the Commonwealth of Independent States after the collapse of the USSR. Ethnically they are all related, intermarriage and religious affinity surely counting for something. But the opposite is true. The Uzbeks loathe the Kyrgyz, who hate the Kazakhs, who mistrust the Turkmen. No one talks to the Tajiks and so on it goes. Upon the collapse of the Moscow administration, terrible massacres and ethnic cleansing claimed unknown numbers of lives until the borders were re-policed and order

Some Kyrgyz have as many gold teeth as real ones – it is a display of status and wealth.

restored. Uzbeks living within Kyrgyzstan fled across the border, bumping into Kyrgyz fleeing the other way. At Andijan, where we are headed, a riot as recently as 2005 was quelled with brutal violence by government troops, the exact death toll unknown but estimated at around 1000 people shot. The Uzbek Government claimed to be dealing with Islamic terrorists, the locals claim it was a peaceful protest for greater autonomy. Whatever it was, a lot of people died here.

We are forced to go the long way round. The drive is through Jalal-Abad, to Ozgun, and on to Osh. Before the collapse of the Soviet empire these borders were all porous and could be crossed at will; now they are some of the most policed and guarded barriers in the world. It defies sense, but there are roads that are cut in two, that stop as dead ends, because of the new frontiers, like Berlin during the Cold War. We inadvertently find ourselves at one guarded post, innocently taking a wrong turn and bumping into soldiers with no warning. I was being a smart arse before but this time is purely accidental and we beat a hasty retreat.

We skirt a stunning blue lake, almost magical in its colours and allure. The road keeps dipping in and out and across the border, locals taking short cuts, but we are totally forbidden from crossing. It is infuriating – we are compelled to detour all day to get to a destination we can actually see just a few minutes' drive away. The ordeal is made worse for me by Jack talking ceaselessly about his sudden attraction to Buddhism. He argues it is the peaceful religion and that he feels a connection to it. I am amazed, as it appears to me to be a slightly bleached version of the same mumbo jumbo and humbug that characterises other religions across the spectrum. Here we are traversing tracts of land that even tiny religious differences have turned into graveyards and he is mesmerised by a variation on the theme. How can his reaction be so different to mine? How can he not see the destructive influence that follows from religious notions of supreme beings and 'God's word' and be blind to the inherent bigotry based on hypocritical and mystical belief that your group is better or superior?

The landscape changes to lush grasslands and fertile fields – it comes as a shock; we have not seen green for a while, certainly not whole fields of grass and feed. Healthy cows and lots of horses dot the farms, and fat women in shapeless clothes waddle along carrying preposterous loads of sticks and sometimes fruit. Roadside stalls sell honey in recycled soft drink bottles and we try to buy a bag of mandarins but the craggy sun-dried farmer refuses any money and shakes my hand enthusiastically instead.

A Lada four-wheel drive is chugging along in front of us, its rear shock absorber actually unconnected to the axle and dragging along the ground, shooting sparks. I have never seen anything like it; it must be like a horse cart to drive, but the farmer seems unconcerned and is pottering along as if nothing is awry.

The traffic thins out. We speed everywhere, ignoring regular police checks and the waving of little orange wands at us. No one bothers chasing and I have been warned that to stop is to be touched for a bribe so I ignore their half-hearted attempts to attract attention. Covered in stickers, Ping looks official, and many policemen wave us through the regular roadblocks without checking anything. We get stuck in gridlock as we get to Osh, an ancient Silk Road trading city, architecturally unimpressive, but the people are as friendly as any we have met since China. The bazaar has a welcome selection of fresh food, pistachios, apricots, nuts, green vegetables, meat without flies … the people look healthier, as does their food. We are welcomed and greeted wherever we go – it is heartening and we wander the night market until late.

Next morning, finding the Uzbek border is a challenge. We drive around lost for a while, then a map drawn on a cardboard box by a cafe stall holder guides us through the backstreets and the chaotic crossing is in front of us. The Kyrgyz stamp us out of their side with barely a look, but the Uzbeks have long forms in Russian that we are supposed to be able to fill in with no idea what each of the confusing boxes is asking. A helpful soldier comes over to see who is holding up the queue and takes us into a booth where a chuckling officer helps us fill in the forms. I lie twice – once about my occupation and the second time about how much we carry in foreign currency. As we are finally waved through, we spot two European backpackers waiting in the rain. Alexander and Lea are from Switzerland, and we offer them a lift to Tashkent. It is a bonus when Lea announces from the back seat that she speaks fluent Russian. She translates whenever we get lost as we drive all day in the sleet and rain through flat farmland straight to Tashkent.

JACK WRITES

27 | Tashkent Ramblings

It was snowing. Like I'd never seen before. It tumbled from the sky silently, unnervingly. Men trudged through it, shoulders towards the wind. Children danced, triumphing in the falling magic. Their eyes fixed upwards and mouths and hands stretching out and away. We walked along with the breeze behind us and large flowers of snow clinging to our coats and sitting in our hair.

We left the hotel early and waved goodbye to the cute blonde Uzbek at the front desk who was sitting glued to the procession of Russian pop stars grinding themselves on machine guns and snipers on MTV. I was hopelessly tired and in the snowy cold I could only follow my feet which followed Dad's adrenaline. His buoyancy annoyed me but only because I was jealous of it. Every morning he would get up ready to go and excited, clapping his hands together, chest puffed out and bouncing from toe to toe.

We sidled through the snow and down into the metro station and made for the old part of Tashkent: Chorsu. All through the train ride people stared and there were whispers and nods of heads in our direction followed by laughter. We couldn't have stuck out more with our bright clothes among the leather jackets and black jeans, our white skin and curly hair rising from the tan, flat shade of the Uzbeks.

Burrowing through Tashkent in the underground train with everyone pointing and giggling or just plain staring directly at us through unblinking furrows, the attention was getting to me. When they stared at us I stared at my shoes and pretended like I was an Uzbek born and bred. I copied everyone by slouching and pouting and that didn't work

The shy man in the purple gown — Tashkent.

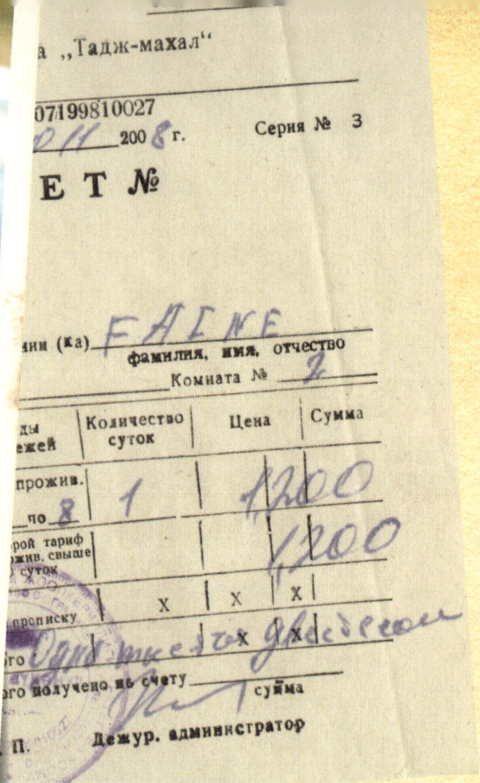

а „Тадж-махал"

07199810027

11 200 8 г.   Серия № 3

Е Т №

ии (ка)   FAINE
          фамилия, имя, отчество
                Комната № 2

ды ежей	Количество суток	Цена	Сумма
прожив. по 8	1	1200	
рой тариф жив. свыше суток			1200
	X	X	X

прописку

го получено на счету   сума

П.   Дежур. администратор

so I cursed my damn skin colour and facial features and focused on my shoes. But even they didn't fit in. Even my shoes, my white Japanese-designed sneakers, were out of place beside the imitation basketball shoes and thick black boots. And then there was Dad, infuriating and not even thinking about being anything but a stranger and shooting some ogling locals little cute waves across the train carriage. Then some brave individual sidled over and asked where we were from and Dad pulled out his usual routine to this question; he clamped his hands together in front of his chest and his feet together at his ankles and he sprung up and down, bouncing around, saying, 'Australia! Kangarooooooooo! [then tapping himself on the chest] Papa Kangaroo, and [now motioning toward me and then cradling an imaginary baby in his arms] baybee kangaroo …!' I rolled my eyes and sunk further down into the train seat.

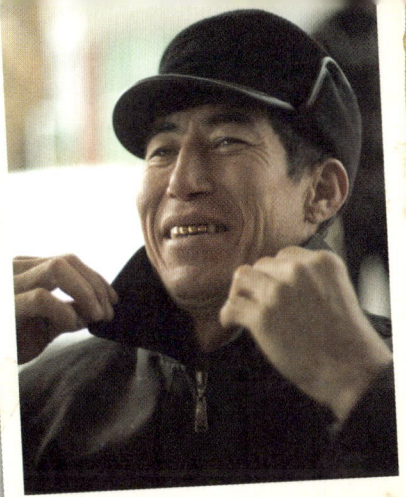

A literally priceless smile, Tashkent, Uzbekistan.

In the former Russian states that are fixated on strong masculine images, Dad's dicking around was met with riotous laughter, back slaps and animated handshakes. And while he basked in the attention of every set of eyes in the carriage, I sat to the side wishing I wasn't travelling with a father who was so blatantly and unashamedly foreign. Just for one day I wanted to walk down the street and escape the stares of little children and the pointing. Just be there to watch, not to be watched and just stumble free around Tashkent and wave to all my Uzbek friends that I've known for years, and have them glance up and nod their heads to me in return, and then I'd feel like I was really truly 'experiencing' this place. Because right now, trading 'You. Know. Nicole Kidman?' and 'You. Know. Skippy?' for smiles and thumbs-up, wasn't doing much for me.

The train ride came to an end and we exited the station to find ourselves in Tashkent's old city – the way things were before the Soviets came. This is the Tashkent where my great-grandmother had grown up. These dirty little lanes disappearing around corners and narrowing in on themselves had been her city, her home. We were walking in her footsteps, squeezing between the mudbrick walls crumbling at the edges and kicking through the rubble strewn across the street and the houses all draped in wires. Children happily hauled school bags home for lunch in the brown muddy suburb and one day long ago, those children were my family heading home to eat *plov* and greasy lunches.

And we continued on and somehow ended up heading through this massive food market with golden teeth flashing out from mouths as they opened to advertise their goods.

After a while the market died out and a small shop selling roasted dumplings appeared. You could smell the big, fatty, juicy dumplings that squirt all kinds of funky oils when you break the doughy seal, and the oil squelches all down your front and across the plate and when you're done you look down and see all that gunk and oil and sort of wish you hadn't looked down, because now you're wondering, 'If that's what I left on the plate, what does it look like inside my belly?' You feel a little sick, but it's food and you have to eat a few more dumplings or else you just would never eat anything, except *plov*. So you scrunch a few more in your mouth and stop looking at what splurts out.

We got to the small shop selling roasted dumplings and there was one big table out the front with a bunch of tea-sipping Uzbeks sitting around loudly. They called out to us and waved hysterically and friendly for us to join them and screamed with laughter when we headed to their table. They jumped up and pulled and offered chairs, calling for cushions from inside. Tea bowls were snatched comically out of hands halfway towards eager mouths, and given to us until our own tea arrived a minute later. Again we were the centre of attention and we fumbled through the usual sign language of 'Kangarooo!' and 'Uzbekistan … biyootiful!', me cringing just a little. More people appeared and there was now a fair group of Uzbeks standing by and watching us eating and communicating. We blundered along hardly understanding anything but the literally golden smiles of the people around us. They muttered, murmured, screamed and yelled things at us, motioning and signalling with sweeping arms until we understood and gave an answer like 'Ohhhh, me? I'm a student' to their repeated words and signals and gestures.

We stuck around sharing confused conversation for a while and they cracked up with laughter when I pulled my camera out to take a photo of one of the men sitting quiet and silent at the other end of the table. He wore a skullcap and purple gown streaming all the way down from his shoulders to his knees. He stared shyly into the middle distance, uncomfortable as I took his picture and the other men roared and tipped his hat out of place and roared louder when I showed them the photo on the back of the camera. The gowned man grew more and more uncomfortable, completely shunning the attention and turning his back on the madness surrounding his photo on my digital screen. The crowd grew larger so that people were no longer coming to see what the foreigners were doing, but what the crowd was about. And the people shuffled and pushed to glimpse the tiny camera screen. Hands reached out for the camera to steady it or turn it in their direction to glimpse the awkward image of the purple-gown man. And every time a new set of hands pawed my camera to get a glimpse, they would stare for a second or two, adjust their eyes and pull their head closer for a better look, and then they would call something out to the purple-gown man and then back off and give a little 'yoop-hei!' in excitement. The crowd was getting really quite big and then the three waitresses working in the fatty dumpling restaurant came out onto the street where this mob had sprawled around us. The oldest waitress tapped me on the shoulder, grabbed Dad by the arm and all three of them posed for a photo, heads cocked to one side and smiling at the camera. The youngest one who was really a bit cute had this great glaring gap in her teeth right at the front and she strained to contain her ruined smile within her lips. The growing group of men cheered and cajoled and joked around, trying to force her to smile. She was so awkward and shy with her closed-lip pout and her cute pointy nose. Her apron picked up dumpling dust as it swept along the floor. The noise grew and I ducked inside to take a quick shot of the young pretty waitress behind the stalls of food. She nodded and posed when I pointed at the camera but she still hid her gap behind her lips. At the last second she shyly dipped her eyes away from me and down at her fresh batch of dumplings. Her flushed cheeks went even redder and her eyes avoided mine.

When I came back outside there was a serious gang of people and some boys pushed up to the front and shoved camera phones in my face and signalled to me to stop still. The phones clicked and they slipped away.

This was all getting a bit ridiculous and Dad and I made eye contact. This attention was too much even for him.

We headed back over to the table where our first tea-sipping friends sat, shook hands with a few choice people, their hands hovering just slightly over their hearts as they stood and bowed to shake our hands and see us off, their golden teeth flashing once more from their mouths. And then we skirted away, out of the swelling crowd and took a breath of fresh air.

Hisobvaraq, account, счет № 10314260

Sana Date Дата	Kirim Income Приход	Chiqim Expenditure Расход	Qoldiq Balance Остаток	Imzolar Signatures Подписи
12.11.08	$500	нал. $500		

перечат долларов сша

12.11.08

PU

← 38

12.11.08

The Khast Imam mosque
in Tashkent.

90

В О
К Н

КВИТА

Приня

для за

М

За что

Сумма
прописы

М.П.

5126576 7

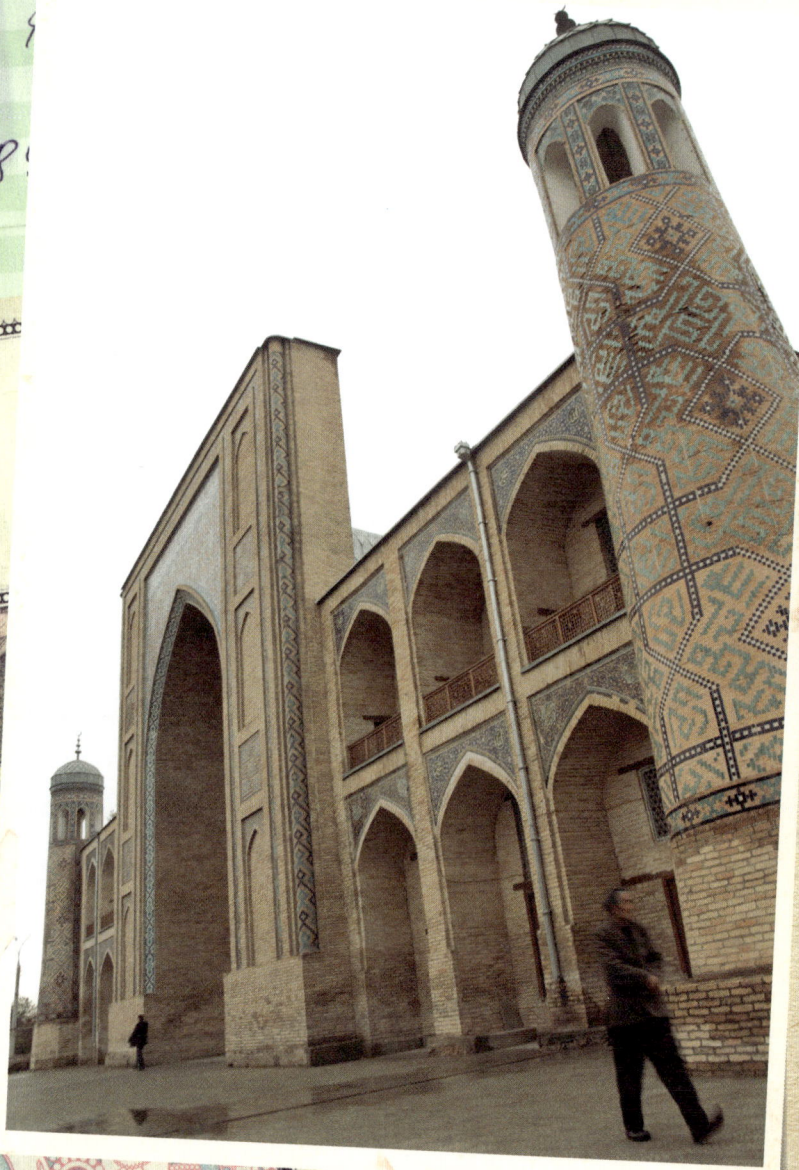

...и сумму принял

...подписей: ст. бухгалтера или бухгал-

ЎЗБЕКИСТОН РЕСПУБЛИКАСИ МАРКАЗИЙ БАНКИ

28 | Visalotto

Here are the rules of the silliest game you can play – Visalotto. Go to a wonderful remote historic city. Spend all your time standing in queues, waiting in travel agencies, arguing with bank clerks. Try not to scream while your exploring time is eaten by mindless bureaucracy.

The single most frustrating thing that happened on our entire trip was securing visas, especially for Central Asia. Getting permits for Ping to go through China was a nightmare, made worse by the Olympics. But that was nothing compared to the former Soviet republics of Kyrgyzstan, Uzbekistan and Turkmenistan – and also Iran – that seem to make it so hard to get a visa it is as if they do not really want you to visit.

A backwards jigsaw is the best way to describe it. Follow closely, this gets complicated and is best done in front of a map. No visas are available at any border crossings under any circumstances. Turkmenistan does not issue visas unless you already have the visa for the next country you are going to. In our case this was Iran, which insists you state exactly the date you want to enter and leave as well as the exact border crossings intended to be used. But this will be dictated by the Turkmen. Catch 22. The Uzbeks have an embassy in Bishkek. But to get there you need a Kyrgyz visa which is only issued in Beijing or Urumqi. Applying for any visa can take weeks of delay, risking a breach of the time limits in the country where you are stuck. That can mean deportation and confiscation of your car. If any link in the chain does not work, the entire trip may have to be abandoned. Horror stories are common. Heard the one about the Dutch biker jailed in Turkmenbashi for breaching their visa rules? Or the Germans driving home from Pakistan arrested at the Iranian border?

In the months before leaving home, I telephoned the Iran Embassy in Canberra dozens of times, but only once did anybody answer, a charming man who told me the name of the only officer at the embassy who could help, what time to ring and a private number to call. At the suggested time I rang that number nonstop for half an hour. No one answered. I called every day for two weeks. I sent countless emails. I wrote letters. I downloaded forms from the internet, but the information I needed was not there. An Iranian visa only has a three-month life span so a visa issued in Canberra in June would expire before we got anywhere near Iran. I sent emails to the Iran Touring Car Club and to several travel agents I found online – none of whom ever replied. I gave up.

It is not possible to get visas for any of the 'stans in Australia as there is no diplomatic representative for any of the Central Asian Republics. I was quoted GBP150 per country plus a GBP500 fee per person by a UK-based visa service, which required our passports be couriered to London for a month as well. To pay more than $2000 was absurd, so we decided there must be a way of doing it on the road, and left it to fate.

In September when we got to northern Laos, I started to plan the rest of the trip. Commandeering a huge dining table to spread out enormous maps, it took all day to figure out a strategy. How would we get from Mongolia to Turkey? We could either go north into Siberian Russia and through Kazakhstan, or on the Silk Road through Kyrgyzstan, Uzbekistan, Turkmenistan to Iran. The Silk Road seemed complex but doable, although the dictatorship of Turk-mad-menistan would always be a lottery. I still wanted to go through Kashgar, but the Chinese at this stage were refusing permission. I drew up a flow chart with several variables: Plan A, B and C.

Iran seemed likely whichever way we went and I learned that it can take months to secure a visa. Online, www.IranianVisa.com seemed professional and we nominated Tashkent in Uzbekistan as the collection point and kept travelling, fingers crossed.

So much could go wrong. If they found out I was a journalist, if they googled my name, we would be refused a visa for Iran and get stuck in Tashkent. We could not go back to China and would overstay our Uzbek visa if we waited for Kazakh visas. Afghanistan to the south was not an option. If we wanted to go to Siberia, we needed visas for Russia. But Russian visas must be applied for where you live, back in Australia.

It was a nightmare.

The Turkmenistan embassy in Tashkent is a high-walled mansion in an otherwise plain residential street. Two armed soldiers lounge around along with a barrel-chested Turkmen security guard. Best practice is to arrive early and put your names on the guards' list. The embassy opens at ten, so we get there at eight, but still are numbers twenty-one and twenty-two.

We come back at ten to find a glum impatient crowd outside. Some are Uzbeks, but most are travellers on their second or third visit to the embassy. All have horrific tales of frustration and inefficiency to recount as we wait literally hours in the cold. Here we are in Tashkent, and our precious time is spent standing in a street staring at a gate. Around lunchtime we are finally allowed through and meet a bored, gold-toothed, Russian-speaking embassy staffer, who waves his hands pointlessly and offers no information we can understand whatsoever. I begin to realise the enormity of the task of getting through these arrangements without being able to speak Russian. There is no information in English at all. Again I feel self conscious and arrogant for expecting the world to speak English.

The Silk Road guidebook recommends Sitara Travel. Kristina is deputised as our fixer, and over the next week becomes our new second-best friend. Kristina comes back with us and translates as we are told it will take at least two weeks for even a transit visa. Her explanations to the man behind the counter that this will be after the expiration of our Iranian visas are met with a shrug of his shoulders and an offer that we return once we have Iranian visas in our passports.

Can it get worse? That night we get the email with the magic code for the visa for Iran, so next morning after half an hour waiting at a locked door outside the Iranian Embassy we see a man who lets us in; to see a man who tells us to wait; for a man who tells us we can apply for the visas – but not today. Nothing can be done and he shuts the window. An urgent email to Hamid in Tehran gets no reply. Next day, the man behind the same counter explains there was a public holiday in Iran and now our code has arrived but we cannot pay for our visa in US dollars because Iran does not recognise the United States, nor will they accept Uzbek currency. Instead, we will have to pay with euro. I have no idea where I can get euro in Tashkent.

Just like the man selling steak knives says, 'But wait, there's more.' Back to Sitara Travel, and Kristina sends me across town to the Central Bank of Uzbekistan. Like Arlo Guthrie's 'Alice's Restaurant', and without exaggeration, this is what happens. I have to painstakingly make my way

- through the security guards
- to an enquiry counter
- then a service desk
- then upstairs to foreign banking to a woman receptionist
- who sends me to see a clerk
- who tells me to queue before a woman at a desk
- who listens to my request and
- sends me to a senior banker who gives me a piece of paper to
- present to a counter in another office
- where I am referred to a teller, who speaks English, and invites me to take a seat. We fill in five forms, all of them different, but all essentially requiring the same information. When I joke that there seems to be a lot of paperwork she rolls her eyes and indicates to me that this is simply how things are done. I am required to open an Uzbekistan bank account and deposit US dollars which get changed to Uzbek Som which then can be exchanged for euro so I can pay the Iranian Embassy.

The bank takes half a day. I feel like screaming. Jack wonders if I have been kidnapped. (I still have an Uzbek bank account.)

With euro in my pocket, we return to the Iranian Embassy to be told that not until the next morning could we see the consul, who would not automatically issue visas but would interview us to ask us some questions, before deciding whether we would be allowed to go to Iran. Next morning, the consul quite charmingly asks us why we want to visit Iran. We explain our drive from Australia to London to him and he nods wisely, and then says it will take one week. I beg his indulgence. 'Why do you want to get to Iran in such a hurry?' I take a chance and say to him, 'Every extra day we can spend in Iran is one day less we need to spend in Tashkent. We would rather spend more time in your beautiful country than here.' He laughs, asks me, 'What is your job?' and, heart in mouth, I spin like a professional and say, 'I am a lawyer.' He nods, smiles, pats our passports, says, 'Very good answer – visa this afternoon,' and we leave the office. The elaborate embossed visas are done that day.

The next morning, back outside the Turkmenistan Embassy, another batch of travellers is waiting and hours pass before our names are called. We have the forms, we have the money, we have the photos, and we have the Iranian visa. We explain everything to the man with gold teeth and he smiles, points to his calendar, counts ten days, points at November 24 and tells us to go. Disaster. If we wait that long we lose our Iranian deadlines and can not possibly get to Paris for Christmas.

Back to Sitara Travel to collect Kristina, then back to the embassy. We wait until every person has been seen and then again see gold-tooth man. Kristina fires off something in rapid Russian, rising to the occasion; sly suggestions are made about extra fees, whatever is required in order to smooth the passage of the Turkmenistan visa. After much discussion, gold-tooth man, wanting to shut the office for the night, assures us that we can apply for our visas now but collect and pay for them at the border near Bukhara. Stupidly, we believe him. Exhausted, heads throbbing, we go away. Another mistake. A very big mistake.

29 | Tashkent

Islam + vodka = Uzbek. Trolley buses, the best flea market ever, a metro station like a Sputnik – this is Tashkent, but no one sees a future.

My Nanna Luba, my father's mother, lived in Tashkent before leaving for the new world around 1923. Walking the streets I pretend that I am in her footsteps. Jack develops an appetite for family history that I struggle to feed. Sadly, she would recognise nothing of what is here now, the Russians and the Uzbeks having rearranged the city to obliterate its past. From our brief visit it is hard to see much of a future either.

Police patrol every intersection and often between them as well. They stop cars at random, extracting bribes and fines under protest from exasperated drivers. The theory is that if you can afford a car you can afford to support the meagre incomes of the police. Trams and trolley buses, crowded and dilapidated, plough through potholed streets; occasionally a latest model BMW or Audi limousine or 4x4 will speed past, often without number plates, immune from regulation. Motorbikes and scooters are banned in Uzbekistan. No one can tell us why.

Boulevards laid out on a European scale host imposing facades of ageing apartment blocks, windows sometimes missing like teeth from a smile. Everything is grimy, except when it snows and instantly the mood changes. Very few new buildings are to be found, the Fine Arts Museum a notable and handsome exception. Inside we browse through a superb collection of weavings, costumes, friezes, carvings, doors, saddles, cloaks, robes, jewellery and paintings. There is almost no one else there.

We take a taxi to the flea market. The driver speaks enough English to say, 'Bush, bad; Clinton – Monica, whoo-hoo.' Jack asks him if he is Muslim. 'Musselman here,' he says, pointing to his head, 'Russkie here,' he says, pointing to his heart. 'Putin very good, Russia good now,' he adds, a sentiment echoed several times over. Vladimir Putin has made Russians proud again, reclaiming Russian greatness. 'We were nothing before,' says a businessman I meet at a cafe.

The flea market at Yangiobod is stupendous. It stretches forever, and mixes old and new, junk and jewels. We buy Soviet-era memorabilia, lead soldiers and vintage embroidery. Jack falls in love with some old cameras, particularly an antique wooden apparatus on a large tripod, where you need a cloak to cover your head while the picture is taken. The lens is Zeiss, the price not unreasonable, but we are spooked by a uniformed customs officer who says, '*Nyet*, no, no export,' as we wander around. There are strict rules on removing antiques classified as cultural heritage and he makes me nervous. Room in the car is also becoming tight as we gather more and more crap on our travels.

Turkmenistan, where we hope to go next, has a rule forbidding dirty cars from entering. This is not a joke – it is true. Ping is filthy, still carrying dirt from Mongolia. At the car wash, Daniel introduces himself in perfect American English. He is a lawyer with Coca-Cola and clearly a member of the local elite. 'Things are getting better here, not like in Kyrgyz … they have no hope, should be carved up, with China, Kazakhs and Uzbeks taking bits. Putin is a great leader; Russia was a mess, not now.' When I go to pay for the cleaning, he has beaten me to it. 'You are my guest in Tashkent,' he protests as I thank him. I spend an afternoon looking for snow chains to fit our tyres. None can be found that are big enough.

We visit Chorsu, the old town. Sher, an accountant, befriends us on the train, German not English his second language. My German is basic but we converse. He takes us to the medressa, an Islamic college, and hands us over to an English-speaking host. 'No radical Islam here, but the government forbids the muezzin from even being heard,' he tells us. The call to prayer, the adhan, can be recited in the mosque but not broadcast as it is throughout Islamic countries from Morocco to Malaysia.

We walk through the university campus, take trams around town, marvel at the Kosmonavtlar metro station dedicated to Yuri Gagarin, the first man in space, as elaborate a train station as you will find anywhere. No photos are allowed as it is regarded as a military installation. No photos also at the shrine that houses the oldest Koran in the world, the seventh-century Uthman Quran. Reputedly claimed as spoils of battle by Timur the Lame (Tamerlane) in the fourteenth century, it was pinched by invading Russians in the 1860s from the holy city of Samarkand and then repatriated from Moscow by Lenin to appease Muslim Russians in 1924. A stain that is said to be the blood of the Third Caliph (prophet) is visible on the open page displayed under thick glass. Shivers go down my spine at the sight of something so old, so revered and over which so much blood has been spilled. There are pilgrims visiting as we are there, bowing, wailing and praying in front of the enormous deer-skin parchment.

Any Russian we meet is looking to emmigrate. 'There is no future here, no life. I cannot trust Uzbeks,' says one Russian who has lived here all his life. 'They hate us and we hate them. I have no respect for any of them, not Uzbeks, not Kyrgyz ... but the police put you in prison if you speak out. No one bothers to vote in the elections. Why vote? Why bother? Nothing works, people don't care. Everyone is corrupt, some people have all the money, the rest of us are poor. How can I go to Australia? Is it good there?'

КВИТАНЦИЯ № 695

200 8 г.

Сумма

70$

ollars

Some Uzbeks have no
Asiatic features

Jon's grandmother
lived in a street like
this in Tashkent.

30 | Samarkand and Bukhara

Fantasies come to life in the twin jewels of central Asia. Your intrepid travellers sample medressa, minarets, scorpion pits and caravanserai, learn of beheadings and torture, and at last appreciate the allure and mystery as well as the elegant beauty of the Silk Road.

From Jon on www.MelbourneToLondon.com

So, this is it ...

I love walking down the ancient cobbled streets of the old city in these two towns, towering fifteenth-century city walls to the side and twelfth-century soaring minarets in the background. Weather-beaten intricately carved double doors keep secret the courtyards within, as I wonder who else has wandered along these stones? What scenes have these streets witnessed, what ordinary and extraordinary things have been happening here for literally thousands of years?

Uzbekistan is as culturally rich and friendly a spot to visit as you can find. Once the infuriating visa system is negotiated (only Turkmenistan is worse ... but I will spare you all the details) the rewards are here. We are in Bukhara for a few days while visas are sorted before we can drive to Iran via Turkmenistan.

Many of the historic sites in both these Silk Road cities have been restored to something approaching their former glory. The effect on visitors is to transport you back to whichever period in the last 2000 years you choose. Mosaic cladding on soaring minarets, carpet traders in every niche of an ancient medressa, torture chambers and steep city walls are all topped off by kebabs at every turn, steaming plov meals, the crispest naan bread and aromatic tea with every meal. Sum-sa – potato-filled pastry (forgive me if I have mashed the spelling) – and guma – parcels, still warm from the clay oven, filled with a mix of chilli and barley – make a great snack while wandering.

But most of all the Uzbeks are very, very friendly. We can barely walk ten steps without being asked where we are from, and having the sort of superficial conversation that limited common language restricts you to. And not always in the name of commerce, although that rich tradition is well exercised too. Fake antiques and 'hand made by my grandmother' embroidery abounds, as well as exquisite calligraphy and gilt-adorned Koran pages ready for framing.

From Jack on www.MelbourneToLondon.com

Fake boobs

I didn't like Bukhara or Samarkand. I found the recreations of the ancient cities like someone who has had plastic surgery. The blemishes that are so important to character had been shined, polished and fixed to an uncomfortable and false perfection. That aside, the Uzbek people were the friendliest we've met this side of Sumatra.

What he originally wrote was that '… the recreations of the ancient cities were like breast implants … impressive but fake' But he toned it down for the blog. It should have stayed like that.

The mood changes as soon as we quit Tashkent. The Uzbeks are charming and not at all as described by the Russians we met in the city. The highway winds along and sometimes across the crazy border, punctuated by a continuous chain of street stalls offering everything from fruit to car parts.

I am bewitched by the ubiquitous felt boots everyone wears, covered by rubber slip-on galoshes. They come in any colour you like as long as it is black. The inserts are of various fit – some ankle high, some calf high, sometimes knee high. They look wonderfully warm and I am about to buy myself a pair in the market when Jack gives me a reality check. 'You look ridiculous, and you'll never wear them again' is his contribution. He is right.

It is about 300ks to Samarkand, and it takes all day. It seems as if we are stopped by security at every intersection. They check papers but sometimes are just curious. The farms are far more prosperous than Kyrgyzstan or Mongolia, the people healthier and happier. The elderly men congregate in cafes and play backgammon, which we have not seen elsewhere until now.

The heavily restored
ancient Bukhara Medressa.

At first we are puzzled at how a nation can be so split between the city and the country. There is almost nothing in common in our experiences of the two. Maybe the impression was formed because we were meeting mostly miserable Russians who, except for the Coca-Cola lawyer Daniel, were unhappy with their lot and that coloured our perception of Tashkent? But if we were travellers around Australia, or the USA, or France, it would be much the same. Paris is not France. New York or LA are not the USA and so on. Why should Uzbekistan be different? It isn't.

Samarkand boasts magnificent domes and minarets, Silk Road signatures, picture-postcard perfect like the Eiffel Tower or the Taj Mahal. At first glimpse it literally takes your breath away. The mosaic tiles glisten in the twilight; the shadows play tricks with perspective. The Registan, a collection of restored, arched fourteenth-century buildings around the showpiece medressa, is the drawcard, a massive complex on three sides creating a huge courtyard or central square. Every nook and cranny is filled with an antique shop, an illuminated scroll calligrapher, souvenir seller or occasionally an actual prayer room. For a modest bribe the soldiers slip you through a steel grille where a slightly dangerous set of ancient, worn, winding internal stairs takes you high to the narrow top of a minaret for a spectacular view over the town.

We joke to each other about a *Chaser*-style stunt, bringing a ghetto blaster to the top of the tower and broadcasting the Rolling Stones or Green Day, instead of the call to prayer. Would they stone you in the square below? Would anyone think it was funny?

Tombs of important figures in Islamic history are dotted around the complex, people who Westerners have never heard of but whose history makes sense when you are here. The tombs of Tamerlane, his two sons and Ulugbek (Tamerlane's grandson but himself also a great leader and inspirational Uzbek hero) are all preserved and venerated. But Samarkand's history goes back to well before the Registan, and we learn of the Samanids, Karakhanids, Seljuq Turks, Mongols and Genghis Khan, who all swept through and conquered what was for hundreds of years one of the greatest cities on earth. It was here that astronomy and algebra were developed by Islamic scholars whose knowledge was later exported to Europe in time for the Enlightenment. It was within these labyrinthine walls that mathematics, astronomy, philosophy and theology were taught to generations of scholars whose libraries were the envy of the known world. It was in these buildings that the pillars of modern civilisation were negotiated and argued hundreds of years ago. Timur's empire spread from Turkey and Syria in the west to Kashgar in the east. His conquests in a succession of bloody uncompromising wars included Pakistan and all of what is now called Central Asia. He pillaged and plundered his way through the neighbourhood, slaughtering and raping, demanding that his soldiers decapitate their foes and return their severed heads to him as proof of their victories. But although the national hero of the Uzbeks dominates Samarkand, it houses other sites for pilgrims including Shah-i-Zinda, the tomb of Qusam ibn-Abbas, who was the cousin of the Prophet Mohammed and the tomb of the Old Testament prophet Daniel on the riverbank. Each is a mosaic jewel in its own right – and together they overwhelm the senses.

Jack accuses me of being dismissive of history as we wander around the town. I refuse to become one of those tourists who walks with the guidebook open on the relevant page declaiming the details of every ruin. I hate missing out on an experience because I have my nose buried in the book instead of looking, smelling and feeling the surrounds. Besides, there is only so much I can absorb, only so many tombs, sarcophagi, ancient frescoes or flying buttresses that I can cope with and process. I argue a guidebook is exactly that – a guide, not a set of instructions. I do not feel compelled to tick off every site on the list. He seems annoyed. We need time apart.

Dinner is interrupted by a bear of a man at the adjoining table who insists we share his vodka. He pours us a glass each, and arms enlaced, we toast Pushkin, the nickname everyone has given Jack. The Russian playwright was famous for his curly hair and since Jack has been cultivating dreadlocks as we travel, something quite unseen in this bit of the globe, the impact is considerable. As we try to eat our meal, the generous neighbour and his table of similarly huge men in black leather coats, their work-worn hands never without a glass, threaten to take over our table too. We share another drink and then make our excuses.

Next morning we head off to Bukhara, the second most famous but less accessible of these two legendary Silk Road cities, scene of famous beheadings and battles for trade routes over thousands of years. The countryside is instantly less fertile and we can feel the desert approaching. It is 300 kilometres, much of it along the valley between the mountains to the north and the desert to the south. We should collect our Turkmenistan visas here and then make our way across the Karakum Desert through the oil- and gas-rich dictatorship, to Ashgabat, then Iran. If we had more time we would make the 1500-kilometre round trip to the Aral Sea, the once vast vanishing waterbody that separates Kazahkstan in the northeast from Uzbekistan, to witness first-hand the famous degraded irrigation land that is one of the greatest environmental catastrophes on earth. But we would need an extra week, a luxury not available to us. It is infuriating to think we are so close, closer than we will ever be, but because of all the time lost and wasted in border and visa hassles along the way, we miss out on a unique experience, one of the most exotic sights in the world, huge fishing trawlers marooned miles from any water.

Bukhara is a gem of a place. Although Samarkand is beautiful, Bukhara has soul. The massive mosaic-covered domed medressa, soaring Kalon minaret and stunning mosque complex is almost empty of tourists. The relaxing central square boasts a swan-filled pond and ancient gnarled mulberry trees shading coffee shops and restaurants. Add to it a fortress unlike any other, the imposing, magnificently preserved fifth-century Ark and a prison with a real bug pit, and this is about as good as the Silk Road gets. To enhance its allure, the old city is still lived in, the buildings less restored and less tampered with than Samarkand, people going about their daily lives amongst the few tourists around. As we wander the back streets and alleyways small children stare and follow, Pied-Piper like. They call out, laugh, chatter and point, dancing and chasing in our wake. The market boasts endless stalls selling gold, jewels and silver adornments for camels and horses and the obligatory carpets, displayed for locals and the few tourists alike. Like Kashgar, it is precisely what we have come to see, to experience.

The rebuilt temples at Samarkand and
Bukhara felt contrived and characterless.

The Samarkand temples were restored under Lenin to appease the local Muslims and gain their support.

An Uzbek pop star shooting a film clip in Bukhara's old city.

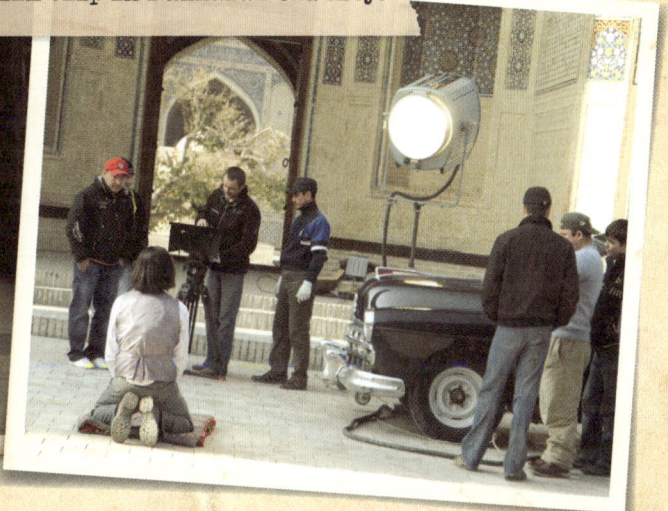

31 | Who Can You Trust?

Is the man in a uniform the most honest or the least trustworthy in central Asia?
Who can we turn to for help? And who can be believed?

Uzbekistan Airways flight 1328 is about to leave Bukhara airport in Western Uzbekistan. I am pacing anxiously up and down the ramshackle building, scanning the faces of the departing passengers. Most of them are in uniforms, military and police, huge wide-brimmed hats with enormous badges above double-breasted brass-buttoned jackets bedecked with medals and insignia in the Soviet style. Jack and I are looking for someone we can give our passports to. In the next few minutes we have to gamble using our passports as chips. We have to find someone we trust, or do a frantic round trip of more than 1000 kilometres on terrible roads all the way back to Tashkent. I cannot believe we are in this situation – even thinking about trusting total strangers not just with our passports but US$200 cash as well! How did we let it get to this?

That afternoon, standing on the ramparts of the fifth-century Ark in the Registan, it seemed our logistical tussles were all but over and the worst of our hassles behind us. We had been to the torture chamber and infamous bug pit at the Zindon where in 1842 English military emissary Colonel Charles Stoddart and his supposed rescuer Captain Arthur Conolly were dragged after years of captivity to be publicly beheaded. Their mission 170 years ago was to assure Emir Nasrullah Khan that the English invasion of nearby Afghanistan would not spread to his lands. The Emir was clearly not impressed, the story being that he was insulted that only middle-ranking officers were sent to pay the Queen's respects. The damp, fetid dungeon that was their home reminded us of the scorpion-infested grave in one of the Indiana Jones films. As always, real life was worse than anything Hollywood could dream up.

We had wound our way through the mosques and mausoleums, medressa and bazaars. We negotiated with blacksmiths over decorative engraved steel knives in elaborate hand-tooled leather scabbards, were no doubt ripped off by elderly gap-toothed women who claimed to have hand-embroidered intricate patterns on colourful fabrics, and marvelled at peasant-style silver jewellery with turquoise and lapis inserts. Sipping sweet tea and almost cracking our teeth on peanut bars brittle with honey and sesame seeds, we spent an hour chatting with other travellers. We scooped up smooth, fresh dips onto endless plates of still warm, soft, round bread.

Our homestay was up a narrow winding alley in the Jewish quarter. As we walked home the night before we had heard prayers coming from the historic synagogue, and invited ourselves in. The gatekeeper asked in Russian if we were Jewish. I smiled and said 'Shalom' and hoped that worked. We borrowed yarmulkes, plopped them on our greasy unwashed hair, in Jack's case dreadlocked and stiffly poking out like a hedgehog. I laughed as the skullcap wobbled precariously as he walked. We took a seat in the tiny room, leaning against the whitewashed wall, and immediately were offered a prayer book. The siddur was dog-eared and the spine loose, and I started to recognise the prayers of Ma'ariv, the evening service, even though it must have been thirty years since I regularly attended synagogue in Melbourne. How these things are imprinted onto our soul!

There was a bare quorum of ten males present, and one of those was a sullen teen playing on his mobile phone and taking no notice whatsoever of the service. Most if not all the others seemed ancient beyond belief. Jack whispered to me that it was his first visit to a synagogue except for his cousin's bat mitzvah! I felt a sudden obligation, somewhat belatedly, to educate him on the etiquette and protocols, but immediately realised the futility. He was totally bored.

The room was square, sparsely furnished and cold. The central raised reading platform, or bima, was carved timber, worn and cracked, painted the same sea-water blue as the doors and windows. The ark, where the Torahs, the scrolls of the law, are stored was dressed with a claret-coloured velvet curtain. A cracked glass framed photo of the Yeshiva Rebbe Schneerson was the only decoration. The New York Lubavitch evangelists would have been delighted.

'If we're lucky someone will ask us home for dinner, and maybe offer you their daughter in marriage,' I quipped to an unamused Jack. We sat and I lip-synched to the prayers for ten minutes until the service was over. The locals tried to quiz us in Russian, then Uzbek, but it seemed no one spoke English.

'Babushka Tashkent,' I offered, explaining that my paternal grandmother lived in Tashkent before leaving for the new world nearly 100 years before. Eyebrows were raised but conversation was impossible. They all drifted away, no hospitality forthcoming. I could barely conceal my disappointment. My assurances to Jack of the inherent hospitality central to Jewish culture were starkly proven wrong. Mongolian peasants in yurts had made us more welcome.

And so next morning, as the mercury roused itself from subzero overnight, we set off again to explore the relics of this jewel of the Silk Road. One final day, before crossing the border to Turkmenistan, of just being tourists in Bukhara. I had dreamt of this for thirty years. We must make the most of it.

We sometimes went days between phone calls, and each ring made me tense – there was always the possibility of a family crisis back home or maybe another ABC radio interview. No one else called. So when my phone rang it meant problems.

'Is Kristina from Sitara Travel, there is problem with visas; you come back Tashkent – sorry' was the news. I leaned my elbows on the ancient stones of the ramparts, looking across the domes and roofs as the sun sank to the horizon, and wondered about the incongruity of mobile telephony interrupting my contemplation of the ancient relics all around me.

'Turkmenistan Embassy refuse you transit visa at border and says if you drive for Iran you come to embassy and get visas,' she continued with her lisping Russian-accented English. 'I am sorry, Mr Jon, but they not change mind, even though he said would be okay just last week, go to border, now he say is not okay ...' Her voice trailed off as she sensed my horror and clenched-teeth fury.

I clamped a hand over my other ear and tried to concentrate to understand despite the scratchy line and her accent. Was she just trying to scam me for money? Did the embassy want a 'special' fee? Did we really need to backtrack for the first time in nearly five months of solid travelling? Was there any other way? Jack was trying to listen in on the conversation sensing this was something other than a social call.

Getting visas was driving me nuts. We needed a Turkmen visa to get through to Iran.

If we drove back to Tashkent to get them, our Iran visas will have lapsed. Catch 22.

'Maybe go to airport, give passports and money to person on plane and he bring to Tashkent, tomorrow I go to embassy. At night get passports back same way, is okay?' suggested Kristina. 'I find good man in hotel he help you at airport,' she offered. 'I text you details, will be okay, you wait.'

Half an hour later, as we sat under the ancient mulberry trees by the tadpole-heavy pool in the town plaza Lyabi-Hauz, Kristina sent me a text message to go to a hotel nearby and ask for Olim. We walked through the bazaars and caravanserai, the archways converted to tourist shops and populated with carpet sellers. Alongside a 900-year-old mosque an internet cafe advertised its services; each was as busy as its neighbour. A film crew provided distraction for the otherwise bored locals, using the massive arched entrances and exquisite mosaic-covered minaret as backdrop for a music video for a local pop star, running cables and dolly tracks across the cobblestones under the watchful eye of soldiers and police. But even that novelty was no substitute for tourists who have all but disappeared for the winter. 'Special price, too cold, no tourist' was the common lament of the touts trying to entice us into their Aladdin caves.

We found Olim's hotel. He was not there. Instead the man behind the counter, Chadrin, made some hurried phone calls, including to Kristina. He spoke good English and in an earnest and efficient way seemed determined to help. There was only one flight to Tashkent, and it was about to leave. We jumped in Ping and in the darkness, spotlights blazing, raced against time to cross town before the plane departed. We had minutes to spare.

As we arrive at the airport, huge concrete tank traps block the road, but we wind our way through and over gutters to cover the last kilometre to the terminal. I ferret out US$200 from our secret stash in the car and put it in an envelope. The flight has already been called. There are several soldiers and police officers still going through security, and it seems logical to me to ask someone in a uniform to be the courier. Chadrin scoffs and explains they are the most corrupt of all and the worst choice. Women, especially if they look like mothers, he says, would be better. A tall man in an airline uniform comes over and in Uzbek demands to know who we are and what we are doing. Chadrin is no interpreter, and I become increasingly frustrated. We have those conversations where someone says a long sentence in Uzbek, I ask what it means, and he says, 'He said nothing.' There are no more passengers left in the airport terminal.

A young woman who speaks English comes through the swing doors behind the airline counter. She is from the Uzbek Tourist Board and explains her job is to ensure smooth passage for foreigners. I explain our predicament to her. She offers to ask the pilot to be our courier, otherwise I will have to go to Tashkent myself. We wait. The tall man in uniform starts shouting, and Chadrin translates that we are being accused of delaying the plane. The airline boss wants me to pay him to secure what he says is the last seat on the plane. I decide I do not like this individual who has all the hallmarks of a standover merchant.

The pilot agrees to carry our passports but refuses to carry any cash. Jack tells me, unhelpfully, to offer a substantial bribe. I tersely tell him to butt out. He goes outside and sulks. I can hear the noise of propellers cranking over. That I even think this crazy scheme might be worth trying is an indication of how disconnected from reality I have become.

I storm out to the car park and confer with Jack. We decide there is no option but for me to get on the plane. I do not even have a toothbrush. I ask the woman behind the counter if I can buy a ticket to catch the about-to-depart plane. The tall uniformed man starts shouting some more, and is apparently insisting that I pay a supplementary fee, a bribe, in order to get a seat on the plane so late. He wants me to pay the equivalent of A$55 to offload a passenger to make room for me. The standard price of the ticket, according to a sign on the counter, is about A$45. I negotiate with the lady at the counter and buy a ticket, one way only, while the man is still shouting at me. I have not got enough Uzbek money, so she fleeces me on a pathetic exchange rate to US dollars. I am putty in her hands. No one can assure me I will get a seat on the flight back the next night. The tall man keeps shouting, leaning into my face as he does. He wants his A$10, his reward for getting me onto the plane despite it being full. I decide to just completely ignore him, and instead busy myself by making sure Jack is okay with driving back to our hotel in Bukhara and being alone for the day. We have not been apart since we left home. He has not driven anywhere on his own and not much at all since we have been on the wrong side of the road. I start to think of all the things that can go wrong. He cheerfully tells me he is looking forward to some space. I wish he had said he will miss me, but he didn't.

I go through security. All the security guards are shouting, waving their arms, hurrying me up because they want to go home. This is the last flight for the day and I am the last passenger. As I go through the metal detector screen and into the departure lounge, everyone is just sitting around, reading books and going nowhere. So why the rush? Amidst the crowd, I notice three people speaking English. I wander over and introduce myself. They work for the Canadian Embassy in Moscow. One of them is the Deputy Head of Mission, Gilles Breton, touring the former Soviet republics on behalf of his government. He asks me what I am doing and I explain my predicament to him. He laughs as he tells me that the Australian and Canadian governments have an intergovernmental agreement that they will look after each other's citizens, where they can. In all of the former Soviet empire, amongst a couple of hundred million people, if I was to look for the very person who should officially help me, it would be him. He was the ideal courier, but it is too late now. We wait another twenty minutes before we are called to the Ilyushin propeller plane sitting alone in the fog. When everyone has boarded there are three empty seats. So much for the bully, demanding payment to free up the last seat.

Mr Deputy Head of Mission and I shout across the aisle all the way to Tashkent, analysing Putin, Russia, the war in Georgia, Central Asia and global affairs despite the engine roar. My head is throbbing as a stress headache sets in. I have not eaten and need a toilet but the plane has none. We land in Tashkent and there are buses to take us across the floodlit tarmac to the terminal. They are taking forever to leave. We get to the terminal, and it is under renovation. The toilets are locked. I am at risk of wetting my pants. I race from the terminal across the car park and relieve myself on a tree. Midstream a car starts, turns on its headlights and I am caught like a roo in a spotlight. I imagine the headlines back home: 'ABC presenter arrested flashing in Uzbekistan'. Behind me the tarmac is covered with Uzbekistan Airlines' fleet of ancient propeller passenger planes in various stages of being dismantled and cannibalised for parts. I catch a taxi back to the very hotel we left just a few nights before, and, arriving well after midnight, greet the night receptionist by name and even get the same room.

Early the next morning, I go yet again to the Turkmenistan Embassy to yet again put my name in the queue. At seven o'clock in the morning, I am already number nine on the list. After breakfast it is a brisk half-hour walk along Shota Rustaveli Street, past the nineteenth-century apartment blocks and shops, through falling snow and I am at the door at Sitara Travel when they open. Kristina is surprised to see me. She telephones the embassy. There is a long and animated conversation in Russian. She hangs up the phone and laughs.

'Papers is lost … we must again do everything new?' she says. I feel like screaming. We grab a cab and go back to the embassy. We wait outside for hours. Kristina tells me she was born in Tashkent, but soon will be leaving to go to live in Moscow. Her husband has a new job and she will look for work in the travel industry.

'Is Tashkent not a good place to live?' I inquire, already knowing the answer.

'No one wants live here, no good now, not good for Russians, only Uzbeks,' she explains. I learn that although she has lived here her whole life, she knows little Uzbek language and has no Uzbek friends. She insists that is not unusual. The two communities have little to do with each other.

The small group outside the embassy exchange travel tips. There is a backpacker from Singapore hoping to get to Europe overland using trains. I meet a loud Spaniard and his Belgian girlfriend who have driven a van from Europe through Turkey, Iran and Turkmenistan and now want to go back the same way. It is their second day at the embassy. They have been told that they are not allowed a second transit visa through Turkmenistan and must find another route back to Europe. They are intending to try to overturn that decision by appealing to the embassy's sense of fairness. Kristina thinks they are wasting their time. If they have to go another way, the detour through Kazakhstan and Russia is thousands and thousands of kilometres extra.

After hours of stamping our feet and walking in circles to try to stay warm, we are called inside. The same slim harassed man with a mouth full of gold teeth is chain smoking in a tiny room tucked into the side of the driveway. He is almost hidden behind piles of paper that threaten to topple over and bury him at any minute. A large framed portrait of his president dominates the room. Kristina flatters and charms him, flirting outrageously. It works. He scratches about and finds our forms. I produce the passports, withholding the bribe money until it is needed. He never asks for it, instead just telling us to come back at five that evening and we will have our visas. I insist Kristina explains that my flight back to Bukhara – if I can get a seat

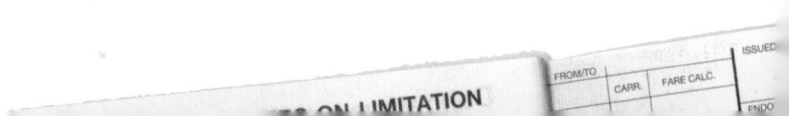

– leaves at six and I will have no time to spare if he is late. He laughs and flashes his gold teeth generously.

We walk through the gated streets to the bank where I change money before we get to the airline head office, a huge building from the 1950s, complete with ripple glass partitions. Sitara Travel has called to book a seat for me on the flight back to Bukhara that night. We are told the plane is full and – of course – I will need to bribe my way aboard. Now I laugh. Payment must be in cash, and the Uzbek som comes in small denomination notes only. My ticket is 56,000 som and I agree to an extra 5000 som as a special fee to the beehive hairdo lady behind the counter.

'This is Uzbek way,' counsels Kristina, who has a fine line in a cynical laugh. She would make a good political analyst.

People carry their money in boxes. No credit card facilities exist. My stack of Uzbek notes for my local trip is the size of a house brick, but people are buying tickets with piles of money that stack up as high as a chair. The higher the stack of notes, the further must be the trip. Europe is a block of notes the size of a loaf of bread. The couple unpacking a shopping trolley must be paying for a family trip to America! The note-counting machines whir ceaselessly.

I wander the streets of Tashkent until late afternoon, buy a box of chocolates to thank Kristina and return with her to collect the passports. The embossed lime-green full-page visas are stuck in, opposite the Iran visas, and I cannot help whooping with relief. The gold-toothed consul laughs.

I race back to the airport and try to buy something to eat. The airport food looks even worse than airport food usually looks. 'Good food?' I plead to the lady behind the counter. 'No, not good,' she admits in deadpan tone, a rare candid moment for anyone in Uzbekistan, or an airport cafe anywhere in the world. I catch the plane back to Bukhara and find Jack relaxed, sitting reading on the bed in our guesthouse as if it was just another day. I am so tired, so stressed and have still not eaten.

JACK WRITES

32 | The Play

Scene I

The following takes place within the confines of the car's cabin somewhere between the Uzbek–Turkmen border and the city of Ashgabat, the capital of Turkmenistan. Radiohead's live album is playing at voice volume, which means that any conversations must take place at a slightly strained level above normal. The landscape of power plants and donkey pumps recedes into hazy fog and Jon is driving, tense and terse after a two-hour wait at the border whilst the customs officials finished their lunch. Jack has just woken from his daily passenger-seat nap and is bored by the ugly desert landscape.

JACK *(yawning, then turning to Jon and speaking at the strained volume)*: If you could have lived in any era of history, any period of time, during a length of, say, twenty years, when and where would it be?

JON *(long pause)*: Umm, I s'pose this era's pretty good ...

JACK: Come on! Don't be boring! Indulge me. Seriously. When would you want to be around? And this era isn't good. It sucks.

Jon doesn't respond, just stares at the road and runs his teeth along the inside of his nail. The Radiohead song hits a long scratchy instrumental. Jack leans forward, picks up the iPod and fiddles with it, forwarding a few songs to a slower, quieter one.

JACK *(now a bit calmer and less strained)*: Are you going to answer ...?

JON: Oh, I don't know ... And besides, what's wrong with this era? We've got better medical practices, standards of living …

JACK (*cutting Jon off*): … Yeah, but that's all bullshit.

JON (*sighing, sick of the weeks of arguing over trivialities*): What? How is it bullshit?

JACK (*ignoring Jon's irritation and happily ploughing on with the hypothetical*): I'd live in America. (*Waiting as if the statement is so profound it has to set in*) Yeah, in America from the 50s through to the 60s. Go and hang with the Beat Generation. Or I'd live around Marco Polo times in Asia somewhere, anywhere in Asia … (*Motions to the country speeding past outside*) See all this when it was real strange and different, something else instead of Coke cans and plastic bags.

Jon stares straight ahead, not showing the slightest interest in the dying conversation. Jack flops back into his seat, giving up on the hypothetical and puts one foot on the passenger dashboard and the other on the door trim.

JON: Can you *not* put your feet up there? You'll break it. How many times do I have to say it? You won't stop till it happens, will you …?

JACK: Relax …

JON: … And don't tell me to relax! Now, can you see if the phone works here, and if it does, can you text your mother?

Jack picks the phone up and after a few seconds turns it off and puts it away.

JACK: Nup, doesn't work.

A long silence follows. The music grows louder and Jack looks at the iPod and can see that Radiohead's droning tones are annoying Jon. He contemplates changing it but leaves it playing just to perturb his father and his gaze returns to the glum grey desert outside the window.

JACK (*after a significant pause*): Well then, how 'bout this one … If you could only listen to one song for the rest of your life, what would it be? *One* song.

JON (*exasperated*): I don't know, Jack …

JACK (*whining*): Come on, Dad!

JON: Jack! I'm trying to drive and it's not easy, all right?

JACK: Come on! One song, Jon! Think about it … It's gotta be perfect, it's gotta make you cry, dance, sing. It's gotta have something to pep you up and to bring you down. It's gotta …

JON: All right, all right then. (*Pretending to ponder for a few moments*) How about

... umm ... umm ... umm ... (*His mind searches for any song famous enough for him to pass it off as having given it significant thought*) ... How about 'Imagine'?

JACK: 'Imagine'! (*Jack picks up the iPod and starts scrolling through lists of songs*) The Beatles ... How lame ...! Are you serious?

JON: What's wrong with 'Imagine'? And it's John Lennon, not the Beatles.

JACK (*still playing with the iPod and staring at the screen*): I dunno. It's just ... not good.

Jack clicks the iPod, turns the stereo up and the soft chords at the beginning of 'Imagine' ring out.

JACK: See. It's just a bit ... plain.

JON (*with a raise of the eyebrows*): You're an idiot sometimes. You know that?

Jon sighs, then sings along and taps his palm on the steering wheel as the chorus hits. They sit in silence as the rest of the song plays through. Without Jon knowing, Jack has toyed with the settings so that the song repeats itself continuously. As the song starts for a second time, Jon chortles.

JON: Is this a test, is it? To see when I'll get sick of it?

JACK (*with a smirk*): Just thought I'd see if you could live with your decision.

Jack turns the volume up and they both sing along periodically. As the song plays through for a third time both Jack and Jon stare fixated at the road, wondering how long the other can bear listening to the same song.

JON: Have you looked at the map of Ashgabat? Do you know where we're going? Where we're staying?

JACK: Nope.

JON: Well ... Can you? And look for something a bit nice. I'm sick of cold showers.

Jack forages for the guidebook, finds it and flicks through to the map of Ashgabat city centre. Jon furrows his eyebrows and tries to block out the fourth repeat of 'Imagine'.

JACK: Ashgabat's fairly big, and there's heaps of hotels. How much do you want to spend?

JON: Well, how much are places?

JACK: Well, it depends on what you want.

JON (*growing agitated*): Well, that depends on how much things are!

JACK (*through clenched teeth*): But it depends on what you want!

JON (*breaking out*): Oh for God's sake! Just choose something. (*Then remembering the Tashkent fiasco when they stayed the first night in flea beds by following Jack's directions*) No, no, no ... read it out to me.

JACK: It's all right, it's all right. I can do it. I'll find somewhere. Hot shower? That's all?

JON (*fed up*): Oh just choose something ...

JACK (*flicking back and forth between pages of the guidebook and muttering map placements to himself*): Relax ...

Before Jon can say it, Jack mocks him in a high-pitched voice.

JACK (*mimicking in a whiney voice*): Don't tell me to relax ...!

Jon exhales and stops at the first traffic light in outer Ashgabat.

Scene II

Jon and Jack are arriving on the outskirts of Ashgabat and they don't yet have a hotel. 'Imagine' is playing for the umpteenth time yet neither person will admit defeat and change the song, and surrounding them is the usual tension that comes when entering a large city. Jack is frantically scouring the Ashgabat city centre map and snapping easily, his eyes following his index finger which is scanning the street map. Jon is silent and focused, but boiling beneath the calm exterior – he is tight and stressed. His true state is given away by his red knuckles gripping the wheel and the veins throbbing in his neck.

JACK (*splaying his arm back and forwards to the left*): Yes! Yes! Yes! Turn left!

JON: It's one way.

JACK: Oh fuck ...

JON (*calm but forceful*): Which way now?

JACK: Okay, ummm. Right. (*slowly, drawn out as if unsure*) I think ...

JON (*slightly aggravated*): I don't need a *think*, Jack. I need to know *which way*?

JACK (*just as uncertain*): Yeah ... go ... um, okay. Go ... right ... then.

Jon rolls his eyes and pleads for inner strength then turns the wheel to the right and his eyes, a picture of concentration, dart from the road to the mirrors to the hotels whizzing past and back again.

JON: Jack! Where am I going?

JACK (*grimacing as he traces his index finger across the map of Ashgabat*): Euh, We ... um ... gotta do a U-turn. Back the other way.

JON (*taking it in his stride*): Okay then ... look for a safe place for a U-turn.

'Imagine' comes to an end and then starts again a few cherished seconds of silence later. Jon indicates then pulls off a dangerous U-turn, accompanied by an orchestra of honking horns.

JON (*to the other motorists*): Yeah, yeah, yeah. I know it was bad. All right, all right! Stop being precious!

JACK: Okay. Nice ... Go straight then turn left.

Jon turns left.

JACK: Oh shit ... umm ... I just saw *that* street sign ...

JON (*drawn out*): And ...?

JACK: And we're in *that* street (*he motions up and down the street with a wave of his hand*). I thought ... you see ... there's *that* fountain (*indicating to the right*) ... and we kinda did that U-turn (*pointing with his thumb behind them*) ... and it sorta, well ... it confused me ... a bit.

JON (*not quite shouting, but close to bursting after a good half-hour driving in crazy Turkmen traffic*): Do you know *where* we are? *Just* tell me! Where? Am? I? Going!?

JACK (*fumbling, stuttering*): Okay, okay ...! Turn around and then, and then, um ... then, we're sweet. I know where we are. It's all good.

Fuming, Jon turns the car around with much effort as the last chorus of 'Imagine' begins.

JACK: All right, the hotel is on *this* street. It's okay, it's cool. Relax ...

JON: Jack! Don't tell me to relax!

Jack retreats as far toward the passenger door as he can go and buries himself in study of the map of Ashgabat. Jon scours the street signs and starts methodically calling out any street or building name he sees. 'Turkmenistan Ministry of Environment' and then 'Turkmenbashi Museum' and then ...

JACK: Yeah, yeah, yeah. All right. Okay. Thank you. I have eyes. You don't need to read it! Now keep going straight.

They drive another few seconds in silent scavenge, eyes peeled and glaring at building names, flickering, catching and focusing on each billboard just long enough to read the words before racing along to the next one. 'Imagine' winds up and as it starts again Jon smashes the off button on the stereo, killing the piano intro mid chord. Jack smiles triumphantly.

JACK *(not sure whether to be victorious or mocking)*: What? Couldn't take it?

JON *(not playing along)*: Cut the shit. Where are we? And where are we going?

JACK *(jumping and pointing, caught off-guard whilst gloating)*: There it is! Just there. *(Pointing over his left shoulder)* Just went past it – it's on the left. Just there. See it? 'Ashgabat Hotel'.

Jon screeches to a frenetic stop and stamps the hazard switch. Glancing over his left shoulder he brazenly launches the car across several lanes and into the driveway of the plush hotel owned by the former president's son. Jack breathes relief, plants the book on the dash and follows Jon into the lobby. Jon stands stiffly upright at the front desk waiting impatiently for the blonde Russian receptionist who is jabbering on the phone in a hushed tone. He raps a pen on his free hand and stares. Jack slouches and plants his elbows on the desktop, cocks his head to one side and looks at his father.

JACK: If you could be any animal, like *anything*, even one that's extinct, like a dinosaur or a dodo, what would you be …?

The strangest city on Earth;
Ashgabat, Turkmenistan

Just one of the countless statues of
the former President of Turkmenistan,
Niyazov Turkmenbashi

33 | Turk-mad-menistan

Jack wrote on www.MelbourneToLondon.com

The Weirdest Place on Earth

Turkmenistan is a tiny country flooded with oil and run by chubby round-faced despots who have built glorious gold monuments of their chubby round faces that gleam and glisten in the harsh desert sun. There is one statue in the capital Ashgabat that reigns supreme above the city of the former president for life, Niyazov, who died in 2006 and it rotates (that's right, it rotates) so that the sunlight is always cast across his gluggy cheeks and fat features.

There are border crossings and then there are border crossings. The Uzbek to Turkmen crossing at Farab is among the worst we endure. Alongside a dry river bed in an open plain, rocks and saltbush as far as we can see, we cruise up to the Uzbek boom gate. They stamp us out in a flash, barely looking at us. A stream of humanity, mostly very round women holding umpteen children and pushing broken prams, is queuing along a barbed-wire race, not unlike the facilities at the MCG to protect the umpires from being pelted as they vacate the field.

The Turkmenistan side of no man's land is dominated by a single building, two storeys, but about the size of a suburban railway station. It is teeming with people, moving around between the different doors and a cluster of ancient caravans perched on barrels to the side, all under the watchful eyes of camouflage-suited soldiers carrying enormous guns. We park Ping and wander in. There is utter chaos. People are shouting, pushing, begging and cajoling half-a-dozen bored, smoking, half-uniformed officers through little half-shut windows and across counters, the noise level and general clatter totally distracting. There is no sense of where to start or who to see, no signs or queues. Light globes dangle from broken fittings, electrical wires poke unprotected from sockets, broken chairs are discarded in corners and desks propped up on upended buckets instead of legs cradle unsteady mountains of papers that seem about to fall onto the filthy floor. Pigeons nest in the ceiling. I lose count of the different people we see to try to get our papers in order, but several hours later just as one serious young soldier stamps our passports at last, and we jump into the car to go through the boom gate, they all go off for lunch. We are sitting in the car, engine running, bonnet nudging the red-and-white-striped pole and the soldiers walk away, leaving one solitary nervous guard who refuses to lift the boom. I show him our stamped passports; he shrugs his shoulders and turns away. I rant and rave, raise my voice, go back inside looking for someone, anyone, who will tell him to let us through but there is no one in the entire building. Jack is laughing at me as I spin myself into a frenzy and tells me to chill. Nothing makes me more determined than being told to chill, so I waste another half an hour knocking on doors and being told 'Nyet' by everyone I find. Beaten into submission, Jack vindicated, much to his delight, we picnic on tinned sardines and water and kick the footy until they all come back to work.

Two burly gorillas in leather coats saunter over and without showing any ID start to go through the car, opening the bags and rifling through the glove box. 'Heroin? Pistol?' they ask, almost showing their disappointment at our answers. One of them lovingly caresses a better than cheap pen he has found in the door storage bin, putting it in his pocket without a second thought. They take long enough to let us know they can make us wait if they want to, then get bored and wave us through. The boom gate goes up, we drive away and we make it into Turk-mad-menistan. It has taken four hours to get across the border. They did not find the secret compartment with the sat phone nor the cash stash. I exhale gratefully. Within the next 20 kilometres we are searched five times at roadblocks and made to pay tolls at little booths for I have no idea what. No one speaks a word of English anywhere, nor any other language that we try – French, German, Arabic all elicit shrugs of indifference. We do not try Hebrew.

Sand and camels remind us that we are entering the desert. The road deteriorates. Astonishingly, cotton farms are on both sides of the road, even though water is scarce. It is 250 kilometres through the Karakum Desert to Mary and the nearby ruins of the ancient biblical city of Merv. A UNESCO World Heritage site, in the eleventh century Merv was dubbed the 'mother of the world' and was the seat of great learning. An ugly Soviet-era town, Mary is the nearest place to stay and we find English-speaking Max running a cheap hotel in the centre of town. There is a wedding in the adjoining restaurant and cars randomly parked all around the hotel. There is no spot to leave Ping without blocking someone in. 'Well, fuck 'em,' says Max as I workshop my dilemma. A caring community is Turkmenistan. I buy 158 litres of diesel for 458,000 Turkmen manat, the equivalent of US$30, which is about A$0.20 a litre and top up the engine oil from a hose that pumps it out free of charge. When I offer to pay for oil the men at the petrol station all laugh at me.

For a World Heritage site, the ruins are a disappointment. A rambling sprawl of barely recognisable remnants of walls, crumbling battlements and a few mausoleums and tombs, the ruins do not capture our attention for long. We decide to head for the capital, Ashgabat, another 350 kilometres away.

34 | Sam

Tired and hot and dry and pissed off because there's some stupid conference on and everywhere's full. We can't find anywhere to sleep so we're bumper-to-bumpering towards this homestay that the guidebook mentions in passing. Shiny new buildings, mostly hotels and banks, shoot up from the decaying roots and shadows of the old city and Dad's got a stomach bug which is making him unbearable. So when we arrive at the homestay, Dad drops dead in bed and I go get him a Snickers bar and then leave him there moaning and groaning and burping and slurping in his own haze of peanut-flavoured pain.

Within two steps from the door of this shabby place we're staying in, two kids yell out to me. The harsh light shines in my eyes, obscuring their faces. They're drunk and swaying from foot to foot and clearly can't see much, but they can see I'm not from around here because I'm wearing clothes with brand names and I don't look at all like a rich local, nor a Russian. They call out to me in English.

'Hay! Where yew fram!?'

I stop and make towards them. 'Awstraliya … You, umm, you know it?' I murmur away scratching my head and wanting to get out of this doomed conversation and explore.

'OOstraliya! What the fuhck are yew dewing here?'

Now, this kid's got a real British accent and he's thrown fuck in the sentence to let me know he speaks good English. I'm sure he's a local of this mouldy slum because he's wearing messed-up thongs and he just looks like that wild, ethnic background of central Asia that's a little bit of every passing horde of rapists and pillagers – Mongol, a little Chinese, Indian, Persian, Turk, Arab and Russian. But why does this kid speak such good English?

'How come you speak such good English? It's impressive,' I say.

'Man, I haf studied overseas for free years. Best free yeahrs of miy life,' and he offers his hand and stumbles a bit because he's quite drunk. 'Call me Sam,' he says as he carefully places his wineglass on a fence post and slaps his right hand down to meet mine and shakes with his free hand hovering light over his heart – central Asian style. Sam laughs. He looks fairly young with bumfluff tickling his cheeks and he wears a wide welcoming smile that's just a little goofy because his teeth clutter his mouth and jut out in different directions. And his nose is all crooked from a break. Strangely, even though his mouth and cheeks spring into a grin his eyes don't sparkle. A constant steady glumness hovers within them.

So, the three of us stand in the last rays of the day's light and Sam and I chat about university and studies. His friend doesn't speak English and is referred to as the 'fuckeeng Russyan'. The fuckeeng Russyan stares blankly at us and fidgets with filthy nuts that he scoops out of his pocket. He spits the shells into the dirt. After a while Sam invites me into his house and we leave his friend on the street. The black soles of Sam's feet kick up dust as he ushers me through his rickety gate.

Sam's house sits in the festering foundations of the old city – the fence falling down and the paint peeling and the stairs crumbling so badly that you have to be really careful when you walk down them so that the tiles don't slip off and you don't fall and break your arse. He nervously shows me through his house and we talk football and surrounding tourist sites and other things that are both boring and nice to talk to a local about. We sit down in his kitchen and make some coffee, bringing it to boil over the stove burner that stays lit all day because gas is cheaper than a match. And we sit in the drab light drifting through the kitchen window and we crack a few jokes and he's smiling this big broad goofy smile that strangely breaks at the end into a pitiful, soul-crushing grimace.

I sit there silently, surveying him in his little world and me in my little world and seeing how our two parallel existences have just forked together in a freak accident. Just like that. And in the aftermath we're really just two strange little beings, two strange little minds wandering the surface of an earth neither of us understands.

And as I'm stirring some sugar in with my coffee there's the first real break in our conversation, and stupid me decides to ask more about his family life.

'So, what's your family like? You live here with your parents? I saw the women's shoes by the door …' And Sam stops stirring his coffee and he looks up at me with those half-Arab, half-Mongol sad, sad brown eyes.

'Yeezsterday, man. Yeezsterday … My mum leyft. Jus' went. But I dunno. She znot reely heppy …' And he hangs his head down into his cup of coffee and instantly a big net of awkwardness has been tossed over us. We're trapped and I can't do anything other than flounder and fluster under this uncomfortable weight pressing down on the conversation. The coffee cools so we can slurp. Only the sound of the gas burning on the stove can be heard throughout the messy little house in the old city. It smells wet and is visibly rotting under foot.

We sit there, neither of us knowing what to say and me planning my exit when this Arab kid barges in the back door yelling into a phone. He absently hugs Sam and nods at me still jabbering on his phone, and Sam turns to me.

'Busseeey man! Always a busy man … Haha!' And we breathe a sigh of relief that the awkward net has been cut and we're released as it falls heavily to the ground. Now free, we start chatting again and then the Arab kid comes over and puts his face, still connected to the mobile, right next to Sam's and they shoot and spit some words to each other and then freeze dead. They simultaneously twist their heads to look at me.

'Um, Jack, we goin' ta go see some girls. You wanna have one?' Sam asks as if he was offering me a refill of my coffee.

'Umm, well …' And I have no idea what to say and I trip over words and I'm hopelessly searching for a way of saying that I'm not really 'into' prostitutes without throwing another net of awkwardness over us. So I decide to just go with 'Nah, my dad's real sick. I shouldn't go too far from him. Y'know?' And Sam translates for the Arab who shifts his whole body and eyes towards me and he furrows his brow and stares deep into me for a split second, before shrugging and recommencing his jabber on the phone. And then just like that he walks out as quickly as he came in and Sam and I are back in the uneasy void, conscious of the slashed net of awkwardness that lies dormant but ever-present on the ground.

Now there's nothing left to say or do and again I'm looking around at his life. Sam gets fidgety and offers me some home-made wine from down in his 'whaddaya call it ... a bassist?'

'A basement?'

'Ah shit. That's it – "basement". Miy Engleesh is disappeering.' And we stumble and fall down his crumbling crappy old stairs and he explains to me. 'Man, yew see this. This all yewsed to be reeyl nice.' Sam pats the wall and it crumbles into his palm. 'Reeeeeyl nice. But now, well, now wiy're not allawed to fix anyfing.' He brushes his hand clean on his thigh.

'Nah, man, it's got a really nice feel to it. Like a home. Y'know the word "ambience"?' And that's me trying to pretend it looks homely and as lovely as a beachside pad, but it looks as if it could instantly collapse, bringing the entire poor old house crashing on top of us and the weak evening light seeping through the cracks would be the last sunlight I'd ever see.

'Yeah weyll, whateva. It's all right, Jack, man, I know yew're just saying that. Yew're a good kid.' He's still drunk and not hindered in what he says as he siphons wine from a gallon bottle into two glasses. 'But yeah, we're not allowed to fix anyting, and in like two or three years or sumtin, the guvenment is goin' tew deestroy it.'

'Huh?'

'Thay'll put me and miy family and miy friends in apartament in one of these big buildings yew seey.' And he motions up the stairs with his chin. 'Where I yam living all miy liyfe, and wheyre miy dad an' grandad liyved all theiyr liyfes, they will, y'know ...' And he claps his hands together and looks at me with those sad brown eyes. He picks up the two glasses and hands me one. 'Cheers, man ...' and the generously filled glasses clink together with a splash of purple jumping out and dripping down to the dusty floor.

We walk up the stairs and the Arab kid is back and he's in the living room, still on his phone. He looks at us, looks at our wineglasses and scoots down the stairs and comes back a minute later with his own glass of wine and sits down with us. The football's on. England versus Germany. England's winning. And I'm sitting here having a relaxed drink whilst watching a match and I could just as easily have been back home in Fitzroy. Back home with friends instead of on the other side of the Gobi Desert, an ocean away from my old mates and my poor mum, who's waking up every morning to an empty bed. Waking up to an almost empty house and occasionally taunted by excited abrupt phone calls from afar and then left alone with the harrowing beep of a dead line. And I'm here in the damp roots of this bulging city, watching an international friendly with two kids who are draining their wine before heading off for a casual romp with a couple of prozzies.

Just then the front door opens and Sam's old man walks in slowly, gaunt and leathery. He stares at me gently for a moment with the same glum brown eyes as his son. He's a little surprised but his regard remains placid.

'*Zdrastvouitie*,' he says and then looks at his son and their big pained eyes connect.

'*Zdrastie*,' I respond, and stand to meet him. He and Sam exchange some words before the father warmly takes my outstretched hand.

'Hello. Welcome to our country,' he mumbles with a difficult smile as his deep eyes flash soullessly across mine before turning down the stairs to get himself a glass of wine. He comes back with an overfilled glass in his hand and watches a few seconds of the match before flipping his mobile out of his pocket and easing out of the room, wistfully scratching his furrowed brow. I turn to Sam whilst his father is out of earshot.

'So, Sam. When are you two off to see these "girls"?' I ask.

'Oooh man, I dunno. Maybiy we are goina goh, we vas just talking,' and he nods to the Arab and then looks over his shoulder for his dad, 'and we thought we'd … umm, y'know,' and he lowers his voice to a mumble, '… go and smoyke liyke some weeyd. You wanna come? It could be fun. Gow for a drive and show our guest, you, like, show you some of the citee and see some friends? You're mohre important dhan girls.'

'Umm … Oh …' And I'm so close to muttering some other piss arse excuse about my dad being sick or something equally as weak and lame, but I don't. 'Why the fuck not?'

And so the night seeps in and eases the day out, and the football match ends. We push up from the couch and put our shoes and coats on. Sam yells to his dad in English.

'Hey, Dad, we are just goin' ta shaw Jack a tour!' and his dad appears. He looks uneasily at Sam, almost says something and then stops himself, takes a sip of wine and stares at the floor.

'Be careful,' he grizzles, almost as an afterthought, and we leave him to bristle about the damp lonely house with his sorry face and leathery wrinkles receding high into his greying hair.

We saunter out onto the pitch-black streets, barren of light where not even shadows exist. The streets are silent and still, but they are surrounded by the noise of newer highways that have been built almost on top of the shack suburb. As we creep through the dark, an occasional outline of a person comes towards us and pauses to greet and embrace Sam and the Arab. Some of the younger outlines almost grovel over Sam and as each one departs he chuckles.

'See, Jack,' Sam explains, 'when I was youngar, I was trouble, man. I was real noht good. Always in fights an stuyff … Miy dad was always of warryin'. But now, peeple are scayred so they respect y'knoy? But miy dad, miy dad … he is gooht.'

'And you're not?'

'I am now.' He chuckles. 'Since corming back from ofarseas I'm good. But before … no gooht.' And Sam seems much more relaxed and free being outside of that old house.

'Yeah sure, man, cool. So … um … what does your dad do?'

'Hmm. Miy dad, he's gooht man. He make sharge of the security of one of tha embassieys. Gooht johb since twenty years.'

'Riiight. That is a good job. Stressful …' and suddenly his father's deep-set eyes make more sense.

So we wander on and in the distance there's a lone streetlight blazing on a street corner, and beneath the bright gaze a small group of men stand or crouch with their hands deeply embedded in their coat pockets to escape the cold. One of them sees us, takes his hands out of his pockets, slaps a few shoulders and shakes a few hands before breaking away and making for us. He's seriously solid and even in the darkness you can see a wry smirk on his face. Like the other boys he must be in his early twenties.

'Semmy!' the breakaway calls out. And Sam and he embrace and spit more words at each other and laugh. 'Jack, man,' says Sam turning to me, 'this is Dimitry. Liyke Dimitry Medvedev, tha mutherfucker.'

And the big Dimitry replies, 'How doo yoo doo, Sir!' and gives a belly of a laugh as he grabs my hand and gives it an almighty shake. And we head off down the street, all four of us; me, Sam, the Arab and now Dimitry as well.

'Dimitry is from Georgia,' explains Sam.

'No way? You come from, er, South Ossetia?' I ask with a grin, as weeks before Russia had invaded Georgia. Dimitry laughs again and continues chuckling for a little longer before stopping in the middle of the street as he searches his mind for the right words in English. He puts his big arm on my shoulder and looks at me.

'Erm … Putin. Putin.' I nod my head. 'Putin, gooht gooht.' And he gives a thumbs up. 'Medvedev …' he says and weighs it up, 'Medvedev … okay … okay …' And then, 'Saakashvili … Prrrresident Georgia Republika … *nyet* gooht. *Nyet* gooht,' he says with rolled eyes, a thumbs down and a wrinkled nose. 'Saakashvili *nyet* gooht …' and he takes his hand off my shoulder, then remembers something and puts his hand back and squeezes my arm. 'But, politic … *Nyet* gooht. Batd for heatd.' And he raps his index finger against his forehead and releases his big belly laugh again. 'But smoking … smoking gooht!' And he takes a cigarette out and jabs it between his lips and playfully shoves Sam along the dark road.

And then we arrive at a house, another rickety damp shack towered over by another bright white monster office block. 'It ah bank,' says Dimitry as I stand there on the splintered veranda gazing up at it. The shack is Dimitry's place and he disappears inside and comes back out with some car keys which he throws to Sam. We walk round a corner closer to the big white bank and we get in a little red Russian car, when suddenly Dimitry remembers something. 'One minute,' he mutters and runs off. We climb out of the car to have a smoke and as we're leaning against the car I look around and see a truck parked at the very end of this dead-end street, right beneath the towering white building. Cramped up in the driver's seat there's a guy reading under the cabin light. A car rolls along at the other end of the street and the reflections of the headlights spray across us, revealing our naked faces and uncovering the blanket of dark over our surroundings. Sam nods toward the other end of the street where the fleeting pan of the headlights reveals two heavy, grave men wearing long trench coats walking toward us. Their clip-clop footsteps echo through the street and they stride past us without a glance and up to the parked truck.

Sam elbows me. 'Watch this, Jack. Watch this,' he says and I watch as the two men in trench coats open the truck's door and fiercely pull the driver out. The two men flash a torch on and shine it in the startled truckie's face. He hands them some papers and the torchlight dips to the sheets, and back to the truckie's face, and again, and again. Then suddenly the light clicks off and the shadows reclaim the scene.

The two men leave the truck and just as they are passing us one gives us a glance and sees me. A foreigner! The torch light flashes on straight in my face and my eyes flame up. Spitfire words are exchanged between Sam and the shadow men. Their hands are clasping my arms. The Arab slinks behind the car and into the safety of the dark. The torch is still burning in my face. Words zing back and forth, louder and faster and piercing. Sam reasons with the men in rumbling tones, and they give short, harsh responses. Then there's silence and the flaming torch is turned off. The two men hover for a few more seconds before disappearing and Sam is left fuming whilst I knead the heat out of my eyes.

'What was that?' I ask, confused. Sam doesn't respond. He just watches the darkness and listens for the clip-clop footsteps to evaporate into the night.

'Them ... them ... farking KGB,' he finally snarls.

'Huh ...? KGB?'

'Tey our country's KGB ...' Sam sighs and plants his hand on the car's bonnet. 'They want to know whu everyone is ... They neeyd to know whu everyone is in this city because ...' He sighs. 'Because maybiy, maybiy we're gooin' to bomb this big special bank or somethingk stupid liyke that. Bastards ...' Sam trails off as he looks up at the starched white bank with his sad brown eyes.

I stop asking questions.

Dimitry comes back, shortly followed by the Arab who shoots me a little cowardly smile. We jump in the car and Sam turns the ignition, flicks the lights on to the ghostly street, pumps the accelerator and kicks the car into action. As we go around the first corner the Arab clicks a tape into the sound system. The stereo jumps to life with 50 Cent blaring out and the Arab, Dimitry the Georgian, and Sam all start nodding and bopping to the hoes and bitches of American gangster life.

The neon lights zoom past. The white gleam of the city shines and throbs as our little red car spins its way between buildings and monuments. Sam screeches around another corner with one hand on the steering wheel and his other hand lighting a cigarette. The white city centre slips past and we pull off a freeway into a quiet little street and roll to a stop in an alley. The Arab scurries out of the car followed by Dimitry, who pauses before shutting the door and sucks on his thumb and then pokes his tongue out. Just Sam and I are left in the quiet street as the others stalk through the shadows. The car engine is cut, as is the music, and Sam starts asking about my life back home. The luxury of life embarrasses me so I turn the focus back to him.

'So ... what do you actually do? Like, for a job?' I ask.

'Nathing really … I yused to be driver. But now, weyll, now I do nathing …' He's embarrassed, but I push him to clarify.

'But you have been to university … in Europe. It's not easy to get a job in your country with Western qualifications?' I ask.

Sam laughs bitterly. 'Yew come fram a goohd country. I seey dat. Here, study in Europe is batd thing. I … I learnt batd ideyas.' He repeats and emphasises 'batd ideyas' and raps his fingers on the steering wheel and scans the street. 'Mebbe one dayy I will gow to Turkiye. I can wurk dair,' he says, and he turns his nervous brown eyes to his fingers that are now drumming the dashboard.

'What yew tink of miy drivink?' he asks me.

'Yeah, you're not bad,' I reply. 'Do you have your own car?'

'I yused to haf my own car. Well, it wasn't mine. I … umm, I yused to wurk for the embassy of our naybor Afghanistan. I was driver for them for one yeayr. But I stopped.'

'Whoaw … Afghanistan Embassy! You must have heard some interesting conversations …' I attempt a joke and Sam's face creases slightly, trying to understand if I'm being serious or kidding.

'I had to stop,' he continues. 'I stopped bycause it is not sayfe.' A shadow of sadness crosses his face. 'A frend of me, he was explosioned, y'know, by a bomb in tha car of tha ambassadar.'

Shit.

And those big, sad, damning eyes still mourn. And I stare at my shoes and exhale. What am I doing here? Why am I torturing Sam into showing me this? Honestly, what is the point in witnessing this kid's embarrassment at such a shambolic country and life? This is the answer to my search for entertainment? This is the answer to my quest to understand and experience other cultures?

The doors of the car open and the Arab and Dimitry flop into the little car. Dimitry looks at me, gives a priceless Russian shrug and says, '*Nyet* marawana …'

Sam looks at me, raises his eyebrows and shrugs as well, 'Dat's life …' and I don't know if he's talking about the joint or his friend being the innocent victim of an assassination attempt on his neighbouring country's ambassador.

The three boys sit muttering and discussing what to do next. The Arab makes phone call after phone call. It's not yet too late, about 9.30 pm, and after some to-ing and fro-ing, they finally nod their heads in agreement.

'Wee gow see sum firends ... okay?' says Sam and with that he flicks the ignition and skids the car back onto the bright highway. We head through the city, back past all the shiny monuments and staggering white buildings all the way to their dark slum suburb. The monumental buildings are still lit up like Vegas. Sam parks the little red car in the same spot where the KGB had grabbed us and we get out.

'First, vee gow get some vootka.' Sam and I walk into a tiny milk bar as the others wait outside. The little shop is full of a family of little children crowded around a Central Asian soap opera and they turn away from the TV and stare at me as I walk up to the counter with Sam. The big mother hauls herself up from the rickety couch and glares at us. Sam shoots some words of which I understand 'vootka' and 'Coca'. She reaches under the counter and plonks a bottle of each in front of us. All the children are still staring at me except for one who's completely engrossed in the TV show. Sam picks up the vodka and begins to violently shake it, jerking and pulling it away and toward his body, then he stops and watches the churning poison inside the glass.

'Ummm, why are you doing that?' I ask.

'Beycause,' he grunts as he starts to jerk the bottle back and forth again. 'Beycause you do dis and vatch fohr a spin in the bottal'. And he puts the vodka back on the bench and asks for another. 'Dhat one is noht goohd.' He picks up the new bottle and shakes it vigorously, then stops and points at the bottle. A perfect tornado of vodka swirls and twirls within the confines of the glass. 'Dat is vhat wee vant ...' We pay half each and break open the Coke as we walk out the door and I feel the children's eyes on my back all the way.

We walk along in the dark sipping Coke and tripping on the broken road.

'Yoo haf vootka Awstraliya?' asks Dimitry and I nod.

'Yoo ... liyke vootka?' he asks and I nod again.

'Me ... liyke vootka biyg!' says Dimitry with his massive grin and he spreads his meaty hands to show just how much he likes his chest-warming liquor. Sam walks quietly along clasping the cool glass to his side.

We eventually get to a corner where there's half-a-dozen Russian guys. They grunt and nod at the Arab who coldly shakes hands with all of them before dipping his head at me and scampering off into the night. They all warmly embrace Sam and Dmitry and when I'm introduced as 'Jeck, Awstraliyann' they all do double-takes followed by hearty handshakes where they drag my hand towards them for a hug. They're all about twenty years old, and wearing baggy clothes and Wu-Tang hats. Their white Russian skin is rancid-looking in the bright fluoro light and when they chuckle their weedy frames and sharp features pulsate. They open and share a pack of cigarettes.

Gripping a cigarette in his teeth, Sam opens the bottle of 'vootka' and raises it above his head. 'To Awstraliyann frendshiyp ...' he toasts and pauses. His gaze flickers from the bottle to me and back to the bottle, 'And to za future ...' He translates to Russian and it's greeted with '*Dah, dah*' and then he flicks the bottle and holds it out in front of himself for everyone else to flick. He takes a slug and grimaces, following it up with a mouthful of Coke and a couple of thumps of his chest. He passes the bottle to me.

'Say someding, I translate and den you hit the bottal with youhr finger den everyone else hit it.'

Oh shit. What do I say ...? Everyone is looking at me and I don't know whether I should praise their country, or them, or Russia, or Eminem ... Shit.

'Erm, to ... umm, your beautiful country ...' and I flick the bottle. Sam stares glumly at me with those dark eyes before translating. They all give an unenthusiastic 'whoop-hei!' and they flick the bottle. I drink and Dimitry slaps me on the back.

'Is gooht!' he says and he passes me the Coke and takes the vodka. Sam puts his hand on my shoulder.

'Take easy. Not tooh much. My fahther saiyd to take cayre of you. Bahtd to mix wine and vootka.'

'Thanks,' I mutter.

The night coasts on by, slug by slug. A few more people arrive. A different Arab (who later explains his family is Iraqi) and his girlfriend who must be Mongolian. She sits to the side watching and they both refuse to drink the vodka.

'Vhey ar Muslim,' Sam explains. 'Mi too ... I'm Muslim, but I drink, smohke, fuck ...' And he doesn't seem proud of it as his eyes sweep across the ground and he scratches at his bumfluff.

Two beautiful brunette Russians appear through the mist and Sam nods his head to one of them and introduces her to me.

'Jack man, this is Daniella,' he slurs and then whispers in my ear, 'Looyks gooht vith mayke-up, but not vith mayke-up she bahtd …' and scrunches up his face in disapproval. Daniella giggles at the English and the fluorescent white light twinkles in her wide green eyes. She holds her eyes on mine before breaking off to gossip with her girlfriend and flirt with the rat-featured Russians. Sam stares darkly at me and gives a little shake of his head as a warning. 'She a slut,' he whispers. And then one of the Russians yells out a toast followed by the round of bottle flicks. He takes a drink and breaks into a Russian rap.

The bottle does another round and it's almost finished. The Coke's long gone and the last mouthful of vodka is passed to Sam. He downs it and gives off a fierce gasp for air, then throws the bottle onto the road where it bounces once and smashes. The Arab and his girlfriend are the first to leave in a screech of rubber as their car lights up the night. Then the brunette girls head off, Daniella kissing me on the cheek and giggling in my ear. One of the rancid Russians slaps her arse as she leaves and she laughs and smiles at him before returning to the mist from which she came. One by one the rest leave until just Dimitry, Sam and I remain. Dimitry takes my hand one last time and grins.

'Goohtbye!' Dimitry laughs and embraces Sam before taking off, sauntering into the darkness.

Sam and I make our way home, keeping one foot in front of the other and stopping every now and then to feel our way along the footpath. The moon occasionally peers out from behind the clouds and its light sweeps between the tree limbs, scattering a white glow across the ground. We walk along in the quiet, our steps the only sound or movement in the streets, but still the ever-present hum of the surrounding highways continues on through the night. The only other display of life is the occasional lit-up government building lording over the petty suburb.

'Do yoo liyke the peeple, my friends, Jack?' Sam asks.

'Yeah, they're fairly … ummm … chilled out,' I respond and Sam nods in agreement, a little bored by my answer. His eyes have lost their sadness and he now just looks tired. I try to build up a little conversation before we say goodbye.

'So, Sam. What's the plan in the future? You going to go to Turkey or what? What do you want to do?'

'What do I wahnt to doo?'

'Yeah.'

'I wahnt to stey here …' he smiles, 'but I canno' get no job,' and he shrugs and starts to look sad again as his eyes return to his feet sweeping along beneath him. We tiptoe further along in awkward silence. He rubs at his eyes and his face nervously.

'Dis is vehry stranje, Jack. You see miy life, and I thihnk it muhst be crayzy for yew.' He pauses and I don't know if it's a question. 'My friends from universitiy, they could nevah undirstaynd this … It's so … very different … I don't think yew even understaynd it?' He brings his eyes from his feet and turns toward me. It's a question.

'Honestly? Yes, it is strange. We come from real different worlds.' And I feel horrible. We've both seen what each world has to offer, and we both know which world is better.

'Maybe it'll change here …' I mumble. Sam chuckles.

'Man, come vit miy, I show yew somethink.' And he crosses the road and heads down a little side street. He keeps chuckling to himself and muttering, 'Maybe it'll change …' followed by a sarcastic, 'Hmph.' And down the side street Sam stops outside a forgotten old house, even more crumbly and destroyed than the others. The roof has big proper holes in it and the windows are all smashed. The gate is lying broken on the ground.

'You szee dis houwse heyre?' he says indicating to the squat and placing his hand on the fence.

'Yeah.'

'Dis howse is tha howse of a frend of me. Frend of my father.' He pulls himself up to sit on the fence. 'Dis man waz takin by KGB. Two years ago dey come and he just … dizapeer. Gowne.'

'What'd he do?' I ask.

'He was oppasichon. Government say he try to kill paresident.'

'And …'

'And what?'

'And was he trying to kill the President?'

'Nah, man. We ahre Muslim peeyple, we don't kill …'

'Right.'

'But he got tayken, just like that. And his wiyfe and kiyds all leayf cos they goht … they've goht nothing. And we nevar seeyn them agaiyn.' The moon drifts behind a cloud and Sam's face becomes a shadow. 'The government duz waht they wahnt.' I hear him exhale and see him brushing his hair back on his head. I can't see where he's looking but I have a feeling his eyes are fixed on his feet again. We stand in the gloom for a few minutes or so and I lean against a tree and exhale too. I stare at the house and imagine the KGB raiding it at night and pulling a half-naked, dark-eyed man out into the street as his family take their last look at their father and husband. Their cries ringing through the shack suburb and falling on the neighbours' fearful ears. Their hollers ringing on and being swallowed by the dark. And still that continuous hum of the highway.

'C'mon, Jack. It's bahtd to think too much.' And Sam lifts up off the fence and starts back towards his house. I kick the tree and follow after him.

We get to the place where Dad and I are staying and the moon reappears out of the clouds. Sam's face is completely flushed and the moonlight shows sags of skin hanging under his eyes. He's on his way down after drinking all day and all night. He can't stand up straight.

'Well, Jack, man, it is a pleashure ...' He smiles wryly with that crowded-teeth grin and puts his hand on my shoulder. I don't know what to say. He's smiling but his eyes are staring daggers at me. I think he hates me.

'Sam, maybe one day it'll change ...' I try to be as earnest as possible. His eyes fall to the ground and he shakes his head, still smiling painfully.

'Maybe ... Maybe ...' And he looks back up at me one last time. The moon is fully out of the clouds and shining bright. The shadows of tree branches sprawl across his face and his crooked nose sticks out in the moonlight. His eyes remain hidden. He's not smiling anymore. I force myself to look him in the eye. His half-Mongol, half-Arab hurt brown eyes stare at me.

'I hate this city,' he says and he turns. He shuffles away and disappears into the cover of dark. His stumbling footsteps are drowned out by the harrowing hum of the highways and, imperious above the city, the white government towers stand strong and tall.

35 | How to Bribe a Policeman

Whereby Australians materialise where we least expect them, lambs are sacrificed and at last Jon bribes a policeman. At last.

I sleep like the dead. My bladder wakes me early and I creep out trying not to wake Jack. The musty mouldy carpet is warm, the concrete outside freezing. I sneak past doors to other rooms and around Ping, parked inside the gates off the street away from prying eyes. There is barely room to get around the car to the toilet in the corner of the yard. It is freezing cold. As I shut the door to sneak back to bed, I am greeted by, 'G'day, where you from?' A tall fit man in tracksuit pants is leaning on the bullbar, running his hand through his fair hair before reaching out to shake mine. His accent is unmistakeable. I wake Jack and we all sit and yarn. Lachy Milne and Helene tell us they have been travelling overland from Beijing since the Olympics. We must have covered much the same terrain but they are using local transport, buses and trains. From Melbourne originally, they have been living in Sydney where he is a doctor and she a physio. It takes ages before Lachy tells us he was at the Olympics as a competitor, a slalom kayaker, not a spectator!

The day before, as we drove from Mary to Ashgabat, Jack had asked me, 'Do you think we are the only Australians in Turkmenistan right now?'

'I reckon we are the only Australians driving through Turkmenistan in a white Toyota,' was my hilarious reply.

We sit under the vines at an unsteady table in this Ashgabat homestay for ages and compare travel notes and plans. Our host Manut, meanwhile, together with his toothless elderly father, busies himself tying up the feet of a tethered sheep and then with no fanfare or forewarning slits its throat and starts to butcher it. Our shoes are splashed with blood before the frenzied rush for cameras. It is a sacrifice for a family feast that is looming, no religious ceremony required. It takes about a minute for the hapless animal to bleed to death, the pink frothy blood collected in a bowl. Lachy and Helene give us an anatomy lesson as the butchering gets under way. Michael from Queensland and Olivier, a Frenchman who lives in Italy, are the other two guests in the homestay, and we recognise them from last week wandering the alleys of Bukhara. Olivier asks if he can get a ride with us to Venice, where his parents will make us welcome, but the prospect of having another person with us for our last three weeks does not appeal and we make our excuses.

Ashgabat reminds me of Dubai, huge glass and steel skyscrapers totally out of keeping with their surrounds. Massive gilt and marble statues of the megalomaniac dictator Niyazov perch amid lush formal gardens, tended by uniformed staff, no doubt delighted to be able to make their contribution to the cult of personality that leaves North Korea looking modest. The last election before he died in 2006 saw a 99.9 per cent vote recorded for 'Turkmenbashi', the father of the Turkmen as he named himself. The Ruhnama, his own attempt at creating a Bible, must by law be displayed in every building in the country, is taught as the primary text in schools, is required reading for obtaining a driver's licence, as well as being represented by massive statues, as high as ten-storey buildings – of a book – in the centre of town. Fountains gush water as if we are not in the desert. Twenty-storey apartment blocks with AstroTurf tennis courts line up like sentries along the main streets – and just a block behind them the people live in slums. The oil and gas reserves that fuel – literally – the entire nation have emboldened the elite and entrenched their absolute grip on power. Turkmenistan would be comical if the tyranny and human rights abuses were not so vicious and frequent.

Driving around the city gets me into trouble. Policemen wait on every corner and soldiers in armoured cars patrol the street. On one of the expansive boulevards that criss-cross this crazy city a big-hatted police officer steps in front of Ping and waves me over. 'Papers,' he demands while sizing up the car and me. My licence disappears into his pocket as soon as he has finished scrutinising it. He waves his arms extravagantly and loudly tells me something in Russian, probably about speeding.

I shrug my shoulders, and he traces '50' in the dirt on our back window with his fingers. He keeps pointing to the city, and I guess he is trying to tell me to go to the central police station to pay a fine and then he will give my licence back to me. I have read in the *Lonely Planet* that the Ministry of Fairness is anything but that, so I write '60' in the dirt on the window, protest theatrically and then put my palms together in apology and whisper, 'Dollars?' He has a quick look around, says 'dollars' with a heavy emphasis on the 's' and takes my licence from his pocket. I slip a five-dollar bill from a stash of small denomination notes kept in my shirt pocket for exactly this possibility, he looks around again and gestures with his fingers to pay more, I make it six dollars and he is happy. We exchange money for licence, I jump back into Ping and we zoom away before he changes his mind. If only it was so simple at home.

This lamb was tethered in the courtyard where we were staying in Ashgabat. The next morning as we had breakfast it was slaughtered.

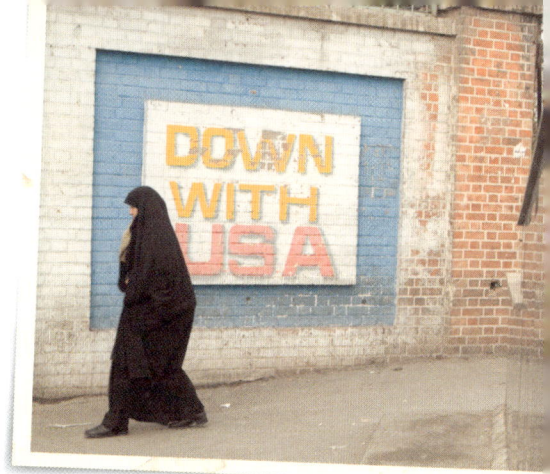

36 | Does the Ayatollah Approve?

Since ancient Persia of the Silk Road is now Iran and is the spindle in the Axis of Evil, we look everywhere for nuclear weapons facilities but can only find kebab stalls.

Four young Germans are in detention at the Turkmenistan to Iran border. They were heading in the opposite direction to us, speak good English and seem amused by their plight. Their sins are twofold – no visas to go on into Turkmenistan, and they were caught taking photos in no man's land, regarded as a military zone and therefore of great sensitivity. They are rash but funny, daring the police to do their worst. Lounging around on the chairs, knowing full well that there is not that much that can really happen to them, time is on their side; they don't really care if they have to wait. They want to sell their car, which they have driven from India, so they can fly home but they could not find a buyer in Iran and want to try to go on to Turkmenistan. I am secretly jealous of their devil-may-care approach, and wish I was less anxious and serious. Jack does too.

It is taking hours – again – to get through the Iranian border post, as the Iranians have a system of forcing drivers of foreign cars to nominate their exact intended route all the way across the country. In a noisy smoke-filled office, jostled by stubble-chinned truck drivers shouting in three or four different languages to each other and anyone else who will listen, I am issued a map with colour-coded highways identifying where we can and cannot go. As soon as it is stamped and cleared and endorsed and embossed and gawd knows what else, we drive exultantly off to the nearest village and buy some lunch. Ping was barely searched, the computers and satellite phone left alone, the guidebooks not confiscated, our lies about having never visited 'occupied Palestine' went unchallenged. So much for the threat posed by foreign devils.

The first mountain town is tiny – stone huts and just one small shop, but a queue outside the baker. I try to send Jack but he is suddenly shy so I join the locals who look sideways and are deeply wary, no smiles or giggles. Is the population of the entire town grubby boys aged ten or twelve? No girls, no adults, it seems. The bakers are two youngsters, dark stubble tinged with flour making for a quite fetching look. They are sweaty, kneading huge piles of sticky dough and robotically rolling it into dinner-plate-sized naan bread. The younger one then sticks his head into a beehive-shaped open-topped oven and somehow gets the dough to stick to the sides of the oven where it stays until cooked. He just intuitively knows the exact moment to grab the baked bread before it peels off the side wall and drops into the flames, and he flips the latest offering onto the pile of steaming fresh loaves on the counter without suffering third-degree burns. The whole choreography is worthy of applause. The bread tastes fabulous.

I am amazed that we have got here. It has been such a nightmare, and gaining entry to Iran is the last logistical hurdle. We should make it to Paris for Christmas now, and I feel lightheaded and want to celebrate, but the Islamic Republic of Iran is not the ideal place for that.

Down the mountains we are astonished to see there are road signs, and in Roman script that we can read! Not since Thailand have there been clear road signs, and we praise the Shah and the Ayatollah – and anyone else who has made such simple things possible – but abandon the approved route at the first major intersection, deciding we do not want to go to Mashhad, which is near the Afghan border. It is more than 100 kilometres in the wrong direction, and although the roads may be better I am sick of being told what to do and where to go. Jack wants to get to Tehran quickly and I am saddle-sore too. Instead, our first stop in Iran is at an unremarkable village called Bojnurd. We wander through the main street, attracting inquisitive stares, eventually finding a cheap guesthouse where they offer us chicken and some salad for dinner in a huge dining room already set up with plastic table cloths on long rows of well-set trestles ready for a function. As the guests arrive the pot-bellied proprietor urgently ushers us upstairs, making sure the TV works for us even though the dreadful Iranian soaps are impossible to watch. When I go down to the car to collect warmer clothes our host is visibly annoyed and nervous about the presence of a foreigner, and a man to make it worse. All the women guests are seated behind a curtain, the men are dancing with each other, live music from local performers on fretted traditional string instruments, like fiddles and also mandolins, in subdued celebration at the other end of the room. A few girls are coming in and out of the hall and quickly cover their faces when they see me, pulling their scarves up to their noses and giggling. In the morning the staff seem only too happy to see the back of us.

There is a massive freeway into Tehran, wide, flat and fast. Infrastructure in Iran is impressive and functional. Every factory or power plant we go past, Jack points and declares 'secret nuclear weapons facility', but jokes aside there are countless army bases, compounds and nondescript buildings with guard towers and barbed-wire perimeter fences, far more frequent than anywhere else we have been. After the mountain passes and winding roads it is a relief to get back to travelling at speed. Jack falls asleep as we sit on 120 kilometres per hour on cruise control, and on a long, boring straight stretch of divided road I struggle to make sense of the horrific scene of a car cartwheeling towards me. Tumbling end on end, airborne like in a movie, glass and debris flying everywhere, it takes a moment before I react. I wake Jack up as I slam on the hazard lights and the brakes, pulling over to the side of the road. Grabbing the still unused first-aid kit from the back of the car, we run across the freeway to the median strip where other helpers have just arrived too. A young man and woman are shaking, standing up after crawling out the windows of the steaming car, which is on its roof, leaking petrol. The woman seems hurt, the man animated and talking. I make the mistake of holding the woman's arm to ask her, 'Okay?' and she withdraws and covers her face with the scarf that has tumbled down to her shoulders. I am taken aback, amazed that her priority in an emergency is to adhere to the morality code of the regime rather than anything else. It is a stupid cross-cultural error on my part, adrenalin racing as we respond to the emergency. Miraculously they are both intact and, although no doubt suffering shock, not seriously hurt, not in need of our first-aid kit nor non-Farsi speaking strangers, no matter how well meaning. We help right the wreck, disconnect the battery to avoid sparks and the risk of fire and go back on our way.

Nearly every vehicle on the road is a Paykan, the Iranian government-produced car, based on the 1967 Hillman Hunter. Until recently Iran was still making them, albeit

IRAN

WE WILL MAKE AMERICA A FACE A SEVERE DEFEAT

The former US Embassy in Tehran has been handed over to a group committed to upholding the values of the 1979 Islamic revolution.

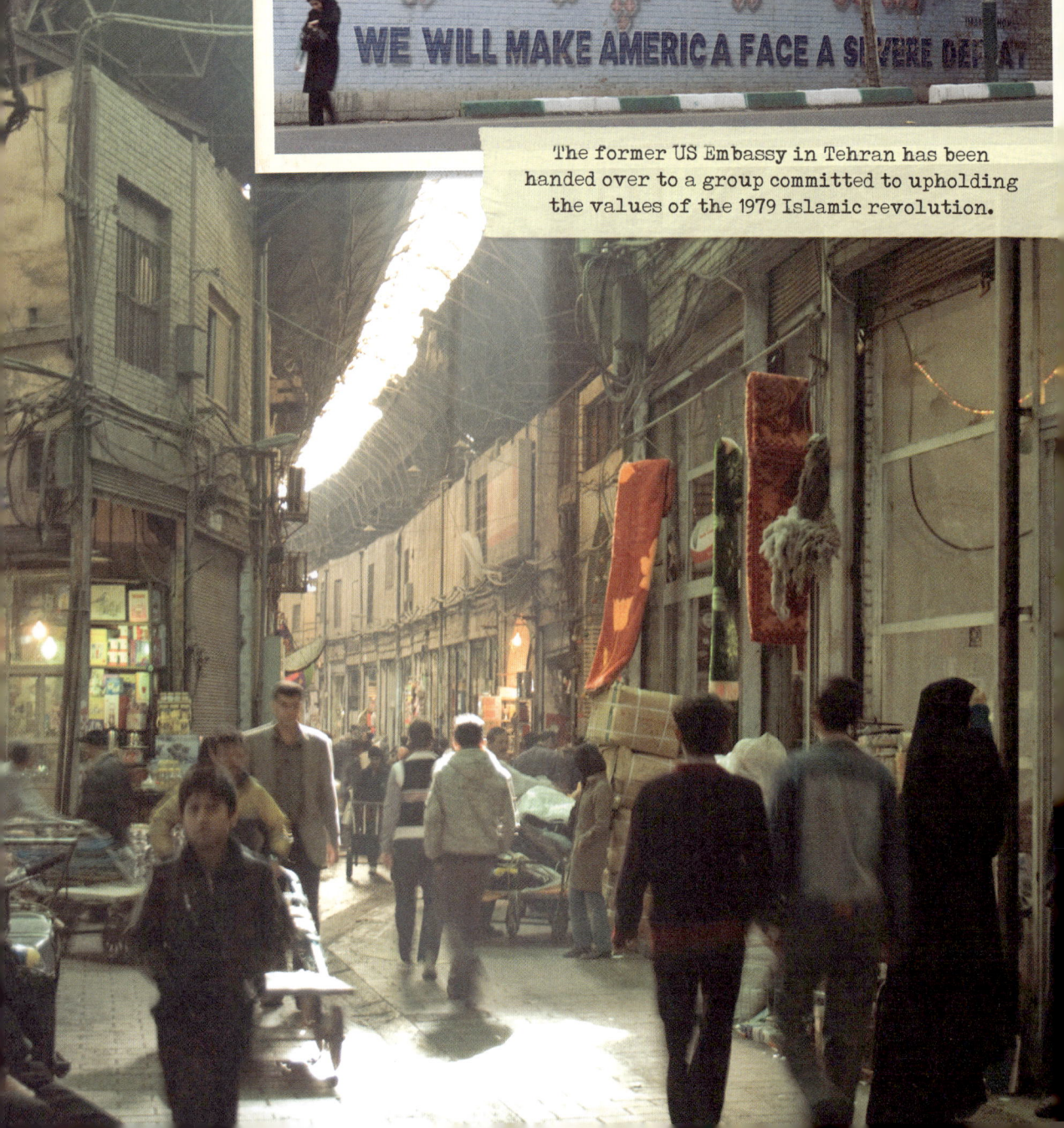

with updates, particularly a Peugeot motor. I was poking fun at them until this crash, but if those two people walked away from an end-on-end rollover, then the Paykan is a seriously tough little car. No airbags, just seatbelts and lots of steel.

Gridlock greets us on the outskirts of sprawling Tehran and it takes two hours of bumper-to-bumper frustration to drive from the edge of the city to a hotel in the middle of town. Traffic congestion is chaotic, reminiscent of Bangkok three months and 20,000 kilometres earlier and the pollution is about as bad too. People in other cars wave and point, smiling and excited to see our exotic right hand drive car. We have been joking about *Lonely Planet* being our Koran, but in this town it seems inappropriate. After settling into a hotel, we walk for hours looking for food and street life, but only finding the usual mix of mobile phone touts, young men selling socks, cheap Chinese animal toys that squawk and, tellingly, a battery-operated crawling soldier with machine gun that lights up as it kills the infidel.

The main bazaar soaks up our first day, a slippery-floored maze of alleyways and dead ends patrolled by gnarled porters with wobbly handcarts and trolleys yelling as they push through the throng. Samovars and cooking utensils, nuts, tea, clothes, shoes, belts, plastic toys, blankets, bathroom fittings, CDs, DVDs, Korans and prayer mats ... it is all here but same old same old; we have wandered the dusty halls of so many markets and bazaars we soon tire of Tehran's offerings and amble off to the museums instead. Amid the magnificence of relics from Persepolis and treasures from the earliest civilisations, a poorly curated but magnificent collection, we stumble upon a hand-holding pair of would-be young lovers who quickly uncouple as soon as we enter the otherwise deserted gallery where they are sneaking a cuddle. Public affection is punished severely if detected by the religious police but judging from our little observations and even though it sounds horribly soppy no amount of religious dogma will stop love.

Girls' eyes are averted in the street as we walk around looking for something other than kebabs to eat, but the more rebellious young women wear the compulsory scarf over just the back of their heads, showing more hair than permitted under the stricter interpretation of the rules. Many sport make-up and fashion is fashion even in Tehran under the Ayatollah. It is strange being somewhere almost totally devoid of Western influence – no billboards for Coca-Cola, no familiar brand names or logos. In a basement cafe off the main shopping street, the nargillah, or water pipe, is as popular with the girls as the boys, and the flirting and socialising is much as it would be in any Western city – but away from the public gaze. Wherever we go in the capital people are incredibly friendly and welcoming, constantly saying 'Iran wants to be friends' and some occasional rude remarks as they apologise for their government. Unlike anywhere else we have been in the world, whether in Central Asia, in China or Asia itself or on other trips everywhere in the world, here in Iran there is almost no activity on the streets, no one sitting around in pavement cafes or tea shops. As soon as the shops shut, everyone disappears.

Across town, the former US Embassy in Tehran – renamed the 'US Den of Espionage' – and its long brick walls are home to colourful political murals proclaiming in Farsi and English 'Death to the USA' and 'The only way to defy the wild wolf of Zionism and the transgressions of the Great Satan the USA is sacrificial resistance; The Supreme Leader'. A human-size portrait depicting the Statue of Liberty as a death angel, together with other wall art declaiming the regime's loathing for all things American, line the street. The American coat of arms at the main gate has had all recognisable features chipped away but left there damaged to show 'the people's' wrath. The massive embassy compound that for years was used by the CIA to prop up the former Shah has been handed over to religious groups and we are politely turned back at the gate as we try to enter. Citizens of the USA cannot get visas to visit Iran at all but we see no other tourists from anywhere the entire time we are in Iran.

On the surface, Tehran functions as any city, people going about their business trying to make a living. But there is unease, a tension that is inescapable. The younger people are, the more likely they will be to have a chat. A deep suspicion undermines our efforts, and our demeanour in Tehran is no different to anywhere else but the reaction from many locals is. Does a paranoid government make for paranoid people? Are the doctrinaire anti-West teachings of the president starting to have an effect? We argue the toss endlessly, workshopping various solutions to the deadlock in the Middle East, intermittently solving and exacerbating the situation depending on the perspective. America should just butt out; America should be more involved; Syria should butt out; Syria should be more involved; the Egyptians should look after Gaza; Saudi Arabia needs to be less selfish; the Israelis need to dilute the influence of the religious extremists; the settlements on the West Bank must be dismantled; the Arabs need to reduce the impact of the religious extremists in their politics; the Iranians are making it worse; the Iranians are making it better; the Sunni need to make peace with the Shia; they are all too corrupt; it is a mess; it is looking better; Tony Blair will fix it; Barack Obama will fix it … we pretty much have it covered.

It is only months after our visit that the disputed presidential election ushers in bloody street riots and mass arrests in Tehran. The restless young modernists use mobile phones, texting, twittering and emailing to organise their democracy campaign and to mobilise people throughout the capital. Only relentless violence from religious thugs and the police puts what I suspect will be a temporary halt to their activism. The repression we see and the censorship has only limited success, much as it has in China. Any regime trying to stop technology will fail – as soon as you block a website a new one emerges. But it is not the exclusive domain of democrats to understand the power and potential of the new and emerging technologies – terrorist groups and the secret police know and understand it too.

The internet sites we have been using to keep in touch with the world are all blocked. Even in China we could read Western news on the BBC and CNN, as well as the Australian media. But here, every news outlet website we can think of is blocked, except www.crikey.com.au the Australian scandal and gossip site which they have probably never heard of! I try to send the editor Jonathan Green an email telling him Crikey has huge potential in Iran, but my email server is blocked, even though Crikey is not, and it will not send. The Ayatollah wins.

37 | Tehran

We drove into Tehran late in the afternoon, or early in the evening, as the cars turned their headlights on and the halogen bulbs of the outer city began to burn brightly across the streets. The glow revealed boys bouncing footballs in front of crumbly old restaurants, and shrouded women sitting with their jet-black headscarves alive with the wind of passing traffic. Their men sold tight apples and sweet little mandies on the side of the road. And racing out to the horizon, the disappearing chain of powerlines silhouetted against the remains of the sunset.

We sprinted to the centre, passing stubbled Persian carefrees sitting in the back of pick-ups who were singing to themselves and to the buzzing ecstatic traffic. Beside the road, hushed women hovered with eyes straight, stern and solemn. Women and children headed off along well-trodden paths to buy naan from glazed- and glittery-eyed bakers who toil and knead in the floury smog of their cracked kitchens. Outside on the street, men meet and greet each other with a leathery slap of hands and they rat-a-tat in their rough and tumble tongue. More people stroll steadily on. And the lights flash a different colour but no one takes notice anyway. The jumbling throttle of the stop-start traffic continues to the tune of scrawls and dotted bumps of Farsi jotted along the road.

Big road signs, big portraits of dark-bearded clerics keep watch over the people and highways with names like 'Abbad Martyr Highway' usher us towards the city. Next to the sign saying 'Abbad Martyr Highway' there's a sombre martyr's face all rugged and respected, pinned up for us to praise.

Then, in the centre, when we finally get there, are illuminated music shops where long-haired wannabes jam guitars and talk amps and the shy shrouded women shuffle past still staring sternly at the ground. Beggars shiver for shelter and chew nothing, just sitting and sometimes teasing wisps of weedy white hair that hang off their sour skin. People give them spare change but don't look back at them, still sitting pondering the cold and munching their gums as steam hisscs up from vents of the ugly underground.

Every now and then gorgeous women walk by with highlighted curls hanging out of their conservative hijabs. Their dark gazes dip to their feet as they scurry past packs of furry men selling shavers on the street, and dart between the beeps and toots of the bottleneck blockage.

The girls are probably headed for a hookah bar to sit cross-legged and smoke long simmering draws of fruity tobacco and talk through the sugared mist. Their angular eyebrows do most of the talking, dipping sharp when serious and rising quick to query and challenge and then relaxing as the women suck down the rumbling smoke. Then when they're all done and finished and refreshing their clammy pores in the cool outside breeze, they pull their scarves a little tighter and a little closer in against the dark and carry on home.

And grand above everything, the silent mountains all jagged and cragged gleam white and glow with snow as the city hums and beeps, and toots and slaps, and swerves and rumbles, and tumbles below.

The Embassy walls display anti-USA propaganda.

38 | The Greatest Disappointment and a Marvellous Rebound

Sturgeons dropping caviar into our laps will surely come our way as we head for the mythical Caspian Sea, the stuff of legends ... or is it?

From Jack on www.MelbourneToLondon.com

Soldiers and pilgrims

And then the Iran-Azerbaijan-Armenia border, where on the Iran side of the river it is safe and passable, but on the other side there is every now and then the shell of a village left over from the Armenia-Azari battles of the 1990s and landmines scattered wherever and everywhere. And it was one of the most beautiful frames we've seen but we couldn't stop and photograph anything because we weren't meant to be there anyway and there were real soldiers kitted out in helmets and guns and sandbags ready to move us on our merry way. And we climbed to a ninth-century Azari fort miles high in the air and as we arrived at the top to look out across the dips of valleys and lips of mountains, all sweaty and puffed and sore-jointed we found that we were not alone but had in fact happened upon a group of mumbling Muslim pilgrims from Tabriz who had climbed to the top to rock and sway to the setting sun. We caught our breath by hardly breathing, and watched and listened. We climbed back down, slipping on our arses and landing in icy muddy gloop.

Tehran's notorious smog is choking us, our coughing and spluttering making us tired and sick. After a few days enjoying the paradox that this epicentre of the strict

Islamic regime also happens to be the most Western city we have been in for ages, we head off north to the Caspian Sea. Men wave from car windows as we trundle along the main expressway, veering across lanes to get a closer look at Ping, such an exotic car, hanging out of windows on one occasion to try to take a photo of us with a mobile phone. There are some women driving but not many. The freeway runs parallel to a railway line and regular new double-decker commuter trains stop at clean unvandalised stations. Maybe the Ayatollah and his mullahs could come and run public transport in Australia?

Lunchtime sees us in a mountain pass between the wide plains west of Tehran and the Caspian to the north, in Rudbar. Stopping for kebabs – again – there is a small garage servicing cars and I inquire about getting an oil change while we eat. Half the village come and watch the performance, photos are taken and the entire service for Ping costs A$15, including oil and filters. I invite the garagiste to fill in the service log of the car, but he cannot write, either in Farsi or any other script, and his friend does it for him to great applause from the crowd. The Toyota service book now proudly boasts entries from Australia, Bandar Lampung, Vientiane, Xian, Urumqi and Iran. Where will the next oil change be? Melbourne?

As we head towards the Caspian Sea, we get into a massive argument. Jack thinks Iran is making great progress despite the best efforts of the West to interfere. I say that Iran – or any other religious state – will never achieve its full potential under the rule of clerics. I think democracy is an essential ingredient to the equitable distribution of the self-evident prosperity. He thinks a theocracy can achieve the same. We both speculate on the ambitions of the emerging generation of graduates – what will they want from Iran and will their view of the future challenge the clerics? What will all these young Iranian university students do when they finish their courses, all tech savvy and worldly? I argue that if governments attempt to constrain the arts and politics, no amount of brainwashing and religious fanaticism will contain their ambition. The constraints on them will create tensions that inevitably will surface. Jack argues that there is evidence all around us that the Iranian economy is going gangbusters under the current regime and they clearly must be doing the right things to have the impressive infrastructure and educational facilities we see everywhere. I describe the clergy as a bottleneck, a constraint on the nation and argue that the prosperity is based purely on oil, not good governance. He says they are clearly facilitating the growth, and are doing a better job at sharing the wealth than the Shah ever did. That the argument gets heated when neither of us really knows enough about the subject is telling. We get angry with each other over not much at all.

The Caspian appears at the end of a grubby road behind the market in the port town of Chalus. We drive through ditches and drains to get to the waterfront. I have conjured up images of paradise, romantic notions of caviar, blue water, golden sands and crisp mountain backdrops for the area famous as the playground for the Persian elite. The reality is that it is a tip: industrial and military facilities lining the shore as far as we can see. Truck repairers, brickyards, crappy clothes stalls, kebab sellers, petrol stations, tyre shops, barbed-wire fences, boat yards and panel beaters. The water is greasy, with plastic bottles and bags and flotsam everywhere, and the shore is a litter trap. Boats at anchor are rusty, listing and nothing seems to be about to go anywhere except the multitude of Iranian navy vessels that are lined up in readiness for war – against who is not clear. We drive along the shorefront for hours, heading north, hoping it will improve. It doesn't.

This is the single greatest disappointment of the trip. Maybe my mind was infected with childhood fairytales about knights on crusade around the Caspian, or was it some movie I have seen that left me with the impression that it would be a thickly wooded idyll, with sturgeon jumping into our laps to leave offerings of fresh caviar; apricots waiting to be plucked from trees, boughs weighed down with juicy fruit. Dream on. Even the weather is against us, as steady rain reduces visibility which might in the circumstances be a good thing. How far do we have to go to get to somewhere vaguely pretty? The road only goes north as far as Astara, where Iran borders Azerbaijan. We go all the way to the border crossing, but it never improves. Without visas for Azerbaijan, that is as much of the Caspian as we can see. We head inland into the lower Caucasus Mountains to Ardabil and the 'spa resort town' of Sara'eyn.

Hotels line the streets in this quaint modern mountain retreat which boasts skiing in winter. There is a little snow about, but touts vie for our attention as we motor into town. The incongruity of coming from the chador-lined streets of Tehran to the swimming costume shops of Sara'eyn is inescapable. Do the religious fanatics in the city know that there are two-piece women's bathing costumes on display in the shop windows in the hot springs resort town just half a day's drive from the capital? Is the inconsistency and double standard indulged for purely financial reasons, the mineral springs being the only source of jobs in the mountains here? I resume hostilities with Jack, arguing it is proof that Islamic fanaticism is a thin veneer imposed uncomfortably and artificially – and temporarily – on Iran with little support amongst the people. He counters citing Nazism and George W. Bush's neo-con views and his second term re-election as examples of extreme views supported by enough people to make an impact but not necessarily supported by every single German or American.

Our hotel has no other guests in it and as we look for dinner there are several kebab stalls open but no customers anywhere. Several shops sell honey, as many as ten or twelve different hues and varieties, labelled and bottled and celebrated like vintage wine. In the absence of any other tourists we are lured into every shop and not-negotiably required to sample everything on offer. The hospitality is wonderful, everyone inquisitive and friendly, outward looking and curious about life where we come from, in complete contradiction of their government's public stance about the evils of the West.

Next morning, setting off into the remote mountains along the border with Armenia and Azerbaijan, we fill up on diesel at a rough and ready truck garage where the cashier accepts payment without bothering to look at the gauge on the bowser. He sits astride a heater in a tiny booth and the fuel is so cheap it is not worth his while to come out into the cold to see how much I owe him. It cost 23,750 rial to fill up with 144 litres of diesel, which is just more than US$2, in total not per litre, which is about one and a quarter cents per litre. And I bought the more expensive low-freeze diesel which costs more than the plain diesel.

Babak fort has been recommended as a 'must see' if in the area so we search it out from the mountain town of Kaleybar. A middle-aged man in the flowing robes of a priest sees us studying the map at the bottom of the mountain, asks us, 'Babak?' and waves to us to follow him. The road winds up in endless hairpin bends and as we get towards a plateau he stops, points ahead and does a U-turn before we can even thank him properly. As we crawl up the steepening road, gravel giving way to dirt giving way to grass and then little more than a walking track, three kids on two motorbikes appear from nowhere and adopt us for the rest of the day. They also ask 'Babak?' and urge us to drop in behind. The path becomes a four-wheel drive then a goat track and we go up as far as we can and park. A hike of about an hour along a narrow trail gets us to the ruins of what must have been an impregnable castle, dating back to the ninth century. Atop a narrow ledge, sheer walls block access from every direction. The surrounding peaks are all further than an archer can reach, and the fort commands an unparalleled view of the surrounding valleys. According to the Lonely Planet, Babak was a cross 'between King Arthur, Robin Hood and Yasser Arafat', which is probably the only place those three have ever been mentioned in the same sentence. What we enjoy as spectacular ruins perched on an astoundingly remote mountain creating a strategic and impregnable hideaway, the locals see as a shrine to a heroic leader who, again, made them great many years ago. It is remarkably well preserved for an unrestored thousand and more years old ruin, archways and brickwork still well intact and safe to clamber around on. As we get our breath back from climbing the trail, a group of middle-aged hikers, all men, arrive and greet us enthusiastically. One speaks English and explains they are from Tabriz and it is their annual walk to come up this mountain. As they eat apples and oranges, insisting we share with them, they also make their midday prayer, unfurling prayer mats from backpacks and devoutly bowing to Mecca, foreheads down and then sitting cross-legged, arms held up shoulder high, palms open to the sky. We sit on the mountain top, these puffed pilgrims from one culture mixing beads of sweat with hiking adventurers from the other side of the world. We share the thrill at soaking up the beauty of the spot and the tranquillity of the moment. The English-speaking leader asks if we are Christian. I have learned that it is an insult to Muslims to say you do not believe in God because that is taken to mean you do not believe in their God either, so I fudge the answer and say, 'Australia is a Christian country,' which seems to satisfy our new friend. Before they leave every one of the twenty-plus hikers in the group shakes our hands, 'salaams' us with hands on heart and wishes us well. It remains one of the most memorable moments of the entire trip.

Conversation with our teenage escorts is limited by language, Jack's basic Arabic of no use with the Farsi-speaking Iranians. 'Ahmadinejad no terrorist' and 'George Bush terrorist' is clear, as is 'Barack Obama no terrorist'. 'Osama – terrorist, Hezbollah maybe terrorist' is equally clear. 'Australia, I love you mine' from Hamid made some sense, Ali saying 'You me mine love' did not. Again and again as the entire trip progressed, the frustration of language gaps crashed down. The most obvious way of getting around the problem is to pay for a guide, but with a professional hand-holder you do not stumble on anything, as the guide's job is to guide you and they make decisions and choices that remove the very spontaneity those moments provide. The trade-off involves compromises.

An intense discussion about iPod shuffle reveals a superstitious side to my son that I have never seen before. He thinks the gadget can detect his mood, and when he needs cheering up it will select songs that meet that need. Some days the shuffle lets him down, other times it reads his mind. Oddly for a random electronic programme it selects some songs over and over. Since we left home he has changed what we listen to. The first month was his favourites, over and over, and then as he bored himself – and me – he started looking further afield. Now we are playing some of the music he put on just in case he was sick of the music he really wanted, which he has got sick of. We now hear Van Morrison, Leonard Cohen, Mark Knopfler, Colin Hay and the Beatles. We even play some classical music, some Beethoven and Mozart that his grandfather introduced him to.

Along the Azerbaijan–Armenia border, we gingerly pick our way down a road that winds beside the Aras River, the border between Iran to the south and the warring former Soviet republics on the other side. It is apparently a road we are not allowed to be on, but no one stops us so we keep going. Again I am appalled at my own ignorance of the history of these hostile neighbours. I did not know they all have closed borders, that Armenia is almost isolated on all sides, only maintaining an open border with Iran. I knew Turkey and Armenia did not get on, but I had no idea that their relations with other neighbours were as bad. Observation towers punctuate the landscape with silhouetted soldiers and their guns underlining the sensitivity of this patch. Just a few months before, shooting broke out along the frontier, where Armenia has annexed what is claimed as a separate state called Nagorno-Karabakh, a state no one in the UN recognises except Armenia. The Iranian side of the river seems safe, but on the other bank we can see burnt-out and bombed houses and buildings that might once have been part of the now destroyed railway line. If the conflict ever resolves and the train could be made to run again, through tunnels and sweeping along this ravine, it would be one of the great rail journeys of the world.

Noticing that we are being monitored at the regular barbed-wire and tank trap checkpoints, it seems curious that our papers are never checked. Is it again a case of our white Toyota with a big aerial on the front and lettering on the side being assumed

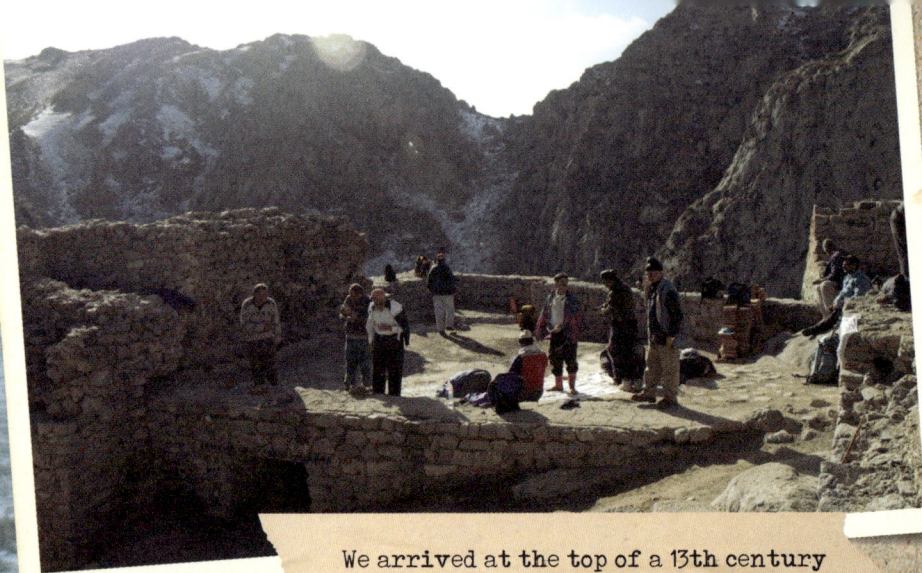

We arrived at the top of a 13th century Azari fort to find a group of elderly hikers from Tabriz who had walked there to sway and pray to the setting sun.

to be some sort of official or UN-type vehicle? We collect a hitchhiking Iranian soldier and give him a lift for an hour to his guard post, through mountainous winding roads touched with fingers of ice but no real snow. He laughs and smiles but with not one word of common language all we can do is offer food, drink and handshakes. The only tourism is when we stumble on the fourteenth-century Church of St Stephanus, founded sixty years after the crucifixion and maintained ever since – for nearly 2000 years – as a place of pilgrimage and worship. Magnificently restored and an oasis of trees and almost European brooks, the stone archways and massive wooden beams would not be out of place in rural France or England. The stained-glass windows celebrating the New Testament are incongruous in the fanatically Islamic surrounds of post-revolution Iran, but the church has thrived in an encouraging sign of respect for history and other people's beliefs. Snow-covered peaks provide a chocolate box backdrop. Inside there are signs offering rooms to rent for travellers and pilgrims but there is no one in attendance and it all seems closed for the winter. It would be a unique experience to stay there a while . . . next time.

We stop overnight in Jolfa and drive towards Mount Ararat, claimed as the true location of Noah's Ark. It is a soaring peak, dwarfing those around it, imposing on the horizon. The road climbs up more mountains this time to the border with Turkey. On a hairpin bend on the mountain pass an overtaking truck nearly wipes us off the earth – the driver as surprised at our presence going up the hill as we are to see him barrelling around the inside of a hairpin bend coming down the mountain. I can still see the panic in the truck driver's eyes as he rounds the bend on the wrong side of the road. But we survived . . . not sure how, but we did.

Hamid and his friends took us up to Babak's fort, in Northern Iran.

39 | The Golden Arches Reappear

In which we cross the Tigris and Euphrates rivers, explore a fourteenth-century castle, sidestep slaughtered sheep and try to find out where dervishes whirl.

Do not stop, do not look, do not appreciate where you are – just shut up and drive. We race across Turkey, barely glimpsing some truly wonderful parts of this magical country. We say farewell to the Silk Road and hello to the first McDonald's.

Another bustling border, but this time it is just as hard to leave Iran as it is to enter Turkey. The authorities are unimpressed with our documents. The map issued at the Turkmen border was actually a passbook. We were supposed to get it stamped at each checkpoint as we drove in order to show we were sticking to the approved route. I shrug my shoulders at the gentle sign language and mime my regrets, accepting the admonishment and explain, 'Well, we are not going back just for the stamps.' There is nothing they can do but wave us through. We get stuck behind a convoy of Chechen Hajis in ancient buses and trucks, in home-made campervans complete with wood-burning stoves. These decrepit fume-belching relics crawl through the mountain pass at jogging speed, blocking everyone from passing any of them, ten or twelve in formation, gasping their way home after the trip to Mecca. When they finally stop, ancient babushkas older than the trucks are lifted bodily from the rear doors, toothless and bent double with sticks. Despite their antiquity, these vintage trucks, which in Australia would be overdue for restoration, have made an astonishing return journey across Saudi Arabia to deliver their human cargo for the once-in-a-lifetime pilgrimage that all devout Muslims are supposed to do before they die.

The first town after the mountain pass is the militarised Dogubayazit, then to the lakeside town of Van where we are greeted by crowds in the streets who chant to us 'Welcome to Kurdistan' in English as we inadvertently drive through a street rally for the illegal independence movement. A bloody guerrilla war was fought here until ten years ago and the rally we stumble upon brings thousands out onto the streets with megaphones, flags, car horns and trumpets blaring as the crowd chant slogans demanding autonomy. Ironically I am on air with ABC Radio in Melbourne in the middle of this illegal rally and if the Turkish authorities knew I was a journalist describing a separatist street demonstration in Kurdish Turkey, I suspect deportation would result. I had declined any interviews for the past month during the particularly sensitive drive through Turkmenistan and Iran, deciding it was silly to take the risk, so it had been a while between radio chats. Derek Guille, the evening host on ABC Radio in Victoria, got a scoop – the first and probably only live report in Western media of something the Turkish government tries to suppress.

It is not only political life that thrives in eastern Turkey. It is such a contrast to Iran to again see people sitting on sidewalk cafes and playing backgammon, girls walking around uncovered and without the awkward self-consciousness we saw in Iran, people laughing and smiling as they greet each other in relaxed and natural familiarity – and at last some food other than kebabs for sale. That marvel of the Western world the cash machine reappears and altogether Turkey is an immediate and stark contrast not just to Iran but all of Central Asia. Iran and the 'stans have a reserve, a reticence about them which we had got used to, but like putting down a heavy backpack after a long hike, suddenly we notice the difference.

Tension between the ethnic Kurds and the government is no doubt fuelled by the endless searches required as we move across Southeast Anatolia. Ping is almost dismantled at one checkpoint, the soldiers doing a more thorough job than anywhere we have been. With several machine guns pointed at us, they empty the entire contents of every bag onto the road, search the tubs of car spares and medicines, even look underneath the car with mirrors on long poles. We try to make the usual jokes but these boys are not for turning and I quickly pull my head in and just do what I am told, no matter how intrusive and inconvenient.

As we mix it with the traffic at the resort town of Tatvan at the western end of the beautiful and unspoilt Lake Van, a baseball-capped kid leans out of the window of a

Jeep and calls out in English, 'G'day, where you from?' I yell back 'Melbourne' before he replies, 'How'd you get that here?' pointing at our right-hand drive 'sticking-out-like-a-sore-thumb' Toyota. I yell, 'We drove it here,' and he laughs loudly and says, 'You *drove* here? Bullshit! … I'm from Canberra,' before his mate in the driver's seat puts his foot down and sadly heads off in another direction before we can ask for help or advice on somewhere to stay.

Blocking a bridge as we cross a ravine is an army tank and a dozen soldiers milling around, agitated and bossy. I slow up expecting yet another luggage and documents check but as we get closer we see carnage and gore like a battle scene. A huge semi-trailer has crested the hill and skidded down the icy bitumen sliding straight into a herd of sheep crossing a very narrow bridge. Unable to stop on the slippery road, he has wiped out all but one, and the soldiers are mediating in a heated exchange between the truck driver and the shepherd. There are guts and heads and bits of sheep all over the place, including some still wriggling under the truck wheels. The local has just lost his entire livelihood and is supported in his outrage by a few others who have come running after hearing the impact. The driver is agitated, although he has my sympathies as the conditions are treacherous and I know how hard it is to stop. The sole survivor of the hapless animals is sitting quietly to the side of the bridge, looking, well, sheepish. We take some photos and drive on, slowing for the conditions to avoid any similar expensive catastrophes.

Wanting to get to the Mediterranean, we map out a route through mountains trying to string the freeways together. It is a long haul – about 900 kilometres in a day – and it nearly kills me. We start at dawn and at last finish at Erdimli on the coast after dark. We barely stop all day. It is a sin to rush through magnificent landscapes and historic towns, but time is not on our side. As we crest the mountain pass behind Osmaniye and glimpse the lights of the waterfront along the Mediterranean Sea glittering all the way down to the border with Syria, it is tempting to turn off south and drop in at Aleppo instead of going west. Next time.

I start to fantasise about driving around the Mediterranean coast, from Spain to Africa, through Morocco and along the northern African coastline to Egypt, then across Sinai, to Aqaba in Jordan and up to Syria and into Lebanon, along the coastal roads of Turkey and Greece and back along the French Riviera. Next time too.

Fuel, when we buy, it is now nearly A$2.60 a litre, not a tankful. It costs the

Moments after crossing from Iran to Turkey. The yellow bus is famous as it is at every kurdish indendence rally in Turkey.

Shepherds use the road and bridges too. If it is icy and the brakes do not work...

TÜRKİYE CUMHURİYET MERKEZ BANKASI

Jack, Jon, Danny, Maddy, Sandy and Rafi at Pamukkale.

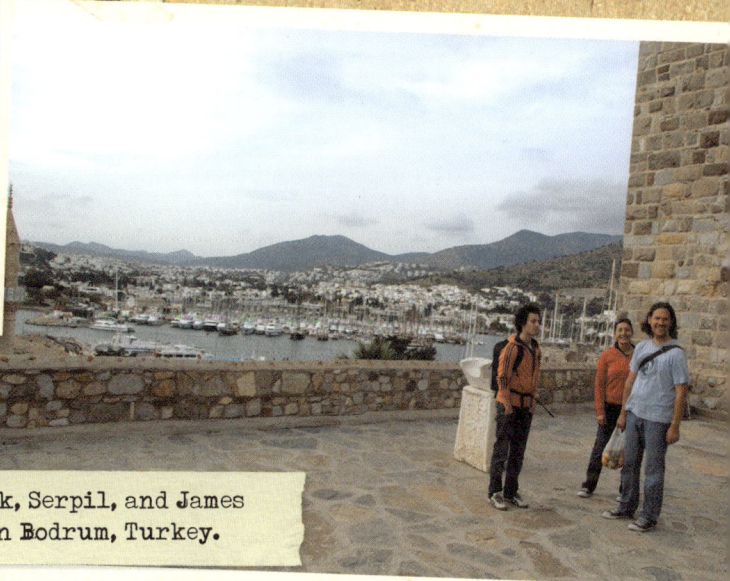

TROIA

TARIH SAATI: DA

TAM / ADULT
15 YIL

Jack, Serpil, and James in Bodrum, Turkey.

satıldığı gun gece

equivalent of A$400 to fill our two 90-litre tanks, even more than it did in the Northern Territory. We watch soccer on TV on a huge wall screen in the restaurant during dinner; the Istanbul team Galatasaray are playing with their new star, the Socceroo Harry Kewell. As soon as we are known to be Australian we are made embarrassingly welcome by the crowd.

We log on to the internet that night and learn of the Mumbai terrorist attacks in India. It is unsettling to think that we have just driven through areas regarded as incredibly dangerous and that our government issues travel alerts warning us not to go, but here are a hundred or more dead and countless hostage in a city that is supposed to be safe in a country where tourists are common.

There is a feeling of sadness as we hit the Turkish coast. It is exciting to see the Mediterranean, a sure sign that we are in Europe and within reach of our goal. But it is also a hint of finality that the exotic and edgy part of our trip is as good as over. It is all safe highways and freeways from here. I suggest to Jack that after all that we have seen, where we have been and what we have done, ultimately it is all a conceit; then I say it is an indulgent conceit. In short time I develop the theme and decide it is a superficial, indulgent conceit, and warming to the task I end up calling it a selfish, superficial, indulgent conceit. We have had several themes during the drive: at first I was reciting the irritating refrain, 'We are the luckiest of the lucky', until Jack threatened to choke me if I said it once more. Then I started saying, 'The more we see the less we know', but he got sick of that too. Now I defer to my new preferred theme: when it boils down, it is all an indulgent conceit, a selfish, superficial, indulgent conceit.

Indulgent because I have taken great liberties with the privileges accorded to me, and also terrible risks. Can anything be more indulgent than that? And a conceit – because we are not really fooling anyone nor pretending that this journey has some profound inner meaning. It was only ever framed as a folly and a folly it has been.

Conversation in the car has taken a distinct focus on the future instead of dwelling on the past. As we started out we were looking back at life in Melbourne, talking through Jack's school exams effort, his toe in the waters of university, life at home and the last nineteen years of our shared time on earth. Now we are looking to the end of the drive, to meeting Jan, to hooking up with some of Jack's friends who are backpacking across Europe. Jack decides he wants to organise an elaborate Christmas lunch in Paris, the full catastrophe – prawns, turkey and pudding. He emails everyone he knows who might be in Paris for Christmas, soliciting offers and allocating jobs. Where can you get berries in Paris in winter? Will there be an oven big enough to cook a turkey? How many of us will there be? When will we know final numbers? He emails Jan for the recipe for summer pudding, he is so enthusiastic.

Cruising the coast road along the Mediterranean, we find a magical route that weaves along the very edge of the rocks, often dropping off with sheer cliffs to the water below. Jack conks out as I drive and sleeps all day as we head inland and on to Denzli and then the next day to Pamukkale. Our plan is to meet friends from Melbourne who are driving eastwards around the world with their children. Sandy works with my sister at a museum in Melbourne, and together with her husband, Danny, and their two primary-school-age kids, Maddy and Raffi, have been on the road for a month longer than us. They have driven in Asia and then shipped their car to California and driven across North America, before shipping their Nissan Patrol to Europe and driving as far as Turkey. They are booked to go to India – to Mumbai, of all places on earth – in a few days. They are frantically changing their plans since hearing of the terror attacks.

Together we wander through the extraordinary white calcium spa waters, the Travertine Pools of Pamukkale and historic ruins of Hierapolis and go together in convoy, two right-hand-drive Victorian-number-plated cars rumbling along the streets of villages and past the fields to the captivating ruins of Aphrodisias, surely as wonderful a Roman ruin as anyone can ask for. It is a wonderful relaxing novelty to sit and talk local gossip, compare travel tales, swap music downloads, just to chew the fat with people from home. We did meet Lachy and Helene in Ashgabat but have not seen many other English-speaking travellers, let alone Aussies. And even that was a novelty, and short lived. The last good sit down yack with other travellers was in Laos.

Sandy and Danny have to get to the port to work out where to send their car instead of Mumbai. We say goodbye and drive to Bodrum on the Aegean Sea. My ABC colleagues Serpil and James have been living with Serpil's parents for six months, taking a break from life in Melbourne, and they have invited us to stay with them on our last stopover before Europe. As we follow the narrow busy road along the coast, we could be in Noosa or on the French Riviera or the Italian coastal resorts – there are signs advertising real estate in English, 'Investment Properties, Water Views', and I start to feel unsettled.

When we see the golden arches and neon signs of the first McDonald's in a very long time indeed, I squawk and wish I could turn around and escape.

Turkish soldier memorials at Cunuk Bair, Gallipoli.

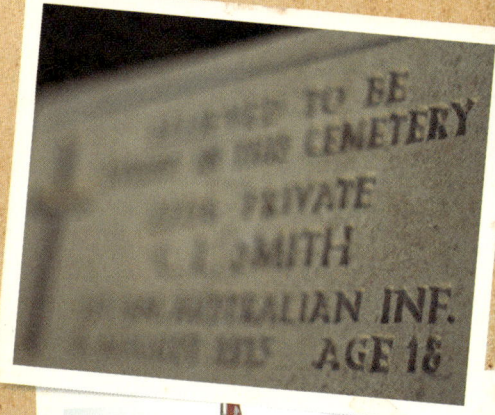

Trenches above the beach where the French landed, Gallipoli.

Cunuk Bair, the highest point on the peninsula and therefore the most vital peak.

Lone Pine, one of the ANZAC memorials at Gallipoli.

JACK WRITES
40 | Turkey by a twenty-year-old

I thought Gallipoli would be a wank. A patriotic and sickening tribute to the soldiers who courageously died for us, a vital moment in the history of Australia and our coming of age and all that crap. Instead, I cried.

We spent two days traipsing along the barren peninsula, gasping at the enormity of death. Walking from mass grave to mass grave, I stared through sizzling tears of horror at the horizon and back down to the memorial stones. The sun set and drenched the peaks and valleys of the peninsula in red, then purple. We walked alongside mass graves breathing out the ages of young boys killed – 'Ohhh … sixteen …' – as if there is a more appropriate age at which to die. We got so caught up in trying to understand the military movements and strategies that we had been sidetracked from the absurdity of men firing sharp little bullets into one another in the names of nations.

The waves lapped at the shore, the rocks rolled and rumbled with the current. The imagination conjured up makeshift camps on the beach with unshaven men in camouflage scampering up and down trenches. With enough concentration the faint echo of machine-gun fire made its way around the cove and the whispers of a long-lost war hung in the air. The distant cries of dying men were heard as shrapnel shells exploded over the other side of the ridge, and men cowered in hiding holes praying that the bayonets didn't find them. In the shallows of the beach the constant pitter-patter of rocks being dragged and dumped continued in the tidal flow.

I looked out to the ocean, an ocean like any other, and the smell of the sea and bush took me home with waves crashing and a film of salt water and foam creeping up the sand. The colour of the rocks and the dense bush took me to Victoria's west coast, down along the Great Ocean Road. The soldiers may as well have been attacking there as the water and the sand and the trees were the same. The scent of pine trees stung my nose and the wind came biting in from the sea, making my eyes water.

I missed home, and hated that.

After a while I got myself together and we continued around the cold wilderness of Gallipoli.

I had never realised how vital Atatürk was in the defence of the peninsula. I never knew that he had led the counterattack that repelled the English. At one of the Turkish memorials at Gallipoli there was a quote of his:

I said to them [the Commanders of the Turkish army] I have total faith and I know that we will defeat the enemy however do not be rushed. I will go forward and when I raise my whip and make a signal, you will come forward all together. Tell your soldiers about this ... I crept forward silently to within 30 meters of the enemy, there was absolutely no sound at Cunuk Bair where there were thousands of soldiers. Lips were moving silently in prayer on this hot night. I paused, lifted my whip over my head and rotating brought it down with a quick movement. It was 4.30am. Bedlam broke out. The English were taken by surprise and didn't know what was happening. To them, sounds of "Allah, Allah" tore the skies in the darkness over the front. Smoke covered all sides and excitement was dominant everywhere. The enemy's bombs tore deep craters in the battlefield. It was raining shrapnel and bullets.

Mustafa Kemal Atatürk

The nationalist overtones that I was expecting were not there. There were modest tributes to the weak remnants of the Ottoman army that had defended their homeland from invasion. They were touching in their simplicity and devoid of jingoistic glory. At each site the feeling of mass death overrode all.

At one area we were driving along a track barely wide enough for just one car. Flanking the track was thin forest and brush, with stripped bark and dead leaves carpeting the ground. Up ahead was a little sign and we stopped: on one side of the sign was a Turkish explanation of the site, and on the other side an English account. On either side of the road were falling-down trenches. The Australian trenches were on the left of the road, and the Turkish trenches on the right, barely four metres apart. Four metres apart. Four metres. Four. Close enough to hear each other snore or sneeze if the deafening drums of war ever stopped for long enough. I jumped down into a trench and again the terrifying stories of the war came to life. The sweaty horror of men, suffering from dysentery, burrowing underground to escape the constant firing and threat of death. And every now and then putting their heads up to fire across at the enemy, and being close enough to see the familiar fear in the eyes of the sorry man who was in the sights of their rifle. Justifying it by muttering 'It's them or me ...'

And then I snapped out of my daydream and all that remained were hollow trenches and the discomfort of standing where men had fallen. A childish part of me wanted to run around playing soldiers and firing from a handgun made from my forefinger and thumb, and another part of me just wanted to scream and cry. So I just stood still and stared at the reality of it all.

The honesty of the whole peninsula shocked me. Although we didn't look for any, the place is apparently riddled with bullets and shells and other things that once harmed. There was no tacky re-creation of scenes, just raw and untouched land that had once been furiously fought over. Down along the southwest point of the peninsula I found a passageway heading underground. I followed it, stepping through mud and over caved-in areas, eventually arriving at a lookout point with another three crumbling passages shooting off from it. I followed one of them another 200 metres or so until it opened just behind a sand dune on the beach where the French had landed and been slaughtered. The passages were lit by cracks filtering sunlight through and along the way I expected skeletal remains to brush against my feet, but all I had to confront were two local kids running in and out of the passageways with sticks for rifles.

Later on, as we made our way to the top of Chunuk Bair, the highest point of the peninsula, we came across a busload of burly Turkish cadet soldiers paying a routine visit to one of the Turkish memorials that dot the high ground of the peninsula (the Anzac and Allied war memorials dot the lower ground). They were hardly older than me. Their big meaty hands slapped into ours as they passed, laughing and running for their army bus that was already moving on to the next site. They kept waving as they took off around a corner.

I guess times change, along with our relationships to places and people.

But Gallipoli wasn't just a landmark for Anzac Cove: it also signified our arrival in Europe.

Just the day before on the small car ferry crossing the Dardanelles Strait, the traditional barrier between Eastern world and Western, Dad turned away from me and stared east from where we'd come. He propped himself against one of the ferry's barriers and wept. I poked fun at him and joked with our friends Serpil and James, who were with us. But then I went and sat alone with the car and watched Dad fling tears into the strait. Short shivers shot up my back: after so much travelling we had finally arrived in Europe.

After Gallipoli we headed for the Greek border. We drove along the Turkish coast and watched the bob and throb and flow of fishing boats rushing to catch dinner before nightfall. Dozens of boats circled just off-shore, only shadows against the drooping sun. Onshore, perched on the rocks, moustachioed men grunted and cast towards the Greek Isles with periodic luck, their ragged old fishing caps shuffling on their heads as they threw the line out with all their might. Then when they steadied and got their balance back, they'd rearrange their hats comfortably on their heads and sit down on the rocks as they slowly and carefully wound in to untangle the unfortunate fish and line. Then they'd do it all again. They'd stand up and take aim, bristling and grunting away another cast as their weathered old hats slipped around their head.

The next day we officially made it to Europe by crossing the Turkey–Greece border. We stopped at the first cute harbour, complete with a medieval hilltop castle. Later that night I strolled off and sat atop that castle wall, with silhouettes of cats creeping across the roof tiles. The sweet smell of fish wafted through the old cobbled streets and made its way up to me on top of the town. I dangled my feet over the wall's ledge, looking out across the flickering city and down to the water. Swaying boats rocked from side to side as tired fishermen scrambled out onto shore. Further along the pier, a pitch-black African wrung out his socks and didn't know where to go. Gorgeous Greek girls with hair that had a life of its own clung together, giggling and smiling, the years of Mediterranean sun glowing off their brown skin. And when the boys revved their car engines I hadn't felt so close to home in a long time.

Anzac Cove. The infamous beach where the Anzacs arrived in 1915.

Jon crying as we cross the Dardanelles. We arrive in Europe.

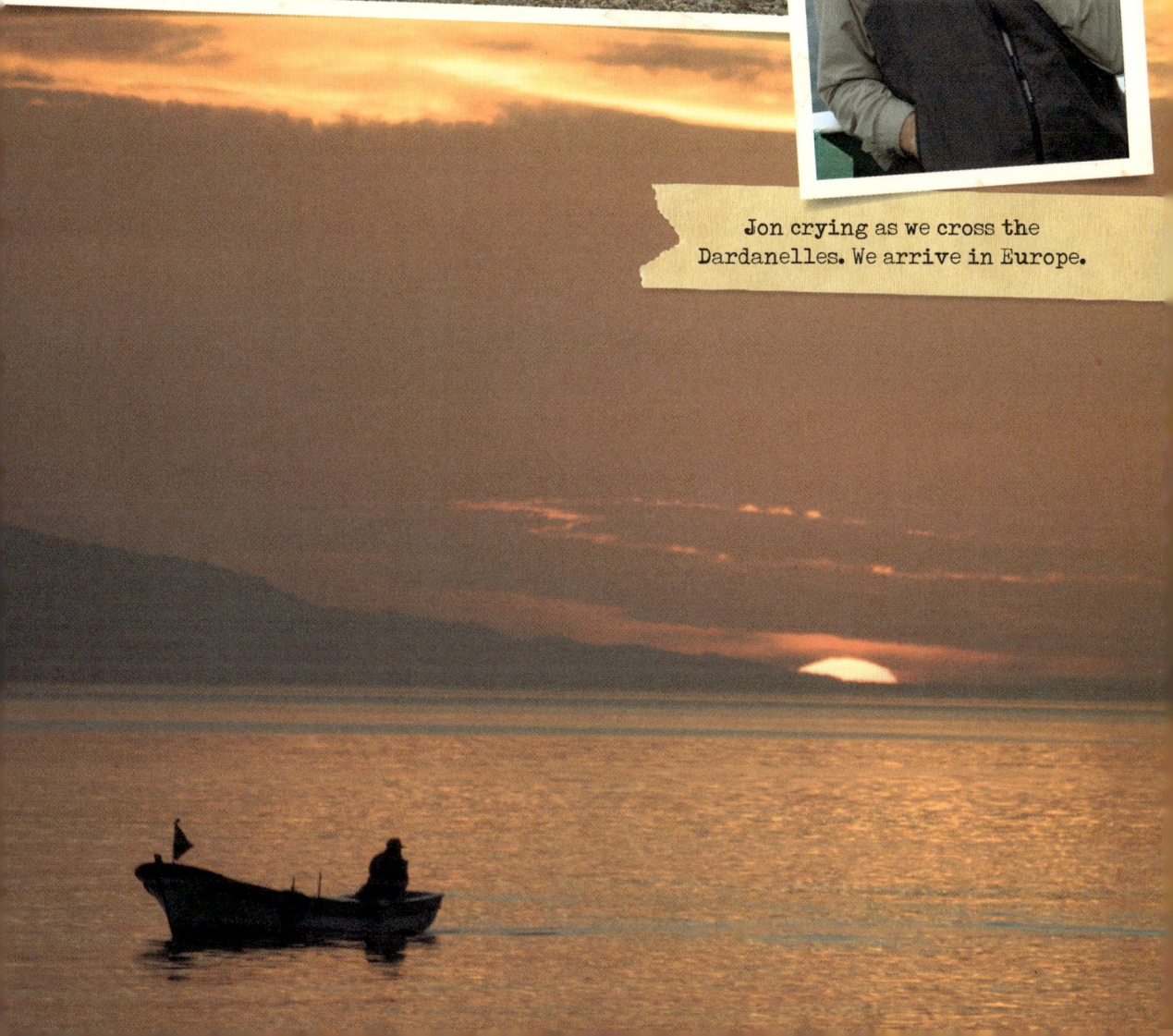

41 | To Gallipoli by a fifty-two-year-old

I do not order you to attack; I order you to die. In the time which passes until we die other troops and commanders can take our place
> – Mustafa Kemal Atatürk, Gallipoli, April 25, 1915

Confronting these men myself I said, 'Why are you running away?'
'Sir, the enemy,' they said.
'You cannot run away from the enemy.'
'But sir we have no ammunition,' they said.
'If you have not got ammunition, you have your bayonets,' and shouting to them I made them fix their bayonets and lie down on the ground. When these men fixed their bayonets and laid down, the enemy also lay down. The moment was gained, and I knew then that we could still win.
> – Mustafa Kemal Atatürk, Gallipoli, April 25, 1915

Bodrum is a resort town gathered around an intact Crusader castle that is also the Museum of Underwater Archaeology. Yilmaz and Sakine, Serpil's parents are wonderful hosts and we do our washing and feel part of the family, albeit for just two nights. They could not be kinder and home cooking is a treat. I have lost about 15 kilos since leaving home, most of it in Mongolia. Sarkine's cooking marks the point where I start to put it back on. The waterfront is stunning, massive tourist charter yachts lined up one after the other waiting to take the rich and the beautiful around the Greek Islands; in summer it keeps them busy but in the first week of December there is no action. Many of the Greek Islands are closer to Turkey than they are to mainland Greece, and the tourism industry is the mainstay of what has also become a retirement playground for Turks and swarms of Europeans. The area is full of relics and historic ruins and Serpil and James come with us as we head off to tour coastal western Turkey and eventually the evocative Gallipoli peninsula.

Our first excursion is the ruins of Halicarnassus, a mausoleum that was one of the original Seven Wonders of the Ancient World, then to Troy where the multilayered excavations explain the successive waves of construction from the Bronze Age, then Mycenaean, the Achaeans, Balkans, Greeks, Romans and Byzantines, as well as Crusaders and Turks. The wooden horse story makes for a corny entrance, but as a site rich in culture and history it has few rivals. Jack had made a study of Homer's *Iliad* for his final year of school and was able to bring the rest of us up to speed as we wandered about the empty ruins. The excavation continues even today and as I stand staring at the uncovered mounds I cannot help but wonder what treasures are still to be unearthed. Can I get a trowel and start scratching away at the soil?

Travelling four up is totally different, especially as Serpil is a native Turkish speaker and can ask for directions each time we get lost. A car ferry carries us across the Dardanelles, the narrow straits between Canakkale and Eceabat. I shed a few tears as the ramps slam shut and the ferry starts to surge; we are saying goodbye to the Asian continent and it is the beginning of the end as we arrive on European soil. I feel a mixture of elation and sadness; looking forward to Paris and looking back to where we have been. I play a mental slide show of Arnhem Land, Komodo dragons, Cambodian jungle and Chinese freeways, the mountain passes and the alpine lakes of the 'stans ... the whole trip rushes through my head as we cross the narrow band of water. I hug Jack, who runs away and hides from my tears inside the sanctuary of the mighty Ping, only to emerge with his camera to document my low emotional threshold. I stare at Ping – our indestructible 4x4, surrounded by little Euro hatches and delivery vans – and distract myself by picking at the stones from the Mongolian steppes still stuck in the tread of the tyres.

Finding lodgings or food in Eceabat requires a choice between the Crowded House Hotel, the Vegemite Bar, and the Boomerang Bar and so on. The entire local economy relies on Anzac tourism. We are happy to add to their turnover, although we are glad to be missing the annual April hordes. As I drive off the steel ramps of the car ferry, a foot passenger steps in front of the car. A tour guide calls out, 'No more casualties in battlefield please,' and we all laugh.

So much has been written about Gallipoli, what more can be said? No matter how much you think you understand or know, it is a confronting place to visit. Paul Keating had recently said he would never visit Gallipoli and that he thought it 'utter and complete nonsense' that Australia was redeemed by the Gallipoli campaign. I agree with his argument but not his conclusion, and do not see why you cannot appreciate the futility of the campaign, the sometimes cynical exploitation of it by all sorts of people keen to make it mean things it maybe did not mean, but still honour the dead on both sides by going there. I have visited the Western Front too and wept at the senseless waste of the young boys' lives, grave after grave. My maternal grandfather fought in World War I for the German Army, Jan's grandfather in the Anzac forces on the Western Front. Jack's great-grandfathers were possibly – unlikely but notionally – trying to kill each other.

At Gallipoli 130,000 soldiers died on both sides, achieving no territorial gain. To take but one of the battles: in the space at Lone Pine equivalent to a suburban footy field, nearly 5000 men died in one week in what was only ever a diversionary attack. Overall, 400,000 dead and wounded on both sides, the Turks suffering twice the casualties of the Allies. More French soldiers died than Anzacs, many of them from North Africa. Many of the Turkish dead were from distant corners of the Ottoman Empire, their memorial stones showing their origins from as far afield as Kosovo, Baghdad and Mosul. But it is the graves of boys from Horsham, Longreach, Stawell, Albany, Moree, Myrtleford and Murray Bridge that get to me and make me cry.

James has been reading Les Carlyon's excellent book *Gallipoli* and can fill us in on many of the finer points of the strategy and geography. The Turks have made generous allowance for Anzac tourists as well as celebrating their own considerable interest in the peninsula, with large but well-written storyboards discreetly placed at important points of interest. It is a clear advantage to have Ping to get about, and we use full 4x4 capacities to go up some of the tracks from the beaches to the battlefields driving in air-conditioned and cushioned comfort where soldiers had to carry their guns, heavy packs and ammunition, all the while dodging bullets and dead friends' bodies as they climbed. Stripping off shoes and socks I wade knee deep in the freezing water off Anzac Cove, trying to imagine what hell it must have been for the soldiers.

We spend two days exploring, and do not see any other tourists except in the town of Eceabat itself.

There is a complete ban on scavenging, and it is a crime for the locals to try to sell shrapnel or other historic mementoes. After years of the battlefields being disturbed by souvenir hunters, these rules are rigorously policed to prevent vandalism and to discourage local school kids. We sit and chat to one local in our hotel well into the night, and he brings out a bucket full of fragments of shells, bits of military hardware, scissors, belt buckles, buttons and bullets he has collected over the years and gives us one each. We offer to pay but he protests it is legal if he gives them to us but illegal if he sells them. He produces his favourite piece – a water canteen, pierced right through by a bayonet, the blade piercing one side and penetrating all the way to the opposite wall of the bottle.

After lunch we farewell Serpil and James, and race the 160 kilometres to the border with Greece. Our original plan to drive through Bulgaria, Romania, Hungary and Austria towards Paris has been superseded by a quirky idea of zipping straight across the northern regions of Greece, grabbing a ferry across to Italy and swapping the stress of eastern Europe for the relative luxury and good food of Italy. A front-seat conference results in a unanimous vote for the soft option. We have had enough queues and hassles at border crossings, enough currency swaps, enough new languages, enough freezing cold mountains. Time to ease up, we decide, and so we do.

Those heroes who shed their blood and lost their lives, you are now lying in the soil of a friendly country. Therefore rest in peace. There is no difference between the Johnnies and the Mehmets to us where they lie side by side in this country of ours. You, the mothers who sent their sons from faraway countries, wipe away your tears, your sons are now lying in our bosoms and are in peace. After having lost their lives on this land they become our sons as well.

– Mustafa Kemal Atatürk, 1934

It was not until nearly twenty years had passed that Ataturk penned those immeasurably generous words.

42 | The Easy Way Out

Riots, freeways, ferries, food, Romeo and Juliet, *Milano, snow in the Alps and the Mont Blanc Tunnel.*

Our first sample of Greece is a riot. The police have killed a student in Athens and the entire country is in uproar. We watch the TV news in a cafe shortly after crossing the border. People are worried about what might happen, but in Kavala there is no immediate local reaction. There are students putting posters on phone poles and on walls, calling for protests, some of them wearing masks to hide their faces as they paste the posters up. We have seen civil unrest in so many of the countries we have been through, it has been following us all the way. Natural disasters have forced route changes, civil unrest has dogged us, military conflict even in southern Thailand and near the Cambodia–Thailand border, earthquakes in Chengdu and Kyrgyzstan, snowstorms in Uzbekistan, riots in Dili and just before we arrived an assassination attempt on the nascent nation's leaders. What next?

Tempting as it is to take any of the clearly signposted turnoffs to Sofia in Bulgaria or Macedonia or even Albania, we stick to the new plan and catch a massive car ferry from Igoumenitsa across to Italy. The prostitutes aboard do a roaring trade with the truck drivers. We sit and read. Tourists with skis strapped to their roofs are heading from Greece to the Swiss or Italian Alps. Our giant 4x4 seems incongruous beside the Euro-boxes in the belly of the ferry. Arriving on the Adriatic coast we rejoice in Italian food and freeways where drivers know what to do. We race through to Padova, then Verona, happy being tourists and enjoying the Christmas fare. Juliet's balcony in the reputed home of the Cappello family, inspiration for Shakespeare's Capulet in Romeo and Juliet, is fairytale material in the light winter snow. Jack has a friend in Milano, a former exchange student at his school, and we survive getting into and out of Milan in order for them to meet up. Negotiating European drivers and roads is such a non-event after what we have had to contend with, yet I recall stressing and sweating about driving here when we have rented cars for holidays in the past. It is all relative after all. Our ascent of the Alps to the Mont Blanc Tunnel is in zero visibility and as we emerge on the Swiss side it is a snowstorm. Overnight in Martigny, we look wistfully at some of the world's most famous ski resorts, Chamonix and Courmayeur, but as this is the first heavy snow for the season there are no lifts running and Ping ploughs on to Geneva.

My distant cousin Michael and his wife Maricella live and work here and make us feel completely at home. We join with them and their son David, a little older than Jack, to celebrate L'Escalade, the festival in Geneva that recognises the 1602 rebellion by the citizens of Geneva against the Duke of Savoy. Jack and David appreciate each other's company and as I prepare to head off to Brittany to meet up with Jan, they decide to spend a few days together. Jack's offer to stay on in Geneva will also give Jan and me precious time together after six months apart and I am grateful and again impressed with his thoughtfulness.

Jack and I part ways. He will catch a train in a week to meet his reunited parents in Paris for Christmas. We try to avoid a soppy farewell. Standing in the snow I grab him in a bear hug and he says to me the sweetest thing I could possibly ask to hear: 'Thank you – and I would not change a thing.' I still do not know if he prepared those words or if they just came to him in the moment but I choked and struggled for something profound to say myself. I failed, but did tell him it had been a privilege and the great adventure of my life, which I would not and could not have done without him. Ping carries me away, the road blurry for my tears.

As I cross the Swiss border into France I realise with a thud that I still have Jack's passport in my bag, and he will need it to get to Paris. A panicked half-hour backtrack and a second farewell and I'm on my way – to embrace my wife.

Corny – but we had to do it.

43 | Paris for Christmas

Jan arrives and we make it to Paris for Christmas – just like we always said we would. Fuss? What fuss?

One thousand kilometres separate Geneva from Roscoff in Brittany, northwest France, where Jan will alight from a ferry in two days. I am determined that nothing will be in my way; no snowstorm, earthquake, volcano or meteor will stop me from being there when she arrives. I do not factor in the contortion and gymnastics involved in paying cash tolls on the French freeways when driving alone in a right-hand-drive car.

It is weird being alone for the first time in six months and I constantly send text messages to Jack, asking if he is okay. He finally tells me to leave him alone. I race across France, barely looking, until I get to Roscoff with half a day to spare. I visit the ferry terminal and make sure the arrival details are all correct and then wait.

Early next morning, I am as nervous as a young lover on a first date. I pace the arrival foyer and try to conjure up something romantic for my first words. Jan finally saunters through the double doors, grinning and looking fabulous. I am not sure if she will slap me or kiss me. I weep and swoop at the same time, swinging her into the air and making her yelp. Everyone stares and I resist the urge to make a speech. Although we have spoken frequently over the phone, it is impossible to communicate meaningfully over that long a time. It has been the hardest part of the journey and now I cannot let go of her. I do not know where to begin bridging the space between us, but we do and we enjoy a wonderful few days in a luxury hotel before heading to Paris, where she is desperate to see Jack.

The party in St Germain is worth the wait. Our two 'extra' children, Theo and Manon, who each lived with us on exchange over the last few years, arrive with Jack, as well as Linda and Ian, close friends from Melbourne and some backpacking mates of Jack's, Sam and Zac. Marcia, who stayed at our home in Melbourne for a six-month pyjama party with Jan while we were gone, is a special guest. A few days later, Christmas lunch at Linda and Ian's rented apartment goes something like this: dips, smoked salmon, oysters, prawns, soup, snails, turkey, vegetables, salads, summer pudding, Christmas pudding, ice cream, patisserie, marzipan, chocolate and cheese. Jack had started planning it months before, distracting himself from the boredom in the desert drives by reciting his favourite foods. My middle sister Susan and her friend Andrew complete the crowd. To see family and friends after so long talking just to each other is utterly exhilarating. There are so many stories to tell. We drive home along the Champs Elysees in bumper-to-bumper traffic, the fairy lights illuminating everything from the Arc de Triomphe to the Eiffel Tower. It has been one hell of a drive and what a magical way to wind it up.

But then Jan and I spend a week, including New Year's Eve, in bed in Paris – not in frenzied clinches but coughing and spluttering our lungs out with a shocking flu. What a waste of our week in the world's most romantic city. I ignore a parking ticket on the Toyota's windscreen, assuming that Victorian registration in Paris gives me immunity, and then panic when Ping has a huge red 'Tow Away' sticker across the windscreen the next morning. I quite liked the idea of someone seeing our oversized Ping with its snorkel and off-road steel wheels parked in Paris in the same way I saw that inspirational Land Rover in London thirty years ago. While it is squeezed in-between the scooters and bicycles illegally on Rue Saint-Andre des Arts, someone does scrawl 'Go Aussie' in the dirt on the door, just above the map of where we have been, and a few notes of greeting are left under the wipers. I reluctantly move it to the incredibly expensive parking station to avoid losing it to the tow truck.

As soon as we recover we head off to Bayeux and then take a ferry from Ouistreham to Portsmouth. Driving off the ferry, I wave our carnet at the UK customs officer who just ignores me and I am back on the proper side of the road, four months after crossing over to the wrong side at the Thai–Cambodia border. I take a few roundabouts to get used to it, but it is such a relaxing experience to drive in sync with the rest of the traffic and to understand the road signs. We potter around the coast of Devon, drop in on Stonehenge and trundle in to stay with Tim, a Melbourne friend, in central London, flouting the congestion charge, on January 7, 2009. Jack arrives by train and we risk arrest taking our photo with Ping outside first Buckingham Palace (not allowed by the anti-terror police) and then the Houses of Parliament at Westminster (only just allowed by the anti-terror police – 'Be quick about it then …'). Big Ben is a fitting backdrop for the final photo before I venture into the wilds of London's outer east and drop Ping off at a shipping company warehouse in Reading. Ping is popped into a box and sent home. We covered 39,231 kilometres in six months and ten days, from our front gate in Melbourne to Trafalgar Square in our car.

We did what we wanted to do. We went north to Ulaan Baatar and then turned left. It's time to go home.

JACK WRITES

I took the Paris metro yesterday with my friend. I was sitting there, clattering and jangling along, and I looked at all the pale faces glowing in the fluoro light. They all looked so ugly and alien. Everyone looked so tired. So fed up with everything and bored. And I just stared at the people all dreaming in their own boggy heads. And no one stared back.

And so, here I am. In Paris. Sitting on the steps of the Sacre-Coeur at Montmartre, the church that overlooks the city from the north. I'm staying with a friend and her boyfriend just around the corner. They live above a little cafe where a Tarantino film is currently being shot and extras dressed in World War II-era clothes crowd the cobbled street. Nazis sip coffees beside newspaper sellers and horses roll past with their carts.

Earlier this morning, with my eyes still droopy and my legs lethargic, I made my way through the morning mist towards the domes of the Sacre-Coeur. I arrived at the top of the hill where the church sits and I took a seat on the steps that lead down to the spiralling snail of Paris. It was cold then, and I haven't moved for a good half hour. It's still cold. The wind is biting at my fingers. Behind me, grandiose and magnificent, stands the stunning cathedral, its peaks disappearing into low-lying clouds. Before me, Paris spreads out with its streets cloaked in fog. Just the roofs and chimneys identifiable through the haze. Somewhere to my right is the Eiffel Tower.

Somewhere to my left is Melbourne. Many things are running through my head. My thoughts flash across a satellite perspective of the earth and then zoom along the path of our journey: Australia, Asia, Central Asia, Turkey, Europe. Snippets of memory flash in and out of my head. Again I feel the hot chicken blood speckled on my leg from Dili. Again I see the peaks of Tiger Leaping Gorge disappearing into the heavens and the rush of water below. Again my insides soar as my mind's eye scans the emptiness of the Gobi Desert. The world towers above me, so massive and intricate, and again I get a glimpse of the belittling bittersweet perspective of myself as a person in a world of people. Just another squirming, thinking, speaking body in the history of humanity.

And I shared all this with my old man. I guess it is pretty strange to spend so much time with my dad. Hours upon hours talking to each other to ward off boredom. Exploring anything that came to mind. His past, mine, the future. Everything. It wasn't always good fun but the tensions and frustrations have made us closer. We know each other's breaking point. We know each other. And in all of these memories there'll be my dad's wild greying hair and his awkward grin, a stable normality in the exoticism.

Yet, clinging to each of my memories is a dash of disappointment that we never had enough time to really soak up a place and get past the superficial layer of a society. There's also a discomfort gnawing at me over the unequal relationship between the tourists and the locals, especially in developing countries. Then there's a tinge of confusion about what it means to be a tourist.

I suppose that's what the distance from home and the introduction to new places does to you. It confuses you and throws up new questions about where you stand in the world. Apparently we're meant to find ourselves when we travel, but it's made me realise just how lost I am in this huge hungry planet.

Finally I arrive at the strange conclusion that it's a pretty stupid idea to cross the world in six months. It's not a wrong idea, just stupid. We didn't have enough time in each place to get a solid base and see much more than the nearest tourist sight. We hardly got past the shallow exterior of a society, and that's what we were really searching for. But that takes years and we only had months. And at nineteen years of age I wasn't going to head off and spend half a year in one place, learn a language and study a society. Maybe that'll come later. But right now the stinging December cold is freezing my fingers and I can't sit here all day reflecting on the past. The sun has risen a touch higher and is shining its way through the Paris fog.

I stand up from the steps and turn to take in the Sacre-Coeur behind me, its spires still lost in the haze. It sure looks proud on top of its hill, a taste of something different sitting on the physical and mental periphery of the city. I turn back to Paris. Grey clouds hovering below fuse with the smoke rising from the streets. There's a certain electricity in the air coming from the metro tunnelling through the rabbit holes underground. There's an energy circulating through the city that comes from the friction of millions of lives all played out in romantic low-rise apartments, all played out within spitting distance from one another. And God, it's cold! A breeze kicks its way along the Seine and flies all the way up to me on the steps as I look out across the rooftops. There's more people out there, doing stuff. Living under those roofs and talking, eating and loving. Just being.

The bells of the Sacre-Coeur ring and that's as good a sign as any. With my hands in my pockets I drop down the stairs into the heart of the spiralling city. I can see the streets and the buildings. I have a job interview in an hour – it's time to go.

44 | Emotion

Jan and I were always planning the big drive for when I stopped working. But a few years ago Jan ruled herself out, so the trip dropped off the list of things to do 'one day'.

A few years later Jan suggested Jack do the overland drive to London with me during his gap year. Jack agreed with one condition – that if he was to sit in the car with his father for six months, he had to be in charge of the music. I agreed without hesitation, trusting his taste in music and his squeamish aversion to torture. As it turned out, he was introduced to more of my music than I was to his. The hits of the 60s and 70s, Bob Dylan or Jackson Browne were more likely to be heard in Ping than Radiohead or Kings of Leon.

Every middle-aged father I have talked to about 'our drive' has had the same reaction to our trip. If I could have a dollar for everyone who has said, 'I wish I could do something like that with my kids ...' There is an unspoken yearning for a closer bond between dads and their offspring. Middle-aged men feel trapped in careers that tie them down, tunnels with no light at the end except for eventual exhaustion and retirement. Financial pressure squeezes the life out of so many of us, and the relentless pace of corporate and now even public sector life makes breadwinners a stressed and often miserable bunch of people. Midlife crises are a dime a dozen, but the solution for everyone is not necessarily a sports car or a motorbike. Mothers complain of the same yearning but not as uniformly as dads. It is not the exclusive preserve of men but so many have said it to me that it is beyond contention.

Taking time out is a huge risk – who are we outside of work? How much of my identity and self was tied up in being on the radio? What am I when I am not a broadcaster? Do I still have ideas? Do I know anything at all? Can I reverse the appalling superficiality and parochialism of what we do to look afresh at the world?

I was not at all sure that I would be welcome back at the studios when my trip was over. Despite the reassurances of the boss and the boss's boss there was always the risk that they would change their minds, or that my replacement would make me look duller than I already was. As it turned out my boss's boss's boss departed while I was away, and a huge shake-up of the division then and there might have been a disaster for someone absent on a folly globetrotting, instead of getting on with the job at hand. And I also must confess I was not sure that I could reapply myself, that I still had the appetite and discipline required for doing the job to the standard I had aimed for over the previous decade. I knew I was utterly tired, getting cynical and accumulating the shift worker's permanent sleep deficit that doctors warn about. And the sad and unpalatable fact is that 774 ABC Melbourne did keep going without me, the Morning Show still went to air, the audience still tuned in. Horrible, really.

How hard would it be to reconnect to the news cycle, to catch up on all the important events and breaking news that happened in six months while we were away? Can I catch up? Or will there forever be this hole, like someone who has lost their memory in a terrible accident, a gap in what I understand about our world? Could I seamlessly re-enter the atmosphere after our half-year orbit?

The other vital part of the equation is whether the parental yearning for time with teenagers is shared by the teenagers themselves? Jack perhaps inadvertently paid me the greatest compliment as we tootled through the middle of nowhere, that 'None of my friends would ever do this with their dads ...' I take that as more an observation of his unlimited tolerance of me, together with his capacity for self-congratulation, than a deliberate endorsement of my parenting techniques. He and his brother Nigel have been sacrificial lambs and close witness to my shortcomings in that department.

Astonishingly, there were only two times in six months when I lost my equilibrium with him. 'If you don't want to be here,' I said a few times, 'here is the credit card, there is an airport and you are out of here.' Thankfully, he does not sulk, and after some earplug time and a nap he always cheered up. I am sure I was ghastly to be with too – and he probably wanted the earth to open and swallow him whenever I did the 'papa kangaroo, baby kangaroo' routine. Can you imagine spending six months with your father, seven days a week, twenty-four hours a day? Jack may be seriously scarred from this experience, will be sending us the counselling bills for years to come, and no doubt at all has heard every growing-up story, joke and confession I am ever going to tell. But I assure you, teenage angst is worse than father stress in anyone's book.

Our trip was never conceived as anything more than an indulgence. We did not raise money for a charity. We did not accept sponsorships. We did not make grand and eloquent claims about uniting peoples across the continents. We just went for a drive.

But if along the way we have achieved anything more than burning a lot of diesel and boosting the profits of Australia's telecommunications giant, then maybe it will be to nudge a few parents into taking a break, risking their careers, their marriages and their solvency and wandering around the outback or the globe with their kids for a while. Travel is the best thing you can do with your time; travel with your kids is the best thing you can do together, and they learn more away from school than when there. It opens their eyes to the world. And if my time is up tomorrow, I know that the family trips we have done will be some of the best times in my life. The return on this risky investment is incalculable.

In front of Buckingham Palace

45 | Mistakes We Made, Things to Avoid

There are millions of questions people have about our trip. I have been corresponding with many overlanders and these are the most common questions asked. I hope the answers are useful if not too blunt.

What time of year? The start of winter was a stupid time to try to cross the Torugart Pass and to enter sometimes impassable parts of the 'stans. Mongolia in summer must be totally different to our experience at the start of winter. For us, no one else was in the countryside, but many of the activities, like eagle hunting, had been stopped for the winter. We avoided the wet season in Asia, but we hit winter in Europe. I had no choice about when I could get a break at work, so it was then or never, but if you have the luxury of choosing your timing, seasons make or break your adventure.

Do you really want to blog? It nearly drove us crazy. It was wonderful to keep family and friends informed, it was fun to get a reaction from the public, but it became a chore. Simple as that. You can spend time on the road living the adventure, or documenting it – but it is a struggle to do both. And once you start, you create a monster. On the positive side, we were astonished at the number of people travelling vicariously with us. It was thrilling and a buzz to read comments but we never expected a fraction of that response. Jack found it unnerving at first, then stimulating.

Is a video camera worth taking? We took a digital HDD broadcast-quality video camera and hardly used it. The enormous amounts of time consumed by editing is time that you do not ever see again. I could not countenance sitting squinting at the laptop in some fabulous remote spot and fiddling for days with edit bars and cross-fades just to create a trophy piece. Lonely Planet TV and the ABC both offered to consider whatever we sent them, but it was not worth it. If you are a professional editor and can whip out something respectable in quick time, maybe. We could not.

Why didn't you make a documentary? The ABC was happy to look at sending a crew to shadow us but discussions did not go past first base. Neither Jack nor I wanted a crew to come with us – it would become their trip not ours. We were not chasing glory, nor wanting it to turn into even more of a circus. We were just going for a drive. A crew making a film have a job to do, and we could anticipate being told, 'Can you just drive through that gorge again the other way so we get the light right …' No thanks.

How far to go in how long a time? We covered nearly 40,000 kilometres in six months. That averages out at about 220ks a day. But some days we did 1000ks and other days we did not go anywhere at all. There are always compromises in any trip, especially one like ours. We wanted to see if it was possible to get from home to London in six months, and we did. It would have been much better to have had nine months, or a year, or two years. But quite simply we did not.

How much do you want to carry? We took clothes we never wore, too many pairs of shoes, a lot of medicine, car parts we never used, tools we did not touch. Some were safety related and not negotiable. EPIRB and satellite phones are essential. They came home unused, but that is how you want it to be and does not mean you can go without them. We took three oil and three fuel filters and used them all. We had spare belts and hoses and did not need them. A second spare wheel would have been comforting, but would have meant a roof rack or elaborate double rear wheel carrier, both to be avoided. We did not equip the car with a winch; if we had one we might have used it once to help other drivers stuck in snow drifts in Kyrgyzstan. We did not take GPS and I only regretted it in big cities in continental Europe, like Milan. We had binoculars, but they never came out of the case. Jack took more camera lenses than he used. We had two portable HDD backups as well as regularly burning photos to CDs. We did not carry a tent. In Asia places to stay are plentiful and cheap. In China camping is unheard of. In Mongolia and beyond it was unsafe and too cold. We took fishing rods and tackle and used them once, in the Northern Territory.

Was the Toyota Prado the right car? Yes. Only the six-stack CD jammed, nothing else broke. Astonishing. Fuel economy was not what I hoped, but we were not pottering along at 90 kilometres per hour, we were climbing mountains or, if on freeways, flying mostly at 120 to 130, sometimes faster. We achieved 13 litres per 100 kilometres.

How much did fuel cost? It is a tricky calculation requiring conversion from sixteen currencies. But here it is: we used 5199 litres of fuel to go 39,231ks. Highest price per litre was A$2.66 in Mongolia; almost as bad was Turkey at A$2.60. Cheapest fuel was Iran where a litre cost less than A$0.02, yes two cents a litre. Overall, after doing currency conversion on each transaction, our diesel bill over the entire journey was A$7539. It took an entire afternoon to calculate that figure, adding up every bill and then converting each currency back to Australian dollars in order to do it!

Is it easier to go the other way? Probably, because visas for the 'stans could all be sourced in London before you head off and they will still be current when you go through central Asia, thus solving the single greatest headache we had. The China visas can be stamped in Ulaan Baatar, but the guiding service will need to be booked well ahead. We had emails from many other overland travellers complaining about their China guides and asking us if we were having the same trouble. One overlander from Spain emailed us that he was stuck at the Mongolia–China border for weeks and felt like he was in jail as he was refused entry into China. His papers were not in order and the Canada-based guide company had made lavish promises they did not fulfil.

How much did it cost? Don't ask.

Some numbers and weird stuff:
by Jon, December 10, 2008 at 8:27 am

- 35,000ks from Melbourne by road you reach Thessaloniki in Greece; 25,000 ks is Kashgar in Western China.

- Jack has taken more than 5000 photos.

- Two punctures: one in Mongolia and the other in no man's land on the Torugart Pass between China and Kyrgyzstan, in the snow.

- No mechanical breakdowns or failures at all. One alarm switch and the CD player have broken. One driving light bulb has blown. Two wheels buckled and were repaired imperfectly, just as well we went for steel instead of alloy wheels which would have cracked or split ages ago. So we have a wonky spare and a slight front-end wobble at speed until at least one wheel can be replaced.

- To those who thought we chose the wrong car . . . we didn't. I could say a whole lot more about this but it could be misunderstood as marketing. To the nice people from the Land Rover Club who wrote on their chatroom before we left that I was an idiot and knew nothing about cars and was heading for disaster, sorry to disappoint you.

- Nothing has been stolen except Jack's notebook and sunglasses, pickpocketed in Thailand. Nothing lost except two guidebooks I cannot find, which could still be buried deep in the car!

- The biggest waste of money was buying tickets for the plane to Dili and then two days later being offered a ride on the cargo ship. Not refundable.

- Equipment not used includes the EPIRB (but good to have it; you do hope you never need it) and binoculars. Various and extensive tools carried and thankfully not used, but again you have to have them. Tyre repair kit not touched . . . you can get tyres repaired everywhere we have been. So that well-travelled kit will go onto eBay!

- The budget . . . well, a work of fiction and I have not dared look at the totals and will not until we get home, because that would spoil the last bit of the trip.

- And more than 1400 comments on this blog . . . and well over 500,000 visitors to the site. We never thought we would get one-tenth of that.

Our Car: by Jon, June 10, 2008

We are driving a 2005 Toyota Land Cruiser Prado Diesel automatic. It had 40,000ks on the clock when we bought it second-hand from a Canberra couple who had driven it around Australia.

Everyone will have a different view on the ideal car for this trip — but for what it is worth, here is what I thought and what I decided. Happy to be told I am wrong!

I decided ABS brakes were essential, as was central locking. I did not want a sunroof, electric seats, and timber veneer on the dash or too many electronic gadgets that can break.

The common rail diesel motor became available in new Prado wagons as we bought ours, but I could not afford a new one — $20,000 more than our three-year-old model which came with about $10,000 worth of extras fitted by the previous owners.

WIM 345 was already fitted with dual battery set-up, snorkel, high lift heavy-duty suspension, cargo barrier, bull bar and extra lights. A modified engine chip has been installed promising better fuel economy. An onboard air compressor operates locking differentials in case of extreme terrain.

MANUAL V. AUTOMATIC

We have always had manual cars. I had not considered an automatic for this trip. Jan suggested, however, that driving on the wrong side of the road for most of the time, juggling maps, chaotic traffic, nerves and other driving challenges might just make an automatic gearbox a sensible choice. After driving a few auto versions of this car I was sufficiently impressed to go with it.

DIESEL V. PETROL

The availability — or not — of fuel dictates diesel. Fuel efficiency dictates diesel. Variable petrol quality dictates diesel. Diesel should cost less. It will be slower and accelerate slower. It makes more noise.

MODIFICATIONS

The Prado has Old Man Emu suspension which the previous owner fitted. It lifts the car a little higher off the road but it does not sway. Steel wheels are stronger than alloy in case of serious ruts and holes on the road surface. Alloys can crack and even break and then cannot be repaired. Steel wheels can be hammered back into shape if dented. New tyres (Cooper All Terrain) and new batteries were fitted. New driving lights (IPF spots), a fire extinguisher, a cradle wired in to an external antenna for the phone, as well as an iPod connection directly to the stereo, have all been treated as essentials. Sheepskin seat covers for comfort finish off our cabin.

OTHER CAR CHOICES

I looked at everything on the market before choosing the Prado. We are not sponsored and I have no connection with Toyota whatsoever.

Reliability was top of our list. Second was parts availability in remote locations. Toyota came first on both measures.

The new 2008 Land Cruiser 200 seems a mighty truck. But it weighs more than an elephant, is heavily electronic and, as a new model, the bugs might not yet be ironed out. It is very expensive.

A previous model big Land Cruiser would have been an option, but on driving the big sister to our car the additional bulk was a penalty that seemed to offer little on- or off-road mechanical advantage. The fuel capacity also does not match the Prado. With just two of us travelling, space was not an issue.

Fuel capacity (2 x 90-litre tanks fitted as standard) and fuel economy were major factors. I was surprised at how thirsty some of the competition was. Land Rovers in particular dropped out of contention here. The Land Rover was my sentimental favourite when I started looking – I had visions of *Born Free* with Elsa the lioness in Africa. But sadly they are now either too soft for this trip (Discovery and Rangie) or too harsh and uncomfortable (Defender). All are too thirsty and lack power. The tank capacity is less than half the Prado and thus its range is less than half!

Mitsubishi's Pajero came a close second, losing out to Toyota only on parts networks. Nissan Patrol was way too thirsty. European cars such as M-Benz, BMW and VW were too expensive and too cushy. The others do not have transfer cases and proper four-wheel drive.

I did a table analysing fuel consumption, tank capacity, range and power. The Prado won hands down on every comparator.

I spent days sifting through ads, the internet and stalking people over the phone. I drove about five cars before chancing on ours on the internet. I got a pre-purchase inspection from the road service organisation (NRMA) and flew to Canberra and drove it home in a day. Upon closer inspection the front off-side guard spot welds had given up (apparently not uncommon with heavy off-road use). The wiring needed a tidy-up from home-made additions but otherwise WIM 345 got a clean bill of health.

Top Ten Photos We Missed

Cambodia: a waving driver steering a wildly modified Toyota Camry, tootling along on the highway with the roof cut off and LPG cylinders welded together between the door pillars serving as an impromptu roll bar, plastic chairs instead of the front seats. Fresh air bags?

Dili: in pitch-black late at night as we drive on the outskirts of Dili, a figure in black balaclava wields a machete at us in a half-hearted attempt at armed robbery as we slow down to negotiate a roundabout. 'Ninja,' says Maria-Gabriella, explaining the hazards of daily life in Timor-Leste's troubled capital.

No Man's Land, Kyrgyzstan: stepping out from his tiny guard post hut in deep snow to wave us down, the border guard, in alpine camouflage, Kalashnikov strapped across his shoulders, is cradling his toddler daughter in a fluffy-collared pink jumpsuit.

Takeshiken, Mongolia-China border: in the middle of a rubble-strewn vacant block in the main street of this frontier town, a matronly Kazakh woman lifts her skirts and, squatting down in the dirt takes a very public crap, oblivious to the passing pedestrians.

Uzbekistan-Turkmenistan border: in the filthy, decrepit toilets adjoining the border a soldier squats to go to the toilet, fully exposing himself; his rifle is slung across the cubicle dividers, his drink bottle and belt hanging off it. In the next cubicle is a customs official in full immaculate uniform and pressed shirt, his back to us, urinating. The wind kicks up snow around them.

Gobi Desert, Mongolia: a snow leopard, appearing from nowhere and running down the track in front of our car, darting left and right before veering off sideways to get away from us.

Cambodia-Laos border: the customs officer sitting under a tree having his breakfast bare-chested with just his sarong on – not quite maintaining his dignity.

Central China: a duck farmer, complete with triangular bamboo hat and pyjama overalls, barefoot but walking along the freeway herding a huge flock of white ducks, waddling twenty wide along the bitumen; the duck herder wrangling them with a long bamboo pole adorned with a rag on the tip, completely ignoring the trucks and traffic whizzing past.

Bayanhongor, Mongolia: a melee outside a bar, haymakers and air swings, hefty men in heavy leather jackets and felted greatcoats, several bleeding from cuts, drunkenly brawling until three policemen arrive and they become instantly subdued and are sheepishly led away.

Tsetserleg, Mongolia: three soldiers huddled around feeding timber into a small fire underneath their Russian jeep to thaw the cheap frozen oil in their motor and their frozen radiator before they can start the engine in minus 13 degrees.

Top Ten Songs from the iPod

1.	More Than Life	Whitley
2.	Nantes	Beirut
3.	Dust Storm	Seagull
4.	Spotlight	The Waifs
5.	Fog Again	Radiohead
6.	Wet and Rusting	Menomena
7.	The Times They Are A-Changin'	Bob Dylan
8.	Gagging Order	Radiohead
9.	Crosses	Jose Gonzalez
10.	Shiver Me Timbers	Tom Waits

47 | Thank you

In Australia:

First – Jan, there is nothing that I can write here that has not been said to you already. But just so everyone else knows – you are amazing! I still cannot believe how hard six months apart turned out to be. What was I thinking? And a massive debt of gratitude to Nigel, the whole family and the many friends – too many to name – who all too readily agreed with Jan when she complained to whoever would listen that we had abandoned her.

Marcia – you are a legend.

Ponch Hawkes, Corey Sleap and Christopher Crocker for photographic advice; Trevor Bear, Sam Bears Outfitters, Russell Street, Melbourne; Damien Kingsbury, Deakin University; Ali Moore, Helen Taylor, Nicole Chvastek, Katrina Palmer, Andrea Carson, Florenz Ronn, Derek Guille, John Standish, Lauren Easter, 774 ABC Melbourne; Steve Kyte, Michael Mason, Sam Guthliebson, ABC Radio Management; Tim Cox, 936 ABC Hobart; Trevor Chappell and Michael Pavlich, ABC Local Radio Overnights; Matt Abraham, David Bevan, 891 ABC Adelaide; Geoff Hutchison 720 ABC Perth; Richard Johnson and Martin Southcott, ABC On-Line; Sue Howard, Melbourne; Brent McCunn, Passport Travel, Melbourne; Johnny Qiu, NMIT; Paul Wilson, *Trailblazer Guide to the Silk Road*; Lonely Planet; UNESCO Asian Highway Handbook; Sandy Khazam and Danny Blay, Melbourne; Tara Whillas, Express Logistics, Brisbane; Carl the hitchhiker at Woomera; Kylie Arnel and Peter Hopton, Perkins Shipping Darwin; Jane Munday, Michels Warren Munday, Darwin; John Flynn, Darwin; the late and much missed Tony Fitzgerald, Darwin; Brian Negus, RACV, Melbourne; David Purchase, Tim O'Brien, VACC, Melbourne; Geoffrey Heard, Melbourne; Kevin Bailey, Honorary Consul for Timor-Leste, Melbourne; Pat O'Beirne and Matthew Brass, Telstra; Chris and Elayne Clash; Zoe Warne, August, Melbourne; David Whiting, Melbourne; Emre Celik, Melbourne; Jonathan Cooper, St John Ambulance, Melbourne; David Guest,

Guest 4 Wheel Drive, Alphington; Candice Seeger-Snowden; Heather Ritter University High School, Andrew MacLeod, UNDP; Rodney Birrell, Mr Funnel; Ian Wilcock, DFAT; Jahar Gultom, Indonesian Consulate; Chris Trueman, Xanana Vocational Education Trust, Dili; Dick Voerwordt; Heather Burge; Adrian Scott; Phil McMillan; Gillian Barker; Felicity and Wayne Wood; Ross Leopold; PEP signs.

Overseas:

Captain Lino and the crew of the MV *Kathryn Bay*; Maria-Gabriela Carrascalao-Heard and Antonio Soares, Dili; Kym Krummel and Dianne Woodward, Sanur, Bali; Mr Seno and Lia Lee Yong, SilKargo, Bandar Lampung and Singapore; Isabelle, Alain and Antoine Mouzard, Phnom Penh, Cambodia; Belinda Pribble, Vietnam; Cathy Williams, Vientiane, Laos; Tracy Cheng, NAVO, Chengdu, China; Jill Howe, Bulgan, Mongolia; Marima Khaumen, Hovd, Mongolia; Jack Ho, Urumqi, China; Ahmed Hamad, Kashgar, China; Kristina and Khadim Nathoo, Sitara Travel, Bishkek, Kyrgyzstan; Erik Fitzgibbon, Tehran, Iran; Serpil Senelmis and James Brandis, Bodrum, Turkey; Mike, Maricella and David Alford, Divonne des Bains, France; Theo Mouzard and Manon Rivière, Paris, France; Tim Jordan, London, UK; Richard Korge, Karman Shipping, UK.

The book:

Richard Smart and Jo Mackay at ABC Books, Patrick Mangan, who edited seamlessly and meticulously for us, Sandra Loy and especially Jessica Dettmann – for making us look like better writers than we are – and grateful thanks to our talented and dedicated designer, Natalie Winter.

And although he did not know it at the time, the Attorney-General for Victoria, Rob Hulls, whose job offer back in 2005 flushed out long-service leave from the ABC – I will be forever grateful.

And to Jan, again, and again, and again … forever.